HOMER'S ILIAD

HOMER'S *ILIAD*

A commentary on three translations

E.V. Rieu, revised by Peter Jones &
D.C.H. Rieu, *Homer: The Iliad*

Martin Hammond, *Homer: The Iliad*

Richmond Lattimore, *The Iliad of Homer*

Peter Jones

Bristol Classical Press

This impression 2010
First published in 2003 by
Bristol Classical Press
an imprint of
Gerald Duckworth & Co. Ltd.
90-93 Cowcross Street, London EC1M 6BF
Tel: 020 7490 7300
Fax: 020 7490 0080
info@duckworth-publishers.co.uk
www.ducknet.co.uk

A catalogue record for this book is available
from the British Library

ISBN 978 1 85399 657 3

Typeset by Ray Davies
Printed and bound in Great Britain by
CPI Antony Rowe, Chippenham and Eastbourne

Contents

Preface

This commentary is based on the following translations of Homer's *Iliad*:

E.V. Rieu, *Homer: The Iliad* (Harmondsworth: Penguin 2003), revised and updated by Peter Jones with D.C.H. Rieu, with new Introduction, book summaries and marginal notes
Martin Hammond, *Homer: The Iliad* (Harmondsworth: Penguin 1987)
Richmond Lattimore, *The Iliad of Homer* (Chicago 1951)

It is designed for those reading the *Iliad* for the first time, and is intentionally limited in scope: its purpose it to elucidate the plot, explain references, say something about the techniques of oral epic poetry and discuss some of the main issues that lie at the heart of this masterpiece of Western literature.

The commentary depends heavily on the work of others. These are, predominantly, the editors of the fine Cambridge series under the general editorship of G.S. Kirk (*The Iliad: A Commentary*, volumes I-VI, 1985-93); M.M. Willcock's smaller but no less excellent *The Iliad of Homer* I-II (London 1978-84) and *A Companion to the Iliad* (Chicago 1976), based on Richmond Lattimore's translation; and Walter Leaf, *The Iliad* I-II (London, 1900-2). The bibliography (pp. 329-32) indicates my weighty debts elsewhere.

William Hazlitt said 'If we wish to know the force of human genius, we should read Shakespeare. If we wish to see the insignificance of human learning, we may study his commentators.' Replace 'Shakespeare' with 'Homer'.

Newcastle upon Tyne   Peter Jones
January 2003

Technicalities

1. I abbreviate the translations as follows: **R-J** = Rieu-Jones (Penguin 2003); **H** = Hammond (Penguin 1987); **L** = Lattimore (Chicago 1951), and always quote them in that order. Where / is used without an abbreviated author reference, the order in which the translations are quoted is also as above.

2. In order to control the size of the book, I do not usually quote the whole passage on which I am commenting (the 'gloss' or 'lemma'), but only a word or two from it. This and the comment itself should be enough to identify what I am talking about. Where the translations are so similar as to require no differentiation, the comment lemma comes from **R-J**.

3. **R-J** sticks to the traditional English spelling of proper names, while **H** and **L** prefer closer transliteration of the Greek originals (thus Ilium/Ilios/Ilion). Since I use **R-J** spellings when discussing the text, I draw attention to the way in which conventional English spelling of Greek names differs from their Greek transliterations:

English	Greek
'ae'	'ai'
'c'	'k'
'-us'	'-os'
'-um'	'-on'
'-es'	'-eus' (end of a name, e.g. Achille(u)s)
'-ous'	'-oos'

The following is a list of names of people that may cause problems:

Achaians = Greeks
Aiakides = grandson of Aiakos, Achilles
Aiakos = grandfather of Achilles
Aiantes = the two brothers Ajax/Aias
Aias = Ajax (the greater or lesser)
Alexandros = Paris
Argives = Greeks
Atreides = son of Atreus (Agamemnon or Menelaus)
Atreus = father of Agamemnon and Menelaus
Danaans = Greeks
Dardanian = Trojan
Kronides = son of Kronos/Cronus, Zeus
Kronion = son of Kronos/Cronus, Zeus
Kronos = Cronus, father of Zeus

Kypris/Cyprian = Aphrodite
Menoetiades = son of Menoetius, Patroclus
Menoetius = father of Patroclus
Oeliades = son of Oileus, the lesser Ajax
Oileus = father of the lesser Ajax
Peleides = son of Peleus, Achilles
Peleion = son of Peleus, Achilles
Peleus = father of Achilles
Telamon = father of the greater Ajax
Telamonian = son of Telamon, Ajax
Tydeides = son of Tydeus, Diomedes
Tydeus = father of Diomedes
Phyleides = son of Phyleus, Meges
Phyleus = father of Meges
Xanthos = Scamander

General Introduction

GI refers to the sections of this General Introduction (pp. 11-43); 'Intro' refers to the introduction to each book (thus 4/Intro = the Introduction to Book 4). *Iliad* and *Odyssey* are abbreviated to *Il.* and *Od.* throughout.

Poetry and history

1. Some features of the Iliad

Homer's *Il.*, composed around 700 BC, covers fifty days in the tenth and final year of a war between the Greeks and Trojans. The Greeks are attacking the town of Ilium (whence *Iliad*, the story of Ilium), in the region called Troy (north-west Turkey; **R-J** maps 1, 2, 3). They are fighting for the return of Greek Helen, seduced back to Ilium by Trojan Paris. The bare bones of the plot of the *Il.* are simply described:

- In Book 1, the Greeks' greatest fighter Achilles is insulted by the expedition leader Agamemnon and withdraws himself and his troops from battle, together with his close friend Patroclus; through his divine mother Thetis, Achilles gets an agreement from Zeus that the Greeks will be slaughtered;
- The slaughter eventually happens in Book 8, and in Book 9, a Greek embassy fails to persuade Achilles to return to battle, despite the massive compensation it offers;
- In Book 16, Achilles permits Patroclus to return to battle to prevent the Trojans under their leader Hector setting fire to the Greek ships, but Hector kills Patroclus;
- In Book 18, Achilles hears of Patroclus' death and his mother Thetis tells him that if he kills Hector in revenge, he will die next;
- In Book 20, Achilles returns to the fighting to take revenge;
- In Book 22, he kills Hector and keeps the body, to mutilate it;
- In Book 24, Hector's father Priam successfully pleads with Achilles for Hector's return. The *Il.* ends with Hector's burial.

Those, at least, are the bare bones of the story as far as *Achilles* is concerned, whose 'anger' is announced in the first line as the engine of the *Il.* This is what the *Il.* is 'about' (cf. **GI** 9). What, then, is going on in the other sixteen books (two-thirds) of the *Il.*, and why? Two initial points need to be made:

- First, the *Il.* and *Od.* are unique among ancient epics for their size: no other that we know of comes near them in this respect; see Griffin (1977). They are, in other words, special efforts; they are not the size they are by mistake.
- But, second, they are also unique for the concentration of their focus. As Aristotle pointed out (*Poetics* 1459a), for all their bulk, each is

driven by a single theme, to which everything else in the story is subservient. There is, in other words, a thematic coherence to the plot. Homer has not enlarged the story merely to create an epic of world-record size, adding on chunks here and there to flesh it out at whatever cost, like a long-running soap-opera: his vision of what is going on may be large and all-encompassing, but it is always germane to the central theme.

On, then, to the reasons for the size of the *Il*.:

A. Homer sets the scene within the context of the battle between the Greeks and Trojans over Ilium. It is a vast cast: he names over a thousand people (individuals, gods and tribes), many of whom appear only once or twice. At the same time, there is no doubt who the twenty or so leading human players are: on the Greek side, Achilles, Agamemnon, Odysseus, Diomedes, Ajax, Menelaus, Nestor, Patroclus and Idomeneus, with minor figures like Antilochus, the 'lesser' Ajax, Meges, etc., and on the Trojan side, Hector, his father Priam, Paris, Greek Helen, whose seizure by Paris started the war, Hector's wife Andromache, Aeneas, the allies Sarpedon and Glaucus, and minor figures like Deiphobus, Agenor and so on.

The leading heroes in particular need to be made real to us, and will be, both on the battlefield and (no less importantly) in discussion with each other and in council together; and on the Trojan side, in addition, in glimpses of life away from the battle, in the town of Ilium itself (e.g. the famous Hector-Andromache scene in *Il*. 6.390-52).

B. Second, the gods feature large in this epic (see **GI** 5-8, below). Homer depicts in detail the tensions of life on Olympus between pro-Greek gods like Athene, Hera and Poseidon and pro-Trojan gods like Apollo, Ares and Aphrodite, the often fruitless attempts of Zeus to impose his will upon them, and the help that the gods, descending from Mount Olympus (their home) or Mount Ida (overlooking Troy from the south), give their favourites on the battlefield. He also describes Achilles' close relationship with his divine mother, Thetis.

In other words, the anger of Achilles has widespread implications among humans on earth and gods on Olympus, fit subject for a great epic. These ramifications need to be described and examined, another function of the non-Achillean books.

C. Third, Homer sets the story in the context of the whole history of the ten-year Trojan war. So while the 'real time' of the *Il*. covers 50 days, Homer creates the impression that he is covering all of it, and even the period before and after it; see Jones (1995). In the course of the *Il*., for example, we hear that Thetis married Peleus (24.60-2), producing Achilles; we see Achilles as a baby (9.485-91), learn of his education (11.831), and find out how Patroclus came to live in his household (23.85-90). We hear how handsome Paris (3.39, 54-5, 64-6) selected Aphrodite as the winner of the golden apple (24.27-30: note that the apple is not mentioned), and was granted Menelaus' gorgeous wife (3.156-8) Helen as his reward; that Paris against all rules of hospitality (13.620-7) seduced her back to Ilium (3.442-6), much to the disgust of his brother Hector (3.39-66). Menelaus then appealed to Agamemnon to gather an expedition to retrieve Helen (7.127, cf. 11.769ff.). The expedition set off with favourable omens (2.299-392), landed, and Protesilaus was the first man killed (2.701-2). Menelaus and Odysseus failed to settle the matter by negotiation (3.205-24) – one Trojan even thought Menelaus should be murdered then and there (11.141) – and for nine years the Greeks laid siege to Ilium without success (2.134-8); see below **GI** 13B(ix) for the strange lack of reference to the art of siege-warfare in the *Il.* Not that Homer says much in detail about this period: a Greek audience did not want to hear about the Greeks' *inability* to take Troy for nine years.

The main exception to this general silence, however, is of the highest importance: it is Homer's account of the Greek raids led by Achilles on neighbouring Trojan towns, to forage for food and increase their wealth by taking booty and captives for ransom. He describes, for example, the seizure of Thebe, where Achilles captured the girl Chryseis (1.366-9), and of Lyrnessus, where Achilles captured Briseis (2.688-93). The importance of this activity becomes clear in the first book of the *Il.*, when Agamemnon threatens to take Achilles' girl Briseis and Achilles raises the issue of the division of spoils that took place after such raids: he does all the raiding, Achilles says, but Agamemnon sits in camp and takes all the rewards (1.165-8, cf. 9.328-33).

The past features frequently in another sense, too – particularly in the mouth of someone like the old Greek adviser Nestor – as a paradigm or example, a model on which present behaviour should be based. Heroes constantly look to the past and use it to relate the experience either of themselves or of their forbears, in order to justify the course of action they think should be taken in the present. Cf. Taplin (1992) 83-109.

D. Fourth, Homer from time to time looks to the future, to what will happen after the *Il.* ends. This will include the death of Achilles (18.95-8), the fall of Ilium (6.448, 15.70-1, cf. 22.410-11), the death of Priam king of Troy and the succession of Aeneas to the kingship (20.302-8), the dispersal of the Trojan women as slaves and the death of Hector's baby son Astyanax (24.727-35), and the destruction of the Greek fortifications (12.10-33). If 'Ilium' were Hisarlik, this would explain why Homer's contemporaries might have been able to see the ruins of the city but could not see those of the Greeks' huge defensive works.

E. Fifth, speeches (statistics here from Lowe [2000] 116-18). There are 666 speeches in the *Il.*, the shortest two lines (Themis, 15.90-1), the longest 172 (Phoenix, 9.434-605). For the record:

- 77 characters speak – 28 Greeks, 28 Trojans and allies, 19 gods, one neutral (Chryses) and one horse.
- Achilles speaks 965 lines (87 speeches), Hector 530 (50), Nestor 489 (31), Agamemnon 445 (43), Odysseus 342 (26), Zeus 337 (37), Diomedes 239 (27), Hera 238 (29), Priam 213 (25), Phoenix 172 (1), Athene 159 (20), Poseidon 158 (16), Menelaus 152 (22), Ajax 129 (17), Glaucus 117 (4), Thetis 116 (13), Idomeneus 115 (12), Apollo 111 (18), Aeneas 104 (6), Andromache 102 (4), Patroclus 83 (11). In all, they take up 6,729 lines of the *Il.* – 43% of the whole epic.
- Speeches carry the moral and evaluative weight of the poem: it is here that the characters reveal the sort of people they are, particularly by their analysis, assessment, and judgement of events and each other, an activity which Homer, broadly, does not carry out in the third-person narrative (though see **GI** 10). Nearly half of the epic consists of speeches and not action – an astonishing statistic. This is a poem where debate, reflection and analysis are as important as action, where a man is revealed as much by what he says as what he does.
- The speeches, inevitably, reveal the balance of power of the poem, but sheer number is not everything. The four speeches of Andromache, for example, or the one of Briseis, are important for their intensity and the dramatic effectiveness of their location in the plot; in terms of line-length, Athene and Apollo combined say far less than Odysseus, but they are gods and their impact is not thereby diminished.

Cf. Kirk (1990) 28-35; Griffin (1986b).

F. Finally, this is poetry, and Homer is a master-poet. His imagination and invention are boundless. One feature in particular stands out: the gloriously rich descriptions with which he invests the heroic world. To some extent, this is part and parcel of the oral poet's technique.

- The repeated formulas in which the poem automatically abounds (see **GI** 2) consist to a large degree in noun + epithet (i.e. adjective) combinations: 'hollow ships', 'white-armed Hera', 'bronze armour', 'Hector of the flashing helmet', 'resourceful Odysseus', 'Zeus who drives the storm cloud' etc. They remind us of the lasting attributes and characteristics of the objects and people described: however evanescent individual people and things may be, there is nothing impermanent about the universal qualities that continue to invest the human and material world and its divinities. At the same time, the epithets can raise questions in our minds: what use is 'swift-footed' Achilles if he spends most of the time sitting in his hut ('an idle burden on the earth', as he admits, 18.104)?
- Important moments, heavy with significance, are expanded (e.g. the greeting the embassy receives from Achilles at 9.185-224, Achilles' battle with Hector 22.25-369); and important objects given careful description (the speaker's staff at 1.234-9, Thetis' gifts to Achilles' at 16.220-7).

- Homer's *c*. 300 similes (see **GI** 12), a magnificent legacy, decorate and deepen moments of drama and tension and generate moments of intense pathos among the slaughter and bloodshed.
See Hainsworth (1991) 1-10, 24-42 and cf. Toohey (1992).

2. Oral poetry

First, some basics, on which later sections of this Introduction will build:
- The *Il.* and *Od.* are the first Greek literature we possess because the Greeks invented a Greek script around the time Homer was composing (i.e. *c.* 750-700 BC), though writing does not seem to have become widespread till *c.* 650-600 BC. But Greeks had been composing and singing poetry *orally* for hundreds, if not thousands, of years before that: we do not possess it because it was not written down. Homer's compositions come at the end of a long tradition of epic song.
- Since Homer's heroes are described as living in a bronze age (all their armour and weapons are bronze), an era ending in Greece *c.* 1100 BC (to be replaced by an iron age), this bronze age must be the age of heroes in which the Trojan war is set. Interestingly, ancient Greeks made various efforts to date the time when the Greek army besieged Ilium, and some, purely by luck, hit on just this period too – by our dating system, *c.* 1200-1100 BC.
- This bronze age is also called the Mycenaean age, because Mycenae in southern Greece was a very rich and important town at the time (the 'rich in gold' kingdom of Agamemnon, as Homer tells us), together with others like Pylos (the kingdom of Nestor), Thebes, Tiryns and so on, all of which have been excavated.
- Presumably, then, in the thirteenth-twelfth century BC there were poets who sang stories of their own time, the bronze age, which were handed down over succeeding generations, all the way to Homer.

In the ancient world and long after, most people assumed that the *Il.* and *Od.* were the work of one man, Homer. In the last two hundred years, however, doubts have been raised about 'single authorship' (as they were at the same time with e.g. books of the Bible and Shakespeare). Those who continued to claim that the Homeric epics, whether written or oral, were the work of one man (i.e. one man composing both, or one man composing the *Il.*, a different man the *Od.*) were called 'unitarians'; while those who argued that editors, sitting in studies, stitched together episodes from many different sources to produce the *Il.* and *Od.* we have today were called 'analysts'. Unitarians argued from what they saw as the coherence of the whole. Analysts pointed to logical contradictions, linguistic oddities and non-Homeric cultural features to argue about which parts were by the 'real Homer', which not; for typical analytical approaches, see Clarke (1981) 156-224.

In the 1930s, however, as a result of working with living oral traditions in Bosnia-Herzegovina, the American Milman Parry produced a third hypothesis: that the poems were oral in style and probably in production too (i.e. the poet did not know how to write), and were the work of a singer (*aoidos*, as the poet calls the singer) coming at the end of a long tradition of oral poetry going back to the Mycenaean period; see Parry (1971), Lord (1960). So if a Homer as Parry imagined him produced the *Il.* ε. 700 BC, the tradition would by then have been at least 400 years old. Further, if Parry is right, many of the problems that worried the analysts might be accounted for by the way in which the oral poet worked. For example, keeping a single, coherent story-line when composing a vast epic on the spot without writing cannot have been exactly easy, or even demanded by the audience; and on the back of a tradition of 400 years of story-telling, the poet had a mass of different sorts of material to choose from, which may have created inconsistencies when he built them into his own version of the *Il.*; see Willcock (1990).

The evidence that the Homeric poems are oral in nature, whether composed with the help of writing or not – 'oral-derived traditional texts' is a useful description – is primarily constructed on the relationship between Homeric language (which is a special poetic language, developed over hundreds of years, never used in ordinary conversation) and the complex metre in which the poem is composed. To put it very crudely, the diction that the oral poet uses provides him with a range of fixed but flexible phrases ('formulas'), even whole sentences, that fit the metre and allow him to compose on the spot: the poet was able to compose because he had at his disposal a range of traditional ways for saying things.

Metre

To illustrate the system:

A. Every syllable of every word in Greek has a fixed metrical length, 'long' or 'short'; and *every syllable counted* when it came to making the verse. To take some proper names by way of example:
- *A-ga-mem-nôn*, four syllables, scans short-short-long-long (ti-ti-tum-tum, if you prefer), as does *Di-o-mê-dês*.
- *A-thê-nê*, three syllables, scans short-long-long (ti-tum-tum), as does *A-khil-leus* and *O-dus-seus*.
- *Pri-a-mos* scans short-short-long (ti-ti-tum), as does *He-ka-bê*.

B. The Homeric verse consists of flexible combinations of six 'feet', a 'foot' being either:
- 'long-short-short' (tum-ti-ti – the 'dactyl'), or
- 'long-long' (tum-tum – the 'spondee').

To illustrate it visually, the numbers across the top representing the six 'feet' of the line:

1	2	3	4	5	6
tum-ti-ti	tum-ti-ti	tum-ti-ti	tum-ti-ti		
or	or	or	or	tum-ti-ti	tum-tum
tum-tum	tum-tum	tum-tum	tum-tum		

C. Homer can use only words that will fit those metrical patterns. Thus *A-ga-mem-nôn* (ti-ti-tum-tum) could fit into the verse only in the position tum-*ti-ti / tum-tum* (for example, in the last four syllables of feet 5 & 6, where indeed his name does crop up regularly, or anywhere in feet 1-4 where tum-ti-ti is followed by tum-tum). If the only space available were, say, tum-ti-ti / tum-ti-ti, 'Agamemnon' was not available for use in that line. Tough. If Agamemnon *had* to feature in it, the poet would have to work out some other way of forming the line, or some other way of indicating 'Agamemnon' (e.g. by calling him *ba-si-leus*, 'lord', ti-ti-tum).

This explains why, for example, Homer has three separate words for 'Greeks' – *Da-na-oi* (ti-ti-tum), *A-khai-oi* (ti-tum-tum) and *Ar-gei-oi* (tum-tum-tum). These give him maximum flexibility for deployment in the line and are used according to metrical need, not because they have any particularly significant meaning in context.

D. But the system is still more complex:
- Assume Homer wants to say *A-khil-leus* (ti-tum-tum) and the metrical space in the line just happens to be tum-ti-ti/tum-tum:
- he will say *di-os A-khil-leus* (*di-os*, tum-ti), i.e. 'godlike Achilles'.
- Assume the space is ti-ti/tum-ti-ti/tum-tum:
- he will say *po-das ô-kus Ach-il-leus* 'feet swift Achilles' (*po-das ô-kus*, ti-ti-tum-ti).

In other words, proper names tend to come 'ready packaged' with epithets to fill certain metrical gaps in the line. And not just proper names either: this sort of system applies, broadly, to all Homeric diction. The language tends to come not in single words but in whole phrases, sometimes indeed whole sentences, already fitted to the metre. At which point it must be strongly emphasised that the system is far more intricate, subtle and flexible than the crudely mechanistic description given here. The poet, emphatically, is not a computer, or a composer of poems-by-numbers.

The language of such a complex system obviously did not spring up overnight. It had been developed and refined by oral poets over hundreds of years, and handed down from one to the other as they learned the business, which is why so much of the language is so old (and some of the words not understood by Homer!). But, given the complexity of the metre, orally recited poetry would have been impossible without some such system, the more highly-developed the better.

This also explains why there is so much repetition in Homer: everything from e.g. 'Agamemnon lord of men', 'swift ships' and 'the murmuring sea' at the level of phrase, through to 'he thudded to the ground and his armour clattered about him' at the level of sentence. Indeed, about one-fifth of Homer consists of repetitions (see, for example, the way in which orders tend to be repeated in exactly the same words when they are given, reported and discussed, e.g. 2.8-70).

Nor does the repetitiveness stop there:

Repeated patterns

(i) The poet has at his disposal a large number of 'templates' which help him to shape and organise common scenes e.g. scenes of arrival (see on 2.167) and arming (see on 3.328-38);

(ii) On an even broader scale, there exist in the Homeric poems story-patterns that are typical of oral-style presentations all over the world (see below on *Gilgamesh*, **GI** 3; for example, there are over 200 versions of the *Od.*'s Cyclops story, from Armenia and Morocco to Finland and Thirsk in north Yorkshire, all following basically the same pattern);

(iii) Again, take Fenik's (1968) work on the construction of the battle scenes. The patterns of such scenes, and the details that go into them, are almost entirely typical, drawn (to put it again with dreadful crudeness) from the poet's construction kit marked 'Building Blocks for Battle Scenes'. Thus it is a common pattern for A to throw at B, miss, and kill C; for A to miss B and B to kill A (B is always Greek here); for A to miss B, B to hit but not pierce the armour, and A to kill B (A again is always Greek); and so on. Typical details include e.g. armour gleaming like fire; brothers fighting from one chariot; fleeing warrior hit in the back; a god intervenes; the son of a prophet is killed, who did (or did not) foresee his death; the capture of horses; and so on and on (the commentary gives examples). But for all their apparent similarities no two battle-scenes are alike – such is Homer's imagination and skill in manipulating the typical into a new format;

(iv) A final example. Homer regularly gives a thumb-nail sketch of characters he is introducing for the first time – especially minor ones – and a typical way of organising this material is as follows (a) 'basic information', i.e. who we are talking about (b) 'anecdote', i.e. a story about them (c) 'contextual information', i.e. what they are now doing; see Beye (1964). This a-b-c pattern has wide application throughout the poem as a means of organising descriptions of e.g. the leaders of the catalogue of Greek ships (e.g. 2.546-56) and especially warriors about to be killed in battle, e.g. at 5.43-8 (a) 43 (basic information) Idomeneus kills Phaestus, (b) 44 (anecdote) Phaestus came from Tarne (c) 45 (contextual information, i.e. what happens now) Idomeneus hits him in the shoulder, kills him and has his armour removed.

(v) The advantage of oral theory is that, quite apart from the all-pervasive formulas, it explains much in Homer that is otherwise difficult to account for, e.g.

- Homer's use of very ancient words and phrases whose meaning the poet probably – certainly later Greeks – did not understand. Take the description of Hermes as *eriounios* (*e-ri-ou-ni-os Her-mês*, ti-ti-/tum-ti-ti/tum-tum, fitting neatly in at the end of the line). Guesses as to its meaning run from 'luck-bringer' to 'runner'. The word must have entered the formular system early on, turned out to be useful and therefore stuck, but over time its precise meaning became forgotten;
- the presence in the poem of a physical and cultural world different from Homer's time (eighth century BC) but characteristic of the bronze age Mycenaean period, e.g. the use of bronze for arms and weapons, the wealth of Mycenae 'rich in gold', the use of chariots in warfare, greaves, all-over body shields ('tower' and 'figure-of-eight' shields), etc.;
- the resemblance of certain parts of the Greek 'catalogue of ships' at the end of Book 2 to the picture of a world bearing some resemblance to the bronze age period;
- narrative inconsistencies, arising from the pressure of on-the-spot oral composition, or the failure to reconcile alternative story-patterns (see e.g. on 9.182); and linguistic oddities too, for the same reason;
- compositional devices typical of oral cultures, such as 'ring-composition' (see below, **GI** 11).

(vi) The oral theory of composition raises a teasing question about the relationship between any version of the *Il*. Homer may have sung at any stage, and our version, which must derive from a written version. If Homer was composing *c.* 700 BC, and writing became common *c.* 650 BC, we would like to know what happened to the poem in this intervening period and how it was transmitted; and who wrote it down, and when? On the other hand, supposing that writing was available in Homeric times (which it could have been), did Homer play any part in the *Il*.'s 'recording', whether because he knew how to write himself, or because he dictated it?

Even more difficult, what was the occasion that would have attracted an audience to listen for thirty or so hours to the *Il*., the length of time it would have taken to sing it? Major festivals, lasting many days and involving games, dancing and song in honour of a god (see e.g. *Homeric Hymn to Apollo* 146-50), may be one possible context; recitation evening after evening by the 'court poet' to listening diners in an aristocrat's palace may be another (see e.g. Demodocus at *Od.* 8.261-369, 471-521). Cf. Taplin (1992) 37-45, though his theory that the *Il*. was composed to be performed on three successive nights is not convincing.

(vii) A note on 'neo-analysis'. This style of analysis is unitarian, and examines *other* epic poems that we know about to try to find the sources from which Homer may have consciously or sub-consciously worked. For example, we have a summary of an epic poem called *Aethiopis*, of which part reads: 'Achilles having put the Trojans to flight and rushed into the city with them is killed by Paris and Apollo. And after a fierce battle over the corpse, Ajax lifts it up and brings it back to the ships, while Odysseus fights off the Trojans. Then they bury Antilochus and lay out the body of Achilles. And Thetis comes with the Muses and her sisters and laments her son.' Apart from the first sentence, the *subject-matter* looks very much like the end of *Il.* Book 17 (the rescue of Patroclus' body) and beginning of Book 18 (Achilles hears of Patroclus' death and Thetis joins in his lament), i.e. Homer may have used this material, in re-worked form, as the basis for the *Il.* at that point. See Willcock (1997) in Morris, etc. (1997), but cf. on 8.80 for objections; and Cairns (2001) 35-44.

3. Homer and history

As we have seen, since Homeric poetry is oral in style and its language of ancient origin, epic poetry was probably handed down by oral poets from bronze age Greece, the so-called 'Mycenaean' age which ended *c.* 1100 BC. If that is so, can we identify a place called Ilium in a region called Troy? And can we then argue that there actually was a real Trojan war? Archaeologists have indeed uncovered a flourishing town in the region which Homer calls *Troia* and has been called the Troad since ancient times (see **R-J** maps 1, 2). This site is called nowadays Hisarlik, and was excavated by Heinrich Schliemann from 1870-90. Hisarlik was built and rebuilt over thousands of years, and levels 6 and 7a, both destroyed violently with signs of burning and fallen masonry *c.* 1270 BC and 1190 BC respectively, seem to be the best bet for a 'Trojan war'. The problem is that, for all the intensive work that has been done there recently, nothing has yet been dug up that connects Hisarlik with any *Greek* military presence at all. Later Greeks and Romans certainly thought Hisarlik was Homer's Ilium, as one can tell from the monuments they left there, but that proves nothing.

At the same time, late bronze age documents of the Hittite empire (central Asia Minor, i.e. modern Turkey) refer to places called Wilusa and Tarwisa located in the north-west of Asia Minor. These may well be Hittite names for Ilium (Greek Wilion/Wilios) and Troia. These documents also talk of a place located overseas called Ahhiyawa, which may well be Hittite for Achaea, i.e. Greece, and describe the people of Ahhiyawa stirring up trouble on the west coast of Asia Minor. Might one such conflict be the historical source of a 'Trojan war'?

But even if it were to be, the problem is that oral epic poets were not ancient historians, working from historical sources (let alone a text). The ancient Greek historian Herodotus pointed out long ago that no king in real life would allow his city to be sacked, his children to be killed and his people to be destroyed because his son had returned home with a foreign female (*Histories* 2.120). Epic poets dealt with traditional stories involving heroes in action, going about their traditional business – winning glory and fame through warfare and adventure. Take, for example, the Babylonian epic of Gilgamesh (two thousand years older than Homer). In both *Gil-*

3. Homer and history

gamesh and the *Il.*, the main heroes Achilles and Gilgamesh are sons of goddesses, with mortal fathers; both are helped by their mothers, who use more powerful gods to support their cause; both heroes are obstinate and passionate, prone to instant decisions; both lose their dearest companions; both are devastated by their loss and take extreme action to try to compensate for it; and so on. See West (1997) 334-401 (336-47 on Achilles and Gilgamesh) with his implied conclusion '[if] the Gilgamesh complex, as we may call it, accounts for major elements in the *Il.*'s plot, structure and ethos ...'. This is not to diminish Homer's achievement, any more than the knowledge that Shakespeare extensively used Plutarch's *Life of Antony* diminishes his *Antony and Cleopatra*; cf. Jones (2000) 33-44.

Likewise, all epic poets created living stories for contemporary audiences by traditional techniques of oral composition, i.e. by stringing together typical sequences of 'themes'. For example, the first book of the *Il.* contains an introduction, a supplication, a prayer, a divine visitation, summoning and dismissing an assembly, a journey by ship, a sacrifice, meals and entertainment, all entirely common to this type of composition. If one added arming/dressing, various types of battle-scene, messenger-scenes, reception-scenes, omens and sleeping, one would have covered the basic compositional elements of the *Il.*

Oral poets also freely introduced material from other epics currently doing the rounds, of which there must have been many. The 'epic cycle' was the term for this mass of epic material, much of which was part and parcel of the oral poet's repertoire. In the *Il.*, for example, Homer refers to the stories about the 'Seven against Thebes', especially those relating to Diomedes' father Tydeus (e.g. 5.800-10), about Heracles (see on 2.638) and about the Calydonian boar (see 9.529-99). Often he takes these stories and changes them, to remove grotesque or discreditable elements (see on e.g. 4.219, 19.326-7); often he hints at them, without going into details. One imagines the audience would pick up the hint (see on e.g. 1.106, 6.403).

The conclusion must be that, even if there had been a Trojan war, the chance of any historical details of it surviving four hundred years of oral poetic manipulation is very remote indeed. As for Hisarlik, even if Homer did base his picture of Ilium on its eighth century BC remains, using it as a sort of mental model for the ancient city – which he may well have done – that proves nothing about the historicity of a Trojan war.

So while the evidence of Homeric language takes us back to origins for this sort of poetry in bronze age Greece, it is very hard to conclude that the Homeric epics as we have them tell us anything substantial about that period. Other evidence also points to this conclusion. For example, written records survive from the bronze age, the so-called 'Linear B' tablets, written on clay which was fired and so survived when the palaces in which they were kept burned to the ground (fourteenth-twelfth century BC). These tablets record in great detail (and in an early form of Greek, which died out with the end of the bronze age) the economic transactions of a hierarchical palace-based society, in which the centralised bureaucracies of great palaces like Mycenae, Cnossus and Pylos organise and control the economic output of the surrounding region. The society of the *Il.* bears no relation at all to this sort of world of (quite apart from the fact that Homeric heroes cannot write).

Again, Hisarlik was without doubt a very wealthy town of very great importance, probably because its position at one end of the Hellespont allowed it to control the lucrative traffic between the Aegean and the Black Sea. It must therefore have had a fleet, presumably stationed somewhere in the gulf which adjoined it at that time (see **R-J** map 1). But Homer never mentions a Trojan fleet, even if he, or the tradition, knew about it. He does not want to raise questions of battles at sea, which would only get in the way of the real heroic action, battles on land. (Hisarlik's power, incidentally, declined as the action of river Scamander slowly silted up the gulf, leaving it land-locked. By Roman times, it had been developed largely as a Homeric tourist site; when the Roman empire became Christian in the fourth century AD, it was gradually abandoned).

In fact, it looks more and more as if the epics are, as Lucian said of all poetry, 'the will of the poet' (*to doxan tôi poiêtêi, How to Write History* 8): Homer is constructing an epic for his time, using his traditional materials to give it a suitably epic gloss; see e.g. on the use of chariots and lack of siege tactics, **GI** 13B(vi), (ix). He reflects the concerns and interests of his own world far more than that of any long-lost past. Why Greeks living on the coast of, or the islands off, western Turkey (ancient Greek Ionia), where Homer probably composed the *Il.* (see on e.g. 2.144, 4.422, 9.4), should have wanted a heroic epic about Greeks fighting their northern neighbours, however, is a very good question. See Morris (1986), who suggests that Homer's vision of heroic culture was constructed to appeal to powerful aristocrats who saw their own world disappearing as more democratic city-state institutions began to develop.

Since it is agreed that Homer's poetry served the needs of Homer's society, scholars rightly spend much time discussing what his poems may actually tell us about that society. Since the poems are not economic or social documents but imaginative epics about a heroic past, this is a difficult and delicate job (what of significance would Little Red Riding Hood tell us of the world in which it was composed?). But at least one thing is certain. Homeric society was, like the rest of the ancient world, agricultural, and the world of the heroes as Homer describes it in the *Il.* is no less agricultural. Heroes they may be, but Achilles, Agamemnon and Hector make their living from the land none the less.

'Pasturing herds is the real work of the day, and a hero may even come across a Nymph while out in the fields, as Bucolion did, or some goddesses, as Paris and Aeneas' father Anchises did; less fortunately, he may meet a rampant Achilles, as Andromache's brothers did. Diomedes raises horses, Andromache personally feeds Hector's, Pandarus paints a moving picture of how he looks after his, Priam accuses his sons of being sheep- and cattle-thieves and himself rolls in the dung of the courtyard when he hears of Hector's death ... values are assessed in worth of oxen and the fighting is constantly being likened to farmers defending their livestock against wild animals' (**R-J**, *Introduction* xxiv); see Strasburger (1982); Griffin (1986a) discusses the sudden shifts in heroic tone this feature can generate.

It is worth noting, however, that Homer's heroic world is one where farming meant predominantly cattle-raising; in Homer's own time, arable farming was the norm – a good example of Homer giving an antique gloss to the world of the poems.

In general, see Edwards (1987) 159-69; Silk (1987) 27-9; on Homer as a predominantly 'dark age' poet, see Dickinson (1986) in McAuslan, etc. (1998); and see Donlan (1998) on the social and political background of the *Il.* and *Od.* being drawn from an 'historical stage of chieftain societies in Greece', with Homer's descriptions of gift-exchange, chiefs with their bands of followers, small-scale raiding, etc., before the development of the city-state. For detailed discussion of many of these issues, see the collection of papers in Foxhall, etc. (1984).

Heroic values

4. The hero's mind-set

The *Il.* is dominated by great individualistic soldiers of the heroic past, arguing with each other in camp and behaving on the battlefield as great individualistic heroes should. Living under the public spotlight, driven by fear of failure in the eyes of others and the shame they will consequently incur, they kill and are killed in search of *kleos*, that 'glorious reputation' which will live on after their deaths. Heroes are supported in this endeavour (or not) by gods who take an intense interest in the fate of their favourites and work openly on their behalf. Cf. Edwards (1987) 150-4.

How historical is all this? General Marshall, who examined American soldiers' attitude to hand-to-hand combat in the Second World War, makes a crucial point in relation to the *average* soldier: 'Whenever one surveys the forces of the battlefield, it is to see that fear is general among men, but to observe further that men are commonly loath that their fear will be expressed in specific acts which their comrades will recognise as coward-ice. The majority are unwilling to take extraordinary risks and do not aspire to a hero's role, but they are equally unwilling that they should be consid-ered the least worthy among those present ....When a soldier is ... known to the men who are round him, he ... has reason to fear losing the one thing he is likely to value more highly than life – his reputation as a man among other men' – quoted from John Keegan *The Face of Battle* (Har-mondsworth 1978) 71-2. This both puts the 'honour' system in context and makes the essential point that the heroes are *not* as other men. They *are* prepared to leap out of the line and take extraordinary risks. This is what makes them heroes. Cf. **GI** 13B(v)(a).

The *Il.* is not the everyday life of country folk. It is a powerfully *imagined* construct, gods and heroes battling it out in a world so distant in the past that Homer has to invoke the Muse to give him the facts (a delightful conceit). The physical and social *mise-en-scène* constructed for the heroes by the poet's imagination and the poetic tradition which he inherited *need* not reflect any contemporary reality known to the poem's listeners. But no poet can escape the world he inhabits; and the issues with which the poem deals must have had powerful contemporary resonances for the audience, or the poems would never have achieved the fame they did.

As the opening words of the *Il.* inform us, the poem is about the emotional reaction – anger – of the Greeks' greatest fighter, Achilles, and its tragic results for himself, his close friend Patroclus and many other Greeks. 'Heroic' behaviour and its consequences in the person of Achilles are the central subject around which Homer builds the *Il.* Within it are contained issues of self-control, power, authority, and compromise (or lack of it) which resonate far beyond the military context in which they are set. Above it all rises the magnificent figure of Achilles, obsessive, complex, extreme, austere, reaping the whirlwind of the decisions he freely makes. How can any community handle a man like Achilles? How can a man like Achilles set about winning the credit he longs for from that community? See Silk (1987) 89-97.

A. The conflict between Achilles and Agamemnon arises from their inability to resolve a constant tension in heroic life: the heroic desire to come out on top against the social need to co-operate. A major driving force of the hero was a commitment to competing, and winning, and showing that he had won (cf. 6.208, 11.783, where the Trojan hero Glaucus and Achilles are given the advice 'always to be the best and excel all others'). On the battlefield, that consisted of killing his opponent and displaying the armour he stripped from him. Not only did the booty so gained indicate a hero's success; the community too showered material rewards on those who fought in the front line and defended them (see on 12.310-28. Note that Sarpedon is not fighting to defend his own Lycian people at this time. Heroes act like heroes whatever the circumstances; they do not *have* to be defending their own people to perform heroics). Such achievements ensured that heroes were given honour/status/high valuation by their fellows (*timê*: the basic meaning is 'value', both financial and social, cf. English 'worth'). This, a hero hoped, would translate into *kleos* at death – a glorious memory that would never die.

B. But what happened when they were dealing, not with an enemy, but their own people? Here the requirement was (as with the gods, **GI** 7) to reciprocate, to give like for like; cf. Donlan (1981-2). This was fine when the 'like' was beneficial, but when it was not – what happened then? At 4.365-418, for example, Diomedes is criticised by Agamemnon for hanging back from battle. His attendant Sthenelus is all for going into immediate 'competition' mode (404-10) – any moment one feels he will land one on Agamemnon – but Diomedes stops him and deals with the situation by saying that Agamemnon is merely trying to encourage the troops to fight. However, when the poet chose to bring a proud, obstinate and volatile hero like Achilles into conflict with an insensitive, overbearing leader like Agamemnon, an explosion was inevitable.

C. Or was it? The point is that there were mechanisms for avoiding such disastrous clashes. As Homer makes clear on numerous occasions, the heroic world is one where the ability to win an argument is rated as highly as the ability to kill an opponent on the battlefield (9.438-43) – where, in other words, the rights and wrongs of the hero's desire to win and assert himself, even over his fellows, can be *debated*; see Schofield (1986). This is one reason why there are so many speeches in the *Il*.; cf. 11.787-8, where Peleus tells Achilles always to be the best, and Menoetius tells Patroclus that it will be his job to give Achilles sound advice. So Phoenix brought up Achilles to be 'a speaker and a man of action' (9.413), and Achilles admits at one point that while he is the best man in battle, others are better at debate (18.105-6). One reason why Agamemnon is an ineffective leader is that he will not listen to good advice; thus he eventually admits he got the decision about Achilles wrong (e.g. 19.137, cf. his praise for Odysseus' good advice 1856-); see Taplin (1990).

D. Most important of all, the heroes are aware that, if they have 'rights', so too do others. If a hero acts shamefully, he is properly rebuked for it: he cannot ride roughshod over others' feelings simply in order to come out on top, and expect to be applauded for it (cf. 23.492-4, where Achilles rebukes two quarrelling heroes: 'it's not right. You would be the first to condemn anyone else who did it'). The control exerted over a hero to do what is 'right' is expressed by the term *aidôs*, 'respect for others, shame, embarrassment', and the rebuke he will rightly receive, *nemesis*, 'anger, disapproval, reproach' if he fails to observe that sanction (cf. 16.498, 17.91-101).

In other words, there is a tension at the heart of the *Il*. between the hero's natural desire for the honour and status to be gained by winning, and his obligations to others to co-operate with them and ensure that their honour is not compromised by his search for his own; see Cairns (1993a, 1993b).

E. It is not surprising, therefore, that the first reaction of Achilles and Agamemnon to the problem raised by the return of Chryseis in Book 1 is to debate it, in open assembly, before the whole army (not that the army plays any part in making any decisions that emerge, then or later, though cf. Thersites' outburst and the reaction to it at 2.211-77). The debate gets nowhere; in fact it serves to entrench the two men deeper in their opposition to each other the more it goes on; and even Nestor is not able to dig them out of it. But the point is that debate was engaged, the issues aired and reconciliation given a chance. That the issue is not resolved is down to the characters of Achilles and Agamemnon.

F. This casts an interesting light on the relationship between Agamemnon and the heroes in the Greek camp. The major heroes bring their own troops to Troy (listed in the catalogue of Greek ships at 2.494-759) and Agamemnon is acknowledged to be their overall leader, but only because he brought more troops than anyone else (2.576). The term *basileus* applied to Agamemnon, 'king' in later literature, means in Homer nothing more than some sort of person of rank. Agamemnon can claim that Zeus supports him as leader (e.g. 1.174-5, backed up by Nestor 1.277-9), but this is not a claim that gives him unfettered authority. Nor does Agamemnon possess the encumbrances of kingship, officials, or a treasury, let alone a 'throne'. In other words, Agamemnon has no innate right to give orders and expect them to be obeyed, as if he were a modern army general; cf. **GI** 13B(iv) on the absence of leadership in battle generally and Taplin (1990) 67-70. Agamemnon can, and does, assert his authority, but the only question is whether anyone will believe him. As a result, when Achilles storms out of the fighting, it is not an act of treachery or rebellion, putting Achilles automatically beyond the pale, but a statement about the wrong Achilles feels has been done to him, and one which no Greek admits he has been unjustified in making, cf. Jones and Wright (1997) 4.

These issues, so central to the *Il.*, presumably also mattered a great deal to Homer's eighth-century BC audience, at a time when the aristocratic world seemed to be losing its innate authority; and they are not exactly irrelevant to us. Through the epic of Achilles, the *Il.* deals with universal human dilemmas.

The human and divine worlds

5. The interdependence of gods and men

A. Homer's portrayal of the gods raises acute questions. What sort of majestic, all-powerful, all-seeing divinities are these who:
- Are subject to time and space (16.515)?
- Quarrel spitefully among themselves in the cause of their favourites, and have to be reined in by a powerful father figure, Zeus, before his will can prevail (8.1-27)?
- Weep at the impending death of their favourites (16.459) and pity the plight of animals (17.441)?
- Then ruthlessly attack men when it suits them (16.788), or leave them to their fate when their time is up (22.213)?
- Can at the same time accuse Achilles of destroying pity (24.44)?
- Are at times endowed with imposing grandeur (13.17-30), but happily

deceive and lie to each other (14.159-311), and are treated by human heroes almost as if they are their equals (1.197-205)?

• Can intend something to happen, and it does not (see Ares and Menelaus at 5.563-72), or can fear that, unless they intervene, someone will cheat destiny (Zeus on Achilles, 20.30)?

These gods are indeed like men and the men (almost) like gods, even more so when one considers that the gods are constructed as a family, with Zeus at their head, and actually have a daily life, like a human family: they live in houses on Olympus, go to bed, sleep, get up, eat, drink, argue and scheme, expend effort over mortals, visit each other, chat, swap reminiscences, beg favours, make love, and so on. Cut them and they bleed (see e.g. 1.595-611, 4.27 cf. 5.339, 870-4; cf. Sissa, etc. [2000] part 1).

As has been well said, religion is rather like a language: it makes perfect sense to those who speak it, but appears gibberish to those who do not. The basic point is that Homer constructs the gods within the context of his own and his world's understanding of divine powers, for his literary purposes. If they look very little like anything we understand as gods, that does not mean that Homer's audience also regarded them as incomprehensible. If the world, for example, seems random and inexplicable, liable to play disagreeable tricks at one moment, agreeable at the next, without any discernible logic to it all, then one can conclude, reasonably, that this is how the powers above must want it to be. Otherwise they would organise things differently (this is not to engage in an argument whether concepts like 'God' are purely linguistic).

None of which, however, is to deny the gods' immortality and absolute power. It is in this sense that Herodotus argued that Homer and Hesiod gave the Greeks their gods (*Histories* 2.53) – there was no other source Herodotus knew of that made a community out of them and informed us of their family relationships, character and everyday activities. Mere ritual – the ordinary form of worship – could never do what the epic poets did. But it is no wonder that later Greeks like Xenophanes and Plato entertained the most serious moral doubts about these divinities.

B. To understand them, we must divorce ourselves from theology, which attempts to present a systematic, coherent and self-consistent exposition of the nature of god, together with creeds and dogmas which impose correct belief on worshippers, all ultimately based on authoritative 'inspired' scriptures which must (by definition) contain The Truth. The ancient had no scriptures, inspired or otherwise. For the ancients, the world was full of gods, who are best thought of as blind forces, like gravity. Belief and dogma are irrelevant to gravity: all one has to do is acknowledge its power when one is on cliff-edges, in the same way that a peasant acknowledged the power of his ruling land-owner without having to sign up to a 'creed' defining the land-owner's characteristics.

Presumably in order to help them envisage, and therefore control, these powers, Greeks personified them; at any rate, natural phenomena like weather and rivers, places like cities, emotions like love and fear, states of the body like sleep and death, were all represented in art and literature as deities, in human shape. So when Homer says that a river made love to woman, he means the god of the river. Male and female gods alike were represented in the great pantheon. There were almost as many gods as there were natural phenomena and human hopes and fears.

C. But there was a catch to all this. Greeks understood that, if a god was not acknowledged by humans, the god became redundant, superfluous – effectively, as far as this world was concerned (and what other world counted?) dead, since no one paid any attention to him or her. Gods, in other words, needed humans as much as humans needed gods.

Further, and paradoxically, men who needed the gods most of all were not the weak or powerless, but the strong and heroic. Gods, being creatures of power, supported only winners. One was a hero *because* the gods supported you: if they did not, how could you have reached the position you had? Observe the delight, for example, with which Achilles welcomes Athene's help to kill Hector (22.222-5). Far from being demeaned by divine help, the hero is enhanced: divine help *proves* he is a hero.

Nevertheless, humans could take nothing for granted. It is a common theme of epic that gods should not quarrel among themselves on Olympus over mere mortals, cf. 1.573-6, 8.427-31, 21.379-80, 462-7. In other words, gods (being gods) can *choose* to do what they like. Divine support is ultimately fickle, whatever expectations men may have about the results of their offerings to the gods. Cf. on 6.147, and see 24.526 for the ultimately care-free gods who, unlike mortals, have no troubles.

At which point, a word of warning. As has been said above, gods are Homer's construct: there is nothing 'objective' about them. They are what the poet wants them to be; they serve the epic he is composing. Likewise, Homer makes them serve the characters in the epic too. When Agamemnon, for example, blames *Atê* for his treatment of Achilles in Book 1 (which he does on a number of occasions, e.g. 19.78-144), or when Priam says that Helen was not to blame for the Trojan war but the gods were (3.164-5; see on 3.164), we should not take these as dogmatic, quasi-theological statements. They must (naturally) represent the sort of thing one could reasonably say about the gods, but they also serve the case that the characters are making at the time. See Cairns (2001) 12-20.

6. Divine intervention

When the gods intervene, there is no doubt about it. At 1.199 Achilles is about to attack Agamemnon when Athene pulls him back by the hair, and 'Achilles was amazed'. It is sometimes suggested that, when a god intervenes e.g. to change someone's mind (as here), it is simply Homer's way of describing a natural mental process ('with a great effort Achilles restrained himself and thought again'), as if the gods were not affecting human actions, merely reflecting them. But Homer is perfectly capable of showing people making up their own minds without divine intervention (e.g. 21.550-70). The point is that this is heroic epic: of course gods intervene to help their favourites, as they do in all epics, all over the world, and their favourites find it very rewarding (see e.g. 5.873-4 and on 1.55, 3.380, 4.40, 5.20). In this particular case, of course, if Homer really is describing what he intends us to see as the working of a normal mental process, it is hard to understand the tug at his hair, Achilles' amazement and his observation of Athene's eyes, not to mention Athene's promise. So in general, when Homer says a god intervenes, it is best to believe him – unless there are very good reasons not to.

Further, at 1.207 Athene urges Achilles to pay attention to what she has to say, 'if you will listen to me'. She is a god – and Achilles has an option? It is in fact a constant feature of the relationship between Homeric heroes and the gods that, when they *talk* to each other, they do so virtually as equals. Achilles here remains completely uncowed by Athene's sudden appearance at 201-5, and addresses her as if she were human. In other words, gods may be superhuman, but they work as one with humans, using the language of normal human exchange. Humans are usually careful to pay attention when the gods tell them not to overstep the mark (contrast e.g. Diomedes at 5.601-6 and Patroclus at 16.702-11, 784-7); but otherwise they are not grovellingly subservient to them (cf. on 22.220). See Jones (1996) for a full discussion of this phenomenon and the sense of the proudly independent hero that it creates, and see Griffin (1980) 172-8 for Homer's broadly rational treatment of the gods, i.e. gods (with a few notable exceptions, e.g. a talking horse at 19.404-17) do not create situations which would seem utterly grotesque or bizarre to human witnesses. Cf. on 16.530; Schein (1984) 45-64; Rutherford (1996) 44-9; Silk (1987) 29-31, 79-82; Taplin (1992) 128-43.

7. Worshipping the gods

Sacred, divinely inspired texts like the Bible and the Koran put correct belief and, to a lesser extent, correct way of life at the heart of worship. Neither was of the slightest interest to Homeric gods. They demanded acknowledgement, and if they did not get it, even as a result of a genuine mistake, they could turn nasty (9.532-40). Acknowledgement of gods was delivered through correct ritual, in return for which humans hoped for divine favour. The relationship was one of *quid pro quo* – you scratch my back and I'll scratch yours.

This might seem to imply that a rich man, who could afford to give the most gifts to a god, would therefore be the most favoured, as if the relationship between man and god resembled a form of commercial exchange. But gifts were a means of reaching gods, i.e. of forming a relationship with inaccessible powers, not of manipulating them; see Parker (1998) 118-25. Prayer-forms reveal the basis of the system:

A. Prayers: at 1.36-42 Chryses prays for help to Apollo. The structure of the prayer is typical and recurs throughout Greek literature: (i) you identify the right god, with various appropriate (here local) titles, in the capacity in which you need him/her (here, to bring destruction), (ii) you recount your past offerings ('if ever before', i.e. you remind them of the existing relationship), (iii) you make your request and (iv) (not here) you promise further offerings if your request is granted. Cf. 10.278-94. The relationship is assumed to be a reciprocal one, involving mutual help and support. Thus Agamemnon is baffled when he claims that Zeus has paid no attention to his numerous sacrifices at 8.236-44; at which point Zeus responds (245-52). At 16.514-31, Glaucus asks Apollo to heal his wound. Apollo does so, but Glaucus expresses no gratitude; he expresses his delight and goes about his business. Love, or submission to the will of the god, does not come into the relationship.

B. Sacrifice: usually combined with prayer, sacrifice was the way to thank or appease the gods. At 1.458, the Greeks 'made/offered prayers' and the sacrifice begins. Note the typical sequence in this common scene:
- purification by washing. Note that cleanliness and good order were associated in the ancient world. When disaster occurs, people pollute themselves to indicate that good order has been subverted, e.g. 18.23-7, 23.38-47, 24.163-5 and cf. 16.795-9; the sacrificial animal too had to be perfect, without blemishes. See Parker (1983);
- prayer;
- throwing grain at the victims (bulls, goats or sheep, cf. 1.66, 316? We are not told);
- slitting their throats and skinning them;
- and then cutting off the thigh bones to be sandwiched in fat, with pieces of meat from the rest of the animal laid on top (to symbolise the whole animal, *Od.* 14.427-8). This was the god's portion, cooked on wooden spits, with libations of red wine poured over it. That done, the sacrifice was over;
- now came the human meal, an event much awaited in real life since, unlike Greek epic heroes, an ancient Greek did not often have beef on the menu. The offal (heart, liver, lungs, kidney, stomach) had been cooked at the same time as the thigh-bones (2.426), and this was eaten first; finally the rest of the meat was kebabed, cooked, drawn off and consumed.

C. Divine protection: Greeks often called the gods to witness institutional-ised relationships in order to win the gods to their side if those relationships broke down. For example, Zeus was the god who oversaw host-guest relationships (*xenia*). Let those be subverted, and Zeus would be called on to witness that he had been disregarded, and should thus take action (e.g. 3.353-4). Menelaus often calls on Zeus in these terms to punish Paris, since

Paris was a guest in his home when he seduced and ran off with Helen. Cf. oaths, E below. It should not be concluded that, because remaining true to oaths and treating guests well may be the moral thing to do, the gods therefore have an interest in compelling humans to behave morally. *Xenia* and oaths are under the gods' jurisdiction. They therefore enforce respect for them. Morality, as far as gods are concerned, does not come into it.

D. Supplication: suppliants too came under divine protection, since Zeus *Hikêsios* was god of supplicants (see Gould [1973]). At 1.15 the priest Chryses 'in supplication/began to entreat' the Greek army. Physical supplication entailed kneeling before someone and holding their knees and chin, partly to restrain them symbolically from movement or speech during the plea, and begging them for help (cf. 1.500-1). Here, of course, Chryses is supplicating the Greek army only metaphorically, but the effect is meant to be the same. The purpose was to humiliate oneself before the supplicatee – something no Greek would normally do – indicating one's abject helplessness and distress. As long as that position and contact were maintained, the supplicatee was almost duty-bound to honour one's request. So when Agamemnon rejects Chryses' supplication, Chryses can pray to Apollo in full confidence that he will punish Agamemnon – and he does.

The 'protection' afforded by supplication, however, does not seem to apply between enemies on the battlefield (see on e.g. 6.45, and 21.70-119) because a suppliant is demanding *pity*, and pity is not an emotion that one associates with Homeric warriors in battle. In fact all human-to-human supplications, in the real time of the action of the *Il.*, are rejected – except the last (24.508-16), where, like Chryses at the beginning, an old man (Priam) comes into the Greek camp to beg for the return of his child and (unlike Chryses' attempt) succeeds. There is surely considerable significance to this moment: after all that he has done to Priam and his family, Achilles in the end takes pity on the old man.

E. Oaths: the gods were invoked to witness the taking of an oath, of which they were made guarantors: all oaths were sworn in their name. Obviously any oath ratified in their name and broken would at once call down their anger. Since the Sun saw everything, and the Earth was mother of all and held under it the Erinyes, gods of vengeance, these gods regularly oversaw oath-taking (see 19.259-60, and on 9.454).

8. Destiny, death and free will

It is worth pointing out that, in most cases, 'destiny/fate' means simply 'the moment you (will) die', and that moment is fixed the moment you are born (cf. 6.487-9, 20.127-8, 23.79, 24.209-10).

But there are occasions when 'destiny' takes on a broader aspect (e.g. 15.58-71), and in these cases it must be remembered that Homer is not a theologian; as Edwards (1987) says, 'fate ... is the will of the poet' (136).

Homer has no rational theory to explain the relationship between fate and free will, except that he often sees them as one and the same: as a result, when he is talking about why people act as they do, he often ascribes a person's motivation to both god and man equally, i.e. as if both are 100% responsible for what happens (see e.g. 9.702-3). This phenomenon is known as 'double determination' or 'over-determination', on which see Lesky (1961).

So when Homer plays the 'Grand Destiny' card, he does not see this as a dreadful imposition on humans; and indeed, when humans face their destiny, they do so with remarkable aplomb and acceptance (e.g. Patroclus at 16.843-54 and Hector at 22.297-305). Homer uses the card primarily for *literary* purposes – to create a dramatic effect at that point in the narrative. See Jones (1996) 114-16; Janko (1992) 1-7; Rutherford (1996) 48.

For Near Eastern parallels to the behaviour of gods in Homer, which are deep and extensive, see West (1997) 33-59, 107-32, 177-90 (the divine comedy).

Features of Homeric plotting and narrative

9. The plot and 'retardation'

Since stories are universally driven by someone's need for something (positive or negative), one way of thinking about a plot is to determine the 'object of desire' that the main character(s) – whoever they are at the time – has/have in mind. In these terms, the *Il.* has seven such plots, beginning with Chryses, then Agamemnon, moving on to Achilles, then the Greeks, going back to Achilles and ending with the Trojans. On two occasions, moving from plot (3) to plot (4), and from plot (6) to plot (7), the plot as defined in terms of the 'object of desire' almost grinds to a halt:

(1) Chryses' 'object of desire' is his daughter Chryseis, whom Agamemnon refuses to return. As a result, Apollo lays the army low with a plague. Agamemnon agrees to return the girl, which solves that problem, but in the process:

(2) Agamemnon now has an 'object of desire', a replacement for Chryseis; he selects Achilles' girl Briseis. Problem solved for Agamemnon, but in so doing he creates:

(3) an 'object of desire' in Achilles, to ensure the Greeks start losing, so that (ultimately) he can return to the fighting and win back the *kleos*/ immortal reputation that Agamemnon's treatment threatens to take from him. So Achilles leaves the fighting, Zeus agrees to help him achieve his ends (Book 1), and the Greeks are so severely beaten (Book 8) that they have no option but to recall their greatest warrior. They therefore send him an embassy (Book 9) offering sensational compensation, which is rejected. This creates a stalemate in the plot. What, then, does Achilles want? Where does the poet go from here? The poet's answer is to turn the spotlight back on the Greeks:

(4) the plot is now driven, as Diomedes says (9.697-709), by the Greeks' 'object of desire', to fight on, win or lose, till Achilles returns. The Greeks therefore carry on fighting, and losing, until:

(5) Achilles relents: his anger has lessened, as he admits, and his new 'object of desire' is to ensure the Trojans are driven back by Patroclus (Book 16). But Patroclus is killed, which prompts:

(6) the return of Achilles, whose 'object of desire' now is no longer revenge on the Greeks but heroic *kleos* from slaughtering Trojans and taking revenge on Hector (even though it will mean his death), which he duly does (Book 22). But the death of Hector solves nothing. Achilles' 'objects of desire' have all turned to ashes in his mouth. There is nothing left for him to desire. All he can do now is die. The poet turns to:

(7) the Trojans, with Zeus now on their side – cf. **(3)** – with their 'object of desire': the return of Hector's body (Book 24). And so the *Il.* ends, in a situation that could hardly be further away from what it was in Book 1.

So while it is true that the anger of Achilles is the engine of the plot and his 'fate' is its main focus, Chryses and Agamemnon actually get the plot going **(1)** and **(2)**, the Greeks keep it going **(4)**, and the Trojans bring it to a conclusion **(7)**.

Looking at the story in these terms has one specific advantage. Homer is often accused of 'retarding the plot'. That seems to mean 'forgetting about Achilles', often for quite long stretches. Books 2-8 come into this category, when the poet focuses on the Greek and Trojan armies and leaders, and Books 13-15, when Zeus' attention is diverted elsewhere, allowing the Greeks to rally. 'Retarding the plot' is, however, an unproductive way of thinking about these episodes, for two reasons.

First, to talk of 'retardation' is to make a judgement about what it is that is being 'retarded', a judgement that depends on knowing the whole story in the first place. But we do not know what the whole story is until we have finished it. We are like someone travelling in a car at night, able to see as far as the headlights illuminate the immediate way ahead. The driver (Homer) may know that there is something really exciting round the corner, but we will not know that till we crash into it. Until that happens, the question to ask is: what are we making of the journey as it unfolds under the headlights before us?

Second, if one thinks in terms of 'objects of desire', one has a better tool for understanding what is going on when Achilles is absent, because there are other 'objects of desire' that come into play. For example, Books 2-8 – plot **(3)** – are dominated not only by Achilles' absence (because of his desire for the Greeks to lose) but also by Agamemnon's presence: his 'object of desire' has been fulfilled, his material status has been restored with the seizure of Briseis, and we get a chance to see what sort of a job Agamemnon makes of it as unchallenged leader. The answer turns out to be 'mixed'. On the other hand, thanks largely to Greeks like Diomedes and Ajax, it looks as if Achilles' 'object of desire', a Greek bloodbath, will not be fulfilled, since in Books 4-7 the Greeks are well on top. All that changes dramatically in Book 8.

Again, in Books 13-15 – plot **(4)** – with Achilles' 'object of desire' now unclear, it is the Greeks' 'object of desire' that holds centre-stage – and their desire to win cannot be faulted in plot terms.

None of this is to deny that Homer uses Books 2-8 in particular to step back and expansively locate the Trojan war in a wider context. But 'retardation' is a negative way of looking at it: seen in 'object of desire' terms, the motivation of these books is better connected with the main thrust of the plot development of the *Il.* than critics have believed.

One can extend the principle. What of the gods and the Trojans? They too have their 'objects of desire'. The pro-Greek and pro-Trojan gods give no ground in their desires for Greek and Trojan victories; but Zeus' 'object of desire' favours Achilles in Book 1, but the Trojans in Book 24, since Zeus demands that Achilles return Hector – a significant commentary on the disastrous pit into which Achilles has dug himself. Hector's 'object of desire', the repulse of the Greeks and the restoration of family life in Ilium, is restrained, almost pessimistic, as he talks things over with Andromache in Book 6; it becomes increasingly grandiose from Book 8 onwards; and ends up as a simple plea for burial in Book 22.

Seen in these terms, one might conclude that the *Il.* is as much 'about' the vanity of human wishes as anything else. But that is the problem: if one decides that the plot of the *Il.* is best described in terms of the characters' 'objects of desire', one will inevitably think about whether those desires are fulfilled (or not), and then be tempted to draw ringing conclusions as a result. That is not to deny such conclusions can be extremely stimulating; it is to point out the problems associated with imposing a single 'model' on a work of literature, since a model necessarily throws up answers which are effectively pre-determined by the remit which the model implies.

10. Homer as narrator and 'focaliser'

A. Homer as narrator of the poem gives the impression of being 'objective', i.e. standing back from the action and simply 'reporting' it, as if he were a city-centre TV camera dispassionately recording everything that happens in the middle of a town. This does not mean he avoids moral or evaluative judgements – far from it – but he places these, again 'objectively', as if simply reporting them, in the mouths of his characters.

Consequently, Homer does not appear to *guide* our responses to the text. He merely tells us what people say, and how they act and react, and leaves us to interpret. For example, after his clash with Agamemnon in Book 1, Achilles took the staff on which he had just sworn an oath, *flung it down* and resumed his seat (245). That one action brilliantly evokes the whole picture of a man in a towering rage (it is typical of Homer to depict emotions and feelings by physical reactions). Again, Homer reports that, when the embassy to Achilles had finished eating and drinking, 'Ajax nodded to Phoenix. But godlike Odysseus caught the signal …' and began himself to speak (9.223). Odysseus' reaction to Ajax's prompting of Phoenix is a delicious moment, but we are moved to ask what its precise significance was. Again, characters sometimes smile; they sometimes fall silent. Homer rarely tells us why. By merely reporting what happens, and making no other comment, Homer invites *our* imaginations to get to work – so much more effective than laying everything on a plate.

At these moments, we get a lively sense of character. Nevertheless, Homer's depiction of character is different from what we might expect in (say) a modern novel or television play. In these, the 'object of desire' tends to be subjective self-fulfilment. Issues like happiness, relationships, life-style and doing your own thing dominate the conversations – do you really love your boy-friend/partner/spouse? Are you neurotic about social situations? Do you worry about what people say about you? Do you envy your sister, and why? Would you drop sweet-wrappers on the pavement? Why do you have so many failed relationships? Are you ashamed of your class background? Do you like your new hair-style? Are you happy with your parents? These are the problems which need solving for characters' desires, some deeply trivial, others of great importance, to be fulfilled.

Homer's world is interested in none of these problems or issues. The inner life of the characters and their private self-fulfilment are not the *main* subjects of exploration by the poet (which makes it all the more striking when that intimate, personal, 'inner self' is revealed, e.g. when Patroclus drops hints about his relationship with Achilles, 11.647-53). When the heroes talk to each other, the subject-matter largely centres on the decisions they choose to take about the demands that they see heroic society placing upon them; and the epic deals with the working out of the consequences of those decisions. Consequently, the conversations of the heroes tend to wind round big ethical issues, i.e. issues of *public*, rather than private or personal, behaviour, relating to what they see are the expectations of the world they inhabit – issues like achievement, honour, status, wealth, shame, humiliation, friendship, reciprocity (returning benefits and injuries) and so on, and the contradictions and problems these issues generate in relation to the smooth functioning of their world. Indeed, one might see the generation of such issue as a key feature of the *Il.*. The poem could have been (perhaps once was) a tale merely of insult, withdrawal and revenge. But the powerful debate in Book 9 about what a hero is worth, the tragedy of Patroclus in Book 16, Achilles' decision in Book 18 to embrace death as the price of revenge and his return of Hector's body in Book 24 move it onto a different plane.

This 'objective' stance of Homer produces another important consequence. Like all the finest artists, he refuses to be drawn into producing 'answers' for us. His characters act and speak and react in a wholly naturalistic way. But when one looks a little more deeply, one is often moved to ask – *exactly* why did he say that? What is the *precise* sequence of cause and effect at work here? Homer does not necessarily tell us. *We* have to make sense of it all. Quite like life, in fact. Nor does Homer leave us with any 'message'; or rather, one can draw as many 'messages' as one likes, but everyone's conclusions will differ, depending on where one looks and what one wants to find.

In this sense, Homer is composing like a playwright. The playwright cannot intervene in the play to explain what is going on, unless he writes his own detailed commentary on every scene (as George Bernard Shaw did). The playwright can only make his characters do things and say things, and leave us to make of it what we will. At one level, this is how Homer composes.

For a detailed discussion of these issues, see Gill (1996), 115-54, and cf. Gill (1990); Silk (1987) 83-97.

B. But the picture is not quite as black-and-white as this, as de Jong (1987) shows (cf. Morris, etc. [1997] 305ff.). There are many ways in which Homer intervenes to manipulate events in an 'unobjective' way that a city-centre TV camera could never do, e.g. when he

- compresses time (e.g. the nine-day plague at 1.53-4);
- pauses to describe an important object (e.g. Achilles' spear at 16.141-4);
- anticipates what is to happen next ('foreshadowing', e.g. 11.603);
- uses the 'if ... not' formulation (e.g. 2.155-6);
- intervenes to make general statements ('gods are stronger than men', 21.264);
- intervenes to make comments of his own (e.g. 'the fool', 2.38);
- invests certain moments with powerful pathos, e.g. the death of a warrior, who is often described as e.g. dying far from home, abandoning his newly-wedded wife, bringing grief to his parents, etc. (e.g. 5.155-8, 11.241-3).

C. Then again, consider the issue of 'focalisation', broadly, the human point of view from which the narrator may be suggesting that an action should be seen. For example:

- when Priam kisses Achilles' hands, they are described as 'those terrible, man-slaying hands that had killed so many of his sons'. That might be an 'objective' description; on the other hand, the impact of the words is powerfully enhanced if they are seen as representing Priam's thoughts at this dramatically charged moment (see on 24.479-80);
- characters freely interpret events in different ways from the narrator, or from other characters. Thus at 1.370-92, Achilles gives an account of the opening scenes of the *Il.* which differs in important ways from the narrator's account – clearly because Achilles sees the situation in his *own* way.
- the past is nearly always related through the mouths of the characters rather than 'objectively' reported in the third-person narrative: it is

made a part of the characters' experience, to manipulate and filter in any way they will;

- at 1.185 Agamemnon says he will come 'in person' (Greek *autos*) to fetch Briseis, but never does – he sends messengers to fetch Briseis (320-2). Yet characters continue to say that this is what he did in fact do, e.g. Achilles 1.356 – at once contradicted by Achilles at 391-507, Thersites at 2.240 and Agamemnon himself at 19.89; Nestor too comes close to it at 9.106-7. Is this simply a mistake? Or should *autos* be translated e.g. 'on my/his authority'? None of these: the characters are surely saying this for a purpose – to stress Agamemnon's guilt by throwing his own words back at him. In other words, characters are made to 'spin' events to suit themselves. What they say is not necessarily an objective account of events.
- Finally, similes are frequently used to give a special emotional colouring to the action (e.g. 6.49-58, and cf. on 'pathos', above).

It is, however, worth stressing that, while manipulation of this sort enormously enriches the epic, it does not go any way to producing 'answers'.

11. Ring-composition

Homer loves descriptions: but a description is a sort of digression, causing the listener to step aside briefly from the continuing action of the poem. When the description ends, Homer has to bring the listener back to the point in the action where the description began. He does this by the device known as 'ring-composition', the words which introduce the description being repeated at the end, sometimes in a complicated 'reverse' pattern. Thus at 1.259 Nestor exhorts the Greeks to listen to him and launches into a tale of his youth to persuade them so to do. At 259 he begins with:

(A) an exhortation to listen to him, and

(B) an observation that the men he mixed with in the past always did so.

He then tells the story, and ends (272-4) by pointing out

(B) that they always listened, so

(A) you should listen too.

Elements in the order 'A B (C) [story/description, etc.] (C) B A' define ring-composition. Indeed, this is an extremely common structuring device for all situations (not merely digressions) – speeches, for example (see Lohmann [1997]). For example, at 5.800-13, Athene rebukes Diomedes for not fighting. She says:

(A) 800 your father Tydeus had a son (i.e. Diomedes), but not much like himself

(B) 801 Tydeus was small but a fighter

(C) 802 even when I told him not to fight he did;

a description of Tydeus fighting ensues; then

(C) 809-10 but I am ordering you to fight

(B) 811-12 you are not a fighter

(C) 812-13 so you cannot be a son of Tydeus.

12. Similes

As we have seen (**GI** 1F), similes play an important part in the narrative. There are a four basic types in Homer, as discussed by M.W. Edwards (1991) 24-41; in general see Moulton (1977):

A. Short similes with a single point of comparison, e.g. 'like nightfall' (1.47), 'like fawns' (22.1).

B. An extended short simile, in the form 'like X, *which/that* …', e.g. 'like fawns, that dash across the plain and exhaust themselves and stop, because they have no more will to resist' (4.243-5).

C. The subject is mentioned, the simile begins 'as when, as, like', and ends 'such was/so X happened' (ring-composition: see **GI** 11) – thus 'X happened, as when Y, so X happened'. For example: 'When warlike Menelaus saw Paris striding towards him in front of the enemy ranks, he was as delighted as a lion that comes across a great carcass and finds it is an antlered stag or wild goat; he is starving and greedily devours it in spite of all the efforts of the quick dogs and strong young hunters to drive him off. So delighted was Menelaus, when his eyes fell on godlike Paris' (3.21-8). Note (A) Menelaus saw (B) he was delighted; [simile]; (B) so he was delighted (A) when he saw.

D. The simile introduces the subject *before* the narrative has reached that point – thus 'as when Y happens, so X happened'. In this case, we have to wait to find out what the precise point of the comparison really is. So at 12.421, the Greeks and Lycians (Trojans' allies) are battling it out round the Greek wall and Homer says: 'As two men quarrel over the boundary-markers in a common field, each with measuring sticks in their hands, fighting for their fair share in a narrow strip of ground: that was the distance they were kept apart by the battlements.' The simile turns out not to be about the fighting so much as the thickness of the wall keeping the two sides apart.

That said, similes rarely follow a simple pattern, and combinations of types are common. Other characteristics features of similes are the way they paint the *whole* picture of a scene, only slowly leading up the actual point of comparison (see e.g. on 16.156); or how they set up expectations of a comparison that are then changed in mid-simile (e.g. see on 11.113-21, 155, 172). They sometimes advance the narrative rather than returning to the precise point at which the simile began (see e.g. on 17.520), and sometimes even hint at events to come (see on 3.23).
   There are over three hundred similes in the *Il.*, occupying *c.* 1,100 lines (7% of the whole):
• Lee (1964) identifies nearly 80 subjects for similes in the *Il.*, which can

be organised into three broad groupings: weather and other natural phenomena (e.g. storms, floods, fires); hunting and herding (e.g. wild animals vs. man or domestic animals); and human technology (e.g. carpentry, weaving, threshing).
- The most common points of comparison with human life and action are lions (forty times in all), birds, fire, cattle, wind and water, and boars.
- Thirty one subjects occur once only: these include mule, ass, worm, rainbow, bean, dew, milk, lead, oil, ivory, trumpet, sandcastle and horse-trainer.
- It is noticeable how many similes add a human perspective in the shape of a hypothetical onlooker, whatever the actual subject of the simile (e.g. 21.347).
- Similes tend to occur at moments of high emotion, drama and tension, often introducing a change of perspective (e.g. the entrance of a warrior), and are especially prevalent in battle-scenes.
- They can generate moments of high pathos, especially when the death of a warrior is set against similes invoking scenes of peace and plenty.
- Throughout, Homer uses the simile to draw comparisons between the experiences of his own audience and the action of the long-distant heroic world he is describing. When similes feature e.g. women squabbling in the street (20.495-7), potters spinning a wheel (18.600-1), a man about to tread on a snake (3.33-5) or a child running after its mother (16.6-10), Homer is summoning up an image his audience would immediately recognise.

The 'classic' summary is by Fränkel (1921). De Jong (1989) 123-36 discusses how similes can also give insights into characters' thoughts. For the Near Eastern parallels, see West (1997) 217-19, 242-52.

13. Battle

A. As van Wees (1996) reports:
- Of the 15,000 lines in the *Il.*, battle takes up some 5,500 lines and consists of 300 encounters.
- There are 170 encounters in which we are given some information about the participants and weapons used – the spear is by far the most favoured weapon – and 130 others in which we know only the names or numbers of the dead.
- Only eighteen encounters involve more than one blow, only six involve more than one exchange of blows.
- Death, unrealistically, nearly always comes quickly and cleanly after a single blow, though there are some odd or gruesome deaths from particularly nasty blows. But the field is not littered with moaning, wounded and dying warriors.
- Out of the 300 encounters there are only twenty-eight duels, i.e. where warriors confront each other and agree to fight. Warriors very rarely launch out into an extended sequence of killings (Patroclus [16.284ff.]

and Achilles [20.455ff.] are among the few exceptions). Hit-and-run is by far the most favoured tactic. The warriors, in other words, tend to look after themselves as best they can. They are not desperate to die.

- Further, of the 230 warriors killed in these encounters, 170 are Trojan, 50 Greek. In all, 281 Trojans are killed, 61 Greeks. There is a continuing debate about the extent to which Homer's mild pro-Greek bias is simply chauvinism or an essential ingredient of the moral universe of the poem. It has been argued that Homer becomes more sympathetic to the Trojans as more are killed.

B. There are, broadly, five basic elements to Homeric battles: mass combat, individuals in combat, speeches (challenges, rebukes, boasts etc.), similes, and divine interventions, cf. Kirk (1990) 15-27. Albracht (2003) offers the best analysis of how Homeric battle actually works. He shows that:

(i) The fighting is dominated by the great heroes, usually on foot, using mainly spear, shield and sword. This does not mean the massed ranks are unimportant. After all, only when the whole army, massed ranks and all, turns and flees, or sets off on a charge, driving the enemy backwards, can one side be said to be winning or losing. It is just that Homer's main interest on the battlefield is to describe the performance of individual heroes – who truly are heroic. Indeed, the outcome of a whole battle often hangs on one man's heroics, e.g. when Patroclus attacks (16.276-83), or failure of nerve, e.g. when Hector flees (16.657). See (v)(a) below for the basic historical realism of this.

(ii) The army's purpose is to break through the enemy line and turn it to flight (the rout), when the pursuers can, effectively, slaughter at will. That, for example, is why a great warrior like Achilles is known as 'swift-footed' (speed in the chase is vital) and *rhêxênôr*, 'breaker of men'. The rout is the moment to be feared above all other – the moment when (as the military historian John Keegan puts it) an army turns into a crowd, 'the strongest fear with which every commander lives'. This is when most men are killed, not when they are fighting in the front line. Homer here reflects a terrifying truth about battle.

(iii) In the course of a battle, particularly during the rout, the lines of battle frequently become disorganised and the men have to be regrouped (e.g. 5.497).

(iv) Battles begin and develop according to the will of the poet, for the most part to show off the abilities and characters of the heroes. There is nothing in the way of a battle-plan, set in motion and controlled by a master-mind, nor of overall strategy or tactics, or even of a united front (e.g. at 20.329 battle is apparently raging, but the Caucones are still busy arming themselves). To that extent, the sense of the independence of the individual heroes, who are thus permitted on the battlefield to do what they like, when they like, is strongly maintained. Cf. 4/Intro.

(v) Two styles of battle dominate proceedings:

    (a) the *stadiê makhê*, 'standing fight': here both lines steadily confront each other, while individual heroes (or small groups) leap out of the line to do battle. They usually thrust with or throw their spear, follow up to finish the enemy off and/or retrieve the spear, and at the same time try to remove the enemy's armour (as plunder), before leaping back (see e.g. 4.517-35). They can leave themselves vulnerable to counter-attack at this moment.

This may all seem rather unreal: it is not. Neil Faulkner, *Apocalypse* (Tempus 2002) 242-6 describes the fighting between Jewish and Roman soldiers at the Temple Mount in AD 70 in such 'Homeric' terms and draws parallels with Agincourt, citing John Keegan *The Face of Battle* (Harmondsworth 1978): 'as movement died out of the two hosts [at Agincourt], we can visualise them divided, at a distance of ten or fifteen feet, by a horizontal fence of waving and stabbing spear shafts, the noise of their clattering like that of a bully-off at hockey magnified several hundred times'. Faulkner goes on: 'There is, in fact, an almost overpowering "terror of cold steel", which ensures that a line which does not flinch in the face of an enemy charge is almost guaranteed to bring the enemy to a halt immediately in front of it ....What men feared when they contemplated crossing the last few yards to close fully with the enemy was not just death or injury, but steel slicing through flesh, agonising and horrific wounds, the possibility of mutilation and permanent disablement'. See **GI** 4 for the heroes' constant willingness to engage in battle in these circumstances.

(b) The 'massed assault', in which the sides amalgamate their lines into a solid block and attempt to smash their way through; this often develops into a *stadiê makhê* (see e.g. 4.446-56, turning into a 'standing fight' 457ff.). Massed assault can also become massed defence (13.126).

(vi) Most of the front-rank heroes use two-man chariots (one driver, one warrior), but their use is restricted. It is worth noting that where a translation says 'horses' in the context of battle, it will usually imply 'chariot' or 'chariots': with the exception of 10.513-14, Homeric heroes do not ride horses (see on 10.498). Chariots:

(a) convey heroes to the battle-front, where they dismount to fight (e.g. 3.27-9);

(b) remain close behind the warrior, in case the warrior needs to get away (e.g. 5.243-50, cf. 11.338-42);

(c) remove warriors at speed in the rout, and pick them up to pursue the routed enemy in the chase (e.g. 16.367-83). When Homer describes warriors making for their chariots, it normally means they are about to turn in flight (e.g. 5.39-83); many warriors and/or their drivers are killed at this dangerous moment. When the rout and chase in particular are on, chariots will get far ahead of their own foot-soldiers. Only very rarely is a warrior said to fight *from* his chariot: 5.13, 8.118ff., 11.531ff., 15.386, 16.377ff., and perhaps 16.809.

Chariots were used for the purposes of massed attack in the Near Eastern and perhaps Mycenaean worlds too; see Wace, etc. (1963) 521-2. They were extremely expensive to maintain and run but, manned by warriors armed with bows and thrusting spears (i.e. lances), and with the horses suitably armoured, could be devastating and therefore worth the outlay. So their use in Homer as little more than a sort of taxi is in a military sense a considerable waste of resources. But one can see why Homer uses them as he does. Homer's is a world of great, individualistic heroes. An élite form of individual transport suits their wealth and status. This may not make much historical sense; but it makes good epic sense.

(vii) It usually takes a special intervention (often by a god) for a rout to be stopped and the fleeing warriors to regroup (e.g. 5.461ff.).

(viii) Great heroes seem to win their spurs not by taking on other great heroes but by the sheer *number* of warriors – often fleeing warriors too – that they cut down (like fighter pilots marking up their kills during the war). This may seem unsatisfactory as a demonstration of heroism, but there is a good reason for it, i.e. that the tradition gives Homer only a certain number of great heroes to deal with, and many of these are known, also in the tradition, to survive the war (e.g. Odysseus). Consequently there are not many 'hero vs. hero' encounters which *can* end in the death of one of them (hence the long list of score-draws which e.g. Ajax fights against Hector in Books 13-16). The way Homer deals with this is to show what a mighty feat of arms it is to cause a rout, to highlight the way in which the great hero achieves this, and then invent lists of minnows whom he can cut down with impunity. This provides the audience with evidence enough of the great hero's abilities, while whetting the appetite even further for the major contests, e.g. Patroclus vs. Sarpedon. And it is to be noted that where great heroes do fight it out against each other, it is often the gods who play a decisive role, never more so than in Achilles vs. Hector at 22.214-99.

(ix) Ilium is a city 'with fine walls', apparently under siege. But the tactics adopted do not seem to bear any relation to siege warfare – the two sides simply meet on the plain outside the city and fight it out. It is as if the onus is on the defenders to drive away the attackers, and all the attackers have to do is camp out, wait for the defenders to attack, and hope to beat them. But it can hardly be called a 'siege' when there is no sign of the art of siege warfare, involving e.g. ladders, undermining walls, bombardment, or even cutting off water supplies, starving the enemy out and so on.

Even when the *Il.* does seem to deal with the subject, with Sarpedon attacking the Greek wall (see on 12.257-64), it is not very convincing: the wall round a hastily fortified camp is not a city wall anyway. But in fact siege warfare *is* known. In his appeal to Achilles, Phoenix describes how the Curetes started bombarding Calydon, scaling it and throwing fire on it (9.588-9). In this respect it is worth noting that the raids which the Greeks carry out all over the Troad to gain booty never seem to require a lengthy siege. Presumably such towns did not have extensive walls to defend them.

Why do the Greeks, after ten long years, not use proper siege tactics against Ilium? Presumably there is a narrative reason, i.e. that the epic tradition asserted that the mark of great heroes was the use of two-man chariots and hand-to-hand combat against other heroes in open field, a style of fighting that siege warfare (if it was to be successful) did not encourage. The tradition therefore simply suppressed it. So it is not surprising that, when Andromache urges Hector to fight a defensive battle, he rejects it; that is not how battle works or heroes behave (6.441-6). His aim is to drive the Greeks away so that they never return (6.526-9). In other words, Ilium will be saved or taken when one army has decisively defeated the other in open combat.

Introductory bibliography

Book-by-book studies

The following have continuous essays/commentary in English on each book of the *Il.* and should be consulted throughout: Frazer (1993); Owen (1946); Pope (1743); Willcock (1976). Toohey (1992) 20-43 is a useful short summary.

Introductions to Homer

As well as the material in **R-J, H** (book by book) and **L**, the following make excellent general introductions to Homer, and to the *Il.* in particular:

Camps (1980), Griffin (1980/2001), Jenkyns (1992), Rutherford (1996), Silk (1987); (more detailed) Edwards (1987), Griffin (1980), Schein (1984), Taplin (1992).

Note that the Cambridge commentaries have useful discussions of various topics, in particular: 'The making of the *Iliad*', Kirk (1985) 1-16; 'The Homeric gods: prior considerations', Kirk (1990) 1-14; 'History and fiction in the *Iliad*', Kirk (1990) 36-50; 'The *Iliad* as heroic poetry', Hainsworth (1993) 32-53; 'The gods in Homer: further considerations', Janko (1992) 1-7; 'Narrator and audience', Edwards (1991) 1-10; 'Composition by theme', Edwards (1991) 11-23; 'Similes', Edwards (1991) 24-41; 'Structure and themes', Richardson (1993) 1-19.

The collection of essays edited by Cairns (2001) is highly recommended. For Near Eastern parallels to the *Il.*, West (1997) 206-17 make fascinating reading.

At the end of each Introduction, I list the main modern sources I have used and other reading matter specific to the Book.

Book 1

GI refers to the sections of the General Introduction (pp. 11-43); 'Intro' refers to the introduction to each Book (thus 4/Intro = the Introduction to Book 4). Note that **R-J** indicates Trojans and pro-Trojan gods with italics, and gods with capital letters.

A note: Greece and Greeks in Homer

Homer (like **H** and **L**) gives the Greeks three names: 'Achaians', *Akhaioi*, men from Achaia, a region of Greece; 'Danaans', *Danaoi*, suggesting that Greeks were descendants of Danaus, an Egyptian king who fled with his fifty daughters, the Danaids, to Argos, to escape forced marriage; and 'Argives', *Argeioi*, men from Argos, an area in the Peloponnese (southern Greece). Homer does not use them in order to exploit subtle distinctions of meaning (see **GI** 2C). **R-J** calls them all 'Greeks' throughout. This has the possible disadvantage of suggesting that the Greeks are fighting as a unified nation at Troy, as if for some great patriotic cause. They are not: each contingent is there because it is under some sort of obligation to help Agamemnon and Menelaus retrieve Helen (1.157-60, 2.286). The Trojan war is personal, not nationalistic.

Interestingly, later Greeks did not call themselves by any of the Homeric names, but 'Hellenes', inhabitants of 'Hellas' (still the Greek name for Greece). Since in Homer 'Hellas' is a small territory in the region where Achilles lives (2.683, 9.395), it is not clear how it became the name for the whole of Greece. The Romans called the Greeks *Graeci*, perhaps because the first Greeks to settle in Italy in the eight century BC came from Graea, opposite Euboea. Roman *Graeci* was adapted to become our 'Greek'.

Homer also frequently refers to a place called 'Argos', but this seems to be a catch-all name for four quite different areas, i.e. central and southern Greece generally, or Thessaly in central Greece, or the Peloponnese, or the specific area where Agamemnon lived (Argos, the Argolid). **H** and **L** stick with 'Argos'; **R-J** translates to suit whichever location seems most appropriate.

Finally, note that the *region* in which the battle is being fought is Troy; the town under siege is called Ilium/Ilios/Ilion. For a reconstruction of the area as Homer may have envisaged it, see **R-J** map 1.

Introduction

The poet begins by calling on the god to sing the epic, and outlines the theme (see notes on 1 below). Such an introduction to an epic is called the 'proemium' (*pro-oimion* 'before-song') or 'proem'. Some have found it

45

odd that Homer does not mention e.g. the Trojans or Hector. But a proemium does not summarise the story. It sets out the major issue that underpins it, in this case, the anger of Achilles and its consequences (cf. *Od*. 1. 1-9).

The first word of western literature is 'anger', promptly described as 'accursed': is that the poet's objective description or evaluative, personal comment? Or should we focalise it (**GI** 10C) through the eyes of Achilles (cf. 18.107-13, where Achilles expresses his regret for it) or of the Greeks, who suffer so much as a result of it? Whatever we may decide, Achilles' anger drives the *Il*. (**GI** 1, 9) and Book 1 lays the secure foundation for what is to come.

Homer does not hang around: he is dealing with only a fifty-day section of the ten-year Trojan war, and after calling on the Muse to sing for him (**GI** 4), he plunges *in medias res* 'into the thick of the action', as Horace puts it (*ars poetica* 148-9 '[Homer] always hurries to the outcome, and whisks the audience *in medias res*, as if they already knew it all from the beginning'). Homer fleshes out the background to the story as he goes along (**GI** 1C) and, incidentally, looks beyond the end of it too (**GI** 1D). So after giving first place to Achilles and his anger, Homer then implicates the gods, saying that Zeus' will was fulfilled in the course of this epic (5). It would not be epic unless gods and humans were equally embroiled. Next, with impressive brevity, he sketches the background to the clash between Agamemnon and Achilles: Agamemnon's refusal to return his captive Chryseis to her priest-father, the insult to Apollo (a pro-Trojan god) that this represented, and Apollo's instant, devastating response – plague. Already Agamemnon is sketched as a leader of no judgement, at odds with his army (22-4) – as he will be for much of the rest of the *Il*. – and a bully (26-32).

When Achilles summons an assembly to find out the reason for the plague, it soon emerges that tension has existed between him and Agamemnon for some time (90-1), as it obviously has done between Agamemnon and Calchas as well (78-9, 106-8). This is all very delicately suggested. Homer is a master of the hint: he drops the implication into the narrative, and says no more.

Homer sets up the action of Book 1 to be played out on three levels: the public, the private and the divine, levels that will interact throughout the epic. The public debate between Agamemnon and Achilles instantly solves the problem of the plague (Chryseis is to be returned), but the conditions Agamemnon attaches to that return raise another issue that turns out to pose even more of a threat to the success of the Greek attack on Ilium. Agamemnon wants compensation for his loss of Chryseis because, he argues, the leader of the expedition has his status to think of: he cannot be seen to lose his share of the prizes (one might compare 'take a cut in salary') while others retain theirs (118-20). But this demand soon turns into a personal battle between Agamemnon and Achilles. The early sparring over conditions rapidly turns into mutual threats and insults, leading to Agamemnon's demand that he be compensated with Achilles' girl Briseis (137-8, 184-5); and the humiliation of Achilles is made final by Agamemnon's insistence that the expedition does not need him anyway (173). So Achilles, with Patroclus, withdraws from the fighting. It is a brilliant description of how a quarrel, between two people looking for a quarrel, escalates. The fears raised by those earlier hints of tension between the two men have been fully realised.

When in the course of this quarrel Achilles considers killing Agamemnon, Athene intervenes. The poet explains why: Hera is deeply concerned for both men (196). So Athene promises Achilles massive future compensation for his present humiliation (194-214), if only he will desist. Achilles agrees, but without sounding very enthusiastic about it (216-18). It is significant that Athene's promise is never referred to again. It was a desperate measure to ensure that Achilles would not disembowel Agamemnon, and it did the job it was designed for. As will soon become clear, Achilles has no interest in gifts to compensate him for Agamemnon's treatment (407-12). As for Nestor's attempted reconciliation of the two men, it merely restates the issue that keeps both men apart; it offers no new way through it. But is this the 'anger of Achilles' announced in line one? No.

In between the handing over of Briseis to Agamemnon and the return of Chryseis to her father, the plot moves on to the second level: the private world of Achilles, asking his divine mother Thetis for help (so much for the value Achilles attached to Athene's promise). It is important to stress the privacy of the communications between the two (cf. on 2.14). The point is that no Greek ever learns that Achilles at this time invoked his divine mother Thetis to intervene with Zeus to ensure the mass destruction of the Greek army. *This* is the anger of Achilles; it is this request that will ultimately bring about his own tragedy because (grim irony) Zeus will indeed fulfil his wishes (18.74-99), and Patroclus will die as a result, and so will Achilles.

The main reason for Achilles' request to his mother is that he knows he will not live long (352) and, despite Athene's earlier promises, is impatient to get back to the fighting and the winning of glory and the immortal reputation that all heroes craved (cf. 488-92, **GI** 4). To do that, the Greeks must start to lose; only then will Agamemnon climb down and right the wrong he has done by taking Briseis. One wonders also if there was an element of reprisal against the Greek army in Achilles' request, because they silently acquiesced in Agamemnon's humiliation of him (299, cf. 16.16-18; see Taplin [1992] 62-3); but whether there was or not, the Greek army will certainly suffer as a result, as the proem has made clear (2-5). All unknown, then, to Agamemnon and the Greek troops, Achilles' plan for revenge against them is launched, with none other than Zeus himself behind it, since he confirmed his promise to Thetis with a nod (524-30). Accursed anger indeed.

Homer now shifts the narrative to the third level, the world of the gods on Olympus, one equally unknown to men on earth, though known to us, thanks to the existence of the omniscient third person narrator Homer (cf. Greek tragedy, where in the absence of such a narrator, or a prophet, or of gods themselves on stage, the divine will remains mysterious). Here Homer indicates the trouble that Zeus' decision to support Thetis' request will cause, especially among the pro-Greek gods who foresee the threat it will pose to the Greek cause (559). When Hera guesses what he has been up to, Zeus imposes his will on her by the threat of physical violence, his superior strength (rather than e.g. wisdom or moral superiority) being the ultimate sanction that he has over all the other gods, as they well know (565-9, 580-1).

So the quarrel on earth has been ended, by the self-willed withdrawal of Achilles. The quarrel on heaven is ended, by Hera's withdrawal of her objections, under compulsion. The gods may then turn to feasting and song – they are gods, after all – but neither on earth nor Olympus have the underlying reasons for the quarrels gone away. From such foundations Homer launches his *Il*.

Main sources for the commentary and related reading
Edwards (1987) 173-87; Kirk (1985); Pulleyn (2000); Willcock (1978).

1.1-7: Proemium

1. *Anger*: as in **R-J**, this is the first word of the *Il*. It announces that the story is driven by someone's feelings. Since the Greek word, *mênis*, is strongly associated with divine anger (Redfield 1979), one immediately wonders which god is angry.

goddess: she is the Muse of epic song and goddess of memory. She is asked to sing through the poet because she alone knows what no human could know – the facts about the heroic past, and especially the gods' rôle in it. The poet can thus claim privileged access to the world of gods and men. Cf. 2.484, 11.218, 14.508, 16.112. Contrast 12.176, where the poet introduces himself into the equation.

Achilles son of Peleus: so it is a mortal who is angry, with an anger that is almost divine. This is not because Achilles is son of a goddess (Thetis); Homer plays down such divine origins (cf. on 10.50), insisting that his heroes are all mortal and equal in their human desire for immortal *kleos*, the reputation that will stay with them after death.

Achilles' father, the mortal Peleus, will play an increasingly important part in the *Il*. as the (absent) father who *will* (after the end of *Il*.) lose his son because of Achilles' decision to kill Hector; in effect, Peleus is in the same situation as the father of Hector, Priam (king of Troy), and for the same reason – the nature of Achilles. See on 19.322.

2. *and its devastation* (**L**): 'accursed' (**R-J, H**) is correct.

Greeks/Achaians: so Achilles' anger brings destruction first and foremost not on the Trojans but on his *own* side – an extraordinary thing to say. One wonders at whom Achilles can be so angry, and why.

3.   *Hades*: not a place but a divinity, god of the underworld.

4.   *warriors* **(R-J)**, *heroes* **(H, L)**: in Homer, *hêrôs* is used to describe a very wide range of people, some distinctly unheroic. The more neutral 'warrior' may be preferable, or even 'war-lord'.

delicate feasting **(L)**: inaccurate. 'Carrion/prey' **(R-J, H)** is correct.

5.   *of dogs, of all birds* **(L)**: **R-J, H** prefer a different text – not 'of all birds' but 'and a feast for the birds'. Homer emphasises the theme of maltreatment of the dead – being left out in the open for scavengers, rather than being properly buried – because Achilles in his anger will himself mutilate Hector's body. Even so, the gods protect Hector's body (24.18-21); and in fact no warrior in the *Il.* is scavenged by dogs or birds, though such a fate is often threatened (but for warriors scavenged by fish, see 21.120-7, 200-4). See on 11.455 for the development of this 'mutilation' theme as a means of raising the emotional stakes as the final battle between Achilles and Hector draws nearer.

6.   *It all began when* **(R-J)**; *Sing from the time of* **(H)**; *since that time when* **(L)**: since any ancient epic is a chunk of a much larger whole – in the case of the Trojan war, embracing anything from the judgement of Paris and seizure of Helen to Ilium's destruction and the return home of the Greeks – the poet must clearly mark out the moment at which his own version of these great events will begin (cf. *Od.* 1.10-21, 8.499). Homer does so here, saying he will start with the quarrel between Agamemnon and Achilles, in the last year of the war. So we should take 'from/since the time' with 'sing' (1) **(R-J, H)** – i.e. sing what happened (death, destruction, etc.) 'beginning from the time when' Agamemnon and Achilles quarrelled. If not, the phrase has to be taken with 'the will of Zeus was accomplished' *beginning from the time when* Agamemnon and Achilles quarrelled **(L)**. That is possible but less likely, since the will of Zeus does not become a factor till *after* the quarrel, when Zeus agrees with Thetis (502-30) that the Greeks should start losing in order for the humiliated Achilles to be welcomed back, with his honour restored. Besides, as the poet goes on to say, it was not in fact Zeus but Apollo who *started* them quarrelling.

7.   *Agamemnon lord of men and godlike (brilliant) Achilles*: 'lord of men' and 'godlike' are both standard epithets; 'brilliant' **(L)** is acceptable, since *dios* 'godlike' is etymologically connected with Zeus (the root of 'Zeus' is *di-*), god of the (bright) day and sky. Agamemnon may be 'lord of men' and the leader of the expedition to Troy but he does not wield absolute authority (though he tries to) over the other leaders. Everything is up for debate and dispute among these strongly independent-minded individuals, with their own troops, from their own regions, at their back. See e.g. **GI** 4F and 13B(iv), 4/Intro, and cf. Achilles' argument at 1.152-60.

1.8-52. 1st day: Agamemnon rejects Chryses' supplication and Apollo sends the plague.

9.   *Apollo*: god of sickness and healing, and of stringed instruments (the bow, cf. 1.45, and the lyre cf. 1.603). He takes the Trojans' side in the war (for reasons Poseidon cannot understand at 21.435-60).

In anger at the king (**H, L**): i.e. at Agamemnon. Many Greek warriors are called *basileus*, usually translated 'king'. They may indeed be 'kings' of a sort, with a line of succession (though no settled constitutional position), back home, but the term means little more than 'war-lord', 'leader' or 'commander' when applied to the head of an army of independent Greek warriors (**GI** 4F).

11.   *not respecting* (**R-J**); *dishonoured* (**H, L**): see **GI** 4A-D.

Chryses: distinguish Chryses, priest of Apollo, from his daughter Chryseis (1.111, 143 etc.) and their town of origin Chryse (1.37, 100 etc., **R-J** map 2).

13.   *(captured) daughter*: Chryseis, captured by Achilles but given by the army as booty to Agamemnon (see on 1.366).

14.   *emblems* (**R-J**); *sacred woollen bands* (**H**); *ribbons* (**L**): the Greek *stemmata* means 'wreaths, garlands', but since they are on a staff they probably indicate that the staff is entwined with wool, the sign of a suppliant (Sophocles, *Oedipus the King* 3). Cf. our flags of truce.

15.   *in supplication* (**R-J**); *began to entreat* (**H**); *supplicated* (**L**): see **GI** 7D.

16.   *the two sons of Atreus*: Agamemnon and Menelaus.

17.   *men-at-arms* (**R-J**); *well/strong-greaved* (**H, L**): **H** and **L** translate accurately. Greaves are leg-guards for the shins, probably made of leather, bronze or (in special cases, 18.612) tin, to protect the legs from low-flying arrows and stones (though in fact no metal examples have been found dateable to between 1100 and 700 BC). Only soldiers depicted on bronze age artefacts are shown wearing them. They were introduced, presumably, when the great tower-shields protecting the whole body went out of fashion (see on 6.117, 7.219). For the bronze age background, see **GI** 2(v), **GI** 3.

18.   *Olympus*: a mountain in north-eastern Greece where the gods had their homes. Zeus, as king of Olympus, is often called 'Olympian'. That is why the Olympic Games were so called: they were held at Olympia, a cult-site of *Zeus Olumpios* in Elis in southern Greece, some 160 miles from Mount Olympus. See **R-J** map 4.

19.   *Priam's town/city*: Priam is king of Ilium, in the region of Troy. 'City' has rather modern overtones of civic rights and organisation absent from this early Greek world.

21.   *respect* (**R-J**); *reverence* (**H**); *giving honour* (**L**): Chryses does not appeal to e.g. the army's sense of pity or justice: he argues that the seizure of his daughter is an insult to Apollo, whose priest he is (14). This will have serious implications if his request is rejected.

29.   *She will grow old* (**R-J**); *old age will come upon her* (**H, L**):

observe how Agamemnon piles on the agony: he goes on to emphasise how far Chryseis will be from home, and the work she will have to do – weaving and, saving the nastiest for last, serving his bed. He comes over as a sadistic bully.

35.   *poured out prayers* (**R-J**); *prayed* (**H, L**): see **GI** 7A.

37.   *Chryse*: home of Chryses and, like Cilla, a town in Troy. Tenedos is an off-shore island (**R-J** map 2).

39.   *Plague god* (**R-J**); *Smintheus* (**H, L**): Smintheus is a name applied to Apollo, meaning 'mouse-god'. Mice were probably associated with plague.

40.   *fat* (**R-J**); *rich* (**L**); *fat-wrapped* (**H**): the thighs were wrapped in fat and burnt for the god; the rest was for human consumption (see **GI** 7B).

42.   *Make the Greeks/Danaans pay*: it is interesting that Chryses does not specifically ask the god for the return of his daughter. First and foremost he wants revenge for the insult done to him. He knows the god will take revenge because an insult to his priest is an insult to the god (and his daughter will automatically be returned).

44.   *in fury* (**R-J**); *with anger* (**H**); *angered* (**L**): note how the emotions in Homer are frequently expressed by physical reaction – the god is furious, as Homer says, and consequently the arrows clash on Apollo's shoulder as he darts down (see **GI** 10A). Apollo is envisaged as a hunter.

47.   *like night(fall)* (**R-J, H**); *as night comes* (**L**): a dramatically suggestive A-simile (see **GI** 12). Apollo the hunter now comes like the night – silent, all-encompassing, and deadly ('darkness' is said to engulf the eyes of those killed in battle, e.g. 4.461).

48.   *shot an arrow*: these are felt to carry the plague, which attacks animals first and then men.

52.   *pyres* (**R-J, H**); *corpse fires* (**L**): typically rapid action, from plague to fires without a pause. It is very Homeric to encapsulate a total experience (lengthy plague, many deaths, destruction of the bodies) in one aspect of it – the burning pyres. The whole army pays the price for their leader's delinquency.

1.53-120. [The nine-day plague.] 10th day: Achilles calls an assembly, at which Agamemnon demands compensation for returning Chryseis.

54.   *Achilles*: anyone *could* have called an assembly. Homer chooses Achilles in order to generate the clash with Agamemnon. Homer commonly uses assemblies to motivate the action (e.g. 2.50, 7.345, 9.9, 19.40 etc.). They follow a regular pattern, some elements of which can be omitted: a leader orders the heralds to summon the troops; they sit; the leader rises, takes the sceptre (bestowing authority to speak) and puts forward a proposal; other leaders respond to it; action is agreed. Cf. **GI** 2(i).

55.   *Hera*: wife of Zeus, and fervently pro-Greek (see 4.1-67; and for her and Athene's rejection by Paris, which caused their hatred of the Trojans, 24.29). The gods have no hesitation in intervening on behalf of their favourites (cf. 5.873-4 and **GI** 5). But since gods rarely cross each other *openly*, Hera will not stop the plague while Apollo is actively spreading it. For the gods who support the Greeks or Trojans, see 20.33-40.

58.   *swift-footed* (**R-J, H**); *of the swift feet* (**L**): the first time Achilles is described with this famous epithet; it is an irony that he will have no use for his swift feet until he rejoins the fighting in Book 20. Cf. on 18.104.

65.   *hecatomb* (**L**): a sacrifice, technically of 100 oxen (*hekaton* '100', *bous* 'ox').

66.   *unblemished*: the animal for sacrifice had to be perfect (**L**, with his 'fragrant smoke', misses this). See **GI** 7B.

69.   *Calchas*: the expedition's main prophet (see e.g. 2.322ff.). A prophet's function is to speak in the name of the god or interpret his will (in this case, Apollo's, 86-7, 96-100). With this gift he is able to understand and make sense of the past and present as well as foretell the future.

71.   *guided the Greek fleet/Achaian ships*: though the *Il.* is set in the tenth year of the war, Homer takes pains to fill in aspects of the earlier years (here, the voyage to Troy). See **GI** 1C.

78.   *I am about to infuriate* (**R-J**); *I shall anger* (**H**); *I shall make a man angry* (**L**): Calchas refers to Agamemnon: he knows his man, cf. on 13.45.

90.   *Agamemnon*: Achilles knows his man as well. There are hints here of previous trouble between the two; cf. 12.211-14, where Polydamas hints at ancient tensions between himself and Hector.

91.   *claims to be far the best/greatest*: the Greek *eukhomai* can mean 'claim to be' or 'be'. So this could also mean 'is the best/greatest'. Is Achilles being sarcastic here?

92.   *matchless/blameless*: *amumôn* is a word of disputed meaning: 'matchless, excellent' is currently in favour.

99.   *without recompense/price or ransom*: an important condition – if Agamemnon wants compensation, he will have to get it from the Greeks.

100.   *Chryse*: the place where the priest Chryses lives.

104.   *heart … eyes*: see on 1.44 for the physical expression of emotion.

106.   *Prophet/seer of evil*: more indications of past trouble, this time between Agamemnon and Calchas. Would the audience pick up here a covert reference to Calchas saying that Agamemnon had to sacrifice his daughter Iphigeneia in order to get the wind that would enable the fleet, becalmed at Aulis, to sail for Troy? See e.g. Aeschylus *Agamemnon* 224-7.

113.   *better than (my wife) Clytaemnestra* (**R-J, L**); *I prefer her to Klytaimestra* (**H**): in the *Od.* (11.422) Agamemnon will bring Priam's daughter Cassandra home from Troy with him: both are killed by Clytaemnestra. Note (114-15) that women in Homer are valued for their beauty (the gift of Aphrodite, goddess of sexual attraction) and skills and intelligence (the gift of Athene: **L**'s 'wit' 115 must be taken in its old-fashioned sense). Cf. 9.388-9.

119.   *would not/cannot be right* (**R-J, H**); *that were unfitting* (**L**): the groundwork of Agamemnon's argument with Achilles is laid. It is not right/fitting for him to lose possessions because that means losing face, and no one who calls himself expedition leader can afford that in Homeric society (see **GI** 4A-B). There is nothing wrong with that position. A leader in the Homeric world demonstrated his status (in terms of material wealth) by ensuring it was on display for all to see, and Agamemnon has now lost an element of it (for the 'reckoning up' of gifts and prizes, see Donlan [1998] 55-6). But a leader also proved he was a leader by demonstrating he was in control, and Agamemnon shows himself incapable of dealing with a man like Achilles. Agamemnon is not an evil man. He is just not up to the job (Redfield [1994] 95). Observe how the argument develops by each man 'capping' the other's claim with a counter-claim; each counter-claim raises the emotional temperature, till argument becomes threat and the situation explodes in a torrent of insults. I call Agamemnon's claim here **Ia**.

1.121-307. The quarrel.

At 1.125-6 ('distributed' **R-J, L**; 'divided' **H**), Achilles says that everything the Greek army has taken is already distributed: it cannot be called back and re-distributed. The background to this is that, during the siege of Ilium, the Greek army raided local towns for plunder, human and material, and the *army* decided who should get what (1.127-8, 162, 276, 368-9, 2.255-6, 11.623-6, 16.56, 18.444-5, but contrast 11.703-5, where Neleus is described as taking what he wanted, and leaving the rest for the people to divide up among themselves. Cf. **GI** 1C).

That is the system and Achilles has no gripe with it. He does not accuse the army of failing to share out the booty properly (125, cf. 2.226-8), nor does he claim e.g. that Agamemnon fixed the initial distribution. His resentment is against Agamemnon for taking advantage of his position as leader of the army to threaten to deprive Achilles of what little he does get when the distribution is made (135-7, cf. 164 Achilles never gets 'a prize equal to yours' **R-J, H**; 'equal to your prize' **L**). Achilles' point is that Agamemnon has done no fighting *at all* to win the plunder (225-31, cf. 2.229-34) – and Agamemnon does nothing to refute him. In other words, Achilles is hinting at the idea that Agamemnon has been cheating, breaking an *unspoken* contract that tied material rewards to performance in battle – which, indeed, seems to lie at the heart of the Homeric hero's understanding of his privileged position in society (12.310-28); Agamemnon, he suggests, does nothing but milk the army's, and especially his own, efforts, simply by dint of his position. This explains the force of Achilles' festering resentments at the injustice which he feels has been done to him. Not only has Agamemnon gratuitously threatened to take his Briseis; this 'leader' has not lifted even a finger to win her, or any other of the booty that the army (thanks largely to Achilles) is able to distribute. If Agamemnon were agreed to be 'the best' by dint of his position, the situation might be different (see on 23.536); but in Achilles' eyes he is not, and therefore his status alone is not enough to justify the way he has acted. Achilles is laying the groundwork for his threat to return home (169-71).

122. *unequalled in your greed* (**R-J**); *most acquisitive* (**H**); *greediest for gain* (**L**): Homeric society is deeply materialistic. Achilles is pointing out that Agamemnon has this otherwise acceptable quality in excess.

126. *right* (**R-J, H**); *unbecoming* (**L**): Achilles (unlike **L**) throws back the same word that Agamemnon used at 119 to justify his demand for compensation. It is a clash of equal 'rights'.

128. *compensate* (**R-J**); *recompense* (**H**); *repay* (**L**): here is Achilles' counter-offer – Agamemnon will be compensated, but *later* (**Ib**).

133. *sit tamely by* (**R-J**); *just sit by* (**H**); *have me sit here* (**L**): Agamemnon rejects Achilles' suggestion (**Ib**) outright, by reducing the argument to personalities: if no new distribution is made, Achilles will be able to keep his prize (Agamemnon means the woman Briseis) while Agamemnon loses his (Chryseis). Agamemnon implies that this is the outcome Achilles is really after, with its implied humiliation of Agamemnon. Agamemnon's counters with a threat (**IIa**): the army *must* make recompense now (i.e. Agamemnon rejects **Ib**) but if not, he himself will take another warrior's prize (137). In other words, Agamemnon is asserting his own absolute authority to do what he likes with anyone else's possessions, in order to restore his own status.

140. *deal with all that later* (**R-J**); *talk for the future* (**H**); *deliberate again hereafter* (**L**): Agamemnon (aware that he has gone too far? Or assuming his proposal will end the argument at once?) makes a sensible concession – a 'cooling off' period while Chryseis is returned.

146. *most impetuous* (**R-J**); *most formidable* (**H**); *most terrifying* (**L**): the Greek *ekpaglos* seems to suggest striking/amazing/excessive behaviour (not the sort of quality desirable in an ambassador).

149-71. *You shameless* (**R-J**); *Oh you, your thoughts* (**H**); *O wrapped in shamelessness* (**L**): Achilles erupts, responding to **IIa** by assuming that Agamemnon's comments were indeed a personal attack on him. Achilles therefore also counters threat with threat – **IIb**, that he will return home at once (169-71). Note the string of personal insults hurled at Agamemnon (149, 158, 159).

155. *Phthia*: Achilles' home, **R-J** map 4.

159. *for Menelaus and you(rself)* (**R-J, H**); *your honour and Menelaos'* (**L**): the first, somewhat oblique, mention of the reason for the Trojan war – not a nationalistic enterprise, but to save Menelaus' and his brother Agamemnon's honour by restoring Helen to her rightful husband Menelaus.

170. *beaked ships* (**R-J, H**); *curved ships* (**L**): the Greek *korônis* suggests a beak or tip, and probably refers to the ships' high, curved, beak-like prows.

173-87. *Run for it, then* (**R-J**); *Yes, run home* (**H**); *Run away* (**L**): Agamemnon calls Achilles' bluff – if bluff it is – accusing him of desertion or even cowardice (*pheugô* 'I run away' is used of men in flight). Ironically, it is Agamemnon who will soon be suggesting the whole army goes home, first as a 'test' (2.73-4), and then for real (9.26-8).

174. *on bended knees* **(R-J)**; *beg* **(H)**; *entreat* **(L)**: the same word as 'supplicate' (see **GI** 7D).

175. *Zeus wise in counsel* **(R-J)**; *Zeus the counsellor* **(H)**; *Zeus of the counsels* **(L)**: Zeus 'wise in counsel' (i.e. 'advice'), being king (*basileus*) of the gods, was therefore patron of the earthly *basileus* (see on 1.9 above, 1.278-9, and cf. 2.196-7, 9.98-9). In fact, Zeus wields power by force (see on 1.401).

177. *Rivalry/strife/quarrelling, war, fighting/battles*: this extreme accusation, true or not, is made by Zeus with justification against Ares (god of war) at 5.891.

184. *Briseis*: daughter of Briseus (cf. Chryseis as daughter of Chryses). Achilles took her while sacking Lyrnessus and Thebe (2.689-1, 19.291-6): on the same expedition he captured Chryseis (1.366-9) and killed the father (Eëtion) and brothers of Andromache, Hector's wife (6.415-24). See on 6.395 and **R-J** map 2.

185. *will come in person* **(R-J)**; *going myself to fetch her* **(H)**; *I myself going* **(L)**: see **GI** 10C for this famous problem.

186. *I am your superior* **(R-J, H)**; *how much greater I am* **(L)**: Agamemnon is publicly asserting his authority to do exactly as he likes, making an example of the mighty Achilles before everyone else. This is a calculated act of humiliation on Agamemnon's part (cf. Achilles' reaction at 201-5; see on 203 below): not only does he signal that the army does not need Achilles (cf. Agamemnon's disparaging remark about Achilles' fighting ability/strength at 178), but he adds insult to injury by confirming that he will indeed deprive Achilles (as he threatened at 137-9) of what is Achilles' by right. What has so far been a matter of increasingly heated debate between the leader of the expedition to Troy and its greatest fighter over a single issue has now developed into a crisis that threatens the success of the whole expedition.

189. *his heart was torn* **(R-J, H)**; *the heart was divided* **(L)**: no Greek passively endures humiliation, let alone one like Achilles, lover of fighting (177) – hence his furious reaction. In scenes of internal debate over what to do, two alternatives are usually offered, and the second usually chosen (here, only eventually – 219-21: even then, Achilles stays his hand but not his anger).

194. *Athene*: another fiercely pro-Greek god (see on 1.55) and supporter of Achilles, sent by Hera to prevent disaster. Observe how, when man and god converse, everyone else on the scene is forgotten, e.g. 5.793-834 (this also occurs occasionally during human conversations too, e.g. 6.119-236).

199. *Achilles was amazed* **(R-J)**; *startled* **(H)**; *in amazement* **(L)**: see **GI** 6 on divine intervention, and the way in which Homer makes it clear that the gods, when they intervene, are really there, often without disguise.

202. *Zeus who drives the storm cloud* **(R-J)**; *who holds the aegis/of* *the aegis* (**H, L**): the precise meaning of the Greek *aigiokhos* is disputed (**R-J** favours the idea that *aigis* means 'storm-wind' in this context). The aegis when it appears as an object, however, belongs to Zeus and was made for him by Hephaestus (15.310 – as if it were originally a thunderbolt?). It is also used by Apollo, but most of all by Athene (2.447-51, 5.738-42, 18.204, 21.400-1). It seems to have been envisaged as a sort of shield with a fringe (cf. 2.447-9). When shaken it terrifies the enemy (15.229-30, cf. 15.307-10) or produces storms (17.593-5). It cannot be destroyed even by Zeus' thunderbolt (21.401).

203. *humiliating affront* (**R-J**); *insult* (**H**); *outrageousness* (**L**): the Greek *hubris* means primarily 'physical assault' but develops into any attempt to humiliate someone and reduce their standing in other's eyes. See **GI** 4A-B.

207. *if you will listen to me/obey me* (**R-J, H**); *but will you obey me?* (**L**): this is not a question in Greek. See **GI** 6 for the casual way in which heroes welcome divine intervention, as if they were on an everyday, almost equal footing with the gods.

213. *the day shall come* (**R-J**); *there will be a day* (**H**); *some day* (**L**): this day will come with Book 9, where Achilles will reject the gifts which here Athene promises that he will be offered. As will soon become apparent from his demand at 407-12, Achilles is already looking for a much bloodier pay-back (cf. on 370-92 for his lack of genuine interest in Athene's promise). One may ask 'Athene is a goddess: does she not *know* what is to happen?' Not necessarily: gods in Homer sometimes know the future, and sometimes do not. The poet plays it according to the needs of the plot at the time.

224. *Atreides* (**L**): i.e. son of Atreus, either Agamemnon (as here) or Menelaus.

226-7. *courage*: Achilles keeps up the attack on Agamemnon's (non-) performance in the field (see on 1.121-307). The ambush seems to call for the greatest daring and bravery (13.276-7): it is the tension and waiting, all working on the imagination to stir thoughts of what might be (283), that make it the ultimate test. See *Od.* 4.269-89, 11.523-32; 14.219.

231. *nobodies* (**R-J**); *ciphers* (**H**); *nonentities* (**L**): because they seem happy to acquiesce in Agamemnon's outrageous behaviour – unlike Achilles. Achilles constructs himself as the lone fighter against injustice.

234. *staff* (**R-J, H**); *sceptre* (**L**): which the speaker was handed when addressing the assembly (23.568). It possesses an almost divine authority, since (next note) it is held by those who transmit ordinances in Zeus' name.

238. *give judgement* (**R-J, H**); *administer the justice* (**L**): the Greek here says 'those who in the name of Zeus safeguard our traditions hold it when they give judgement'. 'Justice' in the Homeric world is to do with tradition – the characteristic way that people have traditionally behaved determines how they should behave, i.e. they should observe common usage and custom. The poet distinguishes between the speaker's staff, which Achilles is holding here, the emblem of a public authority (cf.

18.503-8 for elders, holding staves, giving judgement in a case) and Agamemnon's own staff, also descended from Zeus, which gives him his personal authority (cf. 2.100-8 and 9.98-9).

243. *fall in their multitudes* **(R-J)**; *fall dying* **(H)**; *drop and die* **(L)**: any listening Greek would interpret this to mean that, in the absence of Achilles, the Greeks would *as a matter of course* lose many men. They could not know (and never would) that Achilles was about to enlist help from Zeus himself to ensure this slaughter came about (see on 408).

245. *flung down the staff* **(R-J)**; *threw the staff* **(H)**; *dashed ... the sceptre* **(L)**: this single reaction tells one more about Achilles' emotional state, and more effectively, than a thousand words (cf. on 1.44). Homer uses the gesture with delightful effect in the *Od.*, when Odysseus' inexperienced young son Telemachus addresses the assembly, hurls the staff down in a rage, bursts into tears, 'and all the people pitied him' (2.80-2).

247. *Nestor*: the wise old man of the army – 'three generations' make him about 70 – full of long stories of his youth which (as here) he uses to establish his own credentials as a man of relevant experience and to offer as examples (paradigms) from which others should learn; see **GI 1C**, Willcock (1964), Alden (2000). It is primarily in debate that Nestor is valued. He offers four such pieces of advice + paradigm: here, 7.124-60, 11.656-803 (these three all rebuke the Greeks) and 23.626-50. He is also full of advice on military matters, some of it rather odd e.g. 2.360-8, 4.297-309, 6.67-71, 7.327-43, 9.65-8, 10.204-17, 11.795-802, 14.62-3, 23.306-48.

In general, words rate as highly as action for the Homeric hero, cf. the assembly 'where men win glory', 1.490; and see Schofield (1986), especially 252-8. It is as important for the hero to win arguments in council as battles on the field, since in both arenas, the hero's personal status is at stake (cf. 258 – Nestor says that Agamemnon and Achilles are the best both in debate and war, ludicrous flattery given their recent debating performance; cf. Achilles' judgement at 18.106). See **GI 4C**.

259. *listen to me* **(R-J, H)**; *be persuaded* **(L)**: Nestor constructs his story in such a way that the end of it mirrors the start – known as 'ring-composition' (see **GI 11**).

263-5. *Peirithous ... Theseus*: these are the Lapiths, a tribe from Thessaly. Their king Peirithous invited the Centaurs (half-man, half-horse) to the marriage of his daughter Hippodameia, but they got drunk and tried to rape her. The two sides fell on each other in a battle constructed by later Greeks as one of 'civilisation' vs. 'barbarism' and widely depicted in Greek art (e.g. the Parthenon metopes).

Dryas, shepherd of the people: see **GI 3** for the agricultural background to the *Il.*

271. *my own campaign* **(R-J)**; *in my own right* **(H)**; *single-handed* **(L)**: does this mean that Nestor fought without a chariot or charioteer, as at 11.716-20? Surely not. It means Nestor fought as only Nestor could.

275-84. *though you have the authority* **(R-J)**; *great man though you are* **(H, L)**: Nestor seeks a compromise. He argues that Agamemnon has innate authority from Zeus and is Achilles' superior (because he leads the largest force at Troy – 2.576-80); therefore Achilles should not cross swords with him. Likewise, the army gave Briseis to Achilles first, and they cannot afford to lose the Greeks' greatest fighter; therefore Agamemnon should back off too. Nestor's judgement of the issue between the two men is correct. But he adds nothing new to what has already been said; all he does is define the issue, not offer a way through it.

289. *one* **(R-J, L)**: i.e. Agamemnon.

292. *Abrupt(ly)* **(R-J, H)**: L misses this important word – Achilles is jumping down Agamemnon's throat.

299. *you Greeks gave her*: Achilles acquiesces in the army's willingness to be bullied by Agamemnon into doing nothing about his loss of Briseis. Even if he is not interested in Athene's promise of gifts, she has effectively assured him that his withdrawal will be met with an eventual response from the Greeks; but from this moment on, Achilles has as good as announced that he has broken all ties between himself and the Greeks. All the usual obligations of reciprocal behaviour (**GI** 4) are off. The next move will have to come from the Greek side, if they want Achilles back.

307. *son of Menoetius* **(H)**: i.e. Patroclus, Achilles' dearest companion (17.655, 18.81-2).

1.308-48. Agamemnon has Briseis taken, and the mission to Chryse sets off.

313. *purify itself* **(R-J)**; *purification* **(H)**; *defilement* **(L)**: participants in a sacrifice always purified themselves before the event. Usually handwashing sufficed (cf. 1.449), but after a plague and so many deaths, more comprehensive measures were felt to be required. See **GI** 7B.

316. *murmuring sea* **(R-J)**; *unharvested sea* **(H)**; *barren salt sea* **(L)**: the Greek epithet *atrugetos* is one of those words so ancient that probably even Homer had no idea what it meant; cf. **GI** 2(v). A derivation associating it with sound is in favour at the moment.

317. *curling smoke* **(R-J)**; *curling upwards* **(H)**; *in circles* **(L)**: the smoke and the smell going up to the gods from the fat-covered thigh-bones (their special entitlement – see **GI** 7B) conjure up the whole scene.

321. *heralds*: a catch-all title for people with a wide range of functions – they keep order at meetings, make proclamations, act as escorts, carry messages, run errands and serve food and drink. Talthybius features at 3.118, 4.193, 19.196 and 23.987, helping Agamemnon in a variety of roles.

attendants **(R-J)**; *lieutenants* **(H)**; *henchmen* **(L)**: the Greek *therapôn* means something like the ancient 'squire', i.e. a retainer or helper, but not necessarily a social inferior. In Homer he can be a second-in-command and is often a warrior's charioteer. Patroclus is said to be the *therapôn* of Achilles, as is Meriones of Idomeneus (see on 13.159).

323. *bring her* **(R-J, H)**; *bring back* **(L)**: typically, Agamemnon sends other to do his dirty work for him (as Achilles notes during a later embassy,

9.372-3) – an action which Homer leaves us free to interpret as we wish: is Agamemnon afraid of Achilles? Contemptuous of him? Merely exerting his authority for the sake of it? The order is blunt/stern/ strong (326), as it was to Chryses at 1.25.

327. *unwilling ... embarrassed* **(R-J)**; *reluctantly ... respect* **(H)**; *against their will ... in awe* **(L)**: with brilliant economy Homer shows us, more convincingly than any direct description could, what sort of person Achilles is – by describing the *reaction* of the terrified heralds to the task they face (see on 1.44). One can almost hear the sigh of relief when Achilles gives them a friendly greeting (334-6) – and again, what might Achilles' reaction here tell us about him?

328. *Myrmidons*: the troops that Achilles brought with him from Phthia (2.683-4).

338. *witnesses*: but witnesses to what? Clearly, to what only they *can* be witnesses – the reasonableness of his (Achilles') behaviour as opposed to the lunacy of Agamemnon's (342: for **L**'s 'he makes sacrifice', read 'he is raving mad'). In other words, the Greek disaster which Achilles predicts will ensue as a result of his withdrawal from battle will be Agamemnon's fault, not Achilles' – a reasonable enough argument, were Achilles not about to beg his mother to persuade Zeus to destroy the Greeks.

1.348-430. Achilles appeals to his mother Thetis for help.

348. *unwilling(ly)* **(R-J, L)**, *reluctant* **(H)**: what does this suggestive one-word description of Briseis tell us? Of her feelings for Achilles or Patroclus, or her fear of Agamemnon, or what? Homeric reticence, again, opens up rather than closes down the possibilities. Cf. Briseis' only words at 19.282-300. Compare Achilles' mixed train of thought about her at 9.334-43 with his abrupt analysis at 19.59-60 (where his despair at the death of Patroclus takes precedence over any other sentiments). The 'Briseis painter' (480 BC) depicts the scene; see Woodford (1993) 69.

349. *in tears* **(R-J, H)**; *weeping* **(L)**: it does no discredit to a hero to weep, cf. 9.14-28 (Agamemnon at the apparent collapse of the expedition), 16.2-4 (Patroclus at Greek losses) – unless he is weeping because he is afraid or in pain (like Thersites, 2.266). But what is Achilles weeping about? As the subject of his appeal to his mother Thetis makes clear, it is Agamemnon's treatment of him. The prospect of compensation cannot make up for the present humiliation which he feels so sharply (see on 370-92). Achilles always reacts instantly to the heat of the moment.

352. *Mother*: the immortal sea-nymph Thetis – hence Achilles' position on the beach. She is in close contact with him all the time (e.g. 16.36-7, 18.8-11) and his constant point of reference in extremity (cf. 18.34-7); no other Greek warrior in Troy has a divine mother and such privileged access. Outside Homer, we hear of a story that any child of Thetis would be greater than his father. Poseidon and Zeus therefore avoided making love to her. Another version tells us that Thetis resisted Zeus' advances out of respect for Hera (cf. 24.59-62), for which he punished her by marrying her to the mortal Peleus (cf. 18.429-34). These stories about Thetis have been used in various ways to explain Thetis' role in the *Il.*; see e.g. Slatkin (1986), (1991).

Briefest of lives (**R-J**); *life doomed to shortness* (**H**); *with a short life* (**L**): a key fact about Achilles. If he has only a short time to live (cf. 1.416-18, 505), he cannot afford any loss of honour (*timê*) since that may affect his prospect of an eternally glorious reputation after death (*kleos*).

356. *in person* (**R-J**); *with his own hands* (**H**); *he has taken away* (**L**): L misrepresents the Greek – Achilles, exaggerating, does in fact say that Agamemnon took Briseis 'in person' (see **GI** 10C).

358. *father*: presumably Nereus, since Thetis' sisters are Nereids, 'daughters of Nereus' (18.52).

365. *You know*: clearly Thetis does not know – if she had known, she would surely have commented on Athene's intervention and asked Achilles what all the fuss was about. Note that gods in Homer are not necessarily omniscient: they remember, and forget, to suit the needs of the narrative.

366. *Thebe*: it seems strange that Achilles should have captured Chryseis, who came from Chryse, at Thebe (**R-J** map 2). An ancient commentator explains that Chryseis was visiting Thebe on some religious mission, but whether he was making this up or drawing on a tradition unavailable to us is not known. See on 1.121-307 for these raids.

370-92. *Then Chryses*: we now have a brief summary, with much repetition, of 1.12-348 – events 'focalised' (see **GI** 10C) through Achilles' eyes; cf. de Jong (1985). It is interesting how much of the detail of the actual quarrel he omits, including Athene's intervention (see above on 349). This is further evidence that Athene's promises do not mean much to him; given his short life, he decides to use his mother to hurry things along in his own way.

394. *supplicate* (**R-J, L**); *beseech* (**H**): see **GI** 7D.

if anything you have ever said (**R-J**); *service you have ever done* (**H**); *if ever before now* (**L**): cf. on the prayer form **GI** 7A.

398. *son of Cronus*: i.e. Zeus.

401. *released him* (**R-J, H**): *set him free* (**L**): this is the only time in the *Il.* where Zeus' physical supremacy is said to have been seriously threatened by the gods. At all other times, it is Zeus who threatens (and defeats) the gods e.g. 1.565-7, 589-94; 8.5-27, 15.18-24, 135-7, 162-7; 19.126-31. The gods regularly acknowledge Zeus' *physical* supremacy as the source of his authority e.g. 4.55-6.

403. *Briareus*: a giant who helped Zeus and his Olympian gods defeat the Titans, and then guarded them in the underworld (Hesiod, *Theogony* 711-33). But this particular tale is obscure, not attested elsewhere (who, for example, was Briareus' father?). It has been argued that it is an invention by Homer, to create an obligation on the part of Zeus to Thetis (Willcock [1977]); but in that case is odd that Thetis never mentions it in her appeal to Zeus (1.503-10). Since a god could not be killed, binding, as threatened here (399), was a way of rendering him powerless. In other words, Zeus was about to be supplanted by someone else, but Thetis saved him. This story, then, may somehow, imprecisely, reflect the story about Thetis' child. See on 352 above, and Slatkin (1991) 66-70.

405. *Kronion* (**L**): i.e. son of Cronus = Zeus.

407. *take his knees*: see **GI** 7D for this feature of supplication.

408. *help the Trojans* (**R-J, L**); *bring aid to the Trojans* (**H**): Achilles calculates that, if the Greeks start losing, they will ask him to return, and that will show up Agamemnon for what he is. Like Chryses, Achilles first and foremost wants revenge on Agamemnon, not the return of Briseis (cf. on 1.42) or compensation through gifts, and he is prepared to ask for the slaughter of his own side to achieve it (cf. on 243). It is Achilles' decision to intervene like this that motivates the plot of the *Il.* and leads to the disaster outlined in 1.1-7 (and ultimately his own death). It all arises from his anger at Agamemnon and the knowledge of his own short life; Achilles always gives the impression of a man impatient to take any steps he thinks right to achieve what he wants, and at once, whatever anyone else says or does.

412. *delusion* (**R-J**); *folly* (**H**); *madness* (**L**): the Greek *Atê* suggests some disastrous mental blindness which removes all judgement from you, frequently making you think you are right when you are wrong. As a result, you do something irrational or stupid, with disastrous consequences. It is often associated with unbalanced past behaviour. *Atê* is personified as a god at 9.504-12, and is hurled out of Olympus by a deluded Zeus at 19.95-131, i.e. the characters see it as a force that comes from outside themselves, as if that might possibly absolve them from responsibility for their actions. See on 9.702.

423. *Ethiopians*: the name probably means 'burnt-faced'. People who live far away (by 'Ocean', which Greeks believed surrounded a circular, plate-shaped world and was the source of all rivers, 21.196-7) are often credited with especially agreeable life-styles in which the gods would be keen to share.

424. *yesterday*: something has gone wrong here. These gods, like humans, cannot attend to more than one thing at a time, or be every-where at once (see **GI** 5). But at 222 Athene returned to Olympus to join Zeus and the other gods; and shortly Apollo will attend a sacrifice in his own honour (474). How can it be, then, that they have all been feasting with the Ethiopians since 'yesterday'? Homer has 'nodded' (Horace, *Ars poetica* 359, *indignor quandoque bonus dormitat Homerus* 'I take it amiss when first-rate Homer dozes'; cf. Byron *Don Juan*, stanza 98 'We learn from Horace, "Homer sometimes sleeps"; / We feel without him, Wordsworth sometime wakes.'). But such 'nods' force us to think about why the 'error' has come about, and what advantage, if any, the poet may have thought he gained from it.

1.430-92. Chryseis is returned and the plague ends [11th day].

430. *against his will*: Achilles' anger is driven not primarily by his feelings for Briseis but by Agamemnon's treatment of him.

430-87. *Meanwhile/But Odysseus*: at 1.311 Odysseus left for Chryse to return Chryseis to the priest Chryses and make a sacrifice to Apollo. While Briseis was being returned and Achilles conversing with Thetis, the boat has been sailing on its way, and now arrives, for the handing over of Chryseis, the lifting of the plague, the sacrifice and the return to camp. See on 3.121-244 for the handling of time in Homer.

453. *you heard/listened*: for the prayer-form, see **GI** 7A. Note that Apollo is not called 'Smintheus' here: he is no longer the plague-god.

459. *victims*: see **GI** 7B.

470. *mixing-bowls*: Greek *kratêr* (cf. 'crater'). Greeks drank wine dilute: it was mixed with water to various ratios in the mixing-bowls (**L**'s 'pure' gives the wrong impression), 1-1 being the strongest. Mixing bowls surviving from classical times hold about three gallons. Even the gods mix nectar in a bowl (1.598)! It is odd that the poet should stress the filling of the mixing-bowls *after* their hunger and thirst were satisfied (469): one has to assume that the drinking starts afresh as part of the next ritual (singing and dancing) in honour of Apollo. Note that **L** misses the dancing.

471. *libation* (**R-J, H**); *offered drink* (**L**): a ceremony in which a little wine was poured into each cup, which the recipient then tipped out onto the ground in honour of the god. It commonly accompanies prayers, when ritual, purificatory hand-washing also takes place (cf. 6.266-8, 9.171-7). Libations and prayers often accompany journeys, e.g. 16.220-52, 24.287-321.

477. *rosy-fingered Dawn/with her rosy fingers*: a famous description, referring to light spreading like fingers up across the sky, or to a single finger of light along the horizon.

479. *favourable/ing breeze/stern wind*: Apollo, now appeased, is happy to help the Greek sacrificial party return to camp. The description of the wave hissing round the keel (482) conjures up in one observation the total experience of a boat under full sail.

486. *high up on the sandy shore*: in the absence of a harbour, the Greeks had beached their ships in rows (14.29-36), keeping them upright in runways (2.153) with props and boulders (14.410).

492. *longing for the sound and fury* (**R-J**); *yearning/longed always/for the clamour* (**H, L**): it is not easy for a man like Achilles, who loves fighting (1.177) and for whom life is short, to stay away from battle and also the assembly 'where men win glory', which all epic heroes coveted.

1.493-530. [Eleven-day absence of the gods, beginning at the ninth day, 1.424] 21st day: Thetis supplicates Zeus.

502. *supplication* **(R-J, L)**; *entreaty* **(H)**: for this typical gesture, see **GI** 7D.

503. *Father Zeus*: Zeus is not Thetis' father; she is giving him his traditional title as head of the family of gods (cf. 'father of men and gods', 544), even though most of the gods had been born at the same time as, or before, him, by Uranus and Gaia or Cronus and Rhea.

507. *took/has taken (away) his prize*: see **GI** 10C.

510. *give my son his rights* **(L)**: the Greek says 'compensate my son'.

511-12. *made (her) no reply/answer*: it was not normally done to reject a suppliant. All Zeus can do is to hope Thetis goes away. But why is he so hesitant? Presumably because he fears Hera's reaction (see on 518 below). Might one be tempted to understand Zeus' hesitation for a different reason, i.e. because the plan of Achilles and Thetis will have disastrous consequences (see on the death of Patroclus, 8.470, cf. 18/Intro)?

518. *trouble* **(R-J)**; *grievous business* **(H)**; *disastrous matter* **(L)**: the first sentiment that we know of uttered by the king of the gods to the world is the all too human 'My wife will kill me'. There is a long history behind this Zeus-Hera conflict, mostly generated by Zeus' entanglements with other females (see **GI** 5 and e.g. 14.315-28, and on 19.95-133).

528. *nodded*: a marvellous picture of Zeus' powerful, authoritative gesture, emphasising the brows and hair (obviously abundant for it to roll forward as he nods) and the physical consequences – the mountain shaking. Achilles' desires are now to be fulfilled – cf. 15.58-77 (especially 72-7); 18.74-7 – with tragic consequences.

1.531-611. Hephaestus calms the quarrel between Zeus and Hera over Thetis' pleas.

Hephaestus, the deformed blacksmith god, acts to calm the situation. His intervention emphasises how much the gods are devoted to pleasure: while they have their human favourites, they are not going to ruin a good dinner on Olympus because of them (575-6 'impossible to enjoy/no pleasure in the feast'; see on 21/Intro). So a temporary solution is reached, in order that the gods can enjoy their meal; but from now on Hera will do all she can to thwart Zeus' promise to Thetis. So on earth. The quarrel between Agamemnon and Achilles has ended in the sense that Achilles has lost the argument and withdrawn; but the matter is far from over.

537. *had seen* **(R-J)**; *looked at him* **(H)**; *having seen* **(L)**: Zeus was afraid that Hera might see him and Thetis colluding (522-3), and it now emerges that he was right – she had (cf. 555-9). **H** translates that Hera could tell what had happened merely by looking at Zeus. This is perhaps less likely.

551. *ox-eyed*: presumably because, in the remote past, Hera had been worshipped in animal form. But Homer surely did not think of her as an animal: the epithet is ancient and traditional, used automatically in this context.

561. *Remarkable* (**R-J**); *my dear wife* (**H**); *my dear lady* (**L**): the Greek *daimonios*, here used to describe Hera (in the feminine form *daimoniê*), means that someone is behaving under the influence of a *daimôn* – some unseen divine force – i.e. not in the way one might expect.

567. *unconquerable/invincible hands*: Zeus imposes his will by force, if necessary (cf. on 1.401, and 580-1, 589).

570. *Sky-gods* (**R-J**); *heavenly* (**H**); *Uranian* (**L**): the Greek *ouran*-stem, which **L** uses here, means 'upper air/skies/heavens'. Uranus 'Sky' (Greek *Ouranos*) was grandfather of Zeus. There is no special significance to the usage.

574. *squabbling* (**R-J**); *quarrel* (**H, L**): see **GI** 5C.

591. *hurled/threw me*: gods are often punished by being thrown out of Olympus, e.g. those gods trying to help Hera at 15.22-4 (perhaps the incident being referred to here); Hephaestus again at 18.394-9 by Hera; and *Atê* 19.129-31. Cf. Zeus' threat at 8.13-16.

593. *Lemnos*: the main Greek cult centre of Hephaestus (it contains sources of natural gas and a volcano, both an indication that Hephaestus had a workshop underground). The Sintians (whoever they were) lived on the island.

595. *smiling*: why does Hera smile? Homer leaves us to decide. Unlike *Iliad*ic laughter (see next note), people seem to smile for a number of different reasons, some rather ambiguous. Cf. 4.356 (Agamemnon, perhaps defensively, at Odysseus), 5.426 (Zeus at Athene's joke), 6.404 (Hector, with pleasure at seeing his child), 7.212 (Ajax, bristling with confidence?), 8.38 (Zeus, soothing Athene), 10.400 (Odysseus, with incredulity, at Dolon), 14.222-3 (Hera, at her own cleverness?), 15.47 (Zeus, at Hera's cheek?), 21.434 (Hera, approving Athene), 491 (Hera, making a fool of Artemis), 23.556 (Achilles, approving Antilochus), 786 (Antilochus, in self-mockery?).

600. *bustling*: Hephaestus was lame, so hobbled (18.417), and here he is playing the fool, acting as (of all things) wine-waiter – a job reserved in other traditions, but not in Homer (4.2), for Zeus' favourite beautiful boy Ganymede (20.232-5); or for the goddess Hebe ('Prime of youth') (4.2-4). No wonder the gods break out laughing (cf. **GI** 5A). Simple good humour, or sympathetic laughter – if this is such – is rare in the *Il.*, perhaps occurring only at 6.471 (Hector and Andromache at Astyanax) and 6.484 (Andromache through her tears). It is more normal to laugh at other people's discomfort, e.g. 2.270 (the Greeks at Thersites), 11.378 (Paris at Diomedes), 15.101 (Hera laughing 'with her lips', to suppress her own discomfort), 21.389 (Zeus at the gods fighting), 21.408 (Athene over Ares), 21.508 (Zeus at Artemis), 23.784 (the Greeks at Ajax), 23.840 (the Greeks at Epeius).

601-4. *all day ... Apollo ... Muses*: only the best for the gods.

Book 2

Introduction

Homer immediately puts the plan of Zeus into action, though the way he chooses to do so has not impressed 'analysts' (**GI** 2).

Homer makes Zeus send Agamemnon a deceitful Dream, in the guise of the reliable old Nestor, telling him that this day he will take Ilium (5-34). Since Zeus wants the Greeks and Trojans to get back to the fighting as soon as possible after the recent nine-day halt for the plague (of which the Trojans would have been as fearful as the Greeks), that is a reasonable enough narrative device. Agamemnon, however, instead of following the Dream's instructions, gets the agreement of his senior advisers to test the morale of the troops in assembly *before* they commit themselves to battle again (73-5), and when he has summoned the army, urges them to board ship and get back to Greece as soon as possible (139-41). The men enthusiastically start to do what he has suggested until, on the advice of Athene, Odysseus stops them and reconvenes the assembly (142-210), and he and Nestor get matters sorted out (284-368). So both Zeus' and Agamemnon's plans have completely misfired. It will not be for the first time.

The whole sequence is a bit of a mess. Since Agamemnon really did believe the Dream to be true (36, even though Homer comments that he was stupid to be taken in), why did he decide to test the troops? The Dream said nothing about that. The testing might have made good sense if it had been made clear that the Greeks were nervous about re-starting the war because (say) of the plague or because of the absence of Achilles. No such motivation is suggested. Again, Agamemnon himself seems to realise that the testing could well turn out to be a disaster, because he orders his senior advisers to be ready to dissuade the men from flight (75; see note on 73). But when they do flee, does any senior adviser does anything about it? No. Finally, in his speech to the men urging them to return home, Agamemnon is forced directly to contradict what the Dream had told him (114-15).

It is tempting to wonder whether the same poet as that of Book 1 is at work here (see below). One can, however, find positives out of the episode. First, now that Achilles has departed, Agamemnon is in undisputed charge, though Book 2 casts considerable doubt on his leadership qualities (**GI** 9). Not only does he fail to carry out the Dream's instructions, he turns out to have misjudged the mood of his army completely, and is so immobilised by his men's reaction that he has to leave it to Odysseus to rally them (185-6). One thing, however, does stand to his credit: he admits that his treatment of Achilles was wrong (377-80). Homer is laying the ground-work for Agamemnon's eventual change of heart.

Second, Agamemnon's incompetence gives the poet a chance to shine the spotlight on others, and this surely is the point. Achilles will not return to view again till Book 9. Homer now has ample scope to introduce the other great heroes fighting in Troy, both Greeks and Trojans. Book 2 focuses on the Greeks – in particular Odysseus' and Nestor's powers of persuasion – and the morale of the army, especially as it is conveyed by Thersites (211-77).

Thersites is the one man-in-the-street to be given a voice in the *Il*. An ordinary soldier, he expresses aloud the view that Agamemnon wants to stay in Troy only to enrich himself, and urges the army to sail for home anyway (presumably he has seen through Agamemnon's 'testing' trick). He further adduces evidence of Agamemnon's incompetence as a leader by pointing out that it was he who caused Achilles (a far better man, in Thersites' view 239-40) to withdraw from the field, and he suggests Agamemnon would not have lasted long had it come to a fight between them (242; Thersites presumably remembers Achilles drawing his sword at 1.190).

It is tempting to see Thersites as representing the feelings of the whole Greek army. If he did, it would go some way to explaining why the troops had so instantly charged for the ships when Agamemnon suggested they should. This interpretation is not without its problems because the troops are delighted when Odysseus forcibly beats Thersites back down into his seat. But if the note on 222 is right, Odysseus' actions may be the very reason *why* the army had a change of heart, a change confirmed by the enthusiastic reception they give both his rallying call (333-5) and that of Nestor, warmly backed up (at last) by a hitherto silent Agamemnon (394). The result is that the army return to their huts to eat and ready themselves for battle (398-401).

It is the mark of the leader to able to speak persuasively in public and take his men along with them (see **GI** 4C on the importance of winning words). Odysseus shows his persuasive skills, first, with a combination of carrot and stick in bringing the army to order (190-7, 200-2 – note the use of the sceptre in the latter) and in dealing with Thersites; and second, in his major speech to the army at 284-332 in which he diplomatically expresses sympathy with their desire to return home – it has been a long ten years – but points out that all the omens for the capture of Ilium are coming good. This is a positive, up-beat message, reinforced by Nestor (337-68), who reminds the men of their past oaths and other omens, and hints at what will happen to traitors. These two speeches seem to restore Agamemnon's confidence and he issues a stirring call to battle while admitting (what Thersites had been arguing) that he had been at fault in the matter of Achilles.

There is a third point – the broad perspective that Book 2 offers us. Odysseus' speech takes us back to the time when the Greek expedition was about to set out for Troy: he remembers the mustering at Aulis and the omen (303-30). The catalogue of ships almost relives that moment, with its roll-call of leaders and men. One of the important functions of this book, then, is to give a sense of the whole scope of the Trojan war (see **GI** 1C).

There are, then, positive things to be said about the 'testing' sequence. What can one say, then, of the analysts' argument that this 'testing' sequence is not Homeric? It is noticeable that, when the testing episode is finished, Agamemnon offers a sacrifice and is buoyed up with hopes of beating the Trojans (402ff.). That positive mood would fit very neatly indeed it if it were to be expressed by Agamemnon immediately after he had heard the Dream. In other words, it may be that in some versions of the *Il.* the poet went straight from the Dream to Agamemnon's eagerness to fight, i.e. from (say) 2.22-402. An analyst might well agree with that conclusion.

On the other hand, it is possible that a poet composing within an oral tradition, in which re-working material to fit a new context is taken for granted, might not always get things completely 'right'. Since we shall find this to be the case in a number of other instances in the *Il.*, it is not unreasonable to conclude that Homer *himself* had invented this slightly awkward episode in order to achieve what it delivers – a picture of Agamemnon's incompetence and his reliance on other leaders, the ability of heroes like Odysseus and Nestor to rise to the occasion, the army's morale and the wider picture of the whole war. Since one could easily imagine an *Il.* in which the 'testing' sequence did not appear, Book 2 as we have it may be an example of Homer developing his material to create an epic of unique size (see **GI** 1), but not articulating it with his usual sure touch.

The mustering of the troops for battle and the catalogue of Greek ships ensue, with yet another reminder that Achilles is still out of the picture (771-9). It is matched by the briefest of introductions to the Trojans – our first sight of them – and the catalogue of their troops. Homer will now turn his attention increasingly to the Trojan side.

Main sources for the commentary
Kirk (1985); Willcock (1978).

2.1-207. [Night of 21st day] **Zeus sends a dream that makes Agamemnon think the Greeks are about to win. [22nd day: first day of combat] After a consultation, Agamemnon tests the morale of the men – who charge for the ships to return home. Athene alerts Odysseus, who restrains the senior men and hits out at the ranks.**

2. *sleep*: even the king of the gods sometimes cannot sleep for thinking (see **GI** 5A).

3. *honour Achilles*: as Zeus had agreed at 1.525-30.

11. *long/flowing-haired Greeks*: wearing the hair long was a mark of aristocracy in the fifth century BC in the Greek world, but we do not know if it had any special significance in Homer. Cf. Zeus' long hair at 1.529-30.

14. *Hera's entreaties* (**R-J, H**); *Hera … by her supplication* (**L**): Zeus is never above lying in his own interests. He does not wish Agamemnon to know about the bargain he has struck with Thetis on Achilles' behalf.

28. *he tells/bids you*: note how the dream's words exactly repeat Zeus'; and how Agamemnon will exactly repeat the dream's at 60ff. Such precise repetition is a standard feature of oral poetry, cf. Hera's instructions to Athene at 2.157-65, repeated by Athene at 174-81.

38. *fool. He little knew* (**R-J**); *fool, he/who knew nothing* (**H, L**): it is rare for the poet to use the third person narrative to evaluate a person's actions so directly, but see **GI** 10 for comment of this sort.

42. *tunic*: this is a typical scene of dressing, cf. 10.21-4. Note the logic: under-tunic first, cloak over the top; then sandals; then sword (if one put the sword on first it would interfere with putting on sandals); finally, sceptre. Contrast *Od.* 2.2-4, 4.307-9, 20.124-6 (sword first, then sandals).

45. *sword*: see on 3.334.

46. *sceptre*: this is not the speaker's sceptre (cf. 1.245-6) but Agamemnon's personal symbol of authority, made by Hephaestus (hence 'indestructible') and handed down to him across the generations (see 2.100-8 and on 1.238).

53. *senior* (**R-J**); *elder* (**H**); *princes* (**L**): the Greek *gerontes* means literally 'old men' – correct **L** – but it should not be interpreted too literally. Diomedes, for example, is a youthful hero, but he is always to be found among them. Cf. 14.110-14, where Diomedes argues that lineage is as important as age.

73. *test/make trial of them*: since Zeus has, however falsely, already promised Agamemnon that he will at last take Troy (2.66-7), it seems absurd for Agamemnon now to test the morale of the men. Further, the dream simply told him to remember and not forget the dream (2.33) – nothing about testing, or publishing the news to his council. Finally, Agamemnon has no faith in the men, since (75) he promptly tells the council to dissuade them from fleeing, as if he is convinced they will (unless the Greek means 'dissuade *me*', i.e. stand up after I have tested them and argue against my proposal – which would suggest that Agamemnon wanted a serious debate about the matter. In the event, the men run before anyone has a chance to speak). One senses behind this rather pointless exercise an unspoken desire to find out what effect Achilles' withdrawal has had on morale. At best, the scene gives an insight into Agamemnon's deluded state of mind (see on 111) and ineffective style of leadership (cf. 9.26-8, 14.74-81 where Agamemnon seriously proposes running for home and is slapped down by Diomedes and Odysseus). But it is not convincingly motivated.

79-83. *Friends, leaders*: Nestor proclaims his loyalty to Agamemnon but, oddly, says nothing about Agamemnon's report of the dream's amazing message (we are about to take Troy!) or about the proposal to test the men.

87. *As troops of* (**R-J**); *As when a mass of bees* (**H**); *Like the swarms* *of* (**L**): the first extended simile in the *Il.* (C-type, see **GI** 12). The troops of bees, swarming out, clustering, and settling = the troops of Greeks, coming out, in squads, to the assembly. Bees are orderly creatures, but the Greeks have to be brought to order (97). On the mustering of the troops, beginning with an assembly/council, see Albracht (2003) [I.5-13].

103. *guide and slayer of Argus* (**R-J, H**); *courier Argeiphontes* (**L**): this is the god Hermes, who was the messenger god and guided souls to the underworld, and killed hundred-eyed Argus. Zeus lusted after the mortal Io, and the jealous Hera had set Argus to keep a watch on her.

104. *Pelops*: the first mortal in the list. He gave the sceptre to his son Atreus; Atreus left it to his brother Thyestes; Thyestes then left it to Atreus' son Agamemnon. Homer does not mention the intense, bloody feuding within this family that featured so strongly in later Greek tragedy (e.g. Aeschylus' *Oresteia*).

110. *Ares*: god of war (Mars in Latin).

111-18, 139-41. *Zeus son of Cronus ...*(139) *So I suggest we all* (**R-J**); *No, come, let us all* (**H**)*; Come, then, do as I say* (**L**): = 9.18-28. It is ironic that Agamemnon now lies to the men about the message, also a lie (though he does not know it), that he received from Zeus. He is indeed under a delusion, though not the one he suggests (111, cf. on 1.412 – **L**'s 'futility' is unsatisfactory). On delusion, see 1.412.

119. *what a scandal* (**R-J**); *this is a shameful thing* (**H**); *a thing of shame* (**L**): this elaborates on the earlier point about the disgrace/dishonour of an early return (115).

130. (*numerous*) *allies/companions from other cities*: Agamemnon has just argued that the Greeks outnumber the Trojans in Ilium more than ten to one, but the Trojans' allies from the rest of the region (see 2.816-77) make up the numbers – as if that is somehow cheating. The Greeks also came from all over Greece to win back Helen for Menelaus (2.494-760, cf. 1.152-60). See **R-J** map 5.

134. *nine of great/mighty Zeus' years*: this section elaborates on (122) *no final end in sight* (**R-J**)*; no result* (**H**); *no accomplishment* (**L**).

143. *and listened to his counsel* (**L**): read 'except those who had attended the advisory council'.

144. *like the great/big rollers/waves*: B-simile (the whole assembly was swayed like wind stirring waves). Homer immediately develops the image with a second, D-simile (wind stirring corn) which ends 'so the whole assembly swayed', taking us by ring-composition back to the start of the B-simile. Icaria is a sea north of the island of Samos (the unmarked island opposite the mouth of the River Cayster in the area known as Ionia, **R-J** map 3). Homer often describes natural phenomena occurring in this part of the Mediterranean. It suggests that Homer composed the *Il.* in this region, on or off the coast of modern Turkey.

155. *in defiance of destiny* (**R-J**); *beyond what was fate* (**H**); *beyond fate* (**L**): the prospect of defying destiny is occasionally held out to mark a particularly dramatic turn of events, e.g. 17.319-22, 20.30, 21.517, and

Zeus toys with the idea, but always rejects it (e.g. 16.431-3). Greeks defy destiny once (16.780), a unique occurrence. Otherwise, there are variations on the destiny theme, e.g. Aeneas is told that, as long as he stays clear of Achilles, he will survive the war – a 'conditional' fate (20.335-9, cf. *Od.* 1.32-43); and Achilles claims to have two possible destinies (9.411-14). It is worth remembering that Homer is not a theologian (nor was any Greek, since they had no 'inspired' scriptures to argue about), so Homer plays the 'destiny' card purely to suit his narrative ends. See **GI** 8.

157. *Atrytone*: an epithet applied to Athene. If it is a cult title of some sort, its meaning is unrecoverable. Homer may have thought it meant 'unwearied', but that derivation is most unlikely. For the second time, on Hera's advice, Athene takes a hand to prevent another major disaster (cf. 1.193-222).

167. *came swooping down* (**R-J**); *went darting down* (**H**); *went in speed down* (**L**): note the sequence of events, typical of scenes in which someone departs in order to find and talk to someone: Athene (i) leaves (ii) arrives (168) (iii) finds/comes on X (here, Odysseus) (iv) X is described (here standing still, not touching his ship, in despair) (v) she goes up to/stands beside him and (vi) speaks. Compare e.g. 10.150-8, 18.615-19.7.

170. *not even touched* (**R-J**); *not put his hands* (**H**); *laid no hand* (**L**): another oddity. Why should Odysseus have wanted to lay a hand on his ship? He knew Agamemnon's plan to test the troops was a trick, and that his job was to restrain them.

184. *Eurybates*: Odysseus came from Ithaca. Eurybates is presumably the herald at 9.170. Cf. *Od.* 19.244-8, which suggests Eurybates is a black African.

186. *sceptre*: the one described at 2.100-8. Odysseus here is acting as leader in place of Agamemnon. He has a serious rhetorical problem to face. Agamemnon has told the men to run for it. They have. How can he stop them? One point clearly emerges: that, in the Homeric world, even if the leaders are behaving in the same way as the ordinary warriors (i.e. running for it), they cannot be treated in the same way. Men of high birth and status cannot (almost by definition) be cowards (191), unlike the rank and file (201). Cf. **GI** 4A and 1.121-307 (in relation to the superior rewards which seem automatically due to a leader, whatever his performance). So Odysseus is going to have come up with different arguments to the different groups. He is indeed 'resourceful' (173).

188. *When(ever) he came upon/met/encountered*: the first category of men are members of the advisory council who, Odysseus charitably assumes, have forgotten or did not understand Agamemnon's proposal made at 73-5 ('know/understand' 192; 'Did we not all hear …?' 194). This seems feeble – are they really that forgetful or stupid? – but then Nestor did not seem to know what Agamemnon was planning (see on 2.79-83), so there may be something in what Odysseus says.

190. *You there* (**R-J**); *Friend* (**H**); *Excellency* (**L**): the Greek *daimonios* is used both here and at 200 (see on 1.561).

It does not become ... frightened (**L**): read 'it is not right to threaten you'.

197. *Zeus wise in counsel* (**R-J**); *Zeus the counsellor/of the counsels* (**H, L**): cf. 2.205-6, and see on 1.175.

204-5. *one commander/master/ruler*: here Odysseus' rhetorical problems become much harder (see on 188 above), since the rank and file have simply been *obeying* Agamemnon and know nothing of his ulterior motives. In the event all Odysseus can do is to select those most keen to urge on the retreat (those 'shouting', 198), tell them to go back to their seats (200) and to obey their superiors/betters (i.e. Odysseus, 201), and then accuse them of cowardice and of somehow making themselves all leaders (203), when mob rule is a bad thing (204). This at least raises the issue of the relationship between the leaders and the men, so preparing for Thersites (212).

205. *Zeus son of/ sickle-wielding Cronus* (**R-J**); */devious-minded Kronos* (**H**); */devious-devising Kronos* (**L**): Cronus was famous in myth not so much for his deviousness as for his skill with the sickle, with which he lopped off his father Uranus' testicles (Aphrodite sprang from them as they dropped into the sea). The Greek *agkulomêtês*, lit. 'devising crooked [things]' can be derived so as to mean 'scything off with a crooked [thing]'.

2.207-393. The assembly reconvenes and a common soldier Thersites abuses Agamemnon. Odysseus thrashes Thersites, to applause. Odysseus and Nestor give morale-boosting speeches. The Greeks prepare for battle.

209. *sounding/thunderous sea*: C-simile, recalling 2.144-6.

212. *Thersites*: the name means 'loud-mouth'. Greeks connected an ugly physique with low birth and an ugly mind. His purpose it to get back home at all costs (236, cf. Odysseus at 251) and he argues that all they are doing is gathering booty for Agamemnon, who does not appreciate their efforts anyway (226-34, 238): and to prove it, look, Agamemnon has even insulted Achilles (239-40)! Thersites ludicrously apes Achilles' argument in Book 1 (122, 165-71), as if he were on a par with the Greeks' greatest fighter, and as if Achilles' personal feelings applied to everyone.

222. *at/with him*: at whom were the Greeks angry? Thersites, or Agamemnon? At first glance one would assume it was Thersites, but 270 ('disgruntled though they were' (**R-J**); 'for all their disaffection' (**H**); 'sorry though the men were' (**L**)) seems to suggest that it is Agamemnon. The men were fed up (223) at the recent turn of events that Agamemnon caused (i.e. Achilles' departure and Agamemnon's false appeal to them to depart), and it was these feelings that Thersites was exploiting; but Odysseus' uncompromising treatment of Thersites showed plainly who was in charge (no one likes a loser) and the men, despite their resentment at Agamemnon (270), are persuaded. As usual, naked force wins the day (cf. Zeus, on 1.401).

228. *give you first choice* (**R-J**); *offered to you before all others* (**H**); *give to you first of all* (**L**): see on 1.121-307.

239. *he dishonoured Achilles*: cf. 1.170-1.

241. *Achilles hasn't lost his temper* (**R-J**); *no fury/gall in Achilleus' heart* (**H, L**): really?! Thersites is presumably thinking of the moment when Achilles sheathed his sword (1.220) – a good example of 'focalisation' (**GI** 10C).

247. *stop arguing with your leaders* (**R-J**); *enough of your lone attacks* (**H**); *nor stand up alone* (**L**): Odysseus deploys the argument he used against the ordinary soldier at 2.204, and argues against a return home on the grounds that the outcome of the war is not yet certain (252-3). Further, he points out that Thersites cannot complain at the distribution system (254-6) because it is the army that does the distributing.

260. *Telemachus*: Odysseus' only son, who was born just before Odysseus left for Troy (*Od.* 11.447-9), so would now be nearly ten. He will play a major role in the *Od.*

266. *tear(s)*: see on 1.349.

276. *the great Thersites* (**R-J**); *his proud heart* (**H, L**): **H, L** translate literally here. The meaning is ironical.

279. *rose to speak* (**R-J, H**); *stood up* (**L**): not that Odysseus had been sitting down, but we are now moving into a typical assembly scene, complete with herald (280), which has its own particular format (cf. e.g. 1.58 etc. and 23.567-9). This format assumes that the speaker is seated and then that he rises to speak. The poet drops into this format without thinking – a good example of the way in which the demands of oral poetry cause the poet to 'nod'. The tactful Odysseus is careful to omit all mention of the part Agamemnon played in causing the recent chaos, and both scolds and sympathises with the Greeks (289-97). His speech is appreciated (333-5).

286. *promise they made you/undertook* (**R-J, H**); *fulfilling the promise* (**L**): since this promise was made as the Greeks were leaving Greece (at Aulis, 303), it presumably does not refer to the much earlier episode when Helen was being courted for marriage and all her suitors promised her father Tyndareus that, if the successful suitor (in the event, Menelaus) ever had any problems, they would rally round to help him. The same is true of 4.267, where Idomeneus makes no reference to any promise made to Menelaus.

303. *it seems like only yesterday* (**R-J**); *not so long ago* (**H**); *yesterday and before* (**L**): nearly ten years ago, in fact – but a good example of the way in which Homer tries to give the impression that he is covering the whole war when in fact he is covering only a small part of it (see **GI** 1C). Note Calchas' role in the prophecy – was this one of those occasions when he infuriated Agamemnon by prophesying that it would taken ten years to take Ilium (cf. 1.106-8)?

336. *Gerenian*: neither ancient Greeks (nor Homer?) nor we know what this refers to. Presumably the term is a very ancient one. Nestor takes a stricter line with the Greeks than Odysseus had.

339. *oaths*: these sound more official than the general promises offered at 286 (see note there) and may possibly refer, if obliquely, to
Tyndareus (cf. on 286 above).

344. *firm resolve* **(R-J)**; *unshakeably to your purpose* **(H)**; *your counsel unshaken* **(L)**: Nestor mends bridges with Agamemnon and attempts
publicly to restore his reputation.

356. *Helen's struggles and her groaning* **(H)**; *Helen's longing to
escape and her lamentations* **(L)**: Nestor talks as if Helen were seized
against her will. The tradition was that Helen could hardly wait to run off
with Paris, but Nestor may be 'focalising' the matter differently, in order
to inflame the Greek army at the Trojan treatment of an innocent girl. **R-J**
takes the less romantic view that Nestor is appealing to the baser instincts
of an army that has now been in Troy for nearly ten years fighting to win
back Helen; i.e. the men need revenge against the Trojans for 'all the sweat
and tears' Helen has put them through (cf. the web Helen herself is weaving
at 3.126-8).

360. *take advice from another* **(R-J)**; *listen to another('s words)* **(H,
L)**: Nestor is always full of advice. This recommendation seems absurdly
obvious – how else has the army been organised for the previous nine years
in Troy? Nor is there any specific indication that it is put into effect, unless
the forthcoming marshalling of the army and catalogue of troops are meant
to imply it. But this is unlikely, since even Nestor's men turn out to be
organised on different principles (4.293-300).

378. *lost my temper first* **(R-J)**; *first to grow/be angry* **(H, L)**: this is
the first occasion on which Agamemnon admits that his treatment of
Achilles was at fault and that its effect on the prospects for victory could
be serious. Presumably 'loss of temper first' refers to 1.102-4. The vivid
detail of his instructions to the troops is matched by his prayer to Zeus at
412-18.

381. *eat/food/dinner*: an essential preparation for battle, cf. 8.53-4,
19.155-72. Correct **L**'s 'dinner' (they have only just got up, 41-7).

**2.394-483. The army feeds, Agamemnon offers a sacrifice and a
prayer. Nestor suggests the troops now assemble. The troops are
marshalled with Athene's help.**

394. *like wave(s)* **(R-J, H)**; *like surf* **(L)**: another wind and waves
simile (B-type), cf. 2.209-10, 144-8.

399. *dinner* **(L)**: see on 381 above.

400. *one of the immortal/ever-living gods*: individual troops, coming
from all over Greece, will make their own prayers to their own favourite
god(s).

406. *Aiantes ... Tydeus' son* **(H, L)**: the two Aiantes are here Ajax son
of Telamon and Ajax son of Oïleus; but sometimes they are Ajax son of
Telamon and his half-brother Teucer/Teukros (cf. 8.283-4). Tydeus' son is
Diomedes.

408. *master of the battle/war cry* (**R-J, H**); *of the great war cry* (**L**): effective communication in the noisy chaos of battle – orders and exhortations – required a strong voice.

414. *before/until I bring/have hurled*: Agamemnon's graphically detailed and optimistic prayer is derived from Zeus' false dream (2.29-30). But Zeus is still deceiving Agamemnon, so rejects it (419-20) – the only time in the *Il.* where Zeus accepts a sacrifice (420) but rejects the accompanying prayer (cf. the close calls at e.g. 3.302 prayer rejected, 6.311 offering rejected, 16.250 offering half rejected). For the sacrifice, cf. **GI** 7B.

447. *aegis*: see on 1.202. The troops are not said to see Athene, but she certainly has an effect on them, a god of war inspiring men to battle.

449. *worth a hundred head of cattle/oxen*: values in the Homeric world (a society without money) are frequently expressed in agricultural terms. Cf. 6.234-6.

455-83. A string of similes announces the advance into battle (as often) and also prepares for the catalogue of troops on the Greek side – a high point for a Greek audience, for whom this long list of great heroes who fought in Troy would have been of consuming local and family significance. It is noticeable that such high points are often signalled by expansion and accumulation. The gathering troops are likened to 455 a forest fire (the gleam of their armour), 459 a flock of birds (their extent and noise), and 469 a swarm of flies (number), and 474 the leaders sort them out like goatherds their goats (all D-type); 477 Agamemnon is picked out for special complimentary mention, as resembling deities in his physique (A-type) and 480 standing out in comparison with the troops like a bull among a herd of cows (D-type). This run of similes with no intervening narrative is unique. But Homer is not averse to piling up similes within a significant developing narrative, e.g. 17.735-61 (the retrieval of Patroclus' body, another high point).

461. *Asian ... Cayster/Kaystrios*: the term 'Asia' was originally used of the west coast of Turkey. Cayster is a river which flowed into the sea well south of Ilium, at the later city of Ephesus. See **R-J** map 3.

465. *Scamander*: also called Xanthus, one of the two rivers in Troy (the other being Simoïs). See **R-J** maps 1, 2.

2.484-779. The catalogue of Greek ships.

The catalogue describes the Greek contingents – leaders, ships and number of troops – who sailed to Troy. It moves clockwise round Greece, by region, beginning from Boeotia: central/eastern Greece (494-558), the Peloponnese to the south (559-624), western Greece and its islands (625-44) and northern Greece (681-759), with the south-eastern islands (Crete, etc.) inserted at 645-80. **R-J** map 5 shows the location of each contingent.

The result of this ordering is that the list begins with the Boeotians (494), whose leaders Peneleos and Leitus play very little part in the story (they appear together at 17.597-608) while the Greek leader Agamemnon does not appear till 569 (ninth entry) and Achilles at 685, twenty-first entry (compare the Trojan catalogue, which properly starts with Hector, 816). In other words, the catalogue was not designed to fit the needs of Homer's *Il*. The easiest conclusion to draw is that, since the expedition set out for Troy from Aulis in Boeotia, the catalogue may well be of Boeotian origin, composed perhaps for an epic which (unlike the *Il*.) featured the real-time departure of the expedition. Such catalogues, then, are probably 'givens' for the poet, hallowed perhaps by tradition. He might tinker with them at the margins, but no more. This observation may be supported by the fact that, of the forty-four living leaders named in this catalogue (of whom ten are killed), nine do not appear in the *Il*. again (a feature that also occurs in the Trojan catalogue; see on 2.816-77).

It is not clear how far the catalogue reflects a precise historical reality; on this complex issue, see Kirk (1985), 168ff. He concludes that the catalogue does not represent a single snapshot of Greece at any particular moment but is the consequence of a slow and complex accretion of information gathered through a long and diverse oral tradition going back to Mycenaean times.

This commentary will concentrate on the part in the story played by the leaders mentioned in the catalogue. See GI 2(iv) for the a-b-c pattern to describe many of the contingent entries. It is worth observing that, once battle starts, it goes on till it stops, without strategic interventions from anyone. All the leader can do is try to ensure that at least it begins with everyone in the right place.

484. *Muses*: as usual, the poet appeals to the Muses for hard information (see in 1.1) about an army containing (apparently) 29 contingents led by 44 commanders from 175 Greek localities in 1186 ships containing (one may guess) 100,000 men – a good example of epic exaggeration.

488. *rank and file* **(R-J)**; *mass* **(H)**; *multitude* **(L)**: Homer says (487) that he can deal with the *leaders* by name and origin (and he returns to them at 493 'So I shall list/Yet I will give/I will tell') but not the rank and file. But he says he can deal with the pure *numbers* of the rank and file who came, because here at least the Muses *will* help him (492 'how many came/the many who came/all those who came').

Central/eastern Greece (494-558)

494. *Peneleos ... Leitus*: neither of much importance and both wounded at 17.597-604.

495. *Arcesilaus ... Prothoenor ... Clonius*: Prothoenor is killed at 14.450, the other two at 15.329-42.

505. *Lower Thebes*: because Thebes had already been taken (see on 563-5 below; **R-J** map 4).

512. *Ascalaphus ... Ialmenus*: Ialmenus goes on guard duty at 9.82;

Ascalaphus is killed at 13.518-26 and his father Ares grieves at his death 15.111-16.

517. *Schedius ... Epistrophus*: shadowy figures. Epistrophus never features again, though two Trojans of that name appear at 2.692, 856. Schedius is killed at 17.306-11, and Hector kills another Schedius (son of Perimedes) at 15.515. Pytho (519) is Delphi.

527. *Ajax son of Oïleus*: an important character, the 'lesser' Ajax is so called in comparison with the 'greater' Ajax son of Telamon, the bulwark of the Greeks' defence. His followers, like him, are light-armed (13.714-20) – in contrast with the heavy-armed Telamonian Ajax. He is renowned for his speed (14.520-2) and nearly wins the foot race at 23.758-83; but see on 23.473.

540. *Elephenor*: killed at 4.463-70. He leads the Abantes, the name given to warriors from Euboea.

547. *Erechtheus*: early mythical king of Athens. Athenians claimed they were 'autochthonous', i.e. had never lived anywhere else, affirmed here by the claim that Erechtheus sprang from the soil and was raised by Athene.

552. *Menestheus*: Athens was an important Mycenaean centre, but despite his write-up here Menestheus plays a very small and unimpressive part in the fighting 12.331-77, 13.190-7, 685-90.

557. *Ajax*: a major character, the 'greater' Ajax, son of Telamon, stationed alongside Menestheus. Given his role in the *Il.* as the Greeks' greatest defensive fighter, it is odd that he gets so brief a mention here. Later he is ranked second only to Achilles in battle (2.768-70).

The Peloponnese (559-624)

563-5. *Diomedes ... Sthenelus ... Euryalus*: the Peloponnese is the most important location of historical Mycenaean strongholds, and it cannot be mere coincidence that it sends many top leaders to Troy. These three warriors, of whom Diomedes is the most important, have fathers who featured in another great epic cycle, the Seven against Thebes, which is referred to throughout the *Il.* (see Alden [2000]). In this conflict, which took place *before* the Trojan war, Polyneices, supported by six other epic heroes including Diomedes' father Tydeus and Sthenelus' father Capaneus, tried to remove his brother Eteocles from power in Thebes. He failed (and the maddened Tydeus died sucking out the brains of his enemy Melanippus, a story Homer does not tell); but their sons – Diomedes, Sthenelus and co. – later succeeded, destroying Thebes in the process. We know virtually nothing of this second attack on Thebes. Diomedes and Sthenelus often work in tandem in the *Il.*, e.g. 5.108-327; Euryalus kills four Trojans at 6.20-8 and is beaten in the boxing match against Epeius at 23.677-99.

576. *Agamemnon*: finally appears in the catalogue, ninth in the pecking order. Note that he brings 100 ships, more than anyone else. This makes him nominal leader of the expedition. A fine palace has been excavated at Mycenae. His description here tallies with that at 2.477-83. For **L**'s 'swarming' (581) read 'with many ravines'.

586. *Menelaus*: brother of Agamemnon, husband of Helen, and depicted as an older man, full of courage, but not quite the fighter he once was, e.g. 7.104-14.

590. = 2.356 (see comment for the meaning).

595. *Thamyris*: the theme of a mortal getting above him/herself and being punished is common enough (cf. Niobe at 24.602-9), but it is not easy to see the relevance of the story at this point. It may have had some particular local application now lost on us.

601. *Nestor*: the wise old counsellor, with ninety ships (only Agamemnon has more). His palace at Pylos has been excavated. It is strange that his high-profile son Antilochus is not mentioned.

609. *Agapenor*: neither he nor the Arcadians feature in the fighting. Arcadia is inland; that is why they had to borrow ships from Agamemnon (612) to get to Troy.

620. *Amphimachus … Thalpius … Diores … Polyxeinus*: Amphimachus is killed by Hector at 13.185-96; Thalpius and Polyxeinus do not feature again; Diores is killed at 4.517-26. Nestor describes a fight against the men of Elis (sometimes called 'Epeans' by Homer) at 11.699-761, and mentions some of these places at 755-9.

Western Greece and its islands (625-44)

627. *Meges*: plays a useful part in the fighting, especially in the later books e.g. 5.69-75, 15.518-44, 16.313; at 19.239 he helps to fetch Agamemnon's compensation for Achilles.

631. *Odysseus*: a major character, but with only a feeble twelve ships – perhaps because he had not wanted to come to Troy in the first place (*Odyssey* 24.119)?

638. *Thoas*: ranked in the top nine fighters (7.162ff.) and given a strong commendation at 15.282-4; plays a minor part in the fighting, e.g. 4.527-35. Poseidon disguises himself as Thoas to rally the Greeks (13.216ff.). Oineus (641) is mentioned here to explain why *his* sons – Tydeus and Meleager, both ancient Aetolian heroes – were not at Troy: if they had been, Thoas would not have been leader of the Aetolians. Note that Tydeus' son Diomedes was, of course, at Troy, but as leader of the contingent from Argos (2.559-68), where Tydeus had earlier moved (14.119-20, suppressing the story that Tydeus had been exiled to Argos for killing his uncle). Oineus and Meleager both feature in Phoenix's story to Achilles (9.529-99).

The south-eastern islands (645-80)

645. *Idomeneus … Meriones*: both rank in the top nine fighters

(7.162ff.) and are important figures in the poem. Idomeneus is a son of Zeus (13.449) and an older warrior (13.361, cf. 23.476 and his appearance with Nestor and Phoenix at 19.311). With the third largest number of troops, he is second only to Nestor in seniority if 2.405 is anything to go by. Meriones' father was Molus (10.270). Meriones rescues Idomeneus at 17.605-25. In **L**, for 'Gortyna' read 'Gortyn'.

653. *Tlepolemus*: killed by Sarpedon at 5.628-62, though he does manage to wound Sarpedon in the thigh.

671. *Nireus*: neither he nor his troops from this very small island, on their three ships, appear again. There must be some reason, now lost to us, why they are mentioned.

678. *Pheidippus … Antiphus*: neither is heard of again.

Northern Greece (681-759)

685. *Achilles*: at last! – coming in at twenty-first in the pecking order, with fifty ships, of fifty men each and five ship line-leaders (16.168-97). The poet now briefly explains Achilles' absence (686-94), though without mentioning Patroclus, and gives further detail of his capture of Briseis from Lyrnessus (19.296). Mynes was its king (19.296); we hear no more of Epistrophus. See note on p. 45 for 'Hellas'.

693. *Protesilaus*: first to leap ashore at Troy and be killed, as Homer has to explain. His ship is fired by Hector at 15.704-6.

704. *Podarces*: mentioned at 13.693 as leading the Phthians, though still, as here, a son of Iphiclus (13.698).

714. *Eumelus*: appears only in the chariot race at 23.288, where he has his chariot smashed by Athene (391-7) and comes in last (532). His horses are praised at 2.763-7.

718. *Philoctetes*: again, his absence has to be explained away by Homer. In myth Troy could not be taken without him and his bow, a theme Sophocles explores in his *Philoctetes*.

727. *Medon*: co-leader of the Phthians at 13.693, and killed by Aeneas (15.332), where the story of his youth is elaborated. He is half-brother of Ajax son of Oïleus (2.527).

732. *Podaleirius and Machaon*: both sons of the legendary healer Asclepius and therefore healers themselves. Podaleirius is mentioned again at 11.833; Machaon treats Menelaus at 4.200-19 and is himself wounded and rescued at 11.506-20, cf. 11.595-650.

736. *Eurypylus*: ranked in the top nine fighters (7.162ff.) and plays a useful part in the fighting, e.g. 5.76-83, 6.36, till he is wounded while helping Ajax (11.576-90) and treated by Patroclus (11.808-47, 15.392-404).

740. *Polypoetes … Leonteus*: both Lapiths (see on 1.263-5 for the Lapiths' clash with the Centaurs or (**L**) 'hairy beast men'). They hold the Greek gate against Asius' onslaught (12.127-94).

748. *Gouneus*: he, uniquely, is given no father, and does not appear again; and Cyphus is unknown.

755. *Styx*: a river of the underworld, by which the gods swore the most serious oaths (15.37-8), e.g. 14.271-6. It was Zeus' reward to the Styx for supporting him against the Titans. For the theory of oath-taking, see **GI** 7E. Mortals usually swore by the Furies, see on 9.454.

756. *Prothous*: his last mention in the poem. The catalogue tails away rather feebly with these last two unknowns.

761. *Muse*: a second appeal for information, this time about the best men and horses on the Greek side. Its purpose seems to be to correct the priorities of the catalogue by re-emphasising how central Achilles is to the whole Greek operation: Eumelus may have the best horses (cf. 23.536-8) and Ajax may be the best fighter, *but only while Achilles is absent* (769-70, cf. 7.161, 17.280). This brings the poet back to the main theme of the *Il.*, Achilles' anger and withdrawal (771-3), and allows him to elaborate on how his men, the Myrmidons, passed their time.

764. *son of Pheres* (**L**): read 'grandson of Pheres'.

2.780-815. The goddess Iris alerts the Trojans and their leader Hector to the Greek threat.

783. *Typhoeus*: when Zeus was fighting Cronus and his Titans for mastery of the world, Gaia ('Earth') united with Tartarus ('Lowest Depths') to create the monster Typhoeus, the ultimate challenge (Hesiod, *Theogony* 820-68). Zeus hit him with a thunderbolt and buried him deep in the earth, where he causes earthquakes – the point of this image (cf. the Greek advance at 19.363). The halls of Hades in Homer are envisaged as being just below the earth's surface, but Tartarus stretches infinitely far into the lowest depths.

Homeric epic constructs a world of three basic domains: the sky above, ruled by Zeus; a flat earth, shared by the gods (this naturally includes their home on Mt Olympus), and the sea, ruled by Poseidon; and the underworld for the dead, ruled by Hades, immediately below that. See 15.187-93. Cf. the tri-partite division in Babylonian epic, 'Atrahasis' 1 i, Dalley (1989), p. 9.

786. *Iris*: the messenger goddess.

791. *voice like that of ... Polites*: in other words, Iris made herself like Polites to deliver the message, a common occurrence cf. 2.279 (Athene like a herald), 13.216 (Poseidon like Thoas).

793. *Aesyetes' tomb*: a landmark never mentioned again, like Bramble/Batieia/Thicket Hill (813).

804. *all/each speak different languages* (**R-J, H**); *multitudinous is the speech* (**L**): cf. 4.437-8. It seems a bit late in the war to suggest that leaders and men all speak the same language. Cf. Nestor's equally obvious advice at 2.362-3, as if the war were in its first, not tenth, year.

2.816-77. The catalogue of Trojan contingents.

With Hector heading it up, the Trojan catalogue seems more closely related to the *Il.* than the Greek. But it is much smaller. It lists sixteen contingents as against twenty-nine for the Greeks, and twenty-seven leaders as against forty-five. Seventeen Trojan leaders are killed or said to have been killed (if we count Pylaemenes, 851), as against ten Greeks. Five Trojan leaders are never heard of again, as against nine Greek. Three do appear again, but only fleetingly. Only two – Aeneas and Glaucus – do anything significant and survive. It is remarkable that Paris does not feature in it. Also, the Trojan catalogue has far less information about individual warriors than the Greek does. As a result, a catalogue of just over half the Greek manpower occupies only one quarter of the space (62 verses against 226). Given its low information-density, it looks as if there was no developing tradition of Trojan cities and warriors going back hundreds of years for the poet to draw on. It is surely significant that, of the nearly 350 Trojans and their allies named in the *Il.*, nearly 250 have *Greek* names. See Kirk (1985) 262-3.

The catalogue is arranged by location, as follows: first Troy and its environs (816-43); then European allies (844-50); allies along the Black Sea coast (851-7); inland allies (858-63); allies down the western sea-coast (864-77). See **R-J** map 3.

Troy and its environs (816-43)

816. *Hector*: the greatest Trojan fighter, son of Priam, king of Troy, and overall leader. Killed by Achilles at 22.361. For the full royal tree, see 20.215-241.

820. *Aeneas*: son of Aphrodite and Anchises (5.313). A good fighter, but of a different family branch (20.215-40, especially 230ff.) and not much respected by Priam (13.460-1). He features less than one might expect. According to the Roman tradition, when Ilium fell, he escaped from Troy and brought his Trojans refugees to Italy and founded the Latin race (Virgil, *Aeneid* 1.1-7). See on 13.459.

822. *but with him were* (**L**): with him *in command*, not as other offspring of Aphrodite.

823. *Archelochus and Acamas*: Archelochus is killed by Ajax at 14.463-74, and his resemblance to his father Antenor remarked; his death is immediately avenged by Acamas (475-85), who is himself killed by Meriones (16.342-4).

827. *Pandarus*: famous for his bow, which he uses to no avail against Menelaus (4.89-140) before he is killed by Diomedes (5.171-296).

830. *Adrestus and Amphius*: unambiguously killed by Diomedes at 11.329-34, though Trojans of that name are also killed by Ajax at 5.612-19, Menelaus at 6.37-65 and Patroclus at 16.693-4.

837. *Asius*: leads a foolish single-handed attack on the Greek ditch and wall at 12.96ff. and is killed by Idomeneus (13.384-93).

840. *Hippothous … Pylaeus*: Hippothous is killed by Ajax (17.288-303); Pylaeus does not appear again.

European allies (844-50)

844. *Acamas … Peiros*: Acamas is killed by Ajax (6.7-11); Peiros (= Peiroos) kills Diores (4.517-26) but is himself immediately killed by Thoas (527-31).

846. *Euphemus*: he does not appear again; Mentes appears as leader of the Ciconians at 17.73-4.

848. *Pyraechmes*: killed by Patroclus (16.287-92). At 21.155, Asteropaeus is said to be leader of the Paeonians, having been there only eleven days (cf. 12.102, 17.350-1). Perhaps he took over as leader after Pyraechmes' death?

Allies along the Black Sea coast (851-7)

851. *Pylaemenes*: killed by Menelaus at 5.576-9, though note that at 13.643-59 his son Harpalion is killed by Meriones, and Pylaemenes, weeping, accompanies his body back to Ilium (!) – the most notorious example of Homer 'nodding' (see on 1.424). Correct **L**'s 'Pylaimones'.

856. *Odius and Epistrophus*: Odius is killed by Agamemnon (5.38-42); Epistrophus is not heard of again.

Inland allies (858-63)

858. *Chromis and Ennomus*: these two are urged by Hector to fight for Patroclus' body at 17.215-18 (where Chromis becomes Chromius). Ennomus is said here to have been killed in the river by Achilles (i.e. somewhere in Book 21), but he does not appear in that book.

862. *Phorcys … Ascanius*: Phorcys (presumably this one) is killed by Ajax (17.312); Ascanius helps a rally at 13.792-4, where he is said to have arrived the day before. He is not heard of again.

Allies down the western sea-coast (864-77)

864. *Mesthles and Antiphus*: Mesthles is rallied by Hector at 17.216; Antiphus does not appear again.

867. *Nastes … Amphimachus*: neither appears again, despite the claim at 874-5 that Achilles killed Nastes in the river (see on 858 above).

876. *Sarpedon … Glaucus*: two major allies, oddly coming last (unless the poet is following a geographical route, and the Lycians are furthest away). Sarpedon, son of Zeus (16.459-60), much-respected leader of the allied troops (cf. 16.548-52), heads the attack on the Greek camp, pulling away the battlements (12.397-9), but is killed by Patroclus at 16.502; at this time Glaucus, though wounded at 12.387, is healed and leads a rally

(16.508ff.). At 12.309-28 Sarpedon explains to Glaucus the 'contract' of heroism; and Glaucus has a famous encounter with Diomedes at 6.119-236.

The Trojan army is split into five contingents at 12.88-103 (those who die in the *Il.* are asterisked), under (1) Hector,* Polydamas and Cebriones,* (2) Paris, Alcathous* and Agenor, (3) Helenus, Deiphobus and Asius,* (4) Aeneas, Archelochus* and Acamas,* (5) Sarpedon,* Glaucus and Asteropaeus.*

Book 3

Introduction

The Trojans were briefly introduced and catalogued at the end of Book 2; at the start of Book 3 Homer starts to fill out his picture of the Greeks' enemies. But where and how should he begin? This is an important narrative problem. It is worth imagining the various options Homer might have dreamed up: might he (for example) have begun by showing the Trojans hearing the news of Achilles' withdrawal? Or by depicting an assembly convened to persuade Paris to return Helen? As it is, Homer solves the problem with great brilliance – a duel between Paris and Menelaus, which Paris is on the point of losing when Aphrodite rescues him safely back into Helen's arms in Ilium.

This clever *mise-en-scène* enables Homer to introduce not merely Paris, who started the Trojan war by seducing Helen, but also Helen's husband Menelaus, brother of Agamemnon. He has not featured so far, but is the man for whose sake the war was begun and who stands to lose most if the Greeks are driven out of Troy. With Achilles out of the fighting, the chances of that have considerably increased; but if Menelaus can kill Paris in single combat, he can take his personal revenge on Paris and end the war at one swoop. Menelaus, then, comes into the spotlight for the first time, as does the reason for and background to the whole Trojan war, an issue which has not been relevant to the activity in the Greek camp in the first two books but is obviously vital in the context of the whole epic.

At the same time, Homer's plot-line allows him to set up Paris' brother, Hector, in contrast with Paris (39-75). Hector, leader of the Trojan army and the man who bears the brunt of the fighting, is shown as straight-speaking and contemptuous of his brother's glossy showiness; Paris acknowledges his weaknesses but wins credit for proposing a duel with Menelaus to end the matter once and for all, especially as his first sight of Menelaus in Book 3, as the poet shows, had sent him running for cover (30-7).

But if Paris, then Helen too must be introduced, the reason for the whole war ('Was this the face that launch'd a thousand ships, / And burnt the topless towers of Ilium?', Marlowe, *Doctor Faustus* V i.97). And so it happens: the poet now negotiates her first appearance as well, apparently to witness the battle between Menelaus and Paris (130-8), and then to receive Paris back from the fight. On the second occasion, her movements are overseen by pro-Trojan Aphrodite, goddess of sexual activity, who had brought about the meeting between Helen and Paris twenty (!) years earlier (24.765; see also on 3.66, 380): so Homer introduces another important (divine) figure naturally and effortlessly into the epic.

Helen's first appearance is not without its problems. Homer seems to be introducing her to watch Paris fight Menelaus, but in fact all she does is describe the Greek leaders to Priam from the walls of Ilium (the *teicho-scopia* 'wall-viewing'). After nine years of war and some negotiations between Greeks and Trojans already (205-24, 11.138-41), one would have thought Priam hardly needs this information anyway. What makes it even more difficult to take is that Priam is made not even to know who the Greek leaders are in the first place (he keeps on asking 'Who's that big bloke over there?' and Helen solemnly tells him). After all, it is not as if Homer *needed* to have done it this way: he could easily have made Priam say 'Look! There's Odysseus!' and Helen could have fleshed out the picture with some pithy reminiscences. Even more awkwardly, the number of heroes described is very limited (e.g. Ajax and Idomeneus given the briefest of mentions, 229-33, and no Diomedes or Menelaus at all, let alone the absent Achilles); and even those who are mentioned are not focalised in any particularly significant way through Helen's eyes except for the last pair, Castor and Pollux, Helen's brothers – the one moment when this scene springs to life as a picture of Helen (236-42). Homer also turns down the opportunity of focalising the duel between Paris and Menelaus through Helen's eyes: she is not described witnessing it.

The conclusion is that this episode was originally designed for the *first* year of the war, and has been taken over here with minimal change. If it was originally a catalogue of some sort, it would explain its rather unrepresentative nature (see on 2.484-779). That said, it has its high spots. Antenor chips in with a splendid description of Menelaus' and Odysseus' oratorical abilities (204-54); and the response of the Trojan elders to Helen's beauty when she appears before them is justly famous (150-60). This war is being fought for reasons even these old men can understand, though they wish she would go home at once (159-60).

In her second appearance, Helen is led by a disguised Aphrodite away from the walls of Ilium back to her room to receive Paris. Helen is revealed as a woman full of self-remorse, Paris as a man full of self-importance. When Helen tells Aphrodite that she has had enough of Paris, Aphrodite shows what a god can do to a favourite who crosses her. It is a chilling moment (395-417). Paris and Helen's subsequent love-making, carried out on Aphrodite's instructions, 'replays' the first time they made love twenty years earlier, starting the whole war (441-6; cf. the wider perspective which these books deliver, 2/Intro). Paris is still on fire with her; but Helen? (See on 3.445.)

The book ends with Agamemnon's proclamation that, even though Paris is not dead, Menelaus has won and therefore, under the terms of the oath as he sees it, Helen should now be returned. This lays the groundwork for the next 'move' in the plot – the Trojan response.

It is sometimes claimed that from Book 3 onwards Homer sets before his audience a blanket condemnation of Trojan wickedness, e.g. Taplin (1992) 103-9. That Paris broke the rules of *xenia* (see on 6.216), as Menelaus forcefully points out at 3.351-4, is not in doubt. But how far does the poet invite us to extend that guilt to all Trojans, let alone put this issue at the centre of the moral framework of the epic and argue that (say) it is the reason for Ilium's final destruction?

One immediate point, which always makes decisions of this sort difficult. It is not Homer's practice as third-person narrator to pass outright moral judgements, let alone loud and unambiguous ones: on such issues, broadly, he keeps his counsel and lets his characters do the talking, from their point of view, leaving us in the dark as to his view on the matter. As a result, if there is condemnation of any sort, it has to come from the mouths of the characters who, if they were (say) Menelaus, would condemn the Trojans, wouldn't they (focalisation)?

On the evidence of the text, it seems to me that neither Homer nor any of his characters draws any *consistent* conclusions about Trojan behaviour or guilt: they say what the moment requires to support the case they want to make. Where condemnation is expressed by the characters, it is Paris alone who tends to be on the receiving end of it; even more striking, it is not only the Greeks (3.97-100, 351-4) who make the case against him, but Hector (3.39-57) and the Trojans as well (3.454, they all hate Paris); at 7.390 the Trojan herald expresses the wish that Paris had died before reaching Troy with Helen. But then, on occasions, the Greeks *do* implicate all the Trojans: at 4.155-82 Agamemnon condemns all Trojans for Pandarus' shot (cf. 4.235-49, 6.55-60), as does Menelaus at 13.620-39. On the other hand, Menelaus at one point sees the conflict as a purely *personal* matter, which has caused both sides equally much suffering (3.97-100). As for the gods, they are not to be taken as authorities on humans' moral behaviour anyway. They certainly feel well-disposed to the Trojans as a whole for the sacrifices they make to them (4.44-9). But then, they would, wouldn't they?

The action of Pandarus in shooting at Menelaus at the start of Book 4 is often taken as an indication of Trojan guilt and treachery, but, as I argue in the Appendix, that judgement depends on what one understands by the oath made in Book 3. Trojan Antenor (7.348-53) certainly argues that Pandarus violated the oaths and concludes that it would be wise to return Helen for *that* reason alone. But this is a prudential, not a moral, argument. Antenor makes it because he is afraid of what the gods will do to people who, in his judgement, are oath-breakers. Antenor has nothing more to say about any wider Trojan 'guilt', let alone about Paris' original seduction of Helen.

Homer's picture of the responsibility for and guilt in relation to the Trojan war, in other words, fluctuates: it all depends on speaker and context. But it seems to me that the guilt that may attach to Paris is not extended to cover *all* the Trojans in such a way as to make it a central feature of the argument of the *Il.* in relation to the ultimate fate of Ilium. Homer does not deal in black and white moral judgements in that way. He is not Virgil, who does.

Here it must be said that it is always easy to muddy the waters of guilt and responsibility in Homer by arguing about whether the gods or fate 'forced' someone to act in one way or another, and therefore whether the human involved was 'really' responsible for what he or she had done. See **GI** 8 for the view that, since gods and humans are both *equally* responsible, humans cannot shake off their own responsibilities so lightly.

Main sources for the commentary and related reading
Edwards (1987) 188-97; Hooker (1979); Kirk (1985); Willcock (1978).

1-120. The armies advance to battle, and Paris proposes single combat with Menelaus to end the war. Hector announces the plan, and both sides agree.

2. *like cranes* **(R-J)**; *like birds* **(H)**; *like wildfowl* **(L)**: a B-simile (see **GI** 12), emphasising the chaotic noise of the Trojans (cf. 2.810), in contrast to the silence and unity of the Greeks (7-9). This describes the armies moving from the mustering-place towards the battlefield; they have yet to enter battle.

6. *Pygmies* **(R-J, H)**; *Pygmaian men* **(L)**: the Greek *pugmê* means 'fist' and 'cubit' (about 35 cms), suggesting these are a small, pugnacious people. There were pygmies living in the White Nile region, but no ancients recorded a sighting. Greeks however appeared to know about them. How? Greeks knew that cranes migrated south; this is what Homer observes here; therefore they assumed that he was right about everything else he said in this simile, the details of which were endlessly repeated as reality. The ancients then developed all sorts of fantasies about pygmies on the back of Homer's description here, e.g. vases depicting pygmies' defending themselves against cranes.

10. *As (when) ... the south wind*: D-simile. As usual, an important moment – the first engagement between Greeks and Trojans – attracts a run of similes (see on 2.455-83). Observe the way in which, as often, Homer explores the *human* implications of the image in the simile: dust-cloud = mist on the mountain, and Homer vividly emphasises the mist's impenetrability by describing the ever-present danger it presents to the shepherd. See on 15.669.

16. *Paris/Alexandros*: in 70% of cases Paris is called Alexander in Homer: the tradition uses both names without distinction. **R-J** uses 'Paris' throughout.

17. *leopard*: strange clothing for a warrior to be wearing in the front line: Paris the show-off? Again, a bow would not be a lot of use in the hand-to-hand combat he is inviting (19), and he should have a shield to go with his spears (though unexpected weapon-combinations do occur, cf. Helenus at 13.576-85, who uses a sword first and then his bow); cf. on 13.371. Paris finally puts on proper armour for the duel with Menelaus (330-8). Homer reports without obvious evaluative comment, but it should be noted that Hector thinks he is all appearance (45 'good looks, no strength of purpose or courage' **(R-J)**; 'heart empty of strength or courage' **(H)**; 'handsome ... no strength in your heart, no courage' **(L)**).

21. *(the) warlike/warrior Menelaus*: the epithet 'warlike' (*arêiphilos*, lit. 'dear to Ares', 'Ares-loving') is applied more to Menelaus than to any other fighter, yet he does not appear especially 'warlike' in the *Il.*: Agamemnon fears for him (7.109, 10.240), he can seem too relaxed (10.121), he is not thought to be the greatest fighter (17.26, 587), and so on. One can conclude, perhaps, that if the epithet is traditional, Homer develops his characters in ways different from the tradition.

23. *as/of/like a lion*: C-simile (note the ring-composition (23 'delighted/joy/glad' and 27 'delighted/joy/happy'). Lions, known from northern Greece and Asia Minor (modern Turkey), make up the largest number of simile subjects (40), and hunts regularly provide material for similes, presumably because hunters provide a natural human perspective. Nature is red in tooth and claw in Homer, as man is, and in this particular case, Menelaus. Note that in the simile the lion is chased off by men and dogs – foreshadowing Menelaus' failure to kill Paris? Similes can have anticipatory functions (see on 11.474-82).

28. *he thought/thinking*: note the moral focalisation through Menelaus' thoughts – 'punishment' and 'wrong-doing' are his judgements, not the poet's. For **L**'s 'robber', read 'wrong-doer'.

29. *from his chariot*: the mass of soldiers march to battle on foot (14). But the heroes go to war in two-man chariots and either fight from it or (as here) dismount to fight at ground level; see **GI** 13B(vi). Paris, who has been showing off as the two armies approach each other, now has second thoughts.

33. *snake*: D-simile, though with an element of ring-composition external to it (32 'he retreated/shrank back' and 37 'disappeared/slipped back/lost himself'). For the snake simile, cf. 22.93. This simile and the lion-simile at 23 vividly emphasise the contrast between cowardly Paris and mighty Menelaus.

39. *you parody* **(R-J)**; *you pest* **(H)**; *evil* **(L)**: the Greek says *Duspari*, *dus-* being a derogatory term, *Pari* meaning 'Paris'. Used again at 13.769.

46. *Can you be the same* **(R-J)**; *Is this the man* **(H)**; *Were you like this* **(L)**: in insulting Paris, Hector rehearses the background to and reason for the Trojan war. Homer constantly uses his characters to fill in the action prior to the real-time of the *Il.* (see **GI** 1C).

48. *mixed* **(R-J, L)**; *mingled* **(H)**: the Greek has sexual connotations, ironically in the light of 55 where the same word is repeated ('mixed/have your union/rolled' with the dust).

54. *the lyre*: singing to the lyre could have erotic overtones, depending on what was being sung. Achilles sings the (presumably unerotic) heroic deeds of the past (9.186-9).

57. *coat of stones* **(H)**; *mantle of flying stones* **(L)**: i.e. be stoned to death.

60. *like/as an axe*: C-simile, with human angle. Is Paris mocking Hector here? It seems unlikely, since Paris agrees to fight.

66. *acquires them by his own efforts* **(R-J)**; *would not take them of his* *choice* (**H**); *could have them for wanting them* (**L**): this does not refer to Paris' judgement when he gave Aphrodite the golden apple. The gift he received from that incident was Helen, but here Paris is answering Hector's charge that he is good-looking (54-5) and saying, reasonably, that one can do little about characteristics arbitrarily distributed by Aphrodite (cf. 414-15 – implying she could take them away too). This, of course, does not answer Hector's real charge – that he has *exploited* his looks, bringing shame on himself and trouble to his family (50-1). The poet is here playing with the appearance/worth contrast (cf. on 2.212). For the unpredictable gifts of Zeus, see e.g. 8.141-4, 15.490-3, 17.176-8, 20.242-3.

70. *her goods/possessions*: i.e. which she and Paris had taken with them when they secretly left for Ilium together.

73. *make/swear solemn oaths/truce of friendship* (**R-J, H**); *cut your oaths* (**L**): one 'cuts' oaths in Greek in the sense that the ratifying ceremony involves a sacrifice, i.e. cutting the hair off an animal as a first-offering before cutting its throat (3.273, 292, 19.254).

103. *white ram … black ewe*: the white ram for the (male) Sun god and black ewe for the (female) Earth goddess (cf. *Od.* 11.33). See **GI** 7E. The Greeks say that they will sacrifice to Zeus, perhaps because one of his cult titles was *Xenios*, god of hospitality, whose laws Paris had broken by seducing Helen (e.g. 3.353-4); but clearly the all-powerful king of the gods is the most reliable god of all to have on your side (cf. 107).

121-244: The goddess Iris tells Helen in Ilium of the impending duel. She comes to the walls of Ilium and describes some Greek heroes to Priam.

121-244. Zielinski's first law (named after the man who discovered it in 1899) states that, as a general rule, Homer treats real time in the epic as if everything happened successively, even when it should be happening simultaneously. See, for example, 15.154-220: at 154, Iris and Apollo stand in front of Zeus waiting for instructions. At 157, Zeus tells Iris what to do, and off she goes and does it. When she has fulfilled all her instructions, only *then* does Zeus turn to Apollo and tell him what to do, and off *he* goes and does it. Now, when the poet came to Zeus' instructions to Apollo, he *could* have said e.g. 'As soon as Iris had set off on her mission, Zeus at once turned to Apollo and said …'. But he does not. So while in real life, both actions would have taken place simultaneously, Homer makes no effort to suggest they did. The actions are described as taking place successively, one after the other.

Zielinski's second law states that, when two scenes are running parallel to each other and Homer is cutting from one to the other, the action in scene A (the one *not* being described) is often judged to have moved on in time while scene B is being described. This is what happens here: at 116-17, we are told Hector sent two heralds to fetch the lambs and summon Priam (scene A). At 121-244 we see Helen at the walls of Troy (scene B). When we cut back to scene A at 245, the heralds have already reached Ilium and are gathering everything that is needed for the oath, and Idaeus is telling Priam to come. In other words, we must assume that, while Helen has been on the wall, the heralds have been making their way to Ilium.

The result of both these laws is that, in the real time of the epic, Homer never describes the same period of time twice.

121. *Iris*: note the typical arrival sequence – Iris *came* to Helen's room, *found* her (125) *doing* something (weaving, 125), *went up* to her (129) and *spoke* (129). Cf. on 2.167.

122. *disguising herself* (R-J); *in the form/likeness of* (H, L): gods in the *Il.* do not always disguise themselves before addressing a human (e.g. 1.197-200), and even if they do, they sometimes reveal themselves soon after (e.g. Aphrodite at 3.386-97, cf. on 3.380). Iris usually acts only under someone else's instructions. Perhaps Homer could think of no Trojan who could motivate the action by coming to Helen and describing so accurately what had been taking place, so opted for Iris instead.

128. *suffered/enduring/endured for her sake*: should we 'focalise' this line through Helen's thoughts, or is it an objective narratorial report? Surely the former: Helen expresses her feelings of shame throughout the *Il.* (e.g. 3.172-6, 6.343-53, and cf. her response here 3.139-40).

143. *two waiting-women/maids/handmaidens*: a respectable, aristocratic woman appearing in public would normally do so accompanied and veiled, as Helen is here.

145. *Scaean gate(s)*: plural in Greek, because it has double doors. Ilium has a number of gates (2.809 = 8.58), of which one other is named, the Dardanian (though some argue that it is just an alternative name for the Scaean gate). The gates, defining the point at which the security of the town turns into the threat of the battlefield, are the scene of a number of dramatic encounters, e.g. the meeting of Hector and Andromache (6.237ff.), and the deaths of Hector (22.6) and (in the future) Achilles (22.359-60).

146. *Panthous …*: of these elders, the most significant are (1) Panthous, father of Polydamas. Polydamas will be an important critic of Hector who will act as a 'warning voice' in the second half of the *Il.* (see on 12.60); he does fight as well, 14.449-64, 15.339, 453-7, 518, 17.597-600; (2) Antenor, husband of Theano (6.298) and father of Agenor (see e.g. 4.467) and other Trojan warriors; he accompanies Priam at 3.262.

152. *trilling lightly away* (R-J); *lily-soft song* (H); *delicate voice of singing* (L): B-simile. The Greek *leirioeis*, describing the cicadas' song, in fact means 'thin, spare' (the lily connection is to do with the thinness of their leaves). A cicada's song is hardly soft or delicate.

153. *tower/bastion*: see on 21.526.

156. *No one could blame* (R-J); *No shame* (H); *no blame* (L): this reaction to Helen creates an overwhelming sense of her beauty not because of any physical description but because it is put in the mouths of men who, even though they are old, can still understand why they *and their enemies* have suffered so much for her.

164. *I don't hold you responsible* (**R-J**); *It is not you I blame* (**H**); *I am not blaming you* (**L**): Homeric heroes blame events on either humans or gods equally easily, sometimes both at the same time, e.g. 19.85-7, 409-10 and see on 9.702. Priam, who has always been kind to Helen (as she says at 24.770-1), makes a special case for her here (see **GI** 5C); cf. her evaluation at 6.343-58 where she blames herself, Paris and the gods equally.

173. *to die in misery* (**R-J**); *vile death* (**H**); *bitter death* (**L**): the first of Helen's many self-reproaches, cf. 180 where she calls herself a slut/whore, and 404, 6.344. She repeats her wish that she had died at 6.345-8, 24.764. She dwells on her regret at abandoning her normal relationships (139-40, 174-5, 236-8) and on how long she has been away from Greece (24.765-6). The untenability of her position – everyone rejects her, 3.411-12, 24.775 – her shame (3.242, 6.356, 24.763-4), and the misery this causes her are constant themes.

188. *their ally* (**R-J, H**); *helper* (**L**): the Phrygians, eastern neighbours of Troy, are now their allies against the Greeks (2.862); and the Amazons ('breastless') too, led by Penthesilea, helped the Trojans after Hector died (as we learn from what we know of another epic, the *Aethiopis*).

197. *ram*: in the Greek world it was assumed that there was a connection between looks and performance, and heroes were expected to be tall and impressive (see on Thersites, 2.212 and cf. 3.66). As is indicated by this simile of the ram, and confirmed shortly, Odysseus' outward appearance was unimpressive; he looked like a surly or stupid fellow (220, cf. 223-4). His oratory, however, belied the outward impression (the snow image, 221-3).

202. *manoeuvres and strategies* (**R-J**); *trickery and clever plans* (**H**); *shiftiness and crafty counsels* (**L**): so far Odysseus has been characterised as a persuasive orator (as he will be here) and spoken of in favourable terms (e.g. 2.272-4). But now, for the first time in western literature, we hear of his trickiness. This is perhaps to be expected in one of such a negative outward appearance (see above note about Greek attitudes). In fact there is little sign of his 'manoeuvres and strategies' in the *Il.* (though see on 4.331): these characteristics will be reserved especially for the *Od.* where, even so, his most famous trick, the invention of the Wooden Horse, is never credited to him (Epeius is said to have constructed it, *Od.* 8.493).

205. *once came here* (**R-J**); *Once before* (**H**); *Once in the days before* (**L**): further memory of the early years of the war (cf. 11.138-42; see **GI** 1C).

237. *Castor ... Pollux (Polydeuces)*: later (but not in Homer) known as the *Dios kouroi* (Dioscuri) 'Zeus' sons' by Leda, and worshipped as divinities.

242. *disgrace ... insults* (**R-J**); *shame ... curses/reproach* (**H, L**); further self-reproach from Helen, all the more powerful for being imagined by her as her own brothers' reasons for not fighting.

243-4. *life-giving/teeming earth*: the earth which gives life holds the dead; but Helen, in Troy, knows nothing of her brothers' fate in the land she left. The exquisite pathos of the lines is due in large measure to Homer's refusal to do anything other than report the fact without emotionalising comment (an 'objective' stance, favoured by the poet throughout the epic; see **GI** 10). One can readily imagine the tearful gush in which the modern novelist would have drenched the page at this point.

245-380: The oaths are taken, and the duel begins. Menelaus is cheated of victory by Aphrodite, who rescues Paris.

275. *prayed*: see **GI** 7E for oath-taking. The wine-pouring here, as well as being a normal part of a religious ceremony (see on 1.471), also becomes part of the oath, an image of what transgressors will suffer (spilled wine = spilled brains, 295-301). Note that fire plays no part in this ceremony since this is not a sacrifice to the gods (see **GI** 7B): it is only the blood that counts in oath-taking, and the dead animals are taken away afterwards to be somehow disposed of (310, cf. 19.267-8). That is why the hair is distributed among the leaders (276): normally it would be burnt.

276. *Ida*: for the purposes of the *Il.*, Zeus occupies either Mount Olympus (see on 1.18) or a peak of Mount Ida, overlooking Troy from the south (see **R-J** maps 4, 1).

279. *Powers of the world below* (**R-J**); *you gods below* (**H**); *you who under the earth* (**L**): i.e. the Erinyes (see 9.454, and cf. **GI** 7E).

281. *If Paris/Alexandros kills Menelaus*: there are three sorts of Greek oaths: evidentiary ('I swear that X happened'), confirmatory ('I swear that X happened as Y said it did') and promissory ('I swear I will do X'). This is a promissory oath, accompanied as usual by a blood-curdling condition if the promise is not made good (298-301). Cf. Aristophanes' parody of such oaths at *Lysistrata* 194-239. The oath does not become irrelevant because neither Paris nor Menelaus is killed. See Appendix.

302. *did/would not yet grant their prayers* (**R-J, H**); *none ... would [Zeus] accomplish*: the 'yet' (missed by **L**) shows that the poet is thinking of the destruction of Ilium by the Greeks rather than the fulfilment of the oath.

305. *I am now going back/away* (**R-J, L**); *I shall go back* (**H**): Priam's fear for his essentially archer son against Menelaus is understandable; it is also necessary for Homer to remove Priam since he would make a momentous hostage when Paris is trickily removed from the action by Aphrodite, and Agamemnon declares Menelaus the winner (3.456-60; cf. 24.686-8). For the dead animals he takes with him (310), see on 275 above.

323. *let firm oaths of friendship be made* (**R-J**); *and we make between us a solemn truce* (**H**); *let the friendship and the sworn faith be true* (**L**): see Appendix.

325. *averting his eyes* (**R-J**); *eyes turned away* (**H**); *looking backward*

(L): so as not to be accused of 'fixing' the throw (the 'lots' were probably pebbles).

328-38. *put (on) his … armour*: a typical scene of arming, the structure of which is repeated at 11.17-45 (Agamemnon), 16.131-44 (Patroclus) and 19.369-91 (Achilles), i.e. (in order) greaves, body-armour, sword, shield, helmet, spear(s). Details are varied to suit the occasion, e.g. 333, where Paris (being an archer) has to borrow body-armour from his brother Lycaon (who will be killed by Achilles 21.34-135). As in dressing scenes (cf. 2.42), the logic of the sequence is determined by what is to be worn: note that sword and shield were held in place by straps over the shoulder. Armour symbolises the greatness of the hero; the more elaborate the arming-scene, the greater our expectations. Paris' arming scene is the plainest of them all.

332. *corselet* **(H, L)**: i.e. body-armour.

334. *silver-riveted sword* **(R-J)**; *the hilt nailed with silver* **(H)**; *with the nails of silver* **(L)**: i.e. the bronze blade of the sword was joined to the handle, or hilt, with silver-headed rivets. Such swords are well attested during the Mycenaean period, though they have also been found later.

346. *First … Paris/Alexandros*: it is typical for a spear to be bent back, e.g. 17.44-5; and also typical that a man who throws too weakly to penetrate the armour loses.

355-60. *balanced* **(R-J, L)**; *steadying* **(H)**… *dark death* **(R-J, L)**; *black doom* **(H)**: lines repeated in the later duel between Ajax and Hector at 7.249-54.

362. *ridge* **(R-J)**; *horn* **(H, L)**: it is not clear exactly what this projection, of which there was often more than one, actually was.

380. *with his bronze spear*: but Menelaus has already thrown it. Warriors sometimes take two spears (e.g. Agamemnon at 11.43), but not in this duel (338-9). Homer nods?

380-461: Aphrodite forces a reluctant Helen to go to Paris and make love to him. Agamemnon declares Menelaus the winner of the duel.

380. *Aphrodite … whisked him away* **(R-J)**; *snatched him away* **(H)**; *caught up Paris* **(L)**: as Athene with Achilles at 1.194, gods constantly intervene to help their favourites, sometimes in disguise, usually not (in the *Od.*, they are always in disguise, cf. on 3.122). Since Paris had awarded the golden apple inscribed 'to the most beautiful' to Aphrodite, he was a favourite of hers (and hated by Athene and Hera, whom he had thereby rejected). Concealing in mist is typical (e.g. Apollo saving Hector from Achilles at 20.443-4; 11.751-2).

399. *Mysterious goddess* **(R-J)**; *strange goddess/divinity* **(H, L)**: *daimonios* in Greek; see on 1.561. Helen feels as if she is a helpless pawn in Aphrodite's power, and tells her so in no uncertain terms – even ordering her to marry Paris herself and leave her alone. See **GI** 6 for such extraordinary, but wholly typical, behaviour.

414-15. *detest you … as I have loved you* **(R-J)**; *show a hate … as the love* **(H)**; *hate you … as I terribly love you* **(L)**: chilling words – a god can reverse his or her affections at an instant (cf. on 4.40). One does not cross a deity: no wonder Helen's reaction is terror (418: it is significant how rarely humans in the *Il.* are said to fear the gods). It is hard to believe, as some do, that this whole scene should really be thought of as an 'internal debate' within Helen's mind.

422. *turned to their tasks* **(R-J)**; *turned quickly to their work* **(H)**; *went … to their work* **(L)**: a nice observation. The maids react to Helen's arrival by hurriedly going back to work – Paris' earlier arrival had obviously set them gossiping.

424. *laughter-loving* **(R-J)**; *smiling goddess* **(H)**; *sweetly laughing* **(L)**: an appropriate epithet for the goddess who presides over the pleasures of sexual activity (not of 'love'). She continues to act the part of a maid by drawing up a chair.

427. *attacked him* **(R-J)**; *spoke slightingly* **(H)**; *spoke … in derision* **(L)**: Homer (for once) identifies for us the tone of Helen's words. It is therefore unlikely that, as has been suggested, she suddenly changes her tune to one of loving protectiveness at 433 ('But if you take my advice/No, I would advise you/But no'), cf. 5.337-9. Paris certainly regards her words as 'hurtful/bitter' (438) but is overwhelmed by lust; Helen, especially after Aphrodite's reproach – and the goddess is still present as a maid – has no option but to go quietly (447).

439. *Athene*: but she had had nothing to do with Menelaus' victory. This is Paris' self-serving interpretation to explain away his defeat. In fact it was only Aphrodite who intervened, to save Paris!

445. *Cranae*: Paris remains the same old Paris who seduced Helen away from Menelaus twenty years ago (Homer filling in the background again and 'replaying' for us how the war started in the first place); but Helen has changed. She is making love under Aphrodite's explicit orders – or is she as responsible as the goddess for her decision here (cf. **GI** 8)? Surely not, given her earlier argument with the goddess (see 427 above). With this scene, cf. Zeus and Hera, especially 14.313-28.

448. *Son of Atreus/Atreides* **(H, L)**: Menelaus, who takes Paris' sudden, miraculous disappearance in his stride. Such 'miracles' are taken for granted as an everyday occurrence in a world where gods and men so closely interact, and no Greek has anything further to say about it.

457. *Menelaus has clearly won* **(R-J)**; *Victory plainly rests* **(H)**; *Clearly the victory* **(L)**: oaths were very precise agreements and did not in this instance specifically cater for a non-result (3.276-91, and on 3.281). But there is no doubt what Agamemnon's and the Greek view of the matter is: Menelaus has won on points, and the Trojans should now surrender and hand over Helen, in accordance with the terms of the oath relating to the *loser* (284-91).

Book 4

Introduction

In Book 3 the poet introduced his audience to the pro-Trojan goddess Aphrodite and her favourite Paris, who between them started the Trojan war. Here in Book 4 he lays before us the pro-Greek gods, Athene and Hera, with their insatiable desire for revenge, an emotional commitment that will restart the fighting at this point.

At the end of Book 3 Agamemnon announced that the Trojans must now return Helen. But this is the last thing Hera and Athene want. Their desire is for Ilium to burn and the Trojans to be wiped out for the insult Paris dealt them when he chose Aphrodite over them all those years ago. They must therefore forestall any possibility that the Trojans might accept Agamemnon's offer. After all, the enthusiasm with which both sides settled down to watch the duel between Menelaus and Paris that might have ended the war made it perfectly clear that both sides would rather not fight if they did not have to (3.111-12, cf. their hopes and fears at 4.82-4).

When, therefore, Zeus 'needling/teasing/angering Hera' raises the shocking idea that the war might be settled here and now (16, cf. 3.73-5) – an outcome he *says* he would favour as a result of all the sacrifices the Trojans have made him (44-9) – Hera reveals the depth of her hatred for the Trojans by offering to bargain away three of the Greek cities dearest to her heart (the side she supports!) in return for Ilium's destruction (51-3). Zeus accepts this favourable deal and sends Athene down to re-start the war (69-72). But why does he say that he want the *Trojans* to be first to 'break the oaths made with the proud Greeks' to start the fighting again? Because if a Greek starts the fight, the Trojans might still come up with a settlement offer. But if a Trojan starts it, that will not only guarantee the Greeks' instant retaliation, it will make it clear that the Trojans are not interested in any deals. The point here is that Zeus has indeed been needling or teasing Hera and Athene at the start of the book (5-6): after all, *he* wants war to re-start just as much as Hera does, since he has made a promise to Thetis in relation to it.

Homer now has a problem: how is Athene to re-start the war? She clearly has to persuade a Trojan to do something dramatic to ensure the Greeks retaliate, but, at the same time, she must ensure its consequences are not too severe for her beloved Greeks. Now in Book 3, the oaths declared that, if Paris were killed, the Trojans would give up Helen and end the war; if Menelaus were killed, the Greeks would leave. Paris was nearly killed in Book 3, but rescued by a goddess (Aphrodite); Athene decides that Menelaus must be nearly killed in Book 4, and rescued by a goddess (herself). The delicious simile at 130-1 expresses the relationship at this point between Athene and Menelaus: 'mother' Athene cannot allow her helpless 'baby' to be killed. Helpless indeed amid the scheming of the gods; and it is amusing that Athene, the virgin goddess of war (note 'war-leader/goddess of spoil/spoiler' 128), should be seen as a mother.

Agamemnon's response to Menelaus' wounding is typical. He sees that the war must now re-start and is confident the Trojans will pay the price for (as he sees it) breaking the oaths (155-68), but can think of the prospect of Menelaus' death only in terms of the effect it will have on his own reputation when he gets back to Greece (169-82). There follows the third 'review of troops' (this one known as the *epipôlêsis*, 'tour of inspection') following on the catalogue of ships in Book 2 and Helen's *teichoscopia* in Book 3. This may seem excessive, but it is important to note that each of the reviews is focalised through different eyes – the catalogue is the Muse's 'objective' account (2.484-93), the *teichoscopia* views the Greek army through Trojan/Helen's eyes, and here we have Agamemnon's assessment of his men.

As **GI** 9 argues, however, Agamemnon's review here is in fact much more an assessment that has to be made of *him* as a leader after his 'victory' over Achilles in Book 1. As he shows at once with the general troops, where they are ready for action, he urges them on, and where they hang back, he rebukes them (232-50). So when he moves on to individuals, he finds Idomeneus, the Ajaxes and Nestor (251-326) in a state of readiness, and praises them. Idomeneus replies gracefully enough but implies he does not need encouragement; Agamemnon himself agrees nothing need be said to the Ajaxes; and Agamemnon seems to think Nestor too old to fight, a view that Nestor gently rejects. Odysseus and Diomedes, however, are different cases. Both seems to be hanging back, so both are rebuked. Odysseus replies angrily, though without answering Agamemnon's charge of unreadiness, and Agamemnon immediately backtracks and apologises (358-63); Diomedes, however, excuses Agamemnon's reproaches on the grounds of his respect/awe for the expedition leader (403) and the fact that Agamemnon will carry the can if the expedition goes wrong (412-18).

There is a military point to be made here. It is not surprising that the troops are in different states of readiness for battle. In Homer the various contingents are under the control of their individual leaders, as was made clear during the catalogue at the end of Book 2, and are therefore independent of central command. That is why there is no discussion of tactics before battle begins; there is simply no concept of an overall military strategy in Homer, devised e.g. by a general in consultation with his senior advisers. Indeed, not even anything as elementary as the advance into battle is integrated. Troops just move forward as they will, when they are ready (cf. e.g. 20.329). This must have seemed very frustrating to the man in (apparent) overall charge, and is presumably why Agamemnon went on his *epipôlêsis* to start with, i.e. to do his best, as tactfully as he could, to get all his men all moving together into battle at once. See Albracht (2003) [I.25] and cf. **GI** 13B(iv).

In the light of this, Agamemnon's *epipôlêsis* requires some tact. He cannot just bark out orders and expect to see them automatically obeyed, especially by his senior men. He has to play it cautiously, and on the whole he does quite well; he is even prepared to retract his criticisms. Diomedes' response is especially interesting – he takes Agamemnon's criticism on the chin even though, far from hanging back, he is about to launch out on a tremendous *aristeia* himself (start of Book 5). The contrast with Achilles in Book 1 is obvious. But Diomedes will not forget Agamemnon's rebuke either (9.34-6).

Battle is finally joined (444ff.) It is easy to find the battle-books monotonous and shapeless, but this is because we are not attuned to the world of war 'with all its tears' which at the same time is an activity 'where men win glory'. Homer would not have dwelt on fighting so long if his audience had not found it engrossing. As will become apparent, Homer is enormously ingenious at varying the details of the battles; see **GI** 2(iii) and **GI** 13. There are single combats, duels, massed combats, negotiations, truces, and burials; fights on foot and very occasionally from chariots; advances, retreats and routs. While deaths are generally instant, some are distinctly gruesome, others highly elaborated. The similes and human stories that accompany battle-scenes add colour, pathos and a sense of a wider world to the concentrated slaughter taking place outside Ilium; and the characters of the major heroes and the gods who support them (or not) become evident. There are also moments of the mysterious and supernatural, e.g. divine blood flowing (5.339, 416), Ares and the cloud (5.356), the image of Aeneas made by Apollo (5.449), Athene's helmet of invisibility (5.844), Diomedes wounding gods and Ares disappearing like a tornado (5.864), though such bizarre events are rare in Homer (cf. **GI** 6 and on 6.119-236).

In the battle scenes covering Book 4, variety is the order of the day, as if Homer is giving us a foretaste of his repertoire, and a sense of Greek superiority is established. So where has the plan of Zeus gone, that the Trojans should start winning?

Main sources for the commentary
Kirk (1985); Willcock (1978).

1-72: Zeus wonders whether Hera and Athene would agree to making peace between the Greeks and Trojans. The goddesses, who hate the Trojans, refuse, and Athene descends to re-start the fighting.

2. *Hebe*: means 'prime of youth'; she appears again at 5.722, 905 in other humble roles. In later tradition, Ganymedes (20.232-5) is Zeus' cup-bearer, the young boy with whom Zeus fell in love. But homosexual relationships are not mentioned in Homer.

6. *needling* (**R-J**); *taunting* (**H**); *offensive* (**L**): Zeus is stirring trouble, in order to get the fighting between Greeks and Trojans started again.

though he did not mean what he said (**R-J**); *devious purpose* (**H**); *to* *cross her* (**L**): there is some doubt about what the Greek means, but **R-J, H** add more point than **L**. After this jocular start, however, Zeus soon turns angry (30ff.).

8. *Alalcomene* (**R-J**); *Alalkomenaian* (**H**); *who stands by her people* (**L**): another ancient description for Athene, of disputed meaning. It probably refers to the town of Alalcomene (in Boeotia), where Athene had a temple.

13. *victory has certainly gone to* (**R-J**); *victory certainly rests* (**H**); *the victory now is with* (**L**): see Appendix for a discussion of the 'truce', the oaths and Menelaus' victory, and its relevance to Book 4.

21. *plotting trouble/hardship* (**R-J, H**); *devising evil* (**L**): 4.20-5 = 8.457-62.

27. *sweat(ed)*: see **GI** 5 for the 'daily life' of the gods.

31. *You are impossible!* (**R-J**); *(my) dear wife/lady* (**H, L**): see on *daimonios* (1.561).

34. *raw*: demonstrating just how deeply Zeus understands Hera to hate the Trojans (cf. 8.449): gods, of course, consume only ambrosia and nectar (5.341-2).

40. *When it is my turn* (**R-J**); *Whenever (I) in (my) turn* (**H, L**): observe the ruthlessness of the gods, supporting their own human favourites as far as they can, but jettisoning them, however devoted those favourites have been (44-9), if they have to. Hera confirms the point (51-3), being prepared to bargain away as many as three of *her* favourite cities if this is the only way to destroy hated Ilium (cf. on 3.414-15). It is true, as she says, that nothing she could do would stop Zeus sacking them if he so desired; but she claims she would not even *try* to stand up for them – most un-Hera-like in normal circumstances.

48-9. *my altar*: the gods require nothing but sacrifice (libations of wine and the smell of the burnt offerings) from men, because that is how they are 'honoured' (49).

56. *far too strong* (**R-J**); *far (the) stronger* (**H, L**): see on 1.401.

60. *I am ... (your) wife/consort*: Hera is Zeus' sister as well as his wife. Incest is rife among the gods.

72. *break the oaths* (**R-J, H**); *injury against the oaths* (**L**): i.e. the condition that if the Trojans lost (3.456-60, 4.13), they would surrender and hand over Helen (see Appendix).

73-219: Athene persuades the Trojan archer Pandarus to take a shot at Menelaus. Athene herself takes care to deflect the shot so that it only grazes him, and the healer Machaon is summoned.

76. *like/as when a meteor/star*: D-simile (see **GI** 12), occurring (typically) to herald the start of an important action. A meteor (the likelier translation) was commonly taken as a portent (hence the two armies' awe-struck reaction to it, 79-85). There are nine star/meteor similes in the *Il.* See the list of simile subjects in Lee (1964) 65-73.

86.   *Laodocus*: not mentioned again. For his father Antenor, see on 3.146. Athene obviously cannot appear as herself since the Trojans know she is hostile to them (e.g. 6.94-5).

88.   *Pandarus*: son of Lycaon, from Zeleia (103) near the river Ae-sepus (91, **R-J** map 3), at the head of Trojan troops (2.286). When therefore he is called 'Lycian', the poet can hardly be referring to the region to the deep south of Troy from which Sarpedon comes: 'Lycian' must therefore be some sort of local Zeleian name as well. Pandarus appears in the Trojan catalogue (2.824-7) with the bow he will now use against Menelaus. In the catalogue Apollo gave him the bow; but here its manufacture by a human is described. For **L**'s description of Pandarus as 'blameless', see on 1.92.

89.   *she found/did find*: an arrival scene. See on 2.167.

101.   *Lycian-born Apollo* (**R-J, H**); *Apollo the light-born* (**L**): it is not clear what Apollo's title *Lukogenês* means (it appears only here and 119). *-genês* means 'born', and *luko-* may be to do with wolves or Lycia (cf. Pandarus' father's name Lycaon). A derivation meaning 'light' (**L**) is now rejected. It is worth observing that Athene says nothing about a truce – because there is no truce. Her proposal that Pandarus kill Menelaus would, if successful, effectively win the war for the Trojans, since there would be no incentive for the Greeks to retake Helen if Menelaus were dead (cf. 4.172-82).

105.   *bow*: a famous object, about to play a vital part. Its description is therefore expanded (see on 2.455-83). It is made of the horn of a goat, i.e. strips of horn were fitted into the wooden stave to give it added strength and power. A bow made entirely of horn would have no flexibility.

123.   *iron*: only here is a weapon made of iron (bronze everywhere else, the standard metal of the bronze age heroes, see **GI** 3).

126.   *eager/furious*: typical Homer personification, as if the arrow had a mind of its own.

127.   *you, Menelaus*: an unexpected and striking use of the second person in the 'objective' third-person narrative. The usage, called 'apostrophe', is almost entirely restricted to Menelaus (146, 7.104, 17.679, 23.600) and Patroclus (eight times in Book 16, where he meets his death). It has a strongly sympathetic effect, as if the poet himself has a special feeling for his character or wishes to draw especial attention to him (e.g. Achilles at 20.2).

128.   *the war-leader Athene, daughter of Zeus* (**R-J**); *Zeus' daughter, goddess of spoil* (**H**); *Zeus' daughter, the spoiler* (**L**): the epithet *ageleiê* could mean either 'bringer of spoil/booty' or 'war-leader, leader of the army'.

130.   *like/as (when) a mother*: B-simile – Athene looks after Menelaus as a mother her sleeping child, at the very moment when he is about to be killed by an arrow launched at him on Athene's advice! The simile plays on Menelaus' ignorant helplessness as much as on (the ruthless virgin warrior) Athene's motherliness.

132.   *golden (belt) buckles*: it is not exactly clear what Homer means by a number of these protective items. Assume that Menelaus is hit in the stomach, and the arrow goes through three layers – the belt, the body protection (corselet) underneath at the point where it overlaps (like a double-breasted jacket), and then through the kilt/skirt-piece/guard underneath that.

141. *As (when) a/some woman*: D-simile. Maeonia and Caria are to the south of Troy (**R-J** map 3). The cheek-piece was a luxury item, made from exotic foreign materials: ivory came from Syria, and purple dye from specially treated shellfish from Phoenicia, roughly modern Lebanon. No wonder it was designed for royalty. The introduction of the human perspective, stressing how exclusive the object was, extends the simile beyond the merely visual (is it meant to hint at Menelaus' value to the army?).

151. *arrow-head ... bindings* (**R-J**); *binding ... barbs* (**H, L**): the metal arrow-head was bound ('bindings') to a wooden shaft, but had not sunk right in: the arrow's barbs were still visible.

158. *oath(s)*: see the oath sworn at 3.276-91.

170. *if you die*: Agamemnon has grieved briefly for Menelaus, but is more interested in the effect of Menelaus' death on his own reputation, as if his own honour were of greater importance.

171. *thirsty Argos* (**H, L**): i.e. dry, dusty.

190. *physician* (**L**): too modern a term. 'Healer' (**R-J, H**) is preferable.

191. *medicines* (**H**); *healing salves* (**L**): these would be herbs (**R-J**) of some sort, cf. Agamede's skills at 11.740.

194. *Asclepius*: see on 2.732.

200. *he found/saw*: cf. on 2.167.

214. *barbs (were) broke(n) (off)*: the barbs had not sunk in to the flesh (151), so presumably broke as the arrow was pulled out backwards through Menelaus' protective clothing – a keen little observation.

219. *Cheiron*: there are many myths about this wise centaur (cf. on 1.263-5 for the unwise). In the *Il.* Homer mentions that he was the teacher of Asclepius and Achilles (11.830-1). This briefly acknowledges one tradition about Achilles' upbringing, but since Homer tends to avoid associating his heroes with monsters, however wise, he also gives Achilles a normal upbringing: see 9.485-95, where Phoenix is Achilles' teacher and 18.57, where Thetis raises him. Cheiron was also the donor of the great ash spear from Mount Pelion to Achilles' father Peleus (16.143 = 19.390).

220-421: Agamemnon surveys his troops, praising Idomeneus, the Ajax brothers and Nestor, but rebuking Menestheus, Odysseus and Diomedes.

223-421. *Then you would not*: a third review of the troops, following on from Homer's catalogue of Greeks and Trojans, 2.494-877, and the Trojan perspective on some Greek leaders seen through Helen's eyes, 3.162-244. Here we see Agamemnon using his leadership 'skills' on

Idomeneus, the two Ajaxes and Nestor (praise), Menestheus, Odysseus and Diomedes (blame).

242. *loud-mouths* (**R-J**); *bletherskates* (**H**); *arrow-fighters* (**L**): the Greek *iomôroi* is a term of abuse, but its precise meaning is not clear. 'Bletherskate' (or 'blatherskite'), from the Scottish song 'Maggie Lauder' (popular with the American camp during the war of independence) means 'noisy talkative fellow' (*OED*); 'arrow-fighter', as if the soldiers did not want to fight at close quarters, is less likely, especially as archery was a respectable craft.

243. *like fawns/young deer*: C-simile: a lively image of an inexperienced, easily-frightened, non-combative animal, cf. 22.1. Agamemnon is showing how the good commander verbally shames the slackers (who exist in every army, cf. 2.337ff.).

252. *Idomeneus ... Meriones*: see 2.645-52.

262. *your cup*: presumably the top men had their cup constantly refilled at feasts (cf. 12.311). It was a sign of high status to be invited to great men's feasts; but great men expected something in return, cf. 340-6 below and on 12.310-28.

267. *assurance I gave* (**R-J**); *as I promised* (**H, L**): see on 2.286.

273. *Ajax and Teucer* (**R-J**); *two Aiantes* (**H, L**): the 'two' here cannot include Locrian Ajax since his troops were light-armed (13.712-18), so they must be Ajax and his half-brother Teucer (see on 2.406).

275. *As a goatherd* (**R-J**); *As when from some high point* (**H**); *As from his watching place* (**L**): D-simile, though the 'cloud' of 274 is picked up so quickly that it is effectively a C-simile (there are seven cloud similes in the *Il.*). The human perspective is provided by a lonely goatherd in a cave (the isolation of the viewer is common in similes, encouraging the sense of a specific, personal experience): his fearful reaction to the cloud is the important point, prompting the reader/listener to feel the same.

295-6. *Pelagon ... Bias*: since none of these leaders is mentioned at 2.591-602, and their names are common among both Greeks and Trojans, Homer probably invented them for this occasion. Again, it is odd that Nestor's son Antilochus receives no mention (cf. on 2.601).

297. *horses and chariots (in front)*: cf. on 2.360. Nestor seems to be envisaging a chariot charge (of the sort he engaged in as a young man at 11.746-7, cf. 4.310 'long ago/long experience/from of old'). But Homeric heroes use chariots primarily for transport. See **GI** 13B(vi).

319. *Ereuthalion*: see Nestor's story at 7.132-57.

331. *had not (yet) reached/heard*: Homer clears Odysseus and Menestheus of the cowardice with which Agamemnon charges them (see on 3.202 for Odysseus' reputation for trickery). As Agamemnon demonstrates, it is not difficult to interpret quick-thinking and intelligence as irresponsible self-interest. Not that there has been any evidence of that in Odysseus so far in the *Il.*; Agamemnon's attack on him seems as ill-judged as his next attack, on Diomedes.

345. *take your fill* (**R-J**); *eat* (**H, L**): on the connections between duty and material rewards, see on 1.121-307. Here Agamemnon appeals to the sense of solidarity that should exist in a united army, cf. 9.70-3.

366. *chariots*: at 419 Diomedes appears actually to be *in* his chariot. It is (just) possible that Agamemnon suspects him of cowardice, since chariots could be used to retreat in. At any rate, after Agamemnon's rebuke, Diomedes at once gets down from his chariot to show he means business, cf. Albracht (2003) [I.18].

376. *to Mycenae*: this is the story of the Seven against Thebes; see on 2.563-5 for the role of the fathers and their sons (and see Sthenelus' heated reply below at 4.404). Diomedes and his father Tydeus are commonly compared and contrasted in the *Il.*, as Agamemnon sets out to do here. Agamemnon here is careful to mention that Tydeus came to Mycenae (where Agamemnon was king) and that the Mycenaeans were ready to help him (adding to the point about Diomedes' 'failure' here). The story is referred to again by Athene (5.802-8) and Diomedes himself (10.285-90), with a different focalisation to fit the situation (de Jong [1987] 155-7). It is always assumed by Homeric heroes that worth passes naturally from father to son. Hence the interest in lineage, cf. 7.125-8.

378. *Thebe* **(L)**: read 'Thebes'.

384. *with a message*: presumably that Eteocles should hand the kingship over to Polyneices.

385. *Kadmeians* **(H, L)**: i.e. Thebans, of whom Cadmus was the founder.

389. *try their strength* **(L)**: i.e. challenge them to athletics/games.

400. *better (at) talk(ing)* **(R-J, H)**; *better in conclave* **(L)**: not that Diomedes has yet opened his mouth in the *Il.* Diomedes replies to this jibe with a respectful silence (401) – an effective way of dealing with it.

412. *I am not going to quarrel* **(R-J)**; *I do not resent* **(H)**; *I will find no fault* **(L)**: the comparison between Diomedes here and Achilles in Book 1 is evident: a Homeric hero is not *obliged* to respond to an insult as Achilles did. Cf. 9.34-6, where Diomedes recalls Agamemnon's insult here, and even more pertinently 9.697-703, where Diomedes shrewdly analyses Achilles' recalcitrant behaviour.

421. *might well have quailed* **(R-J)**; *felt the grip of fear* **(H)**; *Fear would have gripped* **(L)**: Homer's imaginary viewer (see on 4.539), drawing the reader/listener into the same response. Diomedes is soon to enjoy a magnificent feat of arms in Book 5.

422-544: Battle is joined. Apollo and Athene urge on the two sides.

422-56. As usual, a climatic moment invites a run of similes (cf. on 2.455-83).

422. *As the waves* **(R-J)**; *As when the sea's* **(H)**; *As when along* **(L)**: D-simile. There are 19 wind-and-wave similes in the *Il.* (we have already meet a run of them at 2.144, 147, 209, 394, 3.10). The relentless onward sequence of the waves is likened to the relentless onward march of the

Greek contingents. Note that the winds blow from a (south) westerly direction onto the beach – perhaps Homer's viewpoint from the coast of modern Turkey?

429. *in silence/silently*: cf. the silent Greek advance after the mustering at 3.8. Homer 'corrects' the noisiness implied by the wave-simile above.

433. *As/like sheep/ewes*: C-simile. Cf. the Trojan babble of noise at 3.2-7. There are nine sheep-similes in the *Il.* (cf. 3.196).

440. *Terror ... Panic ... Strife* **(R-J, H)**; *Terror ... Fear ... Hate* **(L)**: further dramatic expansion: to Athene and Ares' presence are added terrifying abstract forces, personified as deities, driving the armies on (for these abstractions cf. e.g. 5.518, 13.299, 20.48). For **L**'s 'Hate', read 'Strife'.

446-51. *The armies/When they had advanced* **(R-J, H)**; *Now as these advancing* **(L)** *... ran (with) blood*: a scene of general carnage in which a massed assault turns into a standing fight, repeated exactly at 8.60-5. Such scenes commonly feature in battle sequences, e.g. 13.125, 14.388. See **GI** 13B(v)(b). Note that there is no signal to start fighting. The troops engage when they will.

452. *As two mountain* **(R-J)**; *As when two* **(H)**; *As when rivers* **(L)**: D-simile (one of eight river similes), but again anticipated by the 'great roar/loud din/huge sound' of 449. The noise of two powerful rivers crashing together into a deep ravine resembles the noise of the two armies meeting in a single space. A far-off shepherd, silent witness of this awesome natural force, suddenly adds the human perspective, drawing the listeners into the extraordinary experience.

457-544. A complex sequence of deaths, in which the poet shows off the wide range of his wares and a wide variety of ways to die: a death may be a death, but this is not thoughtless composition by rote. Note the structure:

A. five killings + **B.** general perspective.

A.1 two killings + **B.1** general perspective.

A. 457-504. A series of five mostly 'chain-reaction' killings, one leading directly to the next: 1. first a Greek (Antilochus) kills a Trojan with a spear-throw; 2. a Trojan (Agenor) stabs a Greek trying to drag off the body; 3. Ajax kills Simoïsius with a throw (long expansion); 4. a Trojan (Antiphus) misses Ajax with a throw and accidentally hits a Greek (Leucus) dragging off the body; 5. Odysseus, enraged, kills Democoon with a throw.

Observe the gently pro-Greek bias: (i) all the Greeks can throw accurately with the spear; the Trojans stab with it or throw wildly (ii) the Greeks score kills on the attack; the Trojans when a Greek is otherwise occupied (iii) a Greek kill begins and ends the sequence (iv) the big centre-piece (Ajax) is elaborated with an extended description of Simoïsius and a simile and (v) at the end of it all the Trojans retreat. Observe too that all the kills are clean, one-strike affairs, with plenty of variety (they all fall in different ways), including two brief and one long simile. Cf. Friedrich (2003) 53-6, 59-60.

457. *Antilochus*: young son of Nestor. He has played little part so far in the *Il*. One wonders why Homer chose him to launch the fighting.

463. *Elephenor*: Euboean leader (2.540). Elephenor is eager to strip Echepolus of his bronze armour because of its value, financially and as a status symbol (cf. **GI** 4A, 8.191-5, 17.130, etc.); Homeric heroes generally wish to be able to offer *physical* evidence of prowess. This is always a highly dangerous moment, leaving one exposed to counter-attack, **GI** 13B(v)(a).

467. *Agenor*: son of Trojan Antenor (see on 3.146). It is common for A to be stripping B when C kills/wounds him (e.g. 11.256, 13.527, 14.476).

471. *like wolves*: A-simile.

473. *Telamonian* (**H, L**): i.e. the greater Ajax, son of Telamon (2.527-9).

474. *stripling's beauty* (**L**): L misses the fact that Simoïsius was unmarried, all part of the pathos the scene. It is typical to give the dead warrior a brief, poignant but never sentimental history, concentrating on e.g. his youth, the disappointed promise of the young man (in the eyes of wife – if married – children or parents), inability of friends to help, distance from home, and so on, all reported in a severely, 'objective' factual style (cf. **GI** 10B).

475. *Ida ... Simoïs*: Ida, the mountain to the south of Troy, and Simoïs, with Scamander (Xanthus), one of Troy's two rivers. See **R-J** maps 1, 2.

478. *care*: the mention of his parents' loving care, which he was unable to repay, is especially touching (cf. 17.301-2).

482. *like a poplar*: C-simile. Simoïsius was born beside the river-bank; he was not killed beside one, but the poplar tree in the simile, equally well-tended ('trimmed/smooth-trunked' 484), when cut down lies on the bank to season (487). For the tree-simile, cf. the death of Imbrius at 13.178-81.

491. *missed his man/Aias*: it is typical for A to throw at B, miss, and kill C, e.g. 8.118-19, 309-12, 14.460-4.

499. *a bastard son of Priam*: Priam had fifty sons, nineteen by his wife Hecabe, the rest by in-house concubines (24.495-7, cf. 6.244-6). Of these, twenty-two are named and eleven killed in the *Il*.

B. 505-16. Off-field perspective: Apollo rallies the retreating Trojans, Athene the Greeks.

506. *dragged in/away/back the bodies*: both their own men and the Trojans'.

508. *Pergamus*: the citadel of Ilium, the town's highest point.

509. *horse-taming Trojans* (**R-J, H**); *breakers of horses* (**L**): an epithet used only of Trojans; and excavators at thirteenth century BC Hisarlik/Ilium found abundant quantities of horse-bones – a memory from the deep past?

512. *Achilles*: a timely reminder of his absence, which hovers over these books.

515. *Triton-born* **(R-J)**; *Tritogeneia* **(H, L)**: a title restricted to Athene. Its meaning is not known; ancient commentators suggested that, after Athene was born from Zeus' head, she was given to the river Triton to rear.

A.1 517-35. Now the Trojan Peiros (2.844) kills Greek Diores (2.622), and Greek Thoas (2.638) replies by killing Peiros. These are bloodier, more sensational killings: fate intervenes (517), each kill requires two hits (the Trojan scores with a stone and a spear-stab, the Greek with a throw and a sword-thrust) and the details of the Diores' death (shin hit 519, tendons smashed 521, pathetic appeal to friends 523, stabbed in navel and innards pour out 525) are distinctly gruesome. It is worth noting that the warriors may *talk* defiantly about death, but when faced with it they seldom put words into action; like Diores, they usually appeal for help, if they are given the chance, e.g. 13.549, 14.496, 20.463-5, 21.70-96.

521. *shameless* **(R-J)**; *brute* **(H)**; *pitiless* **(L)**: typical personification of the inanimate stone.

527. *Peiros* **(H, L)**: = Peiroös (2.844).

B.1 536-44. General perspective: the carnage.

539. *Anyone arriving* **(R-J)**; *Then no one* **(H)**; *no more could a man* **(L)**: imaginary spectators are typical, see on 4.421 and cf. 13.127, 343. We have witnessed only seven deaths (three Greek, four Trojan) but Homer has created a sense of many more.

Book 5

Introduction

Epics feature great heroes struggling (at a price) for *kleos*, usually on the field of battle. Achilles, however, the Greeks' greatest hero, is off the field of battle till nearly the end, only at 20.382 killing his first Trojan in hand-to-hand combat. Homer therefore has ample scope for showing what the other heroes on the Greek side can do, and he has plenty of major heroes to draw into the action, e.g. Agamemnon, Menelaus, Odysseus, Nestor, Ajax, Diomedes and Idomeneus, as well as minor individuals already mentioned in the catalogue of ships as leaders of contingents, e.g. the lesser Ajax, Eurypylus, Teucer, Meges, Meriones and so on (note the virtual 'check-list' of slayings by major and minor Greek heroes at 38-83 before Diomedes get down to serious business). On the Trojan side, the burden of the fighting falls on Hector, and it is very great. 'Supporting role' is the best that can be said for other Trojans like Paris, Aeneas, Deiphobus and Antenor; the Trojan ally Sarpedon is probably their best fighter after Hector. Otherwise, Trojans are cannon-fodder, produced by the poet at will (note that nearly two-thirds of the Trojans have Greek-derived names, 2.816-77). In all, 281 Trojans are killed as against 61 Greeks, very nearly five to one. This is a Greek epic for a Greek audience.

But though one-third of the *Il.* is taken up with fighting, two-thirds, double that amount, is not, whether on earth or with the gods on Olympus and Mount Ida. Already Homer has kept us absorbed till near the end of Book 4 with hardly a blow being struck; and (to look briefly ahead) if Book 5 is nearly all fighting, half of Book 6 will find us in Ilium with Hector and Andromache, while a duel and the burial of the dead will dominate Book 7; Book 8 plunges us back into full-scale battle again, but Book 9 will be taken up with the embassy to Achilles and Book 10 with an individualistic night raid on the Trojan camp. Even in Book 5 there are two major scenes on Olympus, involving Aphrodite, 352-430, and Ares, 711-904.

Homer depicts in Book 5 a battle swinging back and forth largely through the intervention of individual heroes on both sides. This is not as unrealistic as it sounds, cf. on **GI** 13B(i), (v)(a); and anyway, in a heroic world, if one man starts a rout, another man (usually with divine help) can stop it, cf. **GI** 13B(i). After the slight Greek advantage which Homer described at the start of the fighting (see 4.457-504), the advantage swings dramatically to the Greeks with the brilliant solo feat of arms (*aristeia*) of Diomedes who, despite his wound, starts a Trojan retreat. Climaxes are reached with his victories against Pandarus (290-6, who fired the oath-breaking shot in Book 4), Aeneas (305-12), and the goddess Aphrodite (334-51). At this point Diomedes is warned by Apollo against going too far (440-4), and Apollo sends Ares to help the Trojans.

This evens matters out: Sarpedon's rebuke stings Hector into action but the Greeks hold fast (519-27) and there is a succession of alternating victories. When Diomedes spots Ares in the field, he urges a cautious retreat (601-6). The Trojan ally Sarpedon kills Tlepolemus in a major encounter, Odysseus responds by killing seven Trojans in succession (668-78); but Hector steps in and with Ares' help (699, 702) kills six Greeks (703-10).

The Trojans now seem in the ascendant, but at this point Hera and Athene intervene on the Greek side and, with Zeus' agreement (765-6), use Diomedes (aided by Athene) to wound Ares and drive him from the battlefield. The Greeks are now on top again. Again, one asks the question: where is the Trojan victory that the plan of Zeus was due to bring about? Has Achilles left the fighting in vain? Will Agamemnon turn out to be right that he does not need him (1.173-80)?

Diomedes, the hero of this book, is a young man (9.57-8), aware of his youth and therefore keen to show his pedigree (14.110-27), and with a tendency in debate to jump enthusiastically in when others are silent (7.398-404, 9.30-51, 695-710), often to good effect; self-controlled in the face of Agamemnon's rebuke (4.412ff.), he sometimes knows when to retreat (before gods, 5.443, and man, 5.596ff., 11.345ff.) and sometimes not (8.139-50); he defends himself against cowardice in front of Athene (5.815ff.); he is ready to take on the gods with her help (5.826ff.) – the only mortal to do so in the *Il.* – and he sees through Achilles at 9.697f.; though when he abuses Agamemnon at 9.32ff., he is gently reprimanded for it by Nestor. He is often said, in the absence of Achilles, to be an 'Achilles-sub-stitute', but it is hard to see exactly what that means. If anyone is an Achilles-substitute, it will surely be Patroclus in Book 16. Diomedes is indeed a great fighter, and in his youthful, rather mercurial enthusiasm a different personality from the impulsive, single-minded Achilles, but so are Odysseus, Menelaus and all the other major warriors. At 6.99, Diomedes is even seen by the Trojans as *more* terrifying than ever Achilles was; but on the other hand, the Greeks rate Ajax as next best to Achilles (2.768-9) and Diomedes rates below Ajax at 7.179. After Diomedes is wounded at 11.399-400, he is never seen fighting on the battlefield again. I can see no reason to believe that Diomedes *in particular* is being singled out by Homer for special comparison or contrast with Achilles. See on 11.369; for a comparison between Diomedes and Nestor, see Schofield (1986) 256-8.

We get our first sight of the Trojan leader Hector in action in this book. He does not confront Diomedes at any stage – Homer is saving Hector up for a first major confrontation with someone else, Ajax, in Book 7 – and our first sight of him is not impressive, being rebuked by Sarpedon for leaving all the fighting to the allies (471-92). Hector, however, responds with great vigour. He leads a rally at 493-506 which stops the Trojan rout, carries on the good work with the support of Ares at 590-606 (drawing a double-edged compliment from Diomedes, 601-2) and drives the Greeks back even further with a serious of unopposed slayings at 699-710. He is so effective that Hera and Athene are forced to intervene on the Greeks' behalf. He is, indeed, the Trojans' mainstay in battle, but does the rebuke from Sarpedon raise a slight doubt about his judgement?

Note that most of the information about the typicality of the battle scenes is taken from Fenik (1968); cf. **GI** 2(iii).

Main sources for the commentary
Fenik (1968) 9-77; Kirk (1990); Willcock (1978).

1-94: Athene inspires Diomedes, who goes on the rampage. Athene leads the War-god Ares out of the fighting. Diomedes' onslaught starts a Trojan retreat.

1-8. Diomedes' long *aristeia* ('heroic individual feat of arms') includes victories against Pandarus and even Aphrodite and Ares. There is a pattern to the heroic *aristeia*, consisting of a number of typical elements: a god inspires it (1, 825ff.), the hero's armour is mentioned (4), enthusiasm for battle or some signal of readiness for it is expressed (the fire, 7), the hero advances to attack (8), he scores a number of impressive victories (9-25, 84-94, 144-65, etc.), the enemy counter-attacks (95), there is a moment of danger, sometimes even a wound inflicted (98, 596ff., 793ff.), but ultimately he triumphs (290-6, 855ff.). Cf. Agamemnon's *aristeia* at 11.1-283. Patroclus' entry into battle at 16.284-419 bears a number of structural similarities to the opening 94 lines of Diomedes' *aristeia* here.

5. *like Sirius* **(R-J)**; *like the late summer star* **(H)**; *like that star* **(L)**: B-simile. When armour gleams, it regularly does so like fire or some celestial body (cf. 2.455, 10.153, 19.374ff. – this last passage referring to Achilles' armour when he returns to battle). Heroes entering battle are often described with a simile, e.g. 5.87, 136, 11.67, 16.259 etc.

10. *priest*: when sons of priests/prophets are killed in battle, the poet often appends a (usually ironic) prophetic element e.g. 5.149-51, 11.329-32, 13.663-70. Fathers are often mentioned when their sons are killed, e.g. 5.148, 13.658. Father-son relationships will be dramatised most powerfully in the death of Hector (Priam) and the predicted death of Achilles (Peleus), occurring after the *Il.* ends.

Two sons: brothers commonly fight together, e.g. 5.148, 152, 11.101, 122, 16.317.

13. *chariot ... on foot/dismounted*: warriors on foot frequently take on those (sometimes brothers) in chariots, e.g. 5.608, 11.101. Warriors use two-man chariots (one driver, one fighter) pulled by two horses to get to the battle, then dismount and fight, keeping their chariot close at hand if it is needed for escape (e.g. 11.339-42, 15.455-7). Only very rarely indeed do they fight *from* a chariot, as here. See **GI** 13B(vi).

17. *Phegeus ... did not hit* **(R-J, H)**; *nor struck* **(L)**: very common battle-scene: A throws at B and misses/hits but does not penetrate the armour, B kills A, e.g. 17.43 (Euphorbus and Menelaus), 22.289 (Hector and Achilles). B is always Greek.

20. *Idaeus*: unlike Idaeus, brothers nearly always support each other (11.248, 14.476, 16.319, 20.419). At 11.145, Hippolochus also tries to get away after his brother is killed, but is killed too. Idaeus here (not the Trojan herald of 3.248, 7.276-416) is saved by Hephaestus for his poor father's sake (23-4): gods frequently intervene to save their favourites, e.g. 3.380, 20.318, 21.596.

25. *horses*: like armour (see on 4.463), these are extremely desirable additions to one's wealth and status, and often captured, e.g. 5.273, 319-27, 10.436-41, 17.485-90.

29. *the anger in all of them was stirred* (**L**): read 'panic threatened'.

30. *Athene took … Ares … by the hand*: Athene and Trojan-loving Ares, usually bitter rivals, here agree to withdraw, cf. 15.121ff., and for other divine agreements, 7.17, 20.133. Athene's reference to Zeus' anger (34) reminds us of his plan to allow the Trojans to start winning (1.517-30).

36. *Scamander*: also called Xanthus, the other river round Ilium (see on 4.475).

37-83. A series of killings by individual Greek warriors ensues (such a sequence of slayings by one side is typical, e.g. 6.5ff., 7.8ff., 16.257ff.). This sequence shows how successful Diomedes' onslaught has been – it has almost caused a rout (29) and the Trojans are now in flight (37 the Greeks 'pushed back/turned/bent back' the Trojans). Note that the Trojans are hit in the back, or mounting their chariots to flee. For the a-b-c style of description, which occurs frequently here, see **GI** 2(iv).

39. *hurled out of/from his chariot*: cf. 5.19, 11.143, 16.743.

40. *turning/turned in flight*: cf. 12.427, 13.545, 16.308.

50. *Scamandrius*: named after the local river, cf. Simoïsius after Si-moïs, 4.474.

51. *Artemis*: a moving anecdote. Artemis is goddess of the hunt, who cannot help her favourite now (pathos).

59. *Meriones*: a useful Greek fighter (companion of Idomeneus) who tends to inflict very grisly (and unique) wounds (66-7, a clinically accurate description, in the buttocks and out under the pubic arch, cf. 13.567, 650). This may not be so much a characteristic of Meriones' fighting ability as a reflection on the character of those he kills, who may deserve such a death.

60. *who could turn* (**R-J**); *who had the skill* (**H**); *who understood* (**L**): who is this 'who'? Surely Phereclus rather than his father, though cf. 11.122-42, where sons are punished for their father's guilt.

63. *started all the trouble* (**R-J**); *start of their doom* (**H**); *the beginning of the evil* (**L**): does Homer 'objectively' reports the facts here, or is he passing judgement about guilt or innocence? See **GI** 10.

69. *Meges*: see 2.625-30. A minor warrior, like Meriones (above) he too delivers a very brutal and unique wound here.

70. *bastard*: a common motif, e.g. 4.499, 11.102, 15.333. Raising someone else's child is also typical e.g. 9.481, 13.176, 15.551. Theano is a Trojan priestess of Athene (6.298).

75. *teeth*: teeth often feature in head wounds, e.g. 5.291, 16.348, 17.617.

76. *Eurypylus*: see on 2.736. He is responsible for the third fairly gruesome death in a row. Among the first-rank heroes, only Agamemnon and Achilles are credited with delivering grisly wounds like these, e.g. 11.145-7 where Agamemnon cuts off an arm, as here, 82, and 20.474-83.

84. *So they fought* **(R-J)**; *So they laboured* **(H)**; *So they went*: it is typical for the poet to move from individual encounters to the general scene, e.g. 4.470, 5.627, 6.1-4, 13.491-501, etc.

87. *like a winter torrent* **(R-J)**; *like a river full* **(H)**; *like a winter-swollen* **(L)**: C-simile. Warriors on the rampage are frequently likened to raging rivers or blazing fire (e.g. 11.155, 492). Note the way in which the simile begins at one point in an action-sequence – Diomedes storming along, 87 – but ends at another – Trojan confusion ('thrown into confusion/driven flying/scattered', 93). It is common for similes to move the action along in this way rather than reverting back to the precise moment when the simile began, cf. **GI** 12D.

92. *young men* **(L)**: read 'industrious farmers'.

95-165: Trojan Pandarus hits Diomedes in the shoulder with an arrow, but Athene revitalises him and enables him to distinguish between men and gods.

95. *Pandarus*: the Trojan who had re-started the fighting with his shot at Menelaus (4.122-6). This scene consists of a number of typical elements that recur elsewhere – most especially 5.280-9, 11.320-96, and to a lesser extent 4.124-91 – put together to create this particular version. The elements are (i) 98 arrow wounding (e.g. 11.505), (ii) 106 failure to kill (e.g. 5.280) (iii) 102 boast (e.g. 11.380) (iv) (not here) reply to boast (e.g. 11.384) (v) 111 wounded friend helped (e.g. 11.396).

105. *from Lycia*: not the region to the south of Troy; see on 4.88.

109. *get/step down*: Sthenelus is driving the chariot, while Diomedes fights on foot (5.13).

115. *Listen to/Hear me*: prayers to gods for help in battle are typical, e.g. 16.508. On Atrytone, see 2.157.

116. *if ever in the past/before*: on prayer-forms, see **GI** 7A. Note how Diomedes appeals to Athene in the name of his father Tydeus (cf. 4.376ff., especially 387-90, for Athene's closeness to Tydeus, and 14.112ff. for Diomedes' respect for his father).

122. *removed the heaviness* **(R-J)**; *made his limbs* **(H, L)**: for divine healing, cf. 16.527-8.

127. *mist*: heroes commonly have mist sent over them (e.g. 21.7) or removed from their eyes (e.g. 15.668, 17.640) – but never again so that they can distinguish humans from gods.

131. *Aphrodite*: preparing us for the encounter to come at 5.334ff.

136. *like/as of a lion*: C-simile (similes typically accompany entries into battle), starting and ending with Diomedes' 'determination/rage' (136/143). Diomedes has been wounded, like the lion (138), and is even more determined now (136, 'three times' as much, cf. 5.208) like the lion ('fury/strength' 139). Lions in Homer typically attack farms and grazing animals, often from mountains where they are reared, and are attacked in turn by men.

144-65. Diomedes now goes on a killing sequence of his own, slaughtering four sets of two, three sets of whom are brothers. They are in twos because they are trying to get away in their chariots. Observe the variations: spear and sword deal with the first pair; the next pair's father, the dream-interpreter Eurydamas (149), is high-lighted; so is the next pair's, Phaenops (152), too old to have more children; and the sons of Priam attract a lion-simile. See notes above on 10, 13, 25, the a-b-c pattern (**GI** 2[iv]), 39, 76, 136 for the typicality of these killings.

145. *bronze-heeled* (**L**): read 'bronze-tipped'.

153. *full-grown* (**L**): read 'late-born' (Phaenops can have no more children).

158. *relatives divided* (**R-J, H**); *kinsmen shared* (**L**): a unique element, emphasising the depth of Phaenops' loss.

161. *As a lion* (**R-J, H**); *As among cattle* (**L**): D-simile, nature (as often) red in tooth and claw, like man.

163. *horses* (**L**): read 'chariot'. Heroes do not ride horses into battle (see on 5.13).

166-296: Aeneas and Pandarus attack Diomedes, who kills Pandarus.

166. *Aeneas*: see on 2.820. Now begins the counter-action to Diomedes' assault. It is an example of a 'consultation' pattern, in which (a) Trojans consult (b) they attack, 239 (c) the Greeks stand firm, 252 (d) a Trojan is (usually) hurt, 290. Cf. 12.310ff., 17.483ff.

177. *rites* (**R-J**); *sacrifice* (**H**); *offerings* (**L**): cf. 1.64-7.

187. *flying arrow*: (**R-J, L**); *let fly an arrow* (**H**): 5.98.

190. *Aidoneus* (**L**): i.e. Hades.

194. *cloths* (**R-J, H**); *blankets* (**L**): cf. 2.777, 8.441.

197. *Lycaon*: it is typical for fathers to give their sons advice before they go to war, e.g. 6.206-10, 11.782-9.

203. *fodder ran short* (**R-J**); *short of fodder* (**H**); *going hungry* (**L**): cf. 18.288-92 for shortages at Troy, and its previous vast wealth.

206. *Menelaus* (**R-J**); *son of Atreus* (**H, L**): see 4.125.

218. *No more speeches* (**R-J**); *No more of this talk* (**H**); *Speak no more* (**L**): there is a testiness in Aeneas' voice here at the length and self-indulgence of Pandarus' speech.

222. *bred by Tros* (**R-J**); *Tros' stock* (**H**); *Trojan* (**L**): these are very special horses indeed, as Diomedes knows (265-73), bred by Aeneas' great-great grandfather Tros (correct **L**). Cf. on 5.638.

228. *Or you take on* **(R-J)**; *or you stand up* **(H)**; *or else yourself encounter* **(L)**: the issue of who should drive, who fight from, the chariot was an important one, cf. 17.466-83.

234. *missed/long for [the sound of] your voice*: cf. Automedon's vain efforts to get Patroclus' horses to move after his death, 17.426-40.

252. *Don't talk ... of flight* **(R-J, H)**; *Argue me not* **(L)**: it is common for a hero to reject talk of flight, e.g. 6.440-6, 11.404-10, 14.83ff. Contrast e.g. Menelaus at 17.90-105, Agenor at 21.552-70.

266. *Ganymede*: see 20.232-5, and on 1.600, 4.2.

269. *Laomedon*: was of an earlier generation than Anchises, and a different branch of the family (20.215-40).

273. *heroic/fine/excellent glory*: for the capture of horses, see on 5.25.

276. *Pandarus/Lykaon's son*: see on 5.17 for this combat, interrupted by a series of speeches.

284. *A hit* **(R-J)**; *You are hit* **(H)**; *Now you are struck* **(L)**: boasting and exchanges of boasts are very common, e.g. here, with Diomedes' reply 287-9, 11.378-95, 427-55, 22.278-82.

292. *tongue was cut off* **(R-J)**; *sheared away the tongue* **(H)**; *shore ... through the tongue* **(L)**: a grisly death – fit punishment for such a talker? Cf. on 218, and Saunders in Friedrich (2003) 142-3.

297-430: Aphrodite rescues Trojan Aeneas, but Diomedes stabs her. She complains to her mother Dione; Zeus gently teases her.

297. *leapt/jumped down* **(R-J, H)**; *sprang to the ground* **(L)**: Aeneas had been driving the chariot.

299. *stood over* **(R-J, L)**; *took his stand* **(H)**: it is typical for a warrior to defend the body of a fallen companion by standing over him, e.g. 8.330, 14.428, 17.3.

303. *rock/boulder/stone*: commonly used in battle, e.g. 8.321, 14.410, 20.283-8.

310. *black night*: fainting after a hit is typical e.g. 5.696, 11.355-6, 14.439.

313. *Anchises the ox-herd* **(L)**: read 'when he was herding cattle'. For the agricultural background to the *Il.*, see **GI** 3. Aphrodite similarly rescues her favourite Paris at 3.373.

319. *instructions* **(R-J, H)**; *commandments* **(L)**: see 260-73.

327. *the warrior* **(L)**: i.e. Sthenelus who, having handed Aeneas' horses over to Deipylus, now drives his chariot back to Diomedes.

330. *and he swung* **(L)**: i.e. Diomedes now set off in pursuit of Aphrodite (as Athene had suggested he might, 131-2).

Kypris **(H)**; *lady of Kupros* **(L)**: i.e. Aphrodite, who landed in Cyprus, at Paphos, where she was swept after her birth in the sea (see on 2.205).

333. *Enyo*: a goddess of war.

340. *ichor*: since gods are immortal and live off ambrosia and nectar, they cannot have blood in their veins, because blood is mortal, created from the food mortals eat, and when it is shed, mortals die (though cf. 5.870!). So gods must have something different in their veins – here called *ichor* (for whatever reason). Note that the Greek word, *brotos*, means 'mortal' and 'blood'; and *ambrosia* means 'not-mortal, immortal' or 'no-blood'. Divine horses eat ambrosial food too (369, 'immortal' (**H, L**)). Ambrosia is also used as a perfume and for anointing (see e.g. 14.170-8), i.e. it is the divine equivalent of olive-oil.

349. *seduce the (feeble) wits of (weak) women* (**R-J, H**); *lead women astray* (**L**): Aphrodite is goddess of sexual activity, not love, and Greek males took it for granted that women were especially prone to sexual temptation.

356. *horses* (**R-J, L**); *chariot* (**H**): the Greek says 'two fast horses'. If Homer does actually mean a chariot *without* its horses, that could indeed be propped up against cloud (cf. 8.435). But he could be referring, literally, to the horses, in which case they are leaning for warmth or comfort (as horses do) against it.

365-9. *Iris got in ... down beside them* (**R-J**); *Iris mounted ... down for them* (**H**); *beside her entering ... before them* (**L**): a typical scene of divine chariot travel, cf. 5.768-77, 13.23-36.

371. *Dione*: this is the only place in Homer where Aphrodite is said to have a mother (cf. on 2.205). This scene, where Aphrodite is hurt and runs to be comforted, is paralleled at 21.489-513, where Artemis reacts in the same way.

374. *something wicked*: gentle irony. Aphrodite is *always* up to something wicked.

382. *Endure/have patience*: Dione now offers consolation by referring to three examples of other gods who suffered at the hands of men. None of the examples is mentioned elsewhere in ancient literature, so the details remain obscure. It is possible the examples were invented by Homer for the occasion; cf. Willcock (1964).

385. *Otus and Ephialtes*: two young giants.

390. *Hermes*: patron god of thieves. The idea that Ares might have died if Hermes had not intervened is a dramatic exaggeration on Dione's part, to help Aphrodite put her own wound into perspective.

392. *son of Amphitryon*: i.e. Heracles (Latin 'Hercules'), a paradoxical combination of thug and hero (cf. 403-4 'self-willed monster/criminal wretch/brute') and the only mortal to achieve divine status at death. For his attack on Pylos (of which this episode is a part), see 11.689. His birth is recorded at 14.323-4 and 19.96-133, and his death alluded to at 18.117-19. Cf. on 8.363.

401. *Paeeon*: a god of healing. Note how Hades runs to Olympus for healing too, just like Aphrodite.

407. *how short life is* (**R-J**); *life is not long* (**H**); *lives for no long time* (**L**): further consolation – Diomedes may well pay with his life for his attack on Aphrodite. The tradition does not record any such thing happening.

408. *little/his children*: Homer touchingly portrays Diomedes' death in terms of the reaction of his distant family to it – children here, his wife Aegialea and the household at 412-15. The gentle humour of the scene on Olympus suddenly darkens.

411. *even better than he* (L): the Greek says 'better than you', i.e. than Aphrodite.

414. *best of the Greeks*: note the focalisation of Aegialea's fond thoughts on her 'young [H, L miss this] married husband, best of the Greeks'. It is typical of Homer to emphasise the impact on the family of a warrior's death, cf. 13.170-81, 361-73, 424-44, 17.34-40. Pathos is generated by the sense of the hopes and fears of a whole family resting on one man.

419. *turned mockingly* (R-J); *tease* (H, L): the humour of the episode returns (note Zeus' smile, 426), as Athene pretends Aphrodite has scratched herself on the brooch of some Greek woman she was egging on (as she had once egged on Helen). See on 21.418 for Hera and Athene's hatred of Aphrodite.

431-518. Diomedes pursues Aeneas but is warned off by Apollo. Ares inspires the Trojans. Trojan Sarpedon rebukes Hector, who storms into battle with Ares' support.

434. *had no respect* (R-J); *had no fear* (H); *did not shrink* (L): for human attitudes to gods, see **GI** 6.

438. *fourth time*: compare 16.702-11 (Patroclus) and 20.445-8 (Achilles) for such dramatic moments. Diomedes is the only hero actually to take on the gods, though cf. Achilles vs. Scamander at 21.205-382.

443. *just a little* (R-J); *a little way* (H); *only a little* (L): even after a direct rebuke from a god, Diomedes still does not go into full retreat.

449. *phantom/image*: an extraordinary and unique event (like Artemis and Leto's care for Aeneas). Gods may disguise themselves as humans (e.g. 3.386, 21.600) but they never create a phantom in place of a human. Aeneas seems to attract these rather bizarre episodes, cf. Friedrich (2003) 16ff.

453. *fluttering targes* (H); *fluttering guard-skins* (L): the Greek is difficult to interpret. These are taken to be small shields, in contrast with the (large) ox-hide shields, but what *pteroenta* 'winged, feathered', here 'fluttering', is supposed to mean is unclear. **R-J** evades the issue with 'ox-hide shields, great and small'.

455. *Ares*: invited to leave the fighting by Athene (5.31), he is now invited back by Apollo to end Diomedes' rampage.

462. *Acamas*: see on 2.844. It is typical of gods to disguise themselves as humans and urge on the troops, e.g. Athene at 4.86, Poseidon at 13.45, Apollo at 17.73.

464. *(You) sons of* (R-J, H); *O you children* (L): a typical 'exhorta-tion' pattern, with three elements (i) address to the troops, often insulting, (ii) angry questions, (iii) call to fight, cf. 15.502, 733.

471. *Sarpedon*: see on 2.876. He abuses Hector in a very common type of 'rebuke' pattern: (i) Hector or Aeneas is rebuked (ii) the Trojans rally (497), (iii) the fight evens out, the Greeks hold (498, 522) or the Trojans retreat (Ajax always appears somewhere, 519), e.g. 11.523, 16.538, 17.70, 140, 322. Here Sarpedon contrasts allied determination with Trojan weak-ness. He fights not for the Lycian people, but because this is how a hero should act: fighting and winning *kleos*.

491. *begging the leaders of your ... allies* (H); *supplication to the lords of your far-renowned companions* (L): it seems odd that Sarpedon, having abused Hector for leaving everything to the allies, should now tell him he should be begging the allies to fight. **R-J** is preferable: 'You can plead with the leaders of your allies, but your priority day and night should be to make a determined stand yourself and give no one any grounds for harsh criticism.'

499. *As the wind* (R-J, H); *As when along* (L): D-simile, which seems to start off as a wind-simile but changes direction and ends up comparing whitening chaff to Greeks covered with dust as their charioteers race back to resist the Trojan offensive (warriors fighting from chariots would tend to get ahead of the front line). Demeter is goddess of agriculture. One winnows by batting grain up into the air in a wind. The wind blows away the loosened, light outer casing ('chaff') while the heavier grain inside it falls back to the floor.

505. *as the battle clashed ... their teams* (H); *as they rapidly ... back again* (L): i.e. as the Greeks chariots, which had got ahead of the front line, turned round to rejoin it as a result of the Trojan resistance; see Albracht (2003) [I.45].

506. *the enemy were engaged* (R-J); *pushed their hands' fury* (H); *drove the strength of their hands* (L): H and L translate literally a sentence which seems to indicate that the foot-soldiers, probably on both sides, engaged in fierce fighting.

507. *veil/covering of darkness* (R-J, H); *dark night* (L): darkness/mist often accompanies the rebuke-pattern (16.567, 17.270, 368, 594 etc.).

519-710. General fighting ensues. Diomedes leads the retreat from Hector and Ares.

522. *like the (motionless) clouds*: C-simile, comparing Greek steadi-ness to still clouds when tempests are not raging (which makes it difficult to compare the tempests with the battle, which is raging).

528. *Agamemnon/Atreus' son*: an exhortation-scene (see on 5.464).

544. *substance*: the wealth of the dead man's family is often men-tioned, e.g. 5.613, 708, 16.596.

descent/descended (R-J, H); *generation* (L): it is typical for the family of the dead man to be described, e.g. 4.474, 6.21, 151 etc. A man descended from a river, as here, is engendered by the *god* of the river. Natural forces usually have a divinity associated with them to whom one can pray when one needs their help, e.g. 23.195, where Achilles summons the winds to help light Patroclus' funeral pyre, but they (i.e., the gods of the winds) are at a feast and have to be called away from it first (23.198-201).

554. *As a pair of/two lions*: D-simile. Lions in similes are usually triumphant, even if wounded (5.138); here, uniquely, their death is the main point. See on 5.136 for typical features of lion-similes.

565. *Antilochus*: son of Nestor, and touchingly protective of the older Menelaus (cf. 7.94, 10.240). For one warrior coming to support another, cf. 11.485, 17.128.

576. *Pylaemenes*: see on 2.851. He will reappear, mourning his son, at 13.658-9. The death of Pylaemenes and his unhelpful charioteer Mydon bears striking similarities to the fighter + unhelpful driver deaths at 13.384-99 and 16.399-410. Friedrich (2003) 7-11 discusses these passages, contrasting the fantasy of the passages here and in Book 16 with the deaths 'so concisely, clearly and vividly' portrayed in Book 13, and speculates whether they can be by the same author. Fenik (1968) 63 points out that, bar the fantasies, virtually all the other details of each scene are typical.

580. *Mydon*: a truly fantastic death. A body could not sink up to its shoulders into the sand or dust and stand there upside-down before being kicked over by the horses; the other explanation, that Mydon's body somehow gets hooked up with the chariot, is not supported by the text. See Saunders in Friedrich (2003) 138-40 for discussion.

593. *turmoil of shameless hatred* (**L**): read 'Confusion, the shameless destroyer' – another example of Homer turning an abstract idea into a god.

597. *Like a traveller* (**R-J**); *As when/Like a man* (**H, L**): D-simile. At 5.87, Diomedes was likened to a raging torrent; here he is like a man halted by a raging torrent.

604. *Ares is/goes with him/is there beside him*: Diomedes can see Ares because of Athene's intervention at 128. His call to retreat will be heard (699-702), and this will swing the balance of the fighting back to the Trojans.

612. *Amphius*: note the a-b-c pattern; see **GI** 2(iv).

618. *to strip his armour*: typical, but Ajax is driven back and unable to seize the armour, also typical (4.532-5).

635. *They are liars* (**R-J, L**); *they lie* (**H**): Tlepolemus (from Rhodes, 2.653-4) rebukes Sarpedon for his inability to live up to his parentage, cf. attacks on Diomedes (though by his own side) 4.370-400, 5.800-13.

638. *Heracles*: cf. 20.145-8, which refers to the reason for Heracles' attack on Laomedon. The full story, to which Homer refers elsewhere, is that Apollo and Poseidon had been forced to build the walls of Ilium for Laomedon (Priam's father), but Laomedon refused to compensate them (see 21.441-57; it is not clear why the gods should have been forced into slavery like this – perhaps as a punishment of some sort). So Poseidon sent a sea-monster to terrorise the town, which oracles said could be saved only if the monster was allowed to devour Laomedon's daughter Hesione. Heracles agreed to kill the monster and to save Hesione, in return for Laomedon's famous horses (inherited from Tros, see on 5.222). But when Heracles had done so (with the help of a protective earthwork, 20.145) Laomedon again reneged on the deal. Heracles returned with an army, killed Laomedon and sacked the town. On his return journey, Hera caused him serious trouble, driving him off-course to the island of Cos (14.250-6, 15.26-30); and Zeus punished her for it by hanging her up (a slave punishment), while throwing out of heaven the gods who tried to help her. Hera hated Heracles because Zeus had fathered him by the mortal Alcmene.

654. *Hades famed for his horses* (**R-J**); *the horseman* (**H**); *of the famed horses* (**L**): Hades, god of the underworld, was famed for the horses he was driving when he seized Persephone, daughter of Demeter.

656. *at one and the same time* (**R-J**); *at the same moment* (**H**); *in a single moment* (**L**): it is typical for fighters to attack at exactly the same moment, e.g. 13.581, 601.

662. *his father* (**H, L**): i.e. Zeus.

671. *thoughts raced* (**R-J**); *pondered* (**H, L**): as usual in such scenes of internal debate, the second option is chosen (see on 1.189).

675. *destiny did not intend* (**R-J**); *not fated* (**H**); *not destiny* (**L**): Sarpedon is being saved up for death at Patroclus' hands, much though Zeus would like to avert it (16.433-503).

677. *there he killed* (**R-J, L**); *then he took* (**H**): such 'catalogue' slayings are typical, e.g. 705-7, 8.273-6, 16.415-17, 692-7, 21.209-10 etc.

685-6. *since ... my life must come to an end* (**L**): read as a wish, 'then may I die in your town' and continue 'since it is clear I was not meant to return to my own ...'. Speeches like this are used only by dying heroes (16.492, 844, 22.338) – though also cf. 4.155-82. So Sarpedon is effectively announcing his death. But he does not in fact die here. Friedrich (2003) 93 argues that at one stage in the *Il.*'s development he *did* die here: 'When things do not look all that bad for the wounded man, 686-7 expresses whining despondency; but, on the assumption that Sarpedon's death is imminent, this turns into the noble melancholy of a real farewell'. Friedrich uses this instance to argue for multiple authorship. One could just as well argue that the awkwardness (if there is an awkwardness) arose from Homer himself rethinking his story line and deciding to save up Sarpedon for death in Book 16, as in our version, and failing to readjust here in Book 5 – an interesting insight into the poet's 'workshop'.

696. *mist*: cf. 14.433-9 for fainting and recovery.

711-92. Hera and Athene agree to act against Ares. They arm and tell Zeus their plans. Hera rallies the Greeks.

714. *Atrytone*: see on 2.157. For this whole scene, cf. 8.350-96.

724. *felly/felloe* **(H, L)**: i.e. inner rims of the wheels, supported by the spokes.

726. *naves*: **(H, L)**: i.e. hubs.

739. *aegis*: see on 1.202. It is decorated with the usual terrifying Homeric personifications of abstract ideas, appropriate to Athene, goddess of war (and a match for Ares any day, 766).

741. *Gorgon*: Medusa, who turns to stone any who look on her.

751. *dense darkness* **(L)**: read 'heavy cloud'.

765. *Get to work* **(R-J)**; *to your work* **(H)**; *Go to it then* **(L)**: Zeus encourages Hera's plans to punish Ares, even though it will mean the Trojans are not as successful as they would otherwise be, and will therefore delay his plan, agreed with Thetis, that the Greeks should start to lose. Zeus will respond in a very different way at 8.397 when he has made his will clear and the goddesses intentionally cross it.

778. *like pigeons* **(R-J)**; *like trembling/shivering doves* **(H, L)**: an amusing image for the two, now grounded, goddesses.

782. *Diomedes*: the poet picks up the situation from 699-710, i.e. the Greeks under steady retreat.

788. *Achilles*: a reminder of his absence, cf. 13.95-114.

793-909: Athene rebukes Diomedes, and together they wound Ares. He complains to Zeus.

795. *Pandarus*: he hit Diomedes at 5.99.

800. *unlike himself* **(R-J)**; *little (…) like* **(H, L)**: Athene emphasises Tydeus' courage and the help she gave him, cf. Agamemnon at 4.370-400, who quotes the same story about Tydeus in Thebes as Athene does here, but with a different focalisation (see on 4.376). That Athene (unlike Agamemnon) is only teasing Diomedes is shown by her response at 826-34. See **GI** 11 for the ring-composition.

805. *I invited* **(L)**: read 'I told'.

818. *you told me* **(R-J)**; *the instructions/orders you gave* **(H, L)**: at 5.128-31.

832. *gave his word/pledge* **(R-J, H)**; *protested … promising* **(L)**: Ares never promises in our *Il.* to help the Greeks and fight the Trojans. Is Athene refocalising Ares' departure from the battle at 5.30-36 in the light of his return at 455-61? Or perhaps there was a version of the *Il.* in which he did make such a promise?

835. *dragged Sthenelus* **(R-J)**; *hauled him* **(H)**; *pushed him* **(L**, to be corrected): Athene is in a hurry: she does not stand on ceremony. An amusing touch; Homer does not reveal whether Sthenelus actually realised what was happening to him.

838. *axle groaned/creaked*: the reaction of the chariot to the arrival of a goddess in it – a lovely touch. Athene takes the reins, Diomedes will fight.

844. *[Ares] … was stripping*: the only time in the *Il.* that a god kills a mortal on the battlefield.

851. *reins of his horses* (**L**): read 'reins of Diomedes' chariot'. Ares is on foot.

858. *she stabbed* (**L**): read 'he stabbed'. Ares' great yell is typical, cf. 14.147, 20.48.

864. *air*: Homer is thinking of a tornado. Note how Ares, like Aphrodite, immediately runs home to Olympus when he has been injured (see 905 below).

870. *blood*: cf. on 5.340.

874. *favour(s)*: see **GI** 6. Ares' language throughout this speech is very agitated, but since he has just been rather shamingly wounded by a mortal, though admittedly with Athene's help, it is not surprising.

880. *child you bore* (**R-J**); *you gave birth to* (**H**); *you begot* (**L**): it was said that Athene was conceived by Zeus and *Mêtis* ('cunning intelligence') and born from Zeus' head. See on 4.515 and Hesiod *Theogony* 886-900.

886. *among [the piles of]/grim/stark dead*: cf. 8.455-6, 15.115-18. Ares is not arguing that he might have been killed but that he could have been laid low, as if he had been killed.

890. *I hate you* (**R-J**); *you are (the) most hateful* (**H, L**): in an epic of war it may be thought ironic that Zeus finds Ares the most hateful of all gods, but war is Ares' only function and the gods, like mortals, much prefer to be at peace (1.573-6).

892. *Hera*: Zeus is wrong – it was Athene who started it all – but it is typical of gods not to know what one would imagine gods should know, unless Zeus is cleverly evading Ares' implication that he cannot control his own daughter (879-80). Zeus certainly brings her to heel smartly enough at 8.399-408.

898. *you would have been dropped beneath the gods of the bright sky* (**L**): these gods, 'sons of Ouranos' in (**H**), are the Titans (see on 2.783).

899. *Paeeon*: see on 5.401. Aphrodite was merely scratched; Ares' wound is much more severe and needs a healer.

902. *fig (juice)*: this unique simile emphasises the speed with which Ares is healed. The comparison between divine 'blood' and the action of fig-juice on milk is deliciously unexpected, removing the reader far from the world of Olympus to a homely peasant cottage.

905. *Hebe*: see on 4.2. When Ares is finally restored, he returns 'exulting in his glory/glorying in his splendour/rejoicing in the glory of his strength'. Humiliated gods make a habit of having a bath and putting on their best to recover their self-esteem (cf. Aphrodite at *Od.* 8.362-6) – a neat psychological touch.

908. *Alalcomene* (**R-J, H**); *who stands by her people* (**L**): see on 4.8.

Book 6

Introduction

After the success of Diomedes in wounding and dismissing Ares from the battlefield, Homer continues to make the Greeks drive the Trojans back. There is another run of Greek victories over fleeing Trojans (5-36) featuring known heroes great (Ajax, Diomedes, Agamemnon) and lesser-known small (Euryalus, Polypoetes, Teucer, Antilochus, Leitus, Eurypylus); then Agamemnon orders Menelaus to show no mercy to a captive, and Nestor tells the Greeks to leave picking up booty till they have done with the killing (37-72). It is clear that, at this rate, Ilium is about to be captured, as the poet points out (73-4); and the situation will shortly become even more serious since the poet now plots for Hector, the Trojans' greatest fighter, to leave the battlefield. So Homer takes measures to halt what is virtually a rout, and on Helenus' advice Hector rallies his troops in these most testing of circumstances (103-15), as he had in Book 5 (see 5/Intro). Again, it is noticeable that Hector requires someone else (Helenus, this time) to drive him into action (cf. Sarpedon at 5.472-92).

After all this fighting (beginning at the end of Book 4 and continuing into Book 5 and the start of Book 6), Homer uses the Diomedes-Glaucus encounter, and then Hector's return to Ilium, to open up alternative vistas to those of the unforgiving world of blood and death. Diomedes and Glaucus confront each other in battle soon after Agamemnon's call to Menelaus to show no mercy to the Trojans because of the way the Trojans treated him at home (the reference is to Paris' seduction of Helen), and Nestor's not to strip armour. Diomedes effectively ignores both these instructions. He and Glaucus find they are joined by common bonds of *xenia*, forged by their grandparents (215-33), and as a result part in peace, exchanging armour as they go (234-6). In other words, even on the battlefield, obligations overriding those of slaughter may emerge. One reflects that Paris' trip to Sparta all those years ago, to which Agamemnon has just referred, could have generated such bonds between Paris and Menelaus, and the war never been started, had the obligations of *xenia* meant something to Paris (see e.g. Menelaus' accusations at 3.351-54, 13.620-7). But, overwhelmed by lust, he seduced Helen and the war began.

Hector then arrives back in Ilium to urge the womenfolk to make a peace-offering to Athene (gods, like language, fighting tactics and heroic values, are common across the Greeks and Trojans. For Homer's purpose, it is one world); and visits his family.

First, a different sense of the divine emerges throughout this book. Whereas in Book 5 gods and men worked eagerly in concert (e.g. Athene and Diomedes), here in Book 6 no god features except Athene, and then only to brush aside Trojan wishes in a single contemptuously dismissive line (311). The gods now seem distant and unapproachable. Hector has fighting to do and cannot pray to the gods with filthy hands, he tells his mother (266-8); Helen sees Zeus behind their sufferings (357), and themselves as helpless pawns, their one consolation being that they might make a fit subject for song in the future (357-8); Hector foresees that Ilium will eventually fall (447-9). True, humans can always hope – Hector can pray to Zeus to make his son a fine fighter (476-81), and wish that Zeus may grant the Trojans victory in the end (526-9). But it is a vain hope: note Homer's observation that Hector's women mourned him while he was still living (500). There is nothing unHomeric about this attitude to the gods. Gods can be close, and they can be distant. Here it is men's distance from them that is being suggested – a note that is in fact struck early on in the book when Diomedes, who was given the ability to distinguish men from gods by Athene (5.128), says that he does not know whether Glaucus is human or not (128-9).

Second, Hector, the Trojans' great hero, is to be the foil for Achilles in the *Il.* What sort of a man is he? We have seen him in relation to Paris in Book 3, where he appeared a straight-talking and admirable figure. In Books 5 and in 6, he is without doubt the Trojan's most effective warrior on the field of battle, but on both occasions has needed someone else to tell him what needed to be done. Now Homer focuses on him in relation to the people of Ilium and his family. The crowd scene which greets Hector as he returns establishes the general picture of life in Ilium – danger outside, fear and anxiety inside, and all hopes pinned on Hector, as the women swarm round him (237-41; see Schein [1984] 168-91). Hector will now be seen as a son, talking to his mother; as a brother and in-law, talking to Paris and Helen; and as a husband, talking to Andromache (see a depiction by the 'Inscription painter' in Woodford [1993] 71). In the first two cases, the women recognise that he is exhausted and hospitably offer alleviation: his mother Hecabe with a drink (258-62), Helen with the offer of a rest (354). Andromache goes further, suggesting that he should defend the city close to the walls by the fig-tree rather than fight in the open plain (433). But Hector will remain the same man throughout – the man who will return to the battlefield and fight, whatever is said to him. It is clear that he is strongly influenced by his responsibility as Troy's leading soldier (265, 361-2; see Hooker [1987] in McAuslan, etc. [1998]): his sense of shame at what others would say of him (441-2) and his own desire to live up to his calling (444-6) drive him on, whatever the consequences. Through it all, both Hector and Andromache acknowledge the shadow of death that hangs over Ilium, and over Hector in particular (see above and on 367). Andromache is not made to resent this. Their lives are separate: his in battle, hers with her child and at the loom. In this scene their separate spheres briefly interact, and then they go their different ways (494-6), she in tears, looking back as he goes, he, 'man-slaying Hector', striding off into battle (498). As we shall see, this Hector turns into a less attractive figure when he becomes Zeus' tool in furthering Zeus' plan to honour Achilles.

It is sometimes suggested that Hector's return from the battlefield into Ilium represents a threat to him because he is returning from the world of men in battle to women at home, who attempt to restrain him. But the Trojans return home to Ilium every night after battle. Ilium is not 'the world of women' but of the family – now threatened with destruction by a war from which only their menfolk can save them – and of peace, for which Greeks and Trojans alike most fervently yearn. The moving scene of family life enacted between Hector and Andromache is not about the dangerous 'world of women' but rather draws large what is depicted elsewhere in miniature: what the soldier means to his wife and child, the sense of duty that, in their different worlds, drives him *and her* on, and the desolation his death will bring (cf. e.g. 5.406-15). No man is an island in Homer. Again, Homer widens the perspective on battle: what the family means to Hector is the same as what it means to all warriors, Greek and Trojan alike.

Main sources for the commentary and related reading
Edwards (1987) 198-213; Kirk (1990); Schadewaldt (1959a); Willcock (1978).

1-72. The Greeks enjoy further success. Agamemnon and Nestor urge them to show no mercy.

4. *Scamander/Xanthos*: the same river, 'Xanthus' being the gods' name for it (20.74, **R-J** maps 1, 2).

5-71. The implications of Diomedes' wounding of Ares in Book 5 are worked out in a series of Greek victories against the fleeing Trojans (fifteen are killed; many are in twos, i.e. they are in their chariots trying to get away).

8. *Acamas*: see on 5.462.

12. *Axylus*: note the a-b-c pattern – see **GI** 2(iv) – and the typical references to wealth (14, cf. 5.544) and no one being able to help (16, cf. 5.51).

21. *Aesepus and Pedasus*: a-b-c pattern, with a story of their father Bucolion, son of Laomedon (an early king of Troy, see on 5.638). Cf. on 5.313 for love-making in the open.

22. *nymph*: these are female spirits of nature, demi-goddesses inhabiting localities of every sort, in Homer mostly watery spots. A 'Naiad' is a water-nymph, a 'Dryad' an oak-tree nymph, etc.

26. *Euryalus/son of Mekisteus*: Mecisteus was one of the Seven against Thebes (see on 2.563-5). Correct **L**'s 'Mekistios'.

45. *supplicated* (**R-J, L**); *begged* (**H**): for supplication, see **GI** 7D. No Greeks are taken prisoner in the *Il*. Trojans are said to have been taken prisoner in the past and ransomed, but if they are captured in the present they are always eventually killed (e.g. 10.374ff., 11.126ff. – in both these passages almost the same plea is made as 46-50 here – 21.17ff.). If they supplicate their captors, they never make contact with them or, if they do, the contact is broken before they are dispatched. The sanction implicit in supplication does not seem to be as effective on the battlefield as in other contexts.

55. *concern(ed)*: a telling contrast between Menelaus and the more brutal Agamemnon, with his ruthless call for total ethnic cleansing (57-60).

56. *treat you* **(R-J)**; *best [of] treatment* **(H, L)**: i.e. when Paris came to Menelaus' palace as a guest and seduced Helen away from him.

70. *at your leisure*: see e.g. 15.347 for not picking up enemy armour in the heat of the advance. It was a great temptation for a warrior to stop and seize the evidence of a kill he had made, but this held up the momentum of a successful attack on an enemy in flight, giving them the chance to regroup.

73-118: The prophet Helenus advises Aeneas and Hector to rally the Trojans and then orders Hector to tell the women of Troy to make an offering to Athene to try to stop Diomedes' rampage.

73. *would be driven back* **(R-J)**; *would have fled/climbed* **(H, L)**: sometimes unfulfilled conditions like this are merely rhetorical devices for introducing the next topic; but they may hide genuine alternative versions of the story at this point. See Morrison (1992).

75. *Helenus*: the Trojan prophet (a role filled by Calchas for the Greeks). At 7.44-5 he shows his powers; otherwise he performs as a warrior (12.94, 13.576-600). His words indicate the desperate plight the Trojans are now in – ready to abandon the fight entirely. His purpose is to rally the Trojans and get rid of Diomedes (96); the action follows the common 'rebuke' pattern (see on 5.471).

77. *Aeneas*: one wonders why Homer makes Helenus address Aeneas too, since he will do nothing by way of response. Perhaps Aeneas was meant to hold the line while Hector returned to Ilium (86). If so, the poet does not inform us – it is only Hector who rallies the troops (102-9).

88. *Athene*: Greeks and Trojans share the same gods. Athene has hated the Trojans ever since Paris spurned her; but there is no reason why she might still not be placated on certain occasions. For example, Apollo, hater of the Greeks, was still prepared to lift the plague on the Greeks when Chryseis was returned and sacrifices made, 1.472-4.

87. *mother*: Helenus and Hector are both sons of Hecabe.

89. *opening the door to the sacred chamber let her take* **(L)**: misleading. Hector's mother Hecabe is to open the door to Athene's sanctuary, and then take a robe from her own palace to bring to the sanctuary and offer to Athene. In the event, and rather oddly, it is Theano who opens the gates, lays the offering before Athene and makes the prayer (298-310).

92. *lay/place it on/along the knees*: this sounds rather like the placing of the *peplos* ('robe') on the knees of Athene at the great Panathenaea in Athens every four years. But such ceremonies were not unique to Athens, and there is no need to suspect that later Athenians inserted this scene here.

99. *never so terrified even of Achilles* (**R-J**); *not even Achilles* (**H**); *never did we so fear* (**L**): far from being a mere Achilles-substitute, Diomedes is in Trojan eyes considerably more of a threat (see 5/Intro).

107. *gave ground/way*: the Trojan rally has its effect, and the Greek advance is halted. The Greeks imagine a god had intervened – as gods often did when a rout, the most dangerous of situations to deal with, had occurred. See on 16.715; cf. Albracht (2003) [I.43].

117. *tapped him* (**R-J**); *kept tapping* (**H**); *clashed* (**L**): a famous picture of Hector's great body-shield (oblong or figure-of-eight), slung over his back as he retreats, knocking against his head and heels. Such shields are depicted on Mycenaean artefacts. Hector also carries the smaller, round shield which has a central boss (i.e. a circular bronze base, rising up into a solid bronze knob, e.g. 13.803-4). Here, by a typical confusion, the poet says that Hector's body-shield is 'bossed'.

119-236: Glaucus and Diomedes meet in battle (story of Bellerophon).

In this episode (which the ancient commentator Aristarchus tell us was located elsewhere in other texts of the *Il.*), the Trojan ally Glaucus (from Lycia, 2.876) claims the mythic hero Bellerophon as an ancestor and tells his story. It is pure folk-tale. Bellerophon was favoured by the gods (156-7) but expelled from Argos by Proetus because Proetus' wife Anteia falsely claimed Bellerophon tried to ravish her (157-66). Bellerophon was sent to Lycia, where Anteia's father was ruler (170). There he underwent a number of ordeals designed to do away with him: killing the Chimaera (183), fighting the Solymi (184), killing Amazons (186), and being ambushed (187). But he survived, and as a result, was accepted and given the hand of the Lycian ruler's daughter in marriage (191, as if these were trials for the hand of the king's daughter – a typical folktale theme). They had three children (196), but Bellerophon somehow fell out of favour and wandered off (200), and a son and daughter were killed by the gods (203).

This oddly vague tale with its pointless ending makes little use of other stories featuring Bellerophon, in which he is a son of the sea-god Poseidon. In these he murders Bellerus of Corinth (Bellerophontes = 'Bellerus-murderer') and seeks purification with Proetus in Argos. Proetus sends him to Lycia, where with the help of the winged horse Pegasus he kills the Chimaera. He then tries to reach Olympus on the horse, but Zeus sends a gadfly to sting Pegasus, and Bellerophon is thrown back to earth. There, injured, he wanders off.

Glaucus seems to know nothing about or intentionally omits (i) Bellerophon's divine birth (but cf. 191!), (ii) the murder of Bellerus (so we do not know why Bellerophon is in Argos with Proetus) (iii) Bellerophon's flight to Olympus on Pegasus (so we do not know why he loses favour and starts wandering about). Such manipulation of folktale/myth is entirely normal, however, and it is true that Homer tends to avoid the monstrous and bestial, the grotesque and bizarre (e.g. heroes riding divine horses up to Olympus;

see **GI** 6. It is true, however, that the Chimaera is hardly a household pet). One assumes Glaucus is trying to suppress the discreditable parts of the story (Gaisser [1969] 165-76).

Glaucus' story of his own family's past alerts the listener to the fact that Glaucus is Diomedes' heroic equal, serves as a reminder to Glaucus of the heroic burden resting on his shoulders, but equally illustrates that human life is transient. Is there a general warning about heroic behaviour here? Cf. de Jong (1987) 167. In fact the story of Glaucus' past will serve to bring about reconciliation, not conflict, with Diomedes (215-36); see 6/Intro.

119. *Glaucus*: he and Diomedes meet while they are both in their chariots (from which they leap down at 232). This is not clear from 119-20. Presumably Diomedes was chasing the fleeing Glaucus who decided to turn and fight, and the ensuing dialogue took place before they got down.

128. *if you are one of the immortals*: the poet seems to have forgotten that Diomedes can tell mortals from gods (5.128). Note the complex ring-composition (cf. **GI** 11): A death threat 127, B but if you are immortal 128, C I will not fight 129, because of D the fate of Lycurgus 130-1. There follows the story and then D the fate of Lycurgus 139-40, C I will not fight 141, B but if you are a mortal 142, A advance and die 143.

130. *Lycurgus*: he attacks the god Dionysus (though no reason is given) and is punished with blindness and death (139-40).

132. *nurses/fosterers*: myth told that Dionysus, born from the thigh of Zeus, was nursed and brought up at Nysa. Dionysus is called 'wild/rapturous' because of the effect he has on others.

134. *emblems/wands*: probably the *thyrsus*, wands with a pine-cone at the top, wreathed in ivy and vine-leaves – an emblem of Dionysus.

135. *Dionysus*: he was only a baby at the time. No wonder he was terrified. His reaction to attack by Pentheus in Euripides' *Bacchae* is rather different.

147. *leaves*: on the transience of human life, cf. 21.464-6. Both men and gods know what the real situation of humanity is, and respond as they see fit: in men's case, to transcend death by winning a name that will last for ever, in gods', by supporting their favourites whenever they feel like it (see **GI** 5C).

152. *Ephyre*: another name for Corinth.

154. *Sisyphus*: a trickster. Cf. *Od.* 11.593-600, where he is punished by never being able to roll a rock up to the top of a hill. We know nothing of his son Glaucus, Bellerophon's father.

160. *Anteia*: a version of the biblical story of Potiphar's wife (who played the same trick on Joseph, *Genesis* 39.7-20) and the Greek myth of Hippolytus and Phaedra.

169. *folded tablet … signs/marks/symbols*: whether Homer knew writing or not, Homeric heroes are presented as illiterate. It is not, then, surprising that Homer is so vague about what these 'signs' are. They certainly need not be a dim memory of e.g. Mycenaean Linear B; indeed, the reference to the 'folded tablet' rather suggests a familiarity with alphabetic writing.

171. *journey* **(R-J)**; *went on his way/to Lykia* **(H, L)**: in true folktale fashion, we are not told why Bellerophon *had* to go to Lycia, let alone why the gods should oversee it.

172. *Xanthus*: the river that runs through Lycia (nothing to do with Scamander/Xanthus in Troy). See **R-J** map 3.

183. *Chimaera*: an eastern monster with a lion's head in front, a goat's in the middle and a snake's at the end.

205. *Artemis*: she was traditionally associated with the sudden, but peaceful, deaths of women, as was Apollo of males, cf. 6.427-8, 24.759.

208-9. *always to be the/bravest and /best*: this is the heroic injunction – to be the best, excel others and never bring disgrace on your forbears (cf. on 11.781). Cf. 6.446 – glory for oneself is glory for one's forbears too. See **GI** 4A.

216. *entertained/was host to*: *xenia*, the Greek concept being referred to here, is often translated 'guest-friendship': it means the bond that is sealed between people from separate social units by exchange of goods or services. It generates mutual esteem, trust and obligations between them in perpetuity, almost as if they were kin. So here: Bellerophon was entertained by Oineus, with exchange of gifts, two generations ago. That bond is enough to bind Diomedes and Glaucus into the same relationship when they meet in battle. They greet the discovery with delight (212) and handshakes (233) and reinforce it in concrete terms with their own exchange of armour. Such gifts could travel a long way from hand to hand, e.g. the boar's tusk helmet (see on 10.266-70).

234. *Zeus robbed Glaucus of his wits* **(R-J)**; *took/stole Glaucus' wits away* **(H, L)**: a rare example of the narrator intruding into the narrative to make a judgement about an incident. Homer's 'financial' analysis of the situation seems to cheapen this spontaneous act of mutual respect, as if Glaucus should have thought more about the material loss he was suffering. Perhaps Homer had decided to forget his role as 'objective' epic narrator and openly comment, for once, from the point of view of the values of the contemporary man in the street listening to the poem, who might have been amazed at Glaucus' lack of interest in his tangible assets. Cf. on 23.551.

237-368: Hector arrives in Ilium and meets his mother Hecabe. The offering to Athene is made (in vain), and Hector converses with Paris and Helen.

237. *oak tree*: note its close association with the Scaean gate, cf. 9.354 and 21.549. Presumably it is the spot where Athene and Apollo meet at 7.22, 60. Note that, while Glaucus and Diomedes have been talking, Hector has progressed from the battlefield, which he left at 116, to the gates of Ilium. See Zielinski's second law, at 3.121-244.

244. *fifty*: for Priam's sons, see on 4.499.

255. *It is true, then* (**R-J**); *The sons of the Achaians … must be* (**H**); *Surely* (**L**): Hecabe guesses, only partly rightly, at the reasons for Hector's arrival, and immediately moves to act on her guess with her offer of wine. Her words create a lively sense of a strong-minded woman intent on doing what she can to help out in a situation over which she, ultimately, has no control.

266. *unwashed*: see **GI** 7B.

269. *Go with offerings* (**R-J**); *No, you must go* (**H**); *But go yourself* (**L**): see 5.86-95.

284. *If (only) I could see him/that man*: Hector repeats sentiments about Paris first expressed at 3.39-57: the implied thought is that it is Paris who is to blame for all this, and Hector's feelings boil over (cf. 328).

291. *Sidon*: one of the towns on the coast where the ancient Phoenicians lived (modern Lebanon), via which Homer tells us that Paris and Helen return to Troy. According to another epic cycle, the *Cypria*, Hera drove them there in a storm (cf. her treatment of Heracles, see on 5.638) and Paris promptly took and plundered the city. Sidon was famed for its magnificent glass and purple-dyed cloth (cf. on 3.17 for Paris' taste for exotic gear); the Phoenicians were renowned traders, setting up way-stations all round the Mediterranean (and beyond) in their search for metals.

298. *Theano*: see on 2.146, 5.89; cf. 11.224.

299. *Kisseus* (**H, L**): his name is Kissês (Cissês).

301. *loud cry/wailing*: part of the ritual of prayer, indicative (perhaps) of some great crisis.

311. *shook/turned her head*: 'no' in ancient Greece was indicated by raising the head. For divine rejection of prayers, cf. Zeus at 2.419-20.

313. *Hector made his way* (**R-J**); *Hector had gone* (**H**); *Hector went away* (**L**): one might have expected Hector to have made some progress towards Paris' home while the women offered up their prayers, but see Zielinski's first law (at 3.122-244).

319. *five metres* (**R-J**); *eleven cubits* (**H, L**): an impressive weapon (cf. 8.494). Homer selects this to focus on, leaving us to sense the contrast between Hector the great soldier and Paris the playboy.

326. *What do you think* (**R-J**); *Strange man* (**H, L**): see on 1.561.

337. *gently* (**R-J**); *gentle persuasion* (**H**); *soft words* (**L**): Helen's words were in fact very sharp (see 3.428-36, and notes), but this is how Paris now chooses to represent her words to Hector. Women in the *Il.* usually try to restrain their men from enterprises likely to endanger them (see on 24.208). The fact that Helen urges Paris to return to battle tells us something about her feelings for him.

341. *catch you (up)* (**R-J, H**); *overtake you* (**L**): see 6.515.

342. *made/gave no reply/answer*: a telling one line response – all we need to know about Hector's feelings towards Paris. See on 404.

343. *warmly* (**R-J**); *softly* (**H**); *words of endearment* (**L**): Homer points for us the way the speech is to be taken. Helen admires Hector, and expresses the same feelings in her lament at his death (24.762-75). Hector's reply (359-68) is equally sympathetic. For Helen's self criticism, see on 3.173. Observe that Paris is present in the room as Helen launches her attack on him here (350-8).

356. *blind folly/act*: *Atê*, see on 1.412.

358. *figure in the songs* (**R-J**); *themes of song* (**H**); *things of song* (**L**): or so, modern critics tell us, Homer hopes. But are they right?

367. *whether/if I shall ever … come back*: the meeting between Hector and Andromache is set up as if it were to be their last (see e.g. 407-8, 464, 487 and especially 500-2), though technically Hector spends the next night in Ilium (at the end of the 23rd day – see Book 7).

369-495: Hector converses with his wife Andromache who has their baby Astyanax with her.

371. *he did not find* (**R-J, H**); *he failed to find*: this, strikingly, is the only time that a person going to look for someone else fails to find them (see on 2.167). While Hector is looking for Andromache at home (371) and she is looking for him on the battlefield (386), they are now both *outside* their respective spheres of action.

388. *like a woman possessed/in frenzy/gone mad*: Andromache fears Hector is dead – her reaction will be the same when he is (22.460).

395. *Eëtion*: we learn at 1.366-9 that Achilles was attacking Eëtion's town of Thebe when he took Chryseis (and a lyre, 9.186-8, a horse Pedasus 16.152-4 and much iron 23.827); at 2.689-92 that on this expedition he also took Briseis (cf. 19.291-4); and here (6.414-28) that, on the same occasion, Achilles killed Andromache's father and brothers and ransomed her mother. This tragic past will, for Andromache, turn into an even more tragic future when Achilles also kills her husband (22.325-63). Achilles is central to the past and future of all these women. Cf. on 1.184.

402. *Scamandrius*: it appears usual to name people after rivers, cf. 4.474, 5.50.

403. *Astyanax* (**H, L**): *astu* 'town' + *anax* 'lord'. There is a special pathos about the child's introduction into the scene. The tradition, surely known to the audience, was that when Troy was sacked the Greeks threw him from the battlements. See on 22.59, 24.712-45.

404. *said nothing/in silence*: one silence at 342, where Hector refused to answer Paris; another now, accompanied by a smile, when he sees his child. What might this signify?

406. *possessed* (**R-J**); *Poor man* (**H**); *Dearest* (**L**): see on *daimonios*, 1.561 (do not connect **R-J** 'possessed' with 388). Andromache's speech uses the past to emphasise what Hector means to her in the present – and future, if there is one.

407. *determination/spirit/strength*: see on 12.41 for the development of Andromache's worries about Hector's fearlessness.

417. *strip* (**R-J**); *respect(ed)* (**H, L**): once Achilles was minded to treat the dead with respect (here he does not even strip the body) or take people ransom (e.g. 427). He will no longer (21.100-3, 22.395-404).

418. *cremated/burned*: the normal method of disposing of bodies in the Homeric world (cf. 7.79-80, 23.163-225). The folk-theory was that this finally released the dead from this earth and allowed their souls to find rest in the underworld; it also released the living from fear that the dead would return to haunt them (Rohde [1925] 18-22).

424. *looking after/tended*: see **GI** 3 for the agricultural background to the heroic world.

433. *fig-tree*: features also at 11.167, 22.145. See on 24.208 for women's efforts to restrain excess in their men. Note that Andromache does not ask Hector to stay inside the walls, but to fight defensively just outside them.

436. *about the two* (**L**): i.e. led by the two. This attack is not mentioned in the *Il.*, nor is there any suggestion elsewhere that the wall is weak at this point. But the Trojans are under pressure (cf. Helenus' advice at 6.81) and it is just the sort of thing that a fearful Andromache might say in the circumstances.

440. *Hector … replied/answered*: Hector does not attempt to refute his wife or even argue with her. He merely states his position: that external pressures (441, the shame he would feel) and internal demands leave him no option (444, he has trained himself/learnt to be brave and 445 must win *kleos* for himself and his father – see on 1.352, 4.376 and cf. 7.91, 8.285). He too looks to the future, and a bleak vision it is: the destruction of Ilium (448) and his own death (460-5).

460. *There goes/this is/the wife*: Hector here imagines a time when his eternal *kleos* will be publicly recognised by the Greeks who enslave Andromache (Hector is keen on imagining what people will say about him in public, cf. 7.87-91, 300-2). But this will be at the price of his death and Andromache's eternal grief. That he will prefer death (464-5) indicates his sense of helplessness to prevent it. His world and hers will remain for ever separate. For other such 'death-wishes', cf. 4.182, 8.150, 24.244-6.

471. *burst out laughing* (**R-J**); *laughed aloud/out* (**H, L**): Hector and Andromache are reunited in the terrified reaction of their son. His father understandingly responds by divesting himself of his military insignia. Homer, as usual, just reports and lets us imagine the change of atmosphere, but there is no indication that Hector is renouncing his military calling by this gesture. Quite the reverse – he prays his son may follow in his footsteps.

480. *enemy he has killed* (**R-J, H**); *kill his enemy* (**L**): Hector sees hope for the future. The implication is that he may be dead, but the fighting will still be going on, thanks to his son. This will be some consolation for Andromache (481 'delight/bring joy to his mother's heart' – the duty of a son; cf. Hecabe's pride in Hector at 24.748-59).

484. *tears*: a poignant moment – Andromache was laughing: why is she now crying as well? Homer does not say. Our imaginations race.

488. *before my fated time*: **(R-J, H)**; *fate* **(L)**: see **GI** 8. Hector clarifies the implication of his last words – that he has to die when his time is up, and nothing can either advance or retard that moment (as he recognises when it happens – 22.297-305).

490. *Go home now* **(R-J)**; *go back to the house* **(H, L)**: Hector and Andromache's ways part again, and they go back to their separate existences – the work of the home for her, the work of war for him (492-3). It is a feature of epic that, while the work of men and women is clearly differentiated, there is no obvious sense in which the one is considered inferior or superior to the other. This holds true for the distinction between the sexes as well.

495-529: Hector and Andromache part, as if for the last time, and Hector and Paris meet up and return to battle.

496. *with many a backward look* **(R-J)**; *turning (often)* **(H, L)**: again, a whole world of feeling – the sense that they will never see each other again – summoned up in the single reaction of Andromache, looking back again and again as Hector marches off, with no backward glance, to death.

498. *man-slaying Hector/killer/slayer of men*: a thunderbolt of an epithet, all the more powerful alongside his 'welcoming/pleasant/well-settled' home. For all the warmth and tenderness of the recent scene, Hector is returning to battle, where different values apply.

500. *they mourned*: Homer looks into the women's hearts and reports what he finds there (see on 367 above). Thetis too mourns in advance the death of Achilles (18.52-64, 24.85); cf. also 24.328.

503. *Paris*: we now go back to Paris, who had earlier said he would catch Hector up (341).

506-11. *As a stabled/stalled horse* ('stalled' – i.e. in a stall): D-simile, repeated at 15.263-8 of Hector returning to battle after being revived by Apollo. It begins with an image of the breaking of constraints, but ending up as an image of speed. Horses are noble, aristocratic creatures: this one's pleasure in its beauty and the details of the hair (cf. 3.54-5) suit Paris well.

511. *pasture(s)*: when Virgil imitated this simile (*Aeneid* 11.494) he said these were the pastures of mares (as in **H**). Such a reading might be appropriate for the sex-mad Paris, but the simile pictures someone going not to bed but to battle, on which Paris is said to be not so keen (523 'too ready to give up/you (deliberately) hang back'), though his 'laughing' (514) may belie that (**L**'s 'loved' 511 is not justified by the Greek: read 'accustomed'). The sexual imagery would be quite unsuited to Hector (506 above).

515. *where he yet lingered ... where* **(L)**: there is no 'lingering' in the Greek. Read 'just as he was leaving the spot where'.

521. *strange man*: see on *daimonios*, 1.561. Hector is trying to say something complimentary about Paris in this somewhat strained speech.

524. *shameful/shaming things*: cf. 351, 3.42, 453-4.

Book 7

Introduction

So far Homer has allowed the Greeks to sweep all before them. This, however, is not what Zeus and Thetis had planned. In Book 7, therefore, Homer plots the turn in Greek fortunes. From now on the Trojan counter-attack will gather momentum until the situation is so desperate that, by the end of Book 8, Agamemnon will be ready to agree to the return of Achilles.

Hector is the crucial figure here. He, as we have already seen, is living up to his reputation as the Trojans' greatest hope (e.g. 6.78-80), swinging things round by holding the line and counter-attacking in Book 5, and then rallying the Trojans successfully in Book 6 (106-7). Homer now decides to have Hector continue the good work on the battlefield, and then to replay a device he has exploited once already (Menelaus vs. Paris in Book 3) by matching Hector in a duel against Ajax. This offers the same 'two-birds with one stone' narrative advantage as the earlier duel: it will allow us to get a measure of both Hector, the greatest Trojan warrior, and Ajax, the Greeks' greatest defensive champion, set against each other. The poet can then exploit the outcome. But it also has to be said that two duels in a single day (i.e. this one and Menelaus vs. Paris in Book 3), neither with a definitive result, has raised the suspicion of analytical scholars (**GI** 2), especially as the duel in Book 7 is not very well motivated and nothing hangs on it, unlike the duel in Book 3 whose outcome could at least have ended the war. The matter is discussed by Kirk (1978).

At 1-16, Hector and Paris with Glaucus (13) get to work on the Greek troops, and are so effective that Athene feels the need to intervene again (19-20). A divine initiative between Athene and Apollo then brings about the duel (36-43) – a feeble but necessary motivation (see on 76 for the problem). It is noticeable that Hector accepts the challenge to fight Ajax because his brother, the seer Helenus, assures him that his time to die has not yet come (52-3). One remembers Hector's blunt assessment of a man's destiny at 6.487-9: he will escape it this time. But, we wonder, would he have fought, if Helenus had not told him this? Hector then lays down conditions for the treatment of the body of whichever of them is killed in the duel (76-91, cf. 6.464-5). These things matter to him; the honourable proposal he makes here prefigures Achilles' rejection of his similar pleas at 22.338-54. Hector adds his hopes of the *kleos* he will gain if he wins (87-91), recalling his words to Andromache at 6.444-6. Finally, no Greek initially wants to face him, out of fear (92-3). This reaction tells us all we want to know about the Greek perception of Hector as a warrior.

On the Greek side, their initial reluctance to accept the challenge comes as something of a shock (92-3), but is in keeping with Homer's plan to sketch them in a less confident mood. As for Ajax, Homer's extraordinary description of him and of the Trojan reaction to him at 206-323 tells us in a few, brief strokes what Ajax is like, while the two pre-battle speeches are finely characterised: Ajax, all the more menacing for his refusal to talk about himself and his abilities (226-32), Hector by contrast perhaps protesting a little too much (233-43).

The fight must, naturally, end in a draw, but Homer makes it clear that Hector comes off second best (see on 244-73); indeed, the Trojans can hardly believe their luck that he is still alive (310-11). Though he will have his moments of triumph, Hector's fallibility is already emerging.

It is not a good sign for the Trojans that their greatest champion has been worsted by Ajax, and the poet makes them try one last time to settle the war by agreement. But Paris remains obdurate (as he has to, if the *Il.* is not to end here): he will not return Helen (362; at 11.123-5 we are told that Paris bribed Trojans to oppose Helen's return). The Helen-less deal which the Trojans eventually cobble together is considered by the Greeks, but rejected (400-7); but both sides do agree to the burial of their dead, and after that quietly moving scene is done (421-32), the book closes with both sides taking their evening meal, fearful of what Zeus' thunder might mean (480-1).

Which leaves the question of the Greek defensive wall and ditch round their camp, proposed by Nestor at 336-43 and built at 436-41 (despite Poseidon's worries, calmed by Zeus, at 442-63). This defensive complex has caused problems. It seems odd that Nestor should make the suggestion now, particularly since the Greeks do not seem to be under any particular pressure (as 343 virtually admits); after all, the Trojan rally at 7.1-16 does not read like a major offensive, Ajax has almost beaten Hector in the duel, and the Trojans themselves are in disarray about what to do next (345-6), even seriously considering giving Helen back (350, 393). Then again, 'analysts' (**GI** 2) point out that the wall and ditch are frequently forgotten in the course of the rest of the *Il.*

The motivation for Nestor's plan may not be wholly convincing, but it does suggest that the Greeks are now in a more defensive frame of mind. More important is the narrative *flexibility* that the defensive wall and ditch will give the poet as he plots his way to Achilles' return. First, the defences will allow for major Trojan successes in Book 8 that will be severe enough to suggest to the Greeks that it is time they brought back Achilles, but without immediately threatening the Greek camp: the defences at this point will still hold. But when Achilles refuses to return, the poet can then describe, at whatever length he chooses, the Trojan onslaught on the defences till the moment they *give way*, the Trojans charge in, and the Greek fleet is set on fire. This critical juncture will motivate the return of Patroclus into the fighting in Book 16 – and thus the eventual return of Achilles. The presence of a defensive wall and ditch, in other words, is a device that allows Homer to pace and control the development of the crisis caused by the plan of Zeus. If Homer forgets about these new defences from time to time, that seems typical: he tends to focus his attention on the here and now in the battlefield, often ignoring the wider picture (see e.g. on 11.47-52). All in all, then, though Book 7 is not without its difficulties, one can see why the poet saw advantages in a duel between Hector and Ajax at this point, and having the Greeks build a wall + ditch.

Analysts, worried about both the motivation for the duel and the new Greek defences in this book, have suggested that the building of the wall in Book 7 at any rate is a post-Homeric addition. Their argument depends on a comment from the fifth-century BC historian Thucydides who, using Homer as his source, say the Greeks built the wall *on their arrival in Troy* (1.11.1). If that is what Thucydides read in his text of the *Il.*, then the section of our version of the *Il.* which describes the wall being built in Book 7 must have been put into our text *after* Thucydides' time – a most disturbing conclusion. But Thucydides can be ignored, if we want to argue that he was referring to the defences which, Homer tells us, the Greeks put up when they first landed, round the point where they hauled up their ships (14.32).

Main sources for the commentary and related reading
Kirk (1990); Willcock (1978); Kirk (1978).

1-91: After some skirmishes, Apollo and Athene plan a duel between Hector and a Greek. Hector issues the challenge and offers an agreement about the treatment of the loser's body.

4. *As a god* **(R-J)**; *Like a breeze* **(H)**; *And as to men* **(L)**: D-simile, accompanying (as often) the entry of a warrior into battle (see on 5.5). The simile describes how Hector and Paris answer their men's prayers as a god answers exhausted sailors'.

8-16. Hector and Paris rally the Trojans so effectively – both killing their man and Glaucus joining in the action too (13) – that the Greeks start to turn. This is illustrated by the fact that Iphinous was killed (15) 'leaping up behind his fast mares', i.e. to retreat, and proved by Athene's response who can see (18) the Greeks being slaughtered.

20. *intercept/meet*: the pro-Trojan Apollo descends to prevent Athene rallying her side (he asks her [26] if she wants to 'switch/give victory to the Greeks'). They meet by the oak tree (22), i.e. near the Scaean gate (see on 6.237).

32. *razing this town to the ground* **(R-J)**; *sacking of this town* **(H)**; *be made desolate* **(L)**: cat-and-mouse characterisation from Homer here. Does Apollo really think that Ilium is doomed? Or is he just saying it, to get his way with Athene? She, at any rate, is prepared to agree to a cease-fire for the moment and is surely being economical with the truth at 34, claiming 'That is what I too had in mind/was my thought too/my thoughts also', when all along she had come down to try to turn the tide of battle in favour of the Greeks (26).

40. *mortal/grim/bitter combat*: another duel, not long after the aborted

Paris-Menelaus duel in Book 3. The interest now lies in the question –
Hector versus whom?

44. *Helenus*: see on 6.75. The poet has a narrative problem here – how
to get the message to Hector? A regular device would be for the god to
inform Helenus of the divine intention, cf. Athene descending to instruct
Achilles (1.194) and Odysseus (2.173), Agamemnon's dream (2.6) etc.
Homer rejects that in favour of Helenus somehow intuiting, or even
listening in to, Apollo and Athene's plan (53 'I have (heard) it') – a unique
occurrence in Homer, though a strong index of Helenus' prophetic powers.
See on 76 for Homer's problems here, which may account for this odd
incident.

59. *in the form of vultures* **(R-J, H)**; *likenesses … of vultures* **(L)**: it is
just possible that the poet means 'in the way that vultures do'. At 15.237,
for example, Apollo obviously descends in the way that a hawk does before
he addresses Hector face to face in his own likeness.

63. *Like ripples* **(R-J)**; *Like the shiver* **(H)**; *As when the shudder* **(L)**:
D-simile, but note the ripple/shiver/shudder image started in 63. The
simile, concentrating on the surface of the sea (seen, as it were, from
headland or ship), reflects the aerial perspective of the gods in the tree.

76. *with Zeus for witness*: Hector's conditions relate to the treatment
of the body of the loser, and are never ratified on oath by either side. It is
easy to see why: there was no need. It was normal practice for the bodies
of the dead to be recovered (7.394-6, agreed at 7.408-11). Hector's speech
is significant in relation to his own characterisation, as a man of honour,
and (ironically) because of the way Achilles will maltreat him in death
(22.395ff., see on 11.455).

One can argue about the necessity of the duel because, whatever the
outcome, the fighting will still go on after it (though the death of Hector
would represent a more serious setback for the Trojans than the death of
Ajax for the Greeks). In this it is very different from the Paris-Menelaus
duel in Book 3, where a clear result would indeed have ended the war.
Since there is no convincing *human* reason why a duel is needed, it was
necessary for the gods to motivate it. See on 44 above.

91. *fame/glory*: for *kleos*, see on 6.440.

**92-205: Menelaus is prevented from putting himself forward, and
Nestor berates the Greeks for their cowardice. Ajax wins the lottery to
face Hector.**

93. *afraid/in fear*: it says something for Hector's prowess that the
Greeks hesitate to take up the challenge.

104. *end of you* **(R-J)**; *end(ing) of your life* **(H, L)**: note the sympathetic apostrophe (see on 4.127) and Agamemnon's concern for his brother
(cf. on 2.586), a feeling shared by his attendants who remove Menelaus'
armour 'joyfully' (122).

113. *Even Achilles*: did Achilles *really* avoid Hector in battle? This is surely a face-saving argument from Agamemnon, with little evidence from the text (cf. Achilles' much likelier claim at 9.352-5, and Apollo's advice to Hector at 20.376, which Hector ignores with very nearly disastrous consequences).

125. *Peleus*: an interesting moment for Nestor to remember Achilles' father, whom he had visited in the past (11.766-89); one cannot imagine Achilles shirking the challenge to take on Hector. For the whole speech and Nestor's advice + paradigm sequences, cf. on 1.247. This one is a rebuke.

128. *parentage and pedigree* (**R-J**); *family and birth* (**H**); *generation and blood* (**L**): cf. on 4.376 for the way in which a son's pedigree was judged by his father's. Nestor's point here is that Achilles' father Peleus would never have believed that the sons of such fathers could behave so cravenly.

132. *young as I was* (**R-J, H**); *in my youth as when* (**L**): Nestor usually starts reminiscences with a sentiment of this sort, e.g. 11.670, 23.269, and cf. 4.321, 8.103. These tales probably represent some sort of cycle of epic adventures, sung by local poets, centred round Nestor's town of Pylos, rather like those centred round Thebes, etc. (see on 2.563-5, 9.529).

134. *Pylos*: Nestor's kingdom. See **R-J** map 4. There is a classical Pheia (135) but no Pheia near even one river, let alone two, is known.

136. *Ereuthalion*: Nestor hinted at the story at 4.319. Note the ring-composition (**GI** 11) – A 129-31: you all fear Hector; B 132-5: I wish I were young again; C 136-7: my enemy Ereuthalion had Areithous' armour; D 138-47: story of Areithous; C 148-56 Ereuthalion had his armour; B 156-8: I wish I were young again; A 159-60: you all fear Hector.

161. *Nine*: an interesting ranking of the Greeks' best fighters (in the absence of Achilles and Patroclus), with the top three in the army's view being Ajax, Diomedes and Agamemnon (179-80). Menelaus has, of course, been disbarred (109-22).

164. *two Ajaxes*: the greater (son of Telamon) and probably the lesser (son of Oïleus) Ajax. See on 2.406. Telamonian Ajax wins the lottery.

180. *golden Mycenae*: as it was in the Bronze Age, though not in Homer's time.

196. *out loud*: to show Ajax fears no one. It is difficult to see what the purpose of a silent prayer to a god might be, unless word-magic is implied, i.e. the belief that a god could be called upon successfully only if his proper titles were used. If only the Greeks knew these titles, the enemy could not offer up a successful counter-prayer to the same god. It was therefore important to keep them secret from enemies.

206-321: Ajax and Hector fight, with no clear result.

212. *grim smile* (**R-J, H**); *threatening brows* (**L**): a magnificent picture of the great Ajax – like Ares, awe-inspiring, a tower of strength, grimly smiling, long-striding, brandishing his spear – the 'objective', external physical description inviting us to sense his inner confidence and mastery.

The Trojans' terror and Hector's fast-beating heart (depiction by reaction, followed by Hector's focalised 'thoughts') tell us all we need to know of the effect he has on others.

219. *shield*: for Ajax's uniquely-described shield 'like a tower' (tall, rectangular?), seven ox-hides thick, overlaid with an outer eighth layer of bronze, cf. Hector's at 6.117. Both seem Mycenaean in origin. Ajax's is clearly the huger, heavier piece of equipment, though at 267 it evidently has a boss: surely a mistake, since only the smaller, round shields had those. Ajax's men take it from him when it gets too heavy (13.711-12). For **L** 'carrying like a wall his shield' – few men carry walls – 'carrying his tower-like shield'.

226-32. Ajax's speech is all the more coolly menacing for its understatement and lack of boasting about his own ability (not an 'I' anywhere). Hector's reply (234-43) is all 'I'.

228. *breaker of men* **(R-J, H)**; *who breaks men in battle* **(L)**: this refers to Achilles' ability to break through opposing battle-lines.

241. *tread my measures* **(L)**: a close encounter *during a standing-fight* (to contrast with the chase of 240, missed by **L**) is here likened to dancing. See on 15.508.

244-73. *long-shadowed spear* **(R-J, H)**; *spear far-shadowed* **(L)**: the battle sequence – exchange of throwing spears (244-54), re-use as stabbing spears (255-62), and recourse to stones (262-72) with the promise of swords next (273) – makes up one of the longest fight-scenes in the *Il.*, where most battles are concluded with no more than one exchange of attacks before the fatal stroke is delivered. Note that 7.249-54 = 3.355-60.

Ajax gets the better of it in all three encounters: he hits Hector with the spear throw, wounds him with the thrust and knocks him over with the boulder (so that Hector needs Apollo's help to stand up again, 272). Cf. Ajax's delight at his 'victory' 312 – clearly Ajax's, not Homer's, focalisation of the event – and the Trojans' delight and amazement that Hector survived, 307-10. Since Hector must not die here, Ajax cannot reject the heralds' intervention (which in 'real life' he surely would have done). So Ajax makes the best of a bad job by forcing Hector to offer the stoppage (284-6).

256. *lions*: B-simile. For lions and boars, cf. 5.782-3, 12.42-8.

280. *holds you both dear* **(R-J)**; *has love for both* **(H)**; *beloved* **(L)**: on Zeus' feelings for Hector, see 24.66-70. Ajax is never personally mentioned by the gods in the *Il.*, and he is the one major hero never helped out by the gods in any encounter either, though he is 'inspired' before battle at 13.77-80. This may account for later stories of his hybris, cf. Sophocles' *Ajax* 758-79 (and 815-18, where Ajax remembers his exchange of gifts with Hector here, 299).

299. *exchange/give each other … gifts*: cf. Diomedes and Glaucus, 6.230-3. The idea that Hector and Ajax should become friends (302) stretches credulity somewhat – or is this the sort of ingratiating proposal a beaten man would try to make?

322-432: Nestor proposes the Greeks bury their dead and then build a defensive wall and ditch. [23rd day] The Trojans have a peace-plan rejected, but agree to a truce to collect and cremate the dead, which both sides do.

334-5. *take/carry the bones back home*: a strange proposal. Full cremation on the spot is the way in which bodies of Homeric heroes are dealt with (see on 6.418); further, after the bodies *have* been cremated (430-2), the idea of collecting the bones for transport back to Greece is entirely forgotten. Since transporting bones was an Athenian custom instituted *c.* 464 BC, these two verses were probably inserted by Athenians ('interpolated' is the technical term) to claim Homer's 'authority' for the practice.

337-43. *high-towered walls* (**R-J, H**); *towered ramparts* (**L**): see 7/Intro. Page (1959) 315-24 argues the case for multiple authorship.

352. *oaths* (**R-J, H**); *pledges* (**L**): i.e. the oaths relating to the Paris-Menelaus duel in Book 3. See Appendix and cf. on 11.124.

364. *return the goods* (**R-J**); *give up all the possessions* (**H**); *give all back* (**L**): a pretty feeble compromise from Paris. The Greeks did not attack Ilium to get back Helen's possessions.

381-432. *at dawn*: this heralds the twenty-third day, in which the Greeks reject the Trojan proposal, and the Trojans and Greeks collect and cremate their dead.

421. *the sun of a new day* (**L**): emend. This is still the same day as was heralded by the dawn at 381.

424-6. *to recognise*: the inability to recognise their dead friends before the bodies have been cleaned, and the grief both sides feel as they do recognise them, are all the more touching for being so understated.

433-82: Next morning [24th day], their dead buried, the Greeks construct the defensive wall and ditch. Poseidon's worries about the wall are soothed by Zeus. Greek ships bring in supplies; Zeus thunders all night.

433. *but when the dawn was not yet* (**L**): read 'Before dawn on the next day', i.e. the twenty-fourth day, in which the Greeks build a communal grave-mound and the defensive wall and ditch proposed by Nestor.

441. *stakes*: these seem to have been placed at surface level, in front of the wall, on the edge of the ditch.

453. *Laomedon*: see on 5.638.

461. *break down the wall* (**R-J, H**); *break their wall to pieces* (**L**): the wall's destruction will be described as a future event at 12.17-33. The purpose of this episode is presumably to explain why the wall round Ilium was not visible in Homer's day, evidence that there was a location which the Greeks of Homer's time thought of as Ilium (Hisarlik?).

467-8. *Lemnos … Euneus … Jason*: Lemnos, an island near Troy, was the place where the Greeks had stopped off *en route* for Troy (8.229-35) and Philoctetes had been abandoned (2.722). Jason is the hero of the Argonaut saga. He had an affair with Hypsipyle (daughter of king Thoas, 14.230) on Lemnos, and Euneus was the result. Euneus features at 21.41 and 23.745-7 as a slave-trader (see on 21.43 for one excellent deal he makes), and here as an army supplier.

472. *thence* **(L)**: i.e. from Euneus, not from the special cargo he delivered to Agamemnon and Menelaus.

473. *supplied themselves … in exchange for* **(R-J)**; *bought … paid* **(H)**; *bought* **(L)**: the vocabulary of 'buying' and 'paying' implies money. But this was not in use in Homer's day, when goods were exchanged and bartered, as here. This is the only passage where Homer deals in any detail with the supplying of such a huge army, since such mundane issues were not the proper subject matter of epic. The historian Thucydides, assuming there is solid history behind Homer and trying to make military sense of what is happening in the Trojan war, produces a fascinating discussion of what he thought was really going on in Troy when one has 'allowed for the exaggerations of the poet' (*Histories* 1.9-11).

479. *(kept) thundering* **(R-J, H)**; *in the thunderstroke* **(L)**: this makes a dramatic and threatening close to the day. Presumably the thunder terrifies both sides equally rather than just the Greeks. For the libations to Zeus, see on 1.471.

Book 8

Introduction

The big epic requires the big picture. In Books 2-7, therefore, Homer has chosen to put on hold the plan of Zeus agreed in Book 1, and given us a broad overview of the major champions and armies on both sides, focalised in different ways: we have seen debates and arguments between individuals and in assembly, surveys of the armies, attempts to reach a mutually agreeable settlement, the gods on both sides, interactions with gods through personal contact and public ritual, life at home in Ilium, and conflict on the battlefield, including single combats. Perhaps most important of all, we have been given a sense of the whole sweep of the first nine years of the Trojan war, with the memories of past oracles and the catalogue of ships (Book 2), the Helen-Paris encounter (Book 3), and so on; see Latacz (1996) 127-31. As for the fighting, the Greeks have had the upper hand initially, but the Trojans have been battling back. Throughout, Zeus has shown no inclination to impose himself on proceedings, but has given the pro-Greek and pro-Trojan gods a free hand; throughout, questions have been raised about Agamemnon's abilities as leader; and throughout Homer has kept a balance between the implications of Greek success without Achilles – was Agamemnon right all along and they do need him? – and the sense that, despite that success, Achilles is irreplaceable and his return a matter of urgency. Idly one wonders – was there ever a version of the story in which the Greeks, finding that they *really* did not need Achilles, actually drove the Trojans right back to Ilium before a frantic Achilles appealed to his mother for help to stop them? Surely not: such a plot would seriously lessen our sense of Achilles' indispensability. Nevertheless, the *Il.* constantly invites speculation about possible alternative articulations.

Whatever the balance of play between the forces that has emerged in Books 4-7, Book 8 changes the whole situation dramatically (and compare Book 15, which virtually replays it). Homer brings the plan of Zeus firmly back into view again. Now we can understand the point of all the continuing Greek success in the earlier books: compared with that, the sudden and total reverse in Book 8 is going to seem like a complete catastrophe for them and turn their thoughts even more firmly towards Achilles.

The poet opens the book with a specially summoned council of the gods, at which Zeus makes it clear that any further opposition to his plans will be met with physical violence – an injunction which stays in force (despite various efforts by the gods to circumvent it) till 20.24-5. His orders given, Zeus immediately decamps to Mount Ida, overlooking the plain of Troy, where he can keep an eye on proceedings and intervene to ensure a Trojan victory (47-8). This he does almost at once, directing a lightning flash at the Greek army (75-7), and following it up with a thunderbolt at Diomedes (133-4) who, determined to continue the fight, has nearly killed Hector (118-20); and (such is Diomedes' reluctance to retreat when Hector taunts him) Zeus even has to make a third intervention, thundering from Ida, before Diomedes gets the message (170-1).

The effect on Hector is dramatic. He immediately senses that Zeus in on his side (175-6) and calls on the Trojans to make for the Greek defences, destroy them and set fire to their ships (181-4, cf. 'he would have had the ships in flames' 217-19). It is a turning point for Hector, who from now on is increasingly consumed with confidence that victory will be his – a confidence which becomes more and more blind to the facts. He will realise he has been utterly deceived only when he faces death at Achilles' hands at 22.297-304. See Schein (1984) 179-85.

Zeus' intervention spells disaster for the Greeks, and Hera persuades Agamemnon (218-19) to lead a rally, which is briefly successful; and Zeus even signals to the Greeks that they will not be utterly destroyed (245-6), an important concession given their shattered morale after their earlier success in Books 4-7 and all the signs Zeus is now sending that favour the Trojans. But Zeus then swings the battle back again in the Trojans' favour (335), to such effect that the Greeks retreat right back behind their new defensive wall and ditch (342-7). Hera and Athene can endure this no longer and attempt an intervention from Olympus, which Zeus inevitably spots from Mount Ida (397) and immediately sends Iris to thwart (409-12). The terrified goddesses turn back, and Zeus at once returns to Olympus to reinforce the message to them, in person: he will not be crossed, or he will use overwhelming force against them (454-6).

This raises a tricky narrative problem for Homer. The point is that Zeus' decree means that the pro-Greek deities are now, in theory, excluded from any intervention. Homer realises that this will not wash with goddesses as implacably opposed to the Trojans as Hera and Athene, and that is why he made them test Zeus' resolution at once. They were duly warned off by Zeus, and retreated. But the question is: how long can this go on for? The poet can hardly have goddesses like these sitting idly by, doing nothing, just because Zeus says so; nor, on the other hand, can he have them constantly intervening unless he is prepared to depict Zeus using the ultimate sanction of force against them and throwing them, almost literally, out of the *Il.*

It needs, in other words, more than a decree from Zeus to hold these gods in check. One tactic Zeus adopts is to keep his eyes firmly fixed on the scene of battle from now till the start of Book 13. No god can evade his all-seeing gaze. Another is that Zeus announces that it is *fated* that tomorrow he will give the Trojans one day of victory, involving the slaughter of Greeks in numbers, until Patroclus is killed and Achilles returns to the fighting, i.e. at which point the Greeks will have the upper hand again (470-83). Gods can argue with and try to subvert Zeus; they cannot argue with or subvert destiny. Hera's refusal to say anything in reply (484) speaks volumes, if only we knew what they were. Frustrated fury? Shock? The thought 'At least it is only one day ...'? However we interpret it, Homer immediately makes the sun set (485-6): the fatal 'tomorrow' beckons. On the way Homer handles this divine machinery, cf. Bremer (1987), Emlyn-Jones (1992).

Homer now takes us into both camps to observe their differing reactions to the events of the day represented by Book 8. The Trojans are, naturally, exultant, and Hector, still bursting with confidence (541), is certain that, next day, the Greeks will be driven out of Troy (529-41). The Trojans (for the first time, we feel) are even prepared to camp out on the plain itself right outside the Greek defences, rather than returning back to Ilium at night, as they normally do. Homer describes that scene with quite stunning brilliance (553-65); never before have the Trojans been so much on top. And the Greeks? Their reaction will follow in Book 9.

It is easy to see the Trojan victories in Book 8 as somewhat hollow, the result of Zeus' support rather than any Trojan military excellence. As far as the Greeks are concerned, of course, that is neither here nor there. If Zeus is against you, you run, as Nestor explains to the combative Diomedes (139-44), and the Greeks' agonised council of war in Book 9 will leave no doubt about their feelings of desperation. But there is a second point that needs to be made. All the Greek heroes (bar Achilles and Patroclus) are in the field. It would be quite astonishing if the Trojans were suddenly to be able to drive them back by their own unaided efforts.

But if it is only with the help of Zeus that the Trojans can achieve such ends, how is the poet to achieve the mighty victory for the Trojans that Zeus has promised for the next day (starting in Book 11)? By continuing to allow Zeus, through Hector, to manufacture an easy victory for them, as he has done in Book 8? Or does the poet have another strategy? Indeed he does.

One final point. It is quite common in Homer for an action which is foiled first time round to succeed at the next attempt. So Poseidon refuses to join battle here, but does so in Book 13; and Hera cannot intervene here, but does so in Book 14.

Main sources for the commentary and related reading
Fenik (1968) 219-28; Kirk (1990); Willcock (1978); Willcock (1995); Wilson (1996).

1-52. [25th day: second day of combat] Zeus warns the gods not to help either side, and departs for Mount Ida.

6. *my ruling* (**R-J**); *what the heart urges* (**H, L**): from now on, Zeus will enforce his command that the Greeks start to lose and will intervene to ensure they do e.g. 8.130-44. Pro-Greek gods will fight against this decree, sometimes with temporary success – the route to the fulfilment of Zeus' will is never direct – but Zeus' point that fate is involved (see Intro) will keep them quiet for some time (until Poseidon's pro-Greek intervention in Book 13 and Hera's in Book 14).

13. *Tartarus*: see on 2.783. Its iron gates and bronze threshold are mentioned to suggest how difficult it will be to escape from. See on 1.591 for gods being hurled out of Olympus.

25. *Olympus*: it is hard to see precisely how Zeus can haul up earth and sea and hang it from Olympus when Olympus, a mountain in Thessaly, is itself part of the earth. Zeus may be fantasising wildly here, but the gods understand the point well enough (their horrified silence, 28).

40. *not in earnest* **(R-J, H)**; *not in ... anger* **(L)**: a most odd thing for Zeus to say, destroying the point of all his earlier threats. One might argue that he holds Athene in special affection (cf. 5.877-80), but he reacts uncompromisingly enough towards her at e.g. 8.402-6.

41. *horses*: cf. Poseidon's journey at 13.23-38.

48. *Gargarus*: the highest peak of the Mt Ida range, where Zeus can keep a firm eye on proceedings and make sure no god tries to get round his orders. For its smoking altar (where Hector sacrificed) cf. 22.169-71.

53-197. The Greeks retreat; Diomedes saves Nestor, but Zeus hurls a thunderbolt. Hector mocks Diomedes and urges on the Trojans.

56. *fewer*: see Agamemnon at 2.119-33.

60-5. *advanced/advancing* = 4.446-51. It is typical for battle to begin with the general picture.

66-7. *the morning*: = 11.84-5.

69. *golden scales*: these appear at crucial moments – here, to signal the Greek retreat which will continue (with brief rallies) till Achilles reappears in Book 20, and at 22.209-13 to signal the death of Hector (cf. 16.658). The balance of the 'losing' side always tips down to the earth, signifying the descent to Hades.

75. *thundered* **(R-J, H)**; *crashed* **(L)**: thunder and lightning are regularly taken as signs from Zeus (e.g. 7.479-81, 8.171), lord of the skies and wielder of the thunderbolt. But only in Book 8 does Zeus hurl it at the army (e.g. here and 133), though cf. 17.593-6 where he shakes the aegis at the Greeks. Book 8 is full of omens of this sort, e.g. 133-6, 170-1, 246-52. The wise old Nestor, who gets them right, is contrasted with the youthful Diomedes, who on this occasion does not (but cf. 5.601-6).

80. *Nestor*: in another epic, the *Aethiopis*, Nestor's horse was shot by Paris, the Trojan ally Memnon rode up to finish him off, but Nestor's son Antilochus came to the rescue in the nick of time, losing his own life in the process. 'Neo-analysts', who attempt to find the source of Homer's poetry in other epics, claim this incident here in Book 8 was adapted from the *Aethiopis* by Homer, with Hector and Diomedes replacing Memnon and Antilochus. They may be right, but given the typicality of the episode, it is not possible to say for certain. See **GI** 2(vii) and cf. Fenik (1968) 231-7, who points out the similarities with the scene at e.g. 17.610-18.

81. *trace-horse* **(R-J)**; *one of his horses* **(H)**; *his horse* **(L)**: since a chariot was pulled by two horses and this horse's contortions confuse the other horses (86), it must be a trace-horse, i.e. a reserve, harnessed along-side the other two in case one of the main horses is put out of action. This never, in fact, happens in the *Il.*, in which only trace-horses are killed (here and at 16.467-8).

94. *like a coward*: this seems a harsh judgement on Odysseus when everyone is in retreat (78-80).

97. *did not hear him properly* **(R-J)**; *had no ear for him* **(H)**; *gave no attention* **(L)**: a famous problem – did Odysseus just not hear properly, or did he hear but ignore? The latter would be a serious charge; the former is more likely (cf. Odysseus' heroic stance at 11.404-10). Odysseus and Diomedes often act together, e.g. at 10.242ff. in the night expedition; and in other Trojan war stories, they murdered Palamedes, stole the Palladion, etc.

104. *attendant* **(R-J)**; *lieutenant* **(H)**; *henchman* **(L)**: i.e. Eurymedon (114).

106. *bred by Tros* **(R-J)**; *of Tros' stock* **(H)**; *Trojan* **(L)**: (correct **L**) see 5.319-27 and on 5.222.

113. *Sthenelus*: Diomedes' usual driver (5.108).

120. *Eniopeus*: it is typical for a driver to be killed, e.g. 8.312, 16.463, 737. This is also a rare example of fighting *from* a chariot, cf. **GI** 13B(vi).

131. *against Ilion* **(L)**: i.e. inside.

137. *reins dropped/escaped*: typical, cf. 5.583, 16.403.

143. *will/purpose of Zeus*: for the idea that men cannot resist the gods' will, cf. 2.116, 5.601, 9.23, 14.69 etc.

149. *ran away* **(R-J)**; *to flight* **(H)**; *running before me* **(L)**: heroes did not run for it unless there was no other option. Cf. Hector at 6.441-3.

162. *pride of place*: i.e. at feasts, the warrior's reward for putting his life on the line, cf. 12.311. There is a tremendous confidence about Hector at the moment, heartened as he is by the Greek retreat and Zeus' signs. Hence his contempt for the Greeks' new defences.

182. *fire*: this signals the start of a plan that will be fulfilled at 16.112-23. One might argue with it strategically, since the only way to get rid of the Greeks was either to defeat them outright or otherwise persuade them to sail away, which they could not do if their fleet had been destroyed. But that issue is never raised. See on 15.420.

185. *Xanthos ... Podargos ... Aithon ... Lampos* **(H, L)**: since warri-ors drove two-horse chariots, this line, in which Hector urges on four horses, is clearly not Homeric (it is omitted in **R-J**). Further, the verb in 186 says 'You *two*'. The names of the horses have been lifted at random from different contexts: Xanthos is Achilles' horse 16.149, Podargos belongs to Menelaus, and Aithon/Aithe to Agamemnon 23.295, and Lam-pos is a horse of the Sun god, *Od.* 23.246.

188-90. *before all others ... as for me* **(L)**: emend. The Greek means that Andromache fed the horses *before* she ever fed Hector. Warriors take great care of their horses and talk to them (as here, cf. 19.400-3, where a horse answers back). Zeus even pities and talks to Achilles' horses when Patroclus is dead (17.441-58). The point is that horses are expensive,

aristocratic creatures (see on 5.25), requiring much attention to stay in top
trim, cf. 5.192-203.

189. *wine*: this was probably mixed with the wheat (as in **R-J, L**): the
ancients are known to have given their horses wine. Like the warriors,
horses are also expected to repay their privileged life of luxury with high
performance on the field.

192-95. *shield ... body-armour/corselet*: these are never heard of
again; and is Diomedes not wearing Glaucus' armour (6.234-5)? Hector is
inventing a picture of what they might capture in order to inspire his troops
with the prospect of fantastic booty. **L**'s 'cross-rods' are probably 'hand-
grips'.

**198-252: Hera fails to persuade Poseidon to help the Greeks, but
Agamemnon rallies them.**

203. *Helice ... Aegae*: Poseidon had a cult at Helice (in Greece, **R-J**
map 4), and a palace under the sea at Aegae (see on 13.21), presumably
somewhere off the coast of Turkey, unless Homer is thinking here of Aegae
in Greece.

213-14. *ditch of the wall* (**L**): i.e. all the space (away from the ships)
between the ditch and the wall. This space is filled with Greeks, not
Trojans: the Trojans will cross the ditch and breach the wall in Book 12.

218. *if/had not ... Hera*: as Athene suggested at 8.36, the gods would
advise the Greeks, even if they could not directly help them.

221. *purple cloak* (**R-J, H**); *coloured mantle* (**L**): to draw attention to
himself? Hardly a sensible, let alone effective, tactic in the middle of a
battle. It is never used again.

230. *Lemnos*: during the Greeks' journey to Troy, nearly ten years
ago. Boasts are commonly made during feasts, e.g. 20.83-5.

236-7. *is it one of our ... now* (**L**): read 'have you ever deluded any
mighty leader like this before?' On the Greek concept of reciprocity
between man and god, see **GI** 7A. Agamemnon is always complaining that
he has been 'deluded', e.g. 9.18, 19.88, though with some justification if
he was thinking of the deceitful dream sent him by Zeus (2.8-15). See on
1.412.

250. *Zeus of the Voices* (**L**): i.e. of omens.

**253-349: After some Greek success, Hector wounds Teucer with a
rock, and the Greeks run in panic back to their new defences round
the ships.**

255. *ditch*: the Greeks had earlier been hemmed in between wall and
ditch (212-15).

266. *Teucer*: Ajax's half-brother (see on 2.406). This picture of
Teucer hiding behind Ajax's great shield (7.219-23) is unique.

274. *Orsilochus*: a typical run of deaths, cf. 5.677-8, 704-10.

285. *glory*: see on 6.440 for bringing glory to one's father.

290. *tripod*: this is probably an elaborately worked bronze tripod + cauldron, i.e. a large circular container with three legs attached to it, used for cooking but, in luxuriously decorated form, also given as a show-piece prize or gift, for display.

304-5. *Castianeira ... Priam*: Priam is (in Greek eyes) a barbarian ruler, and therefore has children by many women, cf. Laothoë 22.46-8, and see 24.496-7.

306. *poppy*: a moving C-simile.

312. *Archeptolemus*: the second of Hector's charioteers to be killed (see 118-29).

328. *sinew* (**L**): read 'bowstring'.

335. *Zeus*: the wounding of Teucer in the left shoulder, affecting the hand that holds the bow, leads to a Greek retreat, with Zeus intervening again, this time on the Trojan side (cf. 245-52).

338. *As (when) a ... hound* (**R-J, L**); *as when a dog* (**H**): D-simile. L's 'watches for the beast to turn upon him' suggests the beast might counter-attack, but the Greek means 'follows the beast's every twist and turn'.

345. *reached the ships* (**R-J**); *alongside/beside the ships* (**H, L**): so fierce has been the Trojan attack that the Greeks have taken refuge behind the defensive wall. They are now the ones under siege, the Trojans the besiegers. Night intervenes to save the Greeks from further destruction (8.487-8).

348. *Gorgon*: see on 5.741. Hector is presumably using his chariot (which we have not been told he remounted, cf. 320) to enable him to pick off more quickly any Greeks who have not crossed the ditch.

350-484: Zeus sends Iris to warn Hera and Athene not to help the Greeks. Zeus returns from Mount Ida and foretells further success for Hector till Patroclus dies and Achilles returns to battle.

363. *Eurystheus*: the third of a group of stories about Heracles in the *Il.* (for the Laomedon story, see on 5.638, for Heracles' birth, death and attack on Pylos, see on 5.392). Here, as one of his twelve labours, Heracles is ordered by Eurystheus to fetch the dog Cerberus from Hades; cf. 15.639-40 where we hear of Copreus, who was Eurystheus' message-carrier to Heracles, and 19.131-3, where Zeus grieves over the tasks Eurystheus set him.

370. *Thetis*: see 1.500-10. Thetis did not in fact 'kiss' Zeus' knees, but Athene feels hard done by here and exaggerates what happened between them. Cf. Hera's accurate account at 1.557.

384-96 = 5.733-7, 745-52.

397. *Zeus*: he now intervenes decisively to assert his will, as he had threatened to do at the start of the book (10-12), and returns to Mt Olympus from Ida (8.47) to deliver his lecture to the goddesses (438-40). The goddesses succeeded in their intervention at 5.711ff.; here, they fail.

428. *on man's behalf*: cf. **GI** 5C. Gods, like men, must bow to superior force.

435. *white-plastered/polished/shining*: see on 13.261.

447. *Athene and Hera*: Zeus addresses the two goddesses with rich sarcasm.

455-6. *one hit in your car ... Olympos* (**L**): read 'once hit by the lightning stroke you could never have come back to Olympus in your chariot' – because Zeus was going to smash it to pieces (402-5).

457-62 = 4.20-5.

463-8 = 8.32-7. Hera's comment fits much better here than it does in Athene's mouth at 8.32-7.

470. *At dawn tomorrow* (**R-J**); *In the morning* (**H**); *Tomorrow* (**L**): Zeus reinforces Hera's point about the destruction of the Greeks (465) by promising yet more destruction. This is the first of a number of occasions on which Zeus alerts the listener to the future. The result is that we know what is to happen, but the characters do not. It is a narrative device typical of tragedy, greatly increasing our fears and sympathies for the humans involved – in this case, Achilles' dearest friend Patroclus (whom we have not heard of since 1.345) and (by implication) Hector. The prophecy also comes as a thunderbolt – what has the death of Patroclus to do with Zeus' promise to Achilles? As the omniscient narrator later admits (see on 17.272), Zeus had nothing against Patroclus. One wonders whether Zeus' plan for Achilles' return, with increased honour from the Greeks (see on 1.511-12), is already unravelling, if Patroclus is to be caught up in it so disastrously. For the way in which Homer reveals the future incrementally, piece by piece, with hints dropped here and there but never revealing his full hand at any one stage, see Latazc (1996) 105-6.

471. *a still mightier son of Kronos* (**L**): Zeus is referring to himself.

477. *divinely decreed* (**R-J**); *way of fate* (**H**); *fated to be* (**L**): there is no point in arguing whether Zeus is controlled by 'fate' or not. The poet is not a theologian. The poet wants to alert the audience to the dreadful implications of Thetis/Zeus' plans – this is how it will be – and to provide a plausible reason for the pro-Greek gods staying out of the fighting for a while.

479. *Iapetus*: a Titan, father of Prometheus. See on 2.783.

485-565: Night falls, breaking off the fighting. Hector, full of confidence about the next day, addresses the Trojans. The Trojans spend the night camped on the plain in front of the Greek defences.

490. *river*: i.e. Scamander (**R-J** maps 1, 2).

494. *eleven cubits* (**H, L**): five metres. Cf. on 6.319.

497-541. Hector makes plans to camp out on the plain for the night in front of the Greek defences – so the Trojans will need to bring food from Ilium (505), light fires (509) and ensure guard is mounted round the city (519) – and expresses his hopes that tomorrow he will drive away the

Greeks (527-8) and kill Diomedes (533-4). This is Hector at his most confident (536-41). It is (at the moment) a blameless confidence, based on ignorance of what Zeus really has in mind (Redfield [1994] 138). It will turn out to be utterly misplaced (the ironic 'dear to Zeus/loved of Zeus' at 493, cf. on 13.54) because, unknown to him but not to us, Zeus is using Hector merely as a means to fulfil his plan, whose purpose is to bring Achilles back into the fighting (474). Nevertheless, Hector will enjoy one victorious day, as Zeus has implied (473) and will confirm at 11.192-4, a day that will see Hector becoming less and less open to reason.

533. *to/against the wall*: i.e. the walls of Ilium.

548 + 550-2. *They accomplished ... immortals* + *in its fragrance ... strong ash spear* (**L**): these lines are rightly omitted by **R-J** and **H**. First, they imply that the gods divided up the meat of the sacrifice among themselves – a quite unHomeric idea; second, the sentiment that *all* the gods hated Troy is quite at odds with our *Il.*; third, the lines occur in no manuscript of Homer, but are quoted as being 'by Homer' in a dialogue attributed to Plato (*Alcibiades II*, 149d), in which the speaker says the lines refer to the Trojans camping out. In 1711, Joshua Barnes inserted the lines at this point in the *Il.*

555. *As (when) ... the stars*: a superb D-simile, likening the fires burning on the plain in front of Ilium to the stars on a clear night. It is almost as if the land is a reflection of the sky. Note the human perspective, the shepherd rejoicing (559), picking up the Trojans' 'hopes/high thoughts/hearts' (553), i.e. the simile responds to Trojan joy at their victorious position. Cf. 9.76-7, 232-5 where the Trojan fires strike terror into Greek hearts; see de Jong (1987) 133.

Book 9

Introduction

In Book 8, Homer described how Zeus had turned the tide of battle, and the Trojans swept the Greeks right back behind their new defences. At the end of the book, Hector and the Trojans were all confidence, camped out on the plain in front of the Greek camp. Here at the start of Book 9, after all their successes (even without Achilles) in Books 4-7, the Greeks are in despair at this unexpected turn of events.

A public assembly of the whole army is summoned and Agamemnon, as often, is at panic stations (17-28). Diomedes replies with a powerful rallying speech, committing himself firmly to the cause whatever anyone else does (46-9), which all the Greeks vigorously applaud. One is now half expecting another stand-off of the sort that took place between Agamemnon and Achilles in Book 1, but Nestor at once intervenes. He applauds Diomedes but suggests a more balanced view of the situation is required (60-1). He sensibly proposes to set up an early-warning system against a Trojan attack designed to meet with the listening army's approval – guards by the ditch outside the walls (66-7) – and goes on to defuse any incipient public quarrel between Agamemnon and Diomedes by suggesting that the leading men discuss the matter in private over a meal (i.e. not in public assembly). In this way, he tactfully absolves Agamemnon from the responsibility of replying to Diomedes, and removes Agamemnon from the public arena where fragile heroic tempers like his can easily fray.

In private Nestor proposes a two-pronged approach to Achilles: he must be won round by gifts and winning words (113). Agamemnon agrees he has been in the wrong (115-20), and at once lists fabulous compensation (121-156), an offer meant to solve the problem once and for all. But it comes with conditions: first, that Achilles abandons his anger, i.e. returns to the fighting (157-9); and second, that Achilles acknowledges that Agamemnon is leader (160-1).

The demand may not be tactful – hardly the 'winning words' Nestor suggested at 112, especially the reference to Hades at 158-9 – but it is not unreasonable *from Agamemnon's point of view*. The heroic world works by material compensation for wrongs done. Once the wrong is corrected, the world resumes its normal shape, i.e. one in which Agamemnon is leader and his status as such is acknowledged. Nor, in principle, should the gifts have been unreasonable from Achilles' point of view either (after all, Athene had already proposed that way out in Book 1, and Phoenix will make the same case at 526, 602-5).

Nevertheless, Nestor has seen that, since Achilles left the fighting primarily because of Agamemnon's humiliating and insolent attitude towards him (1.203, 205), it will require more than a cheque in the post, however vast, to get him back; the gifts would have to be mediated to him with those 'winning words'. So Nestor selects Achilles' oldest and most persuasive friends (cf. 9.197, 204, 630, 641-2) to do the job (163-9), quite properly excluding Agamemnon, who would not recognise a winning word if it bit him on the nose.

But Homer now faces a serious narrative problem. If Achilles accepts the offer, the *Il.* ends here. He must therefore refuse it, and in such terms that it is impossible for the embassy to make him an offer which he *will* accept, otherwise they will just keep on coming back again (as Achilles sees, 310-11). So Homer cannot simply make Achilles say 'I want more women from Lesbos', because the embassy would agree at once to as many lorry-loads as he demanded. How, then, can Homer construct a reply by Achilles that justifies his (basically unjustifiable) rejection of the embassy, without making Achilles himself appear completely unreasonable?

Homer has in fact laid the ground-work for the reply already by ensuring that Achilles has never actually *said* that compensation would solve the problem (cf. on 1.213). At 1.216-18, for example, he merely agrees not to kill Agamemnon; and his request to Thetis to intervene with Zeus centres on first, getting Agamemnon to see how deluded he has been in not respecting the best of the Greeks (1.411-12), and second, ensuring his own honour is restored (1.353-6, the subject of Thetis' plea to Zeus, 1.508-10). In other words, it is only the *Greeks'* assumption that compensation will solve the problem. Given heroic material values, the assumption is perfectly reasonable. It is not their fault if it turns out to be irrelevant.

It is important to stress that Achilles' argument does not question the *theory* of compensation. It questions the *nature* of the compensation on offer to *him*: the issue is personal. To put it simply, can gifts alone make up for a humiliating and outrageous personal insult done to a great man like himself by (as he sees it) an inflated second-rater like Agamemnon – an insult so deep that Achilles asked his mother to persuade Zeus that Greeks should die in numbers because of it? As Achilles crucially puts it, Agamemnon has to 'pay back the whole heart-rending insult'/'pay me the full price for all this wrong that pains my heart'/'make good all this heart-rending insolence' (387). Gifts compensate for the loss of Briseis. If that was all that was at stake, there would indeed be no problem (cf. 379-82). But Achilles feels he has lost much more than that – the hurt is emotional ('heart-rending') – and as the speech unfolds it becomes apparent that the key issues are not only his own feelings of humiliation but also his hatred of and contempt for Agamemnon, a leader who thinks he only has to write out a large cheque (which he can transparently afford) to whistle Achilles back into the fold.

So Achilles' intense and powerful speech winds round these two big issues. *But what can the embassy do about these*? And what, for that matter, can Agamemnon? This is why Homer's construction of Achilles' speech is so brilliant: it remains in key with Achilles' character, and therefore seems reasonable, while at the same time putting the issue facing the embassy in such terms as to make Achilles' case unanswerable. All the embassy can do is to try to persuade him to relent and accept the gifts, an attempt doomed to failure because gifts are irrelevant to the problem as Achilles sees it (cf. Achilles' later analysis of his feelings about Agamemnon at 16.72-3). That is why Achilles rejects the embassy, and why his feelings of hurt remain consistent throughout, e.g. 615 in reply to Phoenix, 646-8 in reply to Ajax.

Interestingly, it is the youthful Diomedes who, when the embassy returns, will point out that all the gifts in the world were never going to stop Achilles doing what Achilles' *feelings* moved him to do (698-703). Diomedes understands that the problem lies, not in the theory of compensation or heroic material values, but in the sort of *person* Achilles is, i.e. impossible (cf. Ajax at 628-9, 635-6). The embassy, however, insists on seeing the matter in terms of gifts, even after Achilles' reply to Odysseus in which he unconditionally rejects them. Thus the climax of Phoenix's appeal is that Achilles may lose the gifts if he returns too late (600-5); Ajax insists that Achilles has a good deal – seven girls in place of one, and much more besides (637-9)! But Achilles is not keeping a ledger: he is nursing an explosive grievance against Agamemnon.

Each of the three ambassadors approaches the task of persuasion in a different way. Odysseus dutifully lists the gifts, but buttresses them with a description of the dire plight of the Greeks, their need of Achilles (230-51) and an acknowledgement that Achilles' hatred of Agamemnon may be unbudgeable, but at least he should take pity on his fellows (300-6). This twin appeal to Achilles' sense of pity and need for glory gets nowhere. Phoenix appeals to Achilles' sense of loyalty to his old tutor (culminating at 493-5); his allegory of the *Litae* constructs the embassy not as conveyors of gifts but as suppliants (520); and ends with the story of Meleager who was never given the gifts he was promised because of his obstinacy. That three-pronged attack produces a slight shift in Achilles' position (618-19). Ajax appeals to the ties and obligations of friendship (640-2), which produces another slight shift (650-5): at least Achilles is now prepared to stay on. But the embassy has failed: Achilles has rejected the gifts and will not be rejoining the fighting. It is left to the young Diomedes to get to the nub of the matter – forget Achilles; he is just being Achilles; he will return when he feels like it; meanwhile, we fight on (697-709).

Main sources for the commentary and related reading
Edwards (1987) 214-37; Hainsworth (1993); Griffin (1995); Willcock (1978); Wilson (1996).

1-181. [Evening and night before 26th day] Agamemnon is desperate, and Nestor proposes that an approach be made to Achilles. Agamemnon sketches the compensation he will offer. An embassy consisting of Phoenix, Odysseus and Ajax is sent.

2. *panic*: Trojan confidence at the end of the last book contrasts strongly with the Greek reaction to events here, trapped as they are behind their defensive wall (8.343-7). Homer portrays the panicky emotions of the army alongside their leaders' 'grief', presumably at their losses **(R-J)**.

4. *As the north* **(R-J)**; *As (when) two winds* **(H, L)**: D-simile, which, as it emerges at the end of the simile (8), rather surprisingly reflects the destruction of Greek morale. It is rare for a storm-simile to illustrate human feelings. These north (west) winds blow from Thrace, and would therefore strike the coast of Asia/Turkey and its islands – the sort of observation which a poet living on that coast, but not necessarily on that coast alone, would make. Cf. on 2.144, 4.422. See **R-J** map 3.

10. *heralds*: see on 1.54 for the assembly-sequence. In fact the assembly will make no decisions: Nestor sees to that.

14-15. *like a (dark) spring*: B-simile, almost identical to 16.3-4. See on 1.349 for heroic tears.

18-28. = 2.111-18 + 139-41. In Book 2, Agamemnon was not revealing his true feelings, but testing the army's reaction. Here his true feelings do surface. Agamemnon is often subject to panic attacks when the situation looks really bleak, and relies on others to save the situation, e.g. 14.65-81.

35. *you said/saying I was*: at 4.370-400. See on 4.412.

36. *all this is known* **(H)**; *know all these things* **(L)**: i.e. know how far I am a weakling and coward **(R-J)**, i.e. not at all, as we know from his *aristeia* in Book 5 when he wounded Aphrodite and Ares and captured Aeneas' horses, etc.

38. *sceptre*: in other words, Agamemnon is all show and no delivery, a remark that goes to the heart of Achilles' criticism of him too (e.g. 1.225-32).

42. *If you, for one* **(R-J)**; *If your own heart* **(H)**; *But if in truth* **(L)**: Diomedes here repeats the same accusation against Agamemnon that Agamemnon had made against Achilles at 1.173.

44. *Mycenae*: one hundred ships came with Agamemnon, more than with anyone else (2.576).

48. *We two* **(R-J, L)**; *the two of us* **(H)**; cf. Achilles at 16.97-100.

52-78. Nestor has a difficult task in hand. The Greeks were enthusiastic about Diomedes' attack on Agamemnon (50-1), signalling their willingness to stay and fight. Nestor has to acknowledge that, but without offending Agamemnon who is notoriously touchy in public; he also has to push the debate on without offending Diomedes, whose speech contained no proposals for action. Nestor therefore begins by applauding Diomedes' words but pointing out that he is a young man and has not taken the whole picture into account; and goes on to assert his *own* authority, as an older man, to deal with a situation where internal discord among the Greeks (a clear hint at Agamemnon's inability to lead effectively) will be a disaster.

63. *outlaw(ed)*: Nestor appeals powerfully to the Greeks' sense of community. Discord among them at this moment (which Diomedes' speech virtually invited) will be a disaster: hence Nestor's assertion that anyone who goes for that option is an outlaw from 'clan/brotherhood, law and home/hearth'.

66. *sentries/guards*: the Greeks are now behind their defensive wall, and the guards will patrol outside the wall, between the wall and the ditch.

69. *Agamemnon*: Nestor tactfully puts the words into Agamemnon's mouth for him.

71. *Our* (**L**): read 'Your'.

72. *Thrace*: cf. 7.467-72, where the wine comes from the island of Lemnos. Cf. on 4.345 for the bonds that such feasting creates among the leaders. Agamemnon has a special responsibility here, since he lives off the work of others (see on 1.121-307).

96. *Most glorious/lordly Agamemnon*: Nestor again flatters Agamemnon's power and authority, pointing out that he will get the credit, no matter whose suggestion is adopted (the meaning of **L**'s 'All shall be yours when you lead the way', 102).

99. *sceptre*: see on 1.238.

107. *Briseis*: see 1.346-7, and **GI** 10C.

109. *dissuade* (**R-J, H**); *urged ... not to* (**L**): see 1.275-84. Since Nestor was indeed the only one to attempt an intervention in the quarrel in Book 1, he has some right to take a position here.

112. *talk him round* (**R-J**); *appease* (**H**); *persuade* (**L**): sensitive to Agamemnon's pride, Nestor does not assert himself by demanding a course of action: instead, he suggests how they might consider proceeding, with 'soothing gifts and winning words/kind persuasion' (**L**'s 'supplication' does not reflect the Greek at this point). Agamemnon gratefully takes the bait.

115. *blind folly* (**R-J**); *blindness* (**H**); *madness* (**L**): see on 1.412 and cf. 19.78-144, where Agamemnon reiterates the theme of blind folly, and 2.375-8, where he blames Zeus and himself.

117. *that/this man*: i.e. Achilles – ironic, in view of the fact that (according to Agamemnon) Zeus should honour and love leaders like Agamemnon (1.174-5).

120. *gifts*: the gifts do indeed represent sensational compensation, fully in tune with Athene's promise (1.213-14; compare, for example, what Priam offers Achilles for Hector's body – twelve robes, cloaks, sheets, mantles and tunics, ten talents of gold, two tripods, four cauldrons and a special cup, 24.229-35). Indeed, Agamemnon goes even further than mere gifts, offering Achilles ties of marriage (141-8) and control over seven cities (149-56) as well.

122. *tripods*: see on 8.290.

130. *I chose*: see on 1.121-307.

139. *pick out* (**R-J**); *choose for himself* (**H, L**): in other words, enjoy the privilege that would normally be Agamemnon's alone.

145. *Iphianassa*: even if this is Iphigeneia (whom later Greek authors thought was sacrificed before the expedition set out for Troy), we may still wonder where Electra has gone to. Ancient mythology is fixed only in limited ways.

158. *Hades*: Agamemnon's analogy is extreme, but telling. The god Hades never yields, and is therefore hated. Let Achilles yield, in case people start to hate him too.

160-1. *rank higher* (**R-J**); *the greater king* (**H**); *kinglier* (**L**): cf. Agamemnon's claim against Achilles at 1.185-7.

164. *nobody could say* (**R-J**); *no one can now find fault* (**H**); *none could scorn* (**L**): because Agamemnon's offer is ultimately rejected, it is easy to condemn it out of hand. But Nestor obviously thinks it stands a good chance of doing the job, and he has no further suggestions to make to Agamemnon on that score. Agamemnon, in other words, has delivered his side of the deal as far as the Greeks can see.

168. *Phoenix*: he had brought up Achilles, loved him dearly (9.438-45, 485-95) and would exert the strongest claims of loyalty over him; he had also led the fourth line of Achilles' ships that came to Troy (16.196). Homer never explains why Phoenix is not at this moment among Achilles' absent retinue, nor where the centaur Cheiron fits into all this (see on 4.219). The poet, as often, produces what the moment requires, irrespective of other considerations.

169. *Ajax*: the greatest fighter after Achilles (2.768) and a blunt talker, not given to long speeches (see **GI** 1E and on 625).

Odysseus: ever resourceful and persuasive (cf. 3.221-4).

170. *heralds*: to give the mission an official authority: this is no private initiative. For Eurybates, see on 2.184.

176. *libations*: to bring the gods on-side. See on 1.471.

180. *especial eye for Odysseus* (**R-J**); *Odysseus most of all* (**H, L**): Homer does not tell us why Nestor singles out Odysseus. We can only guess that Nestor thinks Odysseus is the key man here – he, after all, was the man *par excellence* for 'soothing words' – or that Nestor wanted to ensure that Odysseus spoke first (9.223-4)?

181. *Peleion* (**L**): i.e. Achilles.

182-429. Achilles welcomes and feeds the embassy, and Odysseus makes the offer, adding an appeal to Achilles' sense of pity. Achilles rejects it outright, saying he will return home next day.

182. *They walked* (**R-J**); *So they went* (**H**); *So these two walked* (**L**): a notorious problem, the most famous in Homer, highlighted by **L**'s 'two'. Greek possesses verb-, noun- and adjective-forms (called 'duals'), which are used when two people are doing something. These forms are used here with reference to the mission, almost without exception, up to 198 (i.e. up to and including Achilles' welcoming words). The problem is that, as we have just seen, there are *three* members of the mission. One can argue e.g. that Homer has confused the language relating to a three-man mission with the language associated with heralds, of whom two (as here, 170) may be the standard number on such occasions (cf. 1.320ff., 11.139-40); or that dual forms can mean 'more than two' (not true); or that this is a sign of multiple authorship, i.e. the composer of a mission with two ambassadors (Odysseus and Ajax) was overtaken by a later composer who added Phoenix and forgot to change the duals; or perhaps it is a sign of Homer's own re-working, and he himself has 'nodded' over the duals (see on 1.424). It is interesting that, when Homer might have used a dual – Odysseus and Ajax offering a libation on departure from Achilles' hut – he uses the regular plural instead (656-7). We can assume Phoenix is the 'third party', because at 192 Odysseus is said to be 'leader', even though Nestor nominated Phoenix to lead (168); and because Phoenix has been a complete unknown up to this point. Page (1959) 297-315 produces a typically scintillating argument for multiple authorship.

182-224. An extended arrival + reception (*xenia*) scene. For arrivals, see 2.167 (here, 182 'goes' + 185 'arrives', 186 'finds', 187-91 'description of the scene', 193 'goes up to'). This now becomes a reception sequence: 193 rises, 196 'welcome', 199 leads in, 200 seats, [description of food and drink], 221 eat, 222 end meal, 224 talk. Cf. the arrival and reception of Nestor at 11.768-80. Such scenes dominate the *Od.* (see Reece [1993] for a full analysis). The feeding scene may seem out of place here, given that the mission has just eaten in Agamemnon's hut (90), but Achilles is not to know that and, anyway, it is a vital part of the social institution of *xenia*. Achilles' excessively warm greeting (note the strong wine, 203) seems an extremely hopeful sign. Achilles does not enjoy being out of the fighting (1.490-2); now all he can do is sing to himself about the *kleos* (plural) of men (189) – his own, one wonders, or that of others? The 'Triptolemus painter' (480 BC) depicts the scene; see Woodford (1993) 73.

183. *holder and shaker* (L): i.e. Poseidon. They pray to him presumably because they are travelling along the sea-shore and Poseidon is a pro-Greek god.

184. *Aiakides* (L): 'of the family of Aeacus', i.e. Achilles (Aeacus was his grandfather, 21.188-9).

188. *Eëtion*: see on 6.395.

189. *singing*: Achilles cannot carry out heroic deeds; he celebrates them instead.

190. *in silence*: Patroclus says nothing during the whole mission. His silence may be associated with his gentle character (17.204, 670, 19.300, 21.96, 23.252, 281) or his respect for Achilles' authority. It is tempting to think he may be sitting in silent judgement on the whole issue (preparing us for his attack on Achilles in Book 16), but the concept of the 'unmentioned, silent but significant onlooker' is not one that Homer seems to have developed.

197. *greatly I need you* (L): Achilles would never say that! Read 'there is great need of me' (H) or, less pointedly, 'something urgent must have brought you here' (R-J). The Greek does not in fact say what there is a need of, or to whom.

198. *even to this my anger* **(L)**: read 'however angry I am (i.e. with the Greeks)'.

203. *less water* **(R-J)**; *wine stronger* **(H)**; *stronger drink* **(L)**: see on 1.470.

208. *chine* **(H, L)**: the lower back.

209. *Automedon*: see on 16.145.

210. *spitted*: Achilles is making kebabs. When the fire has died down (212), he spreads the embers (213), lays the kebab-laden spits across them on their 'supports/blocks/andirons', salts (214) and roasts them.

220. *firstlings* **(L)**: i.e. the offering of kebabs.

223. *Odysseus caught the signal* **(R-J)**; *noticed* **(H)**; *saw* **(L)**: see on 180 above.

225-306. Odysseus' speech. This is a brilliantly structured rhetorical performance, in five parts: (i) 225-8 – Odysseus thanks Achilles for the meal and comments on his generosity, creating (he hopes) a warm atmosphere in which to negotiate. (ii) 229-31 – Odysseus states the case he intends to make: that Achilles must return, or their ships will be destroyed. This is something of an exaggeration, but it makes the point forcefully enough. (iii) 232-46 – Odysseus describes how the situation arose: the Trojans are near at hand; Zeus favours them with omens; Hector is irresistible and determined, praying for victory; Odysseus himself is afraid the gods may allow it to happen and the expedition be destroyed (cf. 2.229-32, where he argues precisely the opposite case). This is powerfully put, and again, somewhat exaggerated, but Odysseus is pulling the stops out. (iv) 247-8 – Odysseus' recommendation: return to the fight. (v) 249-306 – the five reasons, or 'proofs', why Achilles should return: 249 you will regret it if you do not; 252 your father told you to control your feelings; 260 Agamemnon will offer compensation; 301 take pity on us and you will win great glory; 304 you might well kill Hector.

Observe that, outside the list of gifts, Agamemnon is barely mentioned. Further, the gifts do not form the climax of the appeal, but are hedged in with other considerations – the threat that there will be no going back once the ships are destroyed, the need for Achilles to remember his father Peleus' warnings (cf. on the importance of fathers, 6.440), and the appeal to Achilles' sense of pity and love of honour. It is as if Odysseus suspects that the gifts are not quite the knock-out punch that Agamemnon imagines them to be.

On the other hand, one wonders if it was sensible of Odysseus to leave Agamemnon so thoroughly out of the equation. While it was sound tactics on Odysseus' part to omit the demand Agamemnon made at the end of his speech – that Achilles had to defer to his superior status (160-1) – it was Achilles' personal quarrel with Agamemnon that created the whole problem in the first place (cf. e.g. 16.72-3). One wonders, idly, if any of this was what Nestor was talking about to Odysseus at 180-1 – a masterpiece of Homeric suggestiveness.

225. *You ... your* **(L)**: read 'we ... our'.

233. *next/close to/by the ships*: 8.343-9, 9.76-7.

236. *lightning/lightens*: presumably 8.75-6, 133-4.

239. *mad-dog frenzy* **(R-J)**; *mighty madness* **(H)**; *strong fury* **(L)**: cf. 8.337-42.

240. *His one prayer* **(R-J)**; *He is praying* **(H)**; *He prays now*: how does Odysseus know what is Hector is praying for? The orator in him is working overtime, but not without intelligence.

Dawn: cf. 8.530.

242. *fire*: see 8.180-3.

252. *Peleus*: Odysseus is able to quote Peleus' very words (254-8) because he had been with Nestor when Nestor visited Peleus' palace (11.766ff.). The words Nestor chooses to remember (11.782-3) are different.

255. *hold fast* **(L)**: read 'hold back, restrain'.

256. *consideration* **(L)**: read 'fellow-feeling' or 'good will'.

264-99. For the gifts, see on 122-57, and note at 299 Odysseus' omission of 158-61.

308-429. This speech is all about Achilles' *feelings* in the present, relating to his treatment in the past. It adds up to a devastating critique of the way he has been treated, combining assertions, questions, generalisations, arguments, and outbursts in about equal measure as he circles round and round the problem as *he* sees it. But he is unable to propose a tangible solution to it (a necessary part of Homer's literary strategy, see 9/Intro). Following the analysis of Griffin (1995) 108-9, it can be organised as follows:

308-14: Introduction: I am going to tell you the truth, however inconvenient.

315-45: My grievance against Agamemnon, under two headings (a) one gets no reward for merit, (b) I have put all my efforts into the war on his behalf.

346-63: Agamemnon's situation without me.

364-77: my position without Agamemnon.

378-416: his gifts mean nothing to me: life is what counts.

417-29: the Greeks should return home; Phoenix can stay here if he wants.

See Griffin (1995) 108ff., Edwards (1987) 222-4, Reeve (1973), Claus (1975).

312. *the man who thinks one thing* **(R-J)**; *hides one thing* **(H, L)**: Achilles is talking about *himself* here, as a man who tells the truth, come what may, and is determined to make his position crystal clear. The words can hardly refer to Agamemnon or Odysseus, as some argue, since neither of them is lying. Their offer is genuine, and they want Achilles back. Further, there is nothing in Achilles' speech itself to suggest anyone has been lying to him (344, 375 refer to Agamemnon's cheating of him – i.e. giving something and taking it away again without justification). It is indeed a fine irony that both Achilles and Agamemnon refer to Hades at such significant points in their speeches (158, 312), but this hardly justifies the conclusion that Achilles has sensed what Agamemnon had said about the hatefulness of Hades at 158-61 and noted that Odysseus omitted it (for the opposite view, see Taplin [1992] 66-73).

318. *share* (**R-J, H**); *Fate* (**L**): the Greek *moira* has both meanings, and both can be applied – a true 'ambiguity', a fine word which, these days, is regularly weaselled into meaning 'it is impossible to tell what the author is saying here'. The three short, pithy sayings that make up 318-20 present a powerful image of man desperately trying to control his anger at his treatment: head and heart are battling it out in him.

323. (*mother*) *bird*: Achilles' language is rich in imagery (e.g. 9.385, 648, 18.109-10, 21.282-3, 22.262-4) and the image of a parent and child, with Achilles as the parent, features here and 16.6-11; compare 18.318-22, 23.221-5. See Moulton (1977) 100ff. One can sense Achilles' anger beginning to rise after this point, reaching a climax in the list of furious rhetorical questions at 337-41.

327. *for the sake of … women* (**R-J, L**); *over their wives* (**H**): Achilles here thinks of the female booty he has captured in his various raids, e.g. Chryseis and Briseis, and of the reason for the whole war, Helen.

333. *dole it out* (**R-J**); *share out* (**H**); *distribute them* (**L**): see on 1.121-307 for this system.

336. *wife* (**R-J, H**); *bride of my heart* (**L**): Briseis is not really Achilles' wife, though she had hoped to marry him (19.297-9); Achilles needs to pretend she is in order to make an effective comparison between her and Helen (340-1).

349. *wall*: see 7.436-41.

354. *Scaean*: see on 3.145, 6.237.

356. *As it is/But now*: the Greek *nun de* (lit. 'now but', English 'but/so now') is a key to understanding Achilles. He is constantly assessing what has happened, or what might happen, putting it behind him, *nun de* making an instant decision about what he will do next. Urgent, decisive, responding immediately to the world about him, Achilles makes his decision and takes the consequences. Unfortunately, others have to take them too. Cf. 18.88, 101, 114, 121, 19.23, 67, 148, 203, 275, 319, etc.

363. *Phthia*: Achilles' home. See 2.681-94.

381-4. *Orchomenus … Thebes*: Orchomenus in Boeotia was a powerful and wealthy city in Mycenaean times (its royal tomb is as grand as that at Mycenae). 'Thebes' looks as if it should refer to the other powerful Boeotian city, but it had recently been destroyed (see on 2.563-5); that is why Achilles 'corrects' the assumption and goes on to describe the fabulously wealthy Thebes in Egypt. See **R-J** map 5.

389-90. *Aphrodite … Athene*: see on 1.113.

395. *Hellas*: see note at 1/Intro.

401. *value/worth of (my) life*: at 12.310-21 the Trojan ally Sarpedon argues that heroes receive rich material rewards and are honoured as immortals because they risk death in the front line; and goes on (322-8) to argue that that, since death is unavoidable, a glorious death in battle will demonstrate they are worthy of it (and presumably win them the immortal reputation – *kleos* – that they crave). It is this equation that Achilles attacks: life is worth more than material possessions, even if he were to be rewarded with them (which he is not, 9.320).

405. *Delphi* (**R-J**); *Pytho* (**H, L**): Apollo is the archer-god, and his temple at Delphi (called 'Pytho' here, Delphi's old name) became very wealthy because of the offerings it received from those who consulted Apollo's famous oracle.

407. *tripods*: see on 8.290.

411. *two courses* (**R-J**); *two fates* (**H**); *two sorts of destiny* (**L**): we have heard so far of only one destiny for Achilles, that he will die young (see on 1.352). But in the context of his speech here, it makes sense for Achilles to claim he has the option of a long life, even though one without *kleos*, because Agamemnon's behaviour in Book 1 and response in Book 9 almost seem to Achilles to deny him any prospect of the heroic life he craves (see on 'focalisation', **GI** 10). We never hear of this option again (cf. 18.59-60, 95-6, 458, 21.276-8) – unless Achilles is referring to it at 16.50 (only to deny it), in reply to Patroclus' suggestion at 36.

426. *Phoenix*: he raised Achilles as a child and regards him as his son (9.485-95). Hence Achilles' warmth to him here.

430-622. Phoenix makes his appeal, remembering how he came to Achilles' home and raised him. He appeals to Achilles in the name of the gods of supplication (*Litae*), and tells the story of Meleager who also rejected gifts. Achilles says he will think again about returning home.

434-605. Phoenix's speech is the longest in the *Il*. It can be organised as follows:

(1) The obligations Achilles owes to Phoenix as a result of his upbringing:
434-47: Phoenix's commitment to Achilles.
447-84: how Phoenix came to be welcomed into Peleus' home.
485-95: how Phoenix raised the young Achilles.
(2) The duty Achilles owes to those who are now supplicating him:
496-514: the parable/allegory of the goddesses of supplication, the *Litae*/Repents/Prayers.
515-23: the duty this imposes on Achilles to accept the gifts.
(3) How Meleager missed out on gifts because of his obstinate behaviour, even though he eventually gave in to those supplicating him:
524-99: the story of Meleager.
(4) The moral for Achilles:
600-5: take the gifts now, while they are on offer and before it is too late: that way honour lies.

438. *Peleus*: like Odysseus (252-9), Phoenix too brings Achilles' father into the picture. Fathers are powerful influences; see on 1.1, and cf. on 4.376.

454. *Furies/Erinyes*: the guardians of human oaths and curses. They

live in the underworld and punish anything considered unnatural, especially relating to the family (e.g. children dishonouring parents); sometimes they send *Atê* on the wrong-doer (*Od.* 15.233-4).

455-6. *I ... on my knees* (**L**): read 'he ... on his knees'. It was
traditional for a child to be accepted into the family by being placed in his
grandfather's lap (*Od.* 19.401-2).

458-61. *I then planned ... father-killer* (**R-J**); *My thought ... Achaians*
(**H**); *Then I took it ... Achaians* (**L**): these lines appear in no manuscript of
Homer, but are quoted by the second-century AD essayist Plutarch (*Mor-
alia* 26F), who says the ancient editor Aristarchus removed them because
he was shocked by Phoenix's admission that he had considered killing his
father. They were introduced into the text by Joshua Barnes (1711). The
lines are probably genuine, since the Phoenix story is (somewhat awkwardly) designed to parallel Achilles', e.g. both stories feature a quarrel
over a woman (Achilles and Agamemnon over Briseis in Book 1, Phoenix
with his father over the girl); this involves anger (Achilles and Amyntor)
and supplication (Phoenix is supplicated not to leave his home [465], as the
embassy is supplicating Achilles here); and Phoenix thinks of killing his
father, as Achilles did Agamemnon (1.193-8). See Scodel (1982).

465. *entreat/y/ies* (**R-J, H**); *supplications* (**L**): it is not made clear why
Phoenix's relatives entreated him to stay, but the narrative point is that it
makes a parallel with Achilles being supplicated by the embassy.

495. *a wretched end* (**R-J**); *shameful destruction* (**H**); *hard affliction*
(**L**): Achilles was Phoenix's insurance against a miserable old age (cf.
24.488-9) and lonely death. In later classical times, children were legally
obliged to care for their parents. It is noticeable that the *Il.* hints at another
upbringing for Achilles, with the centaur Cheiron. See on 4.219.

501. *supplicat/e /ing* (**R-J, L**); *prayers* (**H**): Phoenix prepares the
groundwork for the allegory of the '*Litae*/Repents/Prayers' by describing
how men can turn aside the gods' anger by supplicating them (see **GI** 7D)
and offering gifts: if even gods can relent at such an approach, surely
Achilles can too.

502-14. The allegory of the *Litae* is designed to point out to Achilles
where he is going wrong. It puts the embassy on a new footing, as
suppliants (see on 520), and so offers a new perspective from which
Achilles can be invited to consider matters, quite unrelated to his feelings
about Agamemnon or Agamemnon's about him. The general picture seems
to be as follows: 'Delusion/Folly/Ruin' (i.e. *Atê*, see on 1.412), which is
strong and fast, causes A to offend B. A can then choose to supplicate B
for forgiveness (*Litae* being 'supplications', 505-7). If B accepts and the
original offence is wiped off the slate, the *Litae* will bring B benefits (509);
but if not, the *Litae* go to Zeus and ask that *Atê* strike B down (510-12).
Phoenix, in other words, is arguing that Agamemnon has offended; the
embassy has come as Agamemnon's suppliants to Achilles; and he should
accept them, for fear of being struck down himself in the future.

503. *wrinkled*: the *Litae* are represented as slow, wrinkled and with eyes askance, because no Greek willingly abased himself by supplicating another.

513-14. *be given/their honour … others* **(L)**: i.e. you must cultivate a frame of mind that gives the *Litae* that same respect which makes even 'lordly' men yield.

520. *supplicate/in entreaty*: Phoenix here presses home the meaning of the *Litae* allegory.

523. *up till now* **(R-J)**; *before this* **(H, L)**: Phoenix makes it clear that Achilles, having been in the right before, will put himself in the wrong if he rejects the gifts. He will therefore also, by implication, be subject to *Atê* sent by Zeus, 510-12.

529. *The Curetes*: this is a complicated story, especially as it starts with a battle whose explanation does not emerge till 547. The version given here summarises the story in its natural sequence and fills in the gaps left by Homer:

529-46: the goddess Artemis, insulted by Oineus, king of Calydon, sends a boar to ravage his land (in Aetolia, north of the entrance to the gulf of Corinth; **R-J** map 5). Oineus' son Meleager organises hunters, including the Curetes, a neighbouring Aetolian people, and kills it.

547-72: but the Aetolians and Curetes then fight each other over the division of the spoils (the boar's head and hide). In the course of this, Meleager kills the brother of his mother Althaea, and she puts a curse on him. So Meleager withdraws from the fighting, together with his wife Cleopatra (her history is given, 556-65), while Althaea prays for his death.

573-99: as a result the Curetes get the upper hand and look as if they will capture Calydon. Meleager rejects all supplications, until his wife Cleopatra finally succeeds in persuading him to return to the fight. He drives off the Curetes – but never receives the promised gifts.

The story of Calydon, like that of Thebes (see on 2.563-5 and 7.132) and Troy, was essential material for the oral poet, one of the great cycles of stories under which myth was organised. The story of the Calydonian boar in particular was widely referred to and illustrated in the ancient world, since the hunters contained among their number a large number of ancient heroes, e.g. Jason, Theseus, Phoenix, Peleus, Nestor, Atalanta etc. It is interesting that many of these stories involve sieges, but the art of siege warfare is never convincingly described in the *Il.*, perhaps because siege-warfare does not lend itself to what the oral poets considered to be properly 'heroic' man-to-man, spear-dominated encounters between chariot-borne warriors. See **GI** 13B(ix).

Unfortunately, the *traditional* story of Meleager does not fit Achilles' situation very well, and Homer has to do a good deal of re-working to make it relevant. Its central feature, which Homer somehow has to 'forget', is that Meleager killed his mother's brother in a dispute over the boar hunt and she, enraged, threw the smouldering log that represented Meleager's life onto the fire, slowly killing him. This story is quite irrelevant to Achilles. If Meleager is dying, how can he withdraw from battle, be sent endless deputations, eventually return, and drive off the enemy – the story Homer has to tell (573-99) in order to make the parallel with Achilles? No wonder Homer's description of Meleager's anger with Althaea is so bafflingly brief (553-72). Likewise, it is not clear what is going on in the battle between the Aetolians and Curetes at 550-2. Are the Curetes trying to besiege Calydon, but failing because of Meleager? Is Homer trying to draw a parallel between the fighting prowess of Meleager and that of Achilles, if only he would return and fight? Whatever the weaknesses of the story, however, at least the final moral is clear enough. See Willcock (1964), Alden (2000).

537. *deluded* (**R-J**); *blindness* (**H**); *delusion* (**L**): *Atê* again. The fact that Oineus did not snub the goddess *deliberately* makes no difference to Artemis' reaction: all she cared about was the *fact* that she had been ignored. Reasons and excuses carried no weight with these gods.

556. *Cleopatra*: another very condensed story, i.e. Marpessa (Cleopatra's mother) had been seized by Apollo, but her husband Idas rescued her. Since Marpessa had wept like a kingfisher (Greek *alkuôn*) in captivity, they decided to call their daughter Alcyone. Why then does Homer call her Cleopatra? See on 590.

562. *sea-bird* (**L**): read 'kingfisher'.

568. *beat(ing)*: gods of the underworld were summoned by pounding on the earth, gods of Olympus by standing and raising the hands to the skies.

574-5. *elders supplicated/began to entreat*: now the parallels between the embassy to Achilles (supplicating him with gifts to return to battle) and Meleager begin to work. Observe that the last people to try are his best and dearest friends (586) – as the embassy to Achilles is described (198, 204, 520-2, 640-2).

590. *wife*: Cleo-patra at last succeeds in persuading him – a name made out of the same roots as that of Achilles' dearest companion, Patroclus. Her name can hardly be mere coincidence, given that Patroclus is the one who finally persuades Achilles to relent, at least partially, in Book 16. For another invented name, see on 10.314.

598. *got nothing* (**R-J**); *for nothing* (**H**); *no longer ... make good* (**L**): Phoenix switches the terms of the moral at the last minute: not 'take the gifts and fight, as Meleager did' (cf. 524-6), but 'do not miss out on the gifts by returning to battle too late, when the ships are burning'. Achilles does indeed not return till then, but still receives the gifts though by then they are irrelevant (19.243-8).

608. *Zeus decrees it* (**R-J**); *by the will of Zeus* (**H**); *in Zeus' ordinance* (**L**): Achilles is thinking of Zeus' promise to honour him (1.505-30).

609. *by my beaked/curved ships*: Achilles has either forgotten that he has just promised to return home next day (356-63), or he has begun to reassess the situation.

614. *side with him* (**R-J**); *feel love for him* (**H**); *love this man* (**L**): the Greek *phileô* can mean 'love', but its root meaning has to do with taking sides, and this is what Achilles is concerned about here – whose side is Phoenix on? Phoenix as a suppliant has appealed to Achilles. Achilles rejects the appeal because a suppliant throws himself on the supplicatee's mercy, and in Achilles' eyes, Phoenix has done nothing of the sort – he has merely been serving Agamemnon's interests. Hence his rather sharp reply to his old tutor. Nevertheless, Achilles does acknowledge that Phoenix's appeal has affected him (612), and changes his position very slightly: Phoenix and he *together* shall decide tomorrow whether to return home or not (617-19).

616. *rule … privileges* (**R-J**); *take … honour* (**H**); *be king … honour* (**L**): in other words, *if* Phoenix is on Achilles' side, he can expect to share Achilles' power when they get home. This is an odd sentiment at best, and may be a later addition, though it is hard to discern any purpose to it.

622-55. Ajax appeals to Achilles in the name of friendship. Achilles says he will consider returning to battle when the Trojans threaten his ships.

625. *let/'s/us go*: Ajax can take Achilles' hint (621-2) and offers a crisp parting shot rather than a speech, directed at Odysseus at first and referring to Achilles as 'he' until 'but you/your breast' (636). Ajax emphasises Achilles' savage unreasonableness (629), lack of any sense of comradely solidarity (630-2), his proud obstinacy (632-9) and rejection of ties of hospitality and friendship (640-2). It is the longest speech Ajax makes, though it is worth pointing out that he speaks more than Apollo, and of the 29 Greek speakers, he comes eighth in terms of total lines uttered (**GI** 1E).

633. *blood-price*: see 18.497-500, where Hephaestus depicts such a scene of judgement on Achilles' shield. It was the duty of the family to avenge murder, and this could be done either by killing the murderer or by reaching an agreement about compensation (cf. 18.497-503). There are many examples in Homer of homicides in flight from angry relatives, e.g. Patroclus (23.85-90, cf. the simile at 24.480-4).

639. *Be gracious* (**R-J**); *kindness* (**H**); *make gracious* (**L**): this is the word used in asking a god for help.

640. *under your/the same roof*: Ajax hints at the embassy's suppliant status, and invites Achilles to remember the obligations that exist between friends, to honour each other. Though Ajax still brings the gifts into the argument (seven women and much else, 638-9) he ends on a different note – mutual goodwill between comrades.

645. *I agree* (**R-J**); *after my own mind/feeling* (**H, L**): Achilles virtually admits that Ajax has won the argument, but still cannot bring himself to relent, such is his fury at his degrading treatment (646-8). That has been Achilles' bottom line all along, and the embassy has not changed it. But it has changed Achilles' view of the response he should make to the embassy, and now he shifts his position again: he *will* stay on, after all, and even *contemplate* joining the fighting, if Hector sets fire to the ships (651-3). Note, however, that Achilles makes no *promise* to fight, let alone for Agamemnon or the Greeks in general, let alone to *prevent* the firing of the ships in the first place. He is thinking primarily of his own ships (654-5). It is a concession, and better than nothing, but not what Agamemnon was after.

656-713. The embassy returns, and Odysseus reports its failure. Diomedes says it was always going to be a waste of time, and they must just fight on.

678. *has no intention* (**R-J**); *will not* (**H, L**): Homer has another serious narrative problem here. If Odysseus tells the Greeks what Achilles' real position is, i.e. that he would, probably, return when the Greek ships are fired, the suspense and drama of the impending Greek fight for their ships will be spoiled since they will know Achilles is going to come back, and he is bound to save the situation. Homer therefore has to construct a reply by Odysseus that is substantially accurate but does not give away this crucial fact. So, in a pedantic sense, Odysseus' report of the failure of the embassy is accurate in every carefully-worded detail. Achilles *is* indeed angrier than ever (679, cf. 646); he *does* reject Agamemnon and his gifts (679, cf. 378); he *has* told Agamemnon to take responsibility for saving the fleet (680-1, cf. 423-4); he *did* indeed 'threaten' to return home at dawn next day (682-3, cf. 359-61); he *did* say the Greeks should sail home (684-7, cf. 417-20); and Phoenix *is* staying the night, ready to sail home if he wishes (690-2, cf. 426-29). Finally, Odysseus claims that the heralds and Ajax agree with his account (688-9; Ajax certainly does, 627); and indeed, none of them stands up to object to it.

The problem is that the report covers up the concessions that Achilles made to Phoenix and Ajax, and does not make it at all clear that Achilles has decided to stay on. However, the concession made to Phoenix ('we shall think about staying on tomorrow') is clearly not worth reporting, since Achilles over-rides it with his concession to Ajax that he *will* stay on. Again, the concession made to Ajax, even though it means Achilles is now staying on, still makes no promises relating to any future acceptance of Agamemnon's gifts or any involvement in the fighting. Further, even if Hector does fire the ships, which he may not, Achilles could be interpreted as saying that that he will fight primarily to save his own ships, not to rescue the whole army, let alone Agamemnon, from their nasty situation.

In other words, Odysseus is reporting what is the case: that the embassy has failed to meet Agamemnon's requirements, stated at 157-61, and that Achilles is certainly not returning to fight now, and may not return, ever. Odysseus is doing simply what Achilles originally told him to at 421-6. Since these are the facts, Odysseus has no choice but to report them, as unambiguously as possible. In such a situation, pedantic niceties about Achilles' slight shift in position serve no purpose. Odysseus' speech, in other words, has made the Greek army clear where it stands in relation to Achilles: nowhere. The battle, for the moment, goes on without him.

For the disastrous consequences of Odysseus' failure to mention Achilles' compromise position, see on 11.788, 16.61; and cf. Scodel (1989).

702. *He'll/will fight again*: Diomedes 'reads' Achilles to perfection. See on 308-429 (last para.) above, and cf. on 16.61.

When his/the heart ... and (the) god: 'double motivation', i.e. Homer assigns to both man and god equally the responsibility for initiating an action (cf. 600, where Phoenix asks Achilles not to think as Meleager did, nor let a god encourage him to). The problem of personal responsibility for action is an age-old one, and Homer's solution is as good as any: the explanation, that both man *and* god are responsible, are parallel – the one does not exclude the other. It is, in fact, common in Homer, and archaic Greek thought generally, to explain the reasons for a man's actions in terms of external impulses coming from 'outside' him. But the poet does not use this as a means of excusing the characters – though the characters may try to. See on *Atê*, 1.412, and cf. on 3.164.

707. *you, Agamemnon/Atreides*: Is Diomedes getting his own back with these peremptory, if not wholly unjustified, orders to his commander? Cf. 9.32-49 and 4.365-421. Agamemnon will rise to the challenge with an *aristeia* at 11.1-283.

Book 10

Introduction

Book 10 contains a story of a night spying expedition by Diomedes and Odysseus which turns into the slaughter of the sleeping Thracians (Trojan allies) and their king Rhesus and the capture of his famous horses. Since antiquity, it has been considered a later addition to our *Il*. It has not, however, been shovelled into the epic without due care and attention. The poet, whoever he was, has taken care to shape it in such a way as to fit neatly in between Books 9 and 11: the action takes place at night (cf. 9.713), using the 'But X could not sleep' motif, cf. 2.1-2; Agamemnon is aware of the Trojans camped out close to the Greek defences (11-13, cf. 8.553-65); to start with it centres on the watchfulness of the guards (posted at 9.79-88); it mentions the ditch built at 7.440 (194) and refers to Hector's triumph the previous day at 8.486ff. before night intervened (200-1); and night is said to be well advanced before Odysseus and Diomedes set out on their adventure (253), which takes into account the time that would have been taken up by the assembly and embassy to Achilles in Book 9 and the earlier check on the guards. Nor is there anything wrong in principle with a night action. What are sentries for, if such action was not reckoned to be a possibility?

Nevertheless, the action of Book 10 is never referred to anywhere else in the *Il*. Uniquely, it could be removed, and one could not tell the difference. It contradicts the spirit of the end of Book 9, where the leaders applaud Diomedes (710) for suggesting a good night's sleep and telling Agamemnon to set an example next day; the episode with the guards is deadly dull, dragged out to unconscionable length and very little purpose (one could not imagine the Greeks had a crisis on their hands); the 'victory' of Odysseus and Diomedes over a sleeping Rhesus and his men is crude and unheroic; and the Trojans are consistently portrayed in a poor light, ring-composition in speeches is noticeably absent, and generally the language is naturalistic in style – all uncharacteristic of the rest of the *Il*.

We hear of two other versions of this story. One is that the Thracian king Rhesus caused such havoc among the Greeks that Hera and Athene sent Odysseus and Diomedes to kill him at night; the other involved an oracle saying that if Rhesus and his famous horses drank from Scamander, they would be invincible, so Odysseus and Diomedes killed him the night he arrived. Since neither of these scenarios would fit the *Il*. at this point, the poet has adapted the tale, motivating it through the suggestion of a spying expedition that, with the introduction of Dolon, turns into slaughter by night and the capture of Rhesus' horses. The story in itself is exciting enough, but it is not a *bona fide* part of our *Il*.

Euripides' *Rhesus* (if it is by Euripides) turns the story into a tragedy, based broadly on the Homeric version.

Main sources for the commentary
Hainsworth (1993); Willcock (1978).

1-193: Agamemnon and Menelaus cannot sleep for worry about the Greek situation, so they call a council and check on the sentries.

5. *As Zeus* (**R-J**); *As when the husband/lord* (**H, L**): D-simile, but an unconvincing one: it is hard exactly to see how Agamemnon's groans and fear can be likened to lightning flashes. Cf. 17.547-50 for a simile in which war and bad weather are events that Zeus foretells by a rainbow.

12. *fires*: cf. 8.554.

21. *he got up* (**R-J**); *He rose* (**H**); *He stood upright* (**L**): a dressing scene, cf. 29-31, 131-6, 177-8 (note the slightly exotic clothing of these scenes, cf. 3.17). For the general pattern, see on 2.42.

25. *Menelaus*: given how the leaders approved Diomedes' words at 9.710, it may be something of a surprise to find them so depressed here; that said, the situation was desperate at the start of Book 9, and nothing has happened to alter it.

27. *for his sake*: see **GI** 10 for the 'focalisation' of such sentiments through the mind of the character involved.

34. *armour*: what is Agamemnon doing putting on 'armour' over a large lion-skin (24)? One imagined the dressing scene had ended at 24 with him taking up his spear: perhaps that is what is meant by 'armour' here.

38. *spy*: this will in fact turn out to be the main purpose of these night operations, though the first job will be to ensure the guards are doing their job properly.

50. *no son of (the) god(s)* (**R-J, H**); *son neither of a god* (**L**): very few heroes indeed are sons of gods in the *Il*. Since those who are include e.g. Achilles, fated to an early death, and the Trojan allies Sarpedon and Rhesus, both killed in battle (10.494-7, 16.502-3), it does not seem to be much of an advantage (though Idomeneus and Aeneas both enjoy more luck).

56. *the important guard-posts* (**R-J**); *strong company of guards* (**H**); *sacred duty of the guards* (**L**): these were posted by Nestor at 9.66-7, 80-8. It is not made clear that Menelaus is to pick up Idomeneus and Ajax *en route* to inspecting the guards himself. They need specially summoning because their ships are at the end of the line (113). It will take another 124 lines and much tedious to-ing and fro-ing before this unexciting plan is delivered.

57. *son*: Thrasymedes (9.81); Nestor's other son is Antilochus, implied at 170 ('sons').

63. *run after ... order* (**L**): i.e. or come back to Agamemnon after he has given the guards their orders.

65. *wait here* (**L**): read 'there', i.e. with the guards.

69. *compliment* (**R-J**); *the honour* (**H**); *respect* (**L**): Agamemnon adopts a different and more generous tone here to e.g. his review of the troops at 4.336ff., and shows he is willing to roll up his sleeves himself (cf. e.g. 9.10-11, where he tells his heralds to summon the men).

101. *night attack* (**R-J**); *attack at night* (**H**); *darkness* (**L**): but the night always brings fighting to a close in the *Il.*, e.g. 7.282, 8.486-8.

106. *if (ever) Achilles*: Nestor has no reason whatsoever to believe that Achilles will change his mind. Has he forgotten the result of the embassy in Book 9 already?

110. *Aias … son of Phyleus* (**H, L**): i.e. Ajax son of Oïleus (see on 2.527) and Meges (see on 2.627). Diomedes will in fact fetch these (175-9).

123. *he looks to me*: Agamemnon is very solicitous of his elder, and weaker, brother, e.g. 4.148ff., 7.104-22, 10.240, and Menelaus is aware of Agamemnon's responsibilities (2.408-9).

125. *you mentioned* (**R-J**); *you are asking for* (**H**); *you ask after* (**L**): see on 56.

158. *kick* (**R-J**); *foot* (**H, L**): a standard way of waking friends (*Od.* 15.45) and in keeping with the following joky, rather un*Iliad*ic, tone of the exchanges between Nestor and Diomedes.

164. *tough one* (**R-J**); *hard* (**H, L**): it was Diomedes who had suggested a good night's sleep at 9.705.

176. *wake(n) up* (**R-J, L**); *rouse* (**H**): the laborious scenario becomes more complex, as yet another Greek leader is woken, dresses and sent off on a mission – Diomedes, to fetch Ajax son of Oïleus and Meges, to add to Menelaus fetching Idomeneus and Ajax son of Telamon (54) and Agamemnon picking up Nestor, Odysseus and Diomedes. One wonders when something significant is going to happen.

180. *guards/sentries*: the plan to check on the guards conceived at 56 is finally delivered – and lo, they are all awake (more than one can say for the reader/listener).

183. *As/Like dogs*: D-simile, catching well the uneasiness of expectant men on watch, peering into the darkness, listening out for any sound (187-9).

194-298: At the council Nestor suggests a night spying mission on the Trojan camp. Diomedes and Odysseus volunteer.

194. *ditch*: the guards were patrolling between the wall and the ditch (9.87); Nestor now, inexplicably, leads his council over the ditch onto the battlefield, with Meriones and Thrasymedes added to their number from the guard (they will contribute arms and armour, 255, 260).

200. *where/whence … Hector*: see 8.490-1.

208. *intentions* (**R-J**); *plans* (**H**); *what they deliberate* (**L**): Nestor's proposition is a feeble way of motivating the action. It is hard to see what is to be gained by finding out whether the enemy will stay or retreat, since that will become apparent in the morning anyway (though the disguised Hermes uses the same excuse at 24.401); and, in the event, Diomedes and Odysseus who are chosen for the mission do nothing of the sort.

212. *fame/glory*: since the leaders at this council attend the feasts that Nestor promises (217) anyway, and a ewe with its suckling lamb (215-16) hardly represents a cornucopia (cf. the gifts Agamemnon offered Achilles), it must be the glory that will drive the men to volunteer. At any rate, no more is heard of the material rewards.

240. *Menelaus*: see on 123.

245. *Pallas Athene*: she helps Odysseus win the foot-race at 23.774-83, as Ajax son of Oïleus there acknowledges, and cf. 2.166-84, 5.676, 10.278-82, 295, 11.434-8. It is in the *Od.* that Athene's relationship with Odysseus is fully developed.

255-7. *Thrasymedes*: the detail of the shield he gives to Diomedes is picked up at 14.9-11.

263. *tusks/teeth*: the famous 'boar's tusk' helmet, typical of the Mycenaean late bronze age period; tusks with holes bored in them for attaching to such a cap have been found, and the caps are depicted on ivory carvings. Since the poet appears to know so much about its construction, an example may have survived.

266-70. *Autolycus … Meriones*: since Homer chose to give the helmet a distinguished history, he clearly regarded it as worthy of notice. Autolycus is Odysseus' treacherous grandfather (19.395); Amyntor father of Phoenix (9.448). Eleon is in Boeotia, even though Phoenix says his father lived in Hellas (Thessaly, 9.447). Scandeia is the port of Cythera, an island off the southern Peloponnese. For Meriones (from Crete), see on 2.645. The helmet, in other words, has moved from northern Greece to an island off southern Greece and winds up yet further south, in Crete (cf. on 6.216). See **R-J** maps 4, 5.

278-94. *Hear me*: for the form of Odysseus' and Diomedes' prayers, see **GI** 7A.

282. *great deed/thing*: the poet prepares us for this to be more than a spying expedition.

286. *Thebes*: on Tydeus' exploits here, see on 2.563-5, and 4.376-400 (with notes). Observe the focalisation of the story through Diomedes, stressing in particular Athene's help.

294. *gold*: gilding the horns of the bull with gold made the sacrifice that much more precious and therefore more honorific. Cf. *Od.* 3.425-38.

297. *lions*: A-simile.

299-468: Hector invites a Trojan to spy on the Greek camp: Dolon volunteers and sets off. Odysseus and Diomedes catch Dolon, milk him for information and kill him.

299. *Hector did not allow* (**R-J**); *Nor … did Hektor* (**H, L**): a mirror-scene of the Greek council (both leaders awake, both summon a council, both propose a night expedition, both offer a reward, both are greeted with silence – 218, 313, etc.). Hector's scheme serves some marginally useful purpose: if the Greeks are planning flight and not guarding the camp, the Trojans can prepare themselves for their morning assault accordingly (unless, that is, they decide to watch them go, an unlikely event in the world of heroic enterprise, however strategically sound, cf. on 8.182). In fact Hector had already ordered fires to be kindled to light up any Greek retreat (8.507-11).

305. *chariot ... thoroughbreds/horses*: Hector's reward will prompt the horse-mad Dolon (who demands and is promised Achilles' horses, 323-31) to volunteer, and this equine interest lays the groundwork for Odysseus' and Diomedes' assault on Rhesus. Hector is clearly very confident of victory if he thinks he can capture anything belong to Achilles.

314. *Dolon*: the name, obviously invented for this episode, means 'shifty, slippery'.

316. *unattractive* **(R-J)**; *ugly* **(H)**; *evil* **(L)**: looks and character go hand-in-hand, see on 2.212 (Thersites). The poet is already signalling this man is a loser, making his claim on the mighty Achilles' chariot all the more absurd. He has no brothers, only sisters (317), suggesting to the male Homeric world that he is a milksop.

334. *wolf ... weasel/marten*: predatory and ignoble animals (further characterisation of Dolon).

344. *get/go ... past*: if the Greeks give chase too early, Dolon will merely turn back to the Trojan camp.

347. *away from the army* **(L)**: i.e. the Trojan camp.

349. *bent aside ... corpses* **(L)**: read 'lay down among the dead beside the path'.

351. *range* **(L)**: read 'width of a day's ploughing by mules'.

360. *dogs/hounds*: D-simile, unadorned but effective enough, used of Hector (8.338-40) and Achilles (22.188-93).

378. *ransom*: a typical request, e.g. 6.46-50.

385. *where is it ... walk* **(L)**: read 'where are you off to, coming ...'.

401. *big prize* **(R-J)**; *great/mighty gifts* **(H, L)**: Odysseus' smile at 400 indicates how amused he is by the idea of Dolon trying to control Achilles' chariot.

406. *Hector*: Odysseus is clearly thinking of a 'great deed' (202) – killing Hector.

409. *planning* **(R-J)**; *plans* **(H)**; *deliberate* **(L)**: Odysseus asks the questions to which they had been sent to find the answer (208-10) – not that Dolon ever answers them.

415. *Ilus*: after whom Ilium was named (21.215-32, cf. 11.166).

424-35. *in the same parts* **(R-J)**; *Together with* **(H)**; *mixed with* **(L)**: having heard that Hector is in council and the Trojans on guard (415, 418-19), Odysseus now finds out that the allies are asleep, unguarded – and the newly arrived Thracians the most distant and apart of all (434-5).

428-31. *Carians ... Maeonians*: the Trojans' allied troops extend from the north, with the Carians 'by the sea' (i.e. the Hellespont, see **R-J** maps 1, 2), to the south (Thymbra, 430, which lay on the river Scamander well south of Ilium). Dolon's account of the allies does not wholly square with the Trojan catalogue (2.819-77), but that is hardly surprising.

436. *horses*: Dolon, the great horse-fancier, cannot resist sharing his enthusiasm, giving Odysseus the idea for his 'great deed'; Nestor's original scheme promptly disappears out of the window.

447. *Dolon*: he has not actually told them his name.

455. *supplicate/entreat*: see **GI** 7D. The killing of Dolon is brutal, but cf. on 6.45 for supplication in battle.

463. *give you your due share* (**L**): read 'shall call on for help'.

464. *once again* (**L**): i.e. 'with equal success'.

469-579: Odysseus and Diomedes slaughter the sleeping Thracians and their leader Rhesus, take his famous horses and return in triumph.

485. *lion*: brief D-simile, adding little to the scene.

496. *evil/bad dream/nightmare*: this seems to mean that Diomedes appeared to Rhesus in a dream, unless it means that Diomedes was the equivalent of a bad dream.

497. *Oineus' son* (**L**): read 'grandson'.

498. *horses*: note that they do not take the chariot, however fabulous it was supposed to be (438). Yoking horses (who are unyoked at the moment, 474-5) was too lengthy a business, cf. 24.268-77. So they lose the armour too (504 – note how light the chariots must have been for Diomedes to consider carrying one off, cf. 23.533). Observe that the poet still uses the traditional language of the chariot + team, e.g. 513-14, where Diomedes (literally) 'mounted the horses, Odysseus hit [them] with the bow; and they flew to the ships' and 529-31 ('mounted again/got up behind'), cf. 11.519-20.

528. *arms/spoils*: see 462-8.

545. *how did you (two) get hold of/come by/win*: Nestor has forgotten about the original point of the mission. A fine pair of horses is much more important.

567. *tied the pair/horses*: since Odysseus did not bring any horses to Troy, Diomedes stables them. For all their magnificence, we hear no more about them.

576. *baths/tubs*: these sound rather civilised for the rigours of the army camp. Such bathing-scenes are more typical of the palace world of the *Od.* (e.g. 3.464-8, 10.358-64).

Book 11

Introduction

Book 11 begins an extraordinarily dramatic day, signalled by Zeus at 8.470-6, which will see the wounding of major Greek heroes (Book 11), the breaching of the Greek defensive wall (Book 12), a brief Greek rally inspired by the pro-Greek gods (Books 13-14) but soon stifled when Zeus wakes up (literally) to what is going on (Book 15), the firing of the Greek ships and the return to battle and death of Patroclus (Book 16), the recovery of his body from the Trojans (Book 17) and the decision of Achilles to return to battle to take revenge on Hector for Patroclus' death (Book 18).

At the end of Book 9 Diomedes had urged Agamemnon to set an example in battle the next day, to which at the beginning of Book 11 Agamemnon responds with a considerable *aristeia*. As if to highlight it, Homer omits the usual summons to battle and concentrates instead on describing Agamemnon's extended arming (15-44). His armour, decorated with snakes, a Gorgon's head, Panic and Rout, makes a terrifying sight (was it characteristic of Agamemnon to order armour with such images on it?); and when Hera and Athene thunder their approval (45-6), expectations are high.

But we know that Zeus has other ideas (Homer emphasises that the rest of the gods are staying well out of things, 75-9), and he is soon intervening, as he did in Book 8, to ensure that Greek success is limited. He protects Hector (163-4) and then sends Iris down with the crucial message that, once Agamemnon has been wounded, Hector will enjoy complete success for the rest of the day (181-213). Armed with this unambiguous evidence that Zeus is on his side, Hector, confident enough in Book 8 (see on 8.541), will from now on cling to an increasingly blind and ultimately fatal conviction that he cannot lose. When Agamemnon is duly wounded and retreats from battle (251-3, 267-83), Hector leads a rally, and even the exuberant Diomedes realises that the Greeks cannot win (317-19), though this does not stop him taking on Hector and nearly killing him (343-67, cf. 8.130-71).

In Book 8, Homer used interventions by Zeus to drive the Trojans up to the Greek defences. Homer does not drop this narrative tactic yet – it must still be made clear that Zeus is controlling the situation – but introduces an additional device to explain the Greek defeat: in Book 11, he removes a number of major and some minor heroes from the Greek side by having them wounded. Agamemnon has already gone that way; Diomedes now follows (373-400), then Odysseus (434-88), the doctor Machaon (505-20) and Eurypylus (579-93). These will not return to the fighting again in the *Il.*, though they will give advice and some of them even compete in Patroclus' funeral games in Book 23.

This is very bad news indeed for the Greeks, but good news for Homer. Since it would be unthinkable for the Greeks to be so badly mauled for so long if *all* their major heroes were on hand, the poet can now explain why the Greeks are on the back foot for the rest of the day, and will need serious divine intervention (while Zeus is not looking) in Books 13 and 14 to prevent total disaster. Further, the consequence of this narrative decision will be to thrust into the limelight Ajax (most of all), Menelaus and Idomeneus of the major heroes, and minor ones like Oïlean Ajax, Teucer, Antilochus, Meriones and Meges to bear the brunt in Books 12-15. It will also whet the audience's appetite for the return of Patroclus and, eventually, Achilles.

Homer begins the whetting at once. Achilles sees that Machaon has been wounded and sends Patroclus to find out what is going on (598-616). It is a fatal summons, which the poet marks with a rare narratorial intrusion to mark the moment (603). Patroclus arrives in Nestor's hut to make enquiries and is trapped by the old man, who seizes the opportunity to plant in the sympathetic and impressionable Patroclus' mind a message for the hard-hearted Achilles, creating a 'sort of emotional chain-reaction as a route of access to Achilles' (Taplin [1992] 176). In his longest speech in the *Il.* – indicative of this episode's importance – Nestor tells Patroclus a tale of one of his own, most brilliant, single-handed youthful exploits. Its purpose is three-fold:

(1) 670-763: to alert Patroclus to what a single hero can achieve on his own, and the glory he gets from his achievements, 760, in contrast to Achilles, who will get no 'advantage/profit' at all from his brilliance in battle 761-2;

(2) 764-88: to remind Patroclus of the advice of his father Menoetius, to give Achilles wise counsel (787-8);

(3) 789-802: to suggest what that wise counsel should be – that if Achilles remains obstinate, he (Patroclus) should ask to be allowed to return to the fighting, in Achilles' armour (795-802).

With that message ringing in his ears, Patroclus sees the wounded Eurypylus limping away from battle (808). Patroclus clearly expects to hear the worst from him (815-20) and does so (822-35), proving the truth of Nestor's account of the Greeks' desperate plight and the urgent need for help; and even though he knows he ought to get back to Achilles (837-40), he insists on staying to see to Eurypylus' wound. This episode is designed to reinforce Nestor's message to Patroclus: the Greeks are indeed in serious trouble and he or Achilles must act.

Patroclus' decision to attend to Eurypylus back in his hut (841-2) also serves a structural purpose. It creates the space in which the Homer can depict the Trojans sweeping right *into* the Greek camp, a sequence of events the poet would not be able to describe were Patroclus to go straight back to Achilles. This Trojan advance takes place in the course of Books 12-15. We pick up Patroclus again at 15.390-405, where he abruptly abandons Eurypylus, and 16.2ff., when he arrives back in Achilles' hut, weeping with anguish.

Main sources for the commentary and related reading
Fenik (1968) 78-114; Hainsworth (1993); Willcock (1978).

1-83: [26th day: third day of combat] Agamemnon arms for battle. All the gods except Strife stay away, while Zeus watches from Olympus.

1. *Dawn … Tithonus*: Dawn is the goddess Eos, who fell in love with the mortal Tithonus (brother of Priam, 20.237). She persuaded Zeus to make him immortal, but forgot to ask eternal youth for him at the same time.

4. *Hate* (**L**): read 'Strife'.
emblem/portent/sign: whatever this was – the aegis (see on 1.202)?

5-9. *She took … flanks/hands/strength*: = 8.222-6.

12-14. *heart(s) … fathers/land*: = 2.452-4.

16-46. *armour/bronze*: an arming scene, greatly elaborated cf. on 3.328-38. Note the fabulous body-armour made of dark blue-black inlay, gold and tin, 23-8; the snakes, 26, 39 (which always cause fear, cf. 3.33-5); gold rivets/nails in place of the usual silver, 30 (cf. on 3.334); and the amazing shield with Gorgon, 36 (see on 5.741). This is seriously élite armour, worthy of the wealthy leader of the expedition from '(deep) golden Mycenae' (46).

24. *inlay* (**R-J**); *enamel* (**H**); *cobalt* (**L**): enamel, powdered glass fused *in situ* by firing, may be Mycenaean in origin (*c.* 1425 BC) but was never common; and a few examples have also been found in Cyprus *c.* 1200 BC. None has been found in Greece, however, till the sixth century BC; see R. Higgins, *Greek and Roman Jewellery* (Methuen 1980), 23-8. Cobalt, a blue pigment derived from cobalt ore, has been found as a colouring agent in Mycenaean times (Higgins, 42). But it is most likely that the poet is thinking of niello (Higgins, 28), a blue-black alloy of silver, lead, copper (etc.), used to fill in engraved designs on silver or other metals, producing a decorated effect. It was probably inserted in powder form, gently heated till soft and then worked. Niello is commonly found on engraved Mycenaean daggers.

32. *man-covering/enclosing, covering*: this epithet suggests the poet is describing a full-body shield (see on 6.117), but the mention of rings/circles (33) means that the shield is the smaller, circular one.

43. *spears*: since Agamemnon has two, these are presumably throwing spears, but Agamemnon stabs with them anyway (e.g. 95-8). See Saunders in Friedrich (2003) 135-7.

45. *Athene and Hera*: their acclaim heralds the beginning of Agamemnon's *aristeia* (see on 5.1-8 for the typical pattern).

47-52. *The warriors/Then each/Thereupon … behind (them)*: i.e. those who fought from chariots walked across the ditch and waited on the other side; they were followed by their chariots + drivers, who arrived later.

At 12.118-19 it appears that a causeway must have been left over the ditch, so that chariots could cross it without having to go down into the ditch and up the other side (never mind about the stakes lining the top). It must be said that in the battle scenes Homer tends to concentrate on the immediate action in hand, and the whole picture has to be pieced together bit by bit.

54.   *blood*: a sinister sign (cf. Zeus weeping for Sarpedon at 16.458-61), to be fully justified by the most bloodthirsty action yet. Since Zeus is watching and enjoying every moment (80-3), it is likely that the Greeks are going to start to lose.

56.   *break* (**L**): i.e. high ground, rise.

57.   *Po(u)lydamas*: the first appearance of an important figure, whose function will be to advise and warn Hector.

62.   *bale star* (**L**): i.e. baleful, menacing, deadly star. D-simile, the star in question being Sirius, the dog-star, equally menacing at 22.26-31, where it refers to the gleam of Achilles' armour. Stars usually describe armour (see on 5.5), not the movement of a warrior; here Hector's armour is likened to lightning (A-simile, 66). There are fifteen similes in this book, an indication of the extent to which the battle sways back and forth and heroes come and go – moments which attract similes.

67.   *like reapers* (**R-J**); *as bands* (**H**); *like two* (**L**): similes describing the general scene often herald the start of action (e.g. 4.422-56), and this is the third in five lines, soon to be followed by a fourth ('like wolves', 73). A D-simile, it likens the soldiers cutting down the enemy to lines of reapers mowing down the corn, cf. 18.550-6.

72.   *The pressure held their heads on a line* (**L**): i.e. this is a massed assault, and it brings the armies 'head to head' (cf. **H** 'The battle held them even'). See **GI** 13B(v)(b).

73-83.   *Hate/Strife … (being) killed*: at 3-12, Strife urges on the Greeks. She is in her element here, the very personification of battle, but all the other gods are heeding Zeus' warning, delivered to them at 8.5-27, to steer clear. Zeus is still on Olympus, where he had arrived from Mount Ida to rebuke Hera and Athene (8.438-9); he will return to Ida at 11.183.

84-180: Agamemnon enjoys success, and the Trojans retreat.

84-5.   *Right through/For as long/So long … falling/under them*: = 8.66-7.

86.   *mid-morning meal* (**R-J**); *dinner* (**H**); *supper* (**L**): this is a very long day indeed, the next day not beginning till Book 19. Since Homer tells us the battle was equal during the morning as the sun rose (84-5), and signals the advent of evening at 16.779 when 'the sun began to drop – towards the time when the ploughman unyokes his ox', the woodman's meal here must be taken mid-morning. It all makes for a sensational afternoon and evening's events, covering Books 11-18.

90.   *broke the enemy line(s)/battalions*: the retreat of the Trojans signals the start of Agamemnon's *aristeia*. It ends with Agamemnon's wounding at 252-4 and retreat at 283.

92-100. *Bienor ... Oïleus*: the first of three pairs that Agamemnon kills in sequence in his opening attack (Isus + Antiphus 101-21, Peisander + Hippolochus 122-54). For killing pairs, cf. Diomedes' achievements and notes on 5.10ff. and 5.144-65.

94. *oppose/face*: not all charioteers are so courageous, see e.g. on 5.576.

98. *brain*: a grisly death, typical of Agamemnon: see on 5.76, and cf. 12.185-6. Note the stab, cf. on 43.

102. *bastard*: typical, see on 5.70.

103. *one/single chariot*: for two men in a chariot killed by one on foot, see 5.159.

104. *before/once ... by Achilles*: typical, cf. Lycaon at 21.35-47. Note that they were shepherding flocks when caught, cf. **GI** 3 and see **GI** 1C for raids of this sort.

105. *knees* (**L**): i.e. spurs.

108-9. *spear ... sword*: see 5.144-7.

113-21. *As a lion*: superb D-simile, with a most unexpected point of comparison emerging at the end. It begins with a lion killing fawns, and one imagines it will end 'So Agamemnon (main subject) killed the brothers'; then at 116 the doe is introduced, unable to save her fawns and running in terror, and that turns out to be the point of the simile when the comparison is made at 120 – so the *Trojans* (main subject) could not *save* the brothers because they, like the doe, were in flight (121). It is not uncommon for similes to change direction like this: see 155, 172 below.

124. *gold*: no wonder Antimachus could offer a large ransom (131-5), but the mention of his name is enough to do for the two brothers (138-42). That Paris needed to bribe people to support him in not giving up Helen throws interesting light on e.g. the Antenor-Paris exchange at 7.350-64.

128. *reins*: typical, see on 8.137.

131-5. The brothers' appeal is almost identical to that at 6.46-50.

140. *Menelaus ... Odysseus*: more filling in of the past (cf. 3.205-24, and see **GI** 1C.).

147. *like a log/log-like*: A-simile, describing another of Agamemnon's grisly slayings (see on 98 above).

150-62. *Footsoldiers ... wives* (**R-J**); *soldiers cut down ... wives* (**H**); *footmen ... vultures* (**L**): Homer now pictures a scene of general carnage, with a fine simile and image of empty chariots, before focussing on the Trojan retreat and Zeus' intervention (163-209).

155. *As a raging fire* (**R-J**); *As when annihilating/obliterating fire* (**H, L**): D-simile, suggesting at the start that Agamemnon will be the main subject, likened to a raging fire, but turning out at the end to be about the Trojans, mown down by Agamemnon's onslaught, cf. on 113-21 above. For fire similes, cf. 20.490-4.

160. *empty chariots*: typical, see 15.453, 16.370-1, 379.

163. *Zeus*: Homer 'explains' why Hector had not been rallying the Trojans.

167-70. *Ilus ... fig tree ... Scaean gates ... oak tree*: for these four Trojan landmarks, see 10.415, 21.558 (see note here), 24.349; 6.433 and 22.145; on 3.145; and 6.237, 7.22, 9.354.

171. *each side endured the other* (**L**): read 'waited there for the others'.

172. *like cattle/cows*: again (see 155 above), a C-simile which likens the Trojans to cattle stampeded by a lion; halfway through, the focus changes to the lion (175) killing a cow, and the simile turns out to be not about the Trojans as the main subject but Agamemnon on the rampage (177). Cf. on 155 above.

181-283: Zeus descends to Mount Ida and tells Hector to re-join the battle when Agamemnon is wounded. This happens, and Agamemnon leaves the field.

194. *the sun sets/goes down*: as it will at 18.239-41, hurried on by Hera, who wishes to see an end to Hector's promised day of success as soon as possible (see 8/Intro).

202. *As long as*: as usual, the message is repeated in almost exactly the same words to the recipient (cf. e.g. 2.160-5 = 176-81).

211-14. *Hector ... Greeks/Achaians*: = 5.494-7, 6.103-6.

218. *Muses*: at moments of high drama, especially turning-points, the Muses are summoned to ensure the story is accurate. See on 1.1 and cf. 2.484.

224. *grandfather Cisses*: (not Kisseus, cf. on 6.299). Theano, daughter of Cisses, was priestess of Athene and married to Antenor (see 6.298-300). One of their sons was Iphidamas. As we learn here, Iphidamas was raised by his grandfather Cisses, who married him to another of his daughters (i.e. Iphidamas' aunt!). See on 5.414.

233. *missed*: the battle sequence is typical – A misses, B hits but fails to pierce, A kills B. Cf. 13.601-17, 22.273-330.

239. *against him* (**L**): i.e. dragged the weapon (and Iphidamas) towards himself.

241. *unbreakable sleep* (**R-J**); *bronze sleep* (**H**); *brazen slumber* (**L**): H, L translate literally. Sleep and Death are twin-brothers (16.672), sons of Night (Hesiod *Theogony* 211-12); cf. 14.259, where Night rescues Sleep from Zeus. Sleep is bronze because it cannot be broken. The relationship between Sleep and Death has been much pondered since Homer articulated it. Gilgamesh recognises it too: 'the sleeping and the dead are just like each other, Death's picture cannot be drawn' ('Gilgamesh' X vi, in Dalley [1989] p. 109).

242. *pitiable/unhappy*: emotional focalisation by the poet who promptly drops back into severe, 'objective', factual mode, generating further intense pathos, cf. e.g. on 4.474 and in general **GI** 10. The fact that Iphidamas is a Trojan does not weaken the poet's sympathetic impulse.

250. *fallen brother*: for brothers supporting brothers, cf. 11.428, 14.476, 16.320.

252. *struck/stabbed*: the wound foretold by Zeus at 191. Cf. 4.467-8 for a soldier exposing himself to attack as he bends over to retrieve a body.

257. *dragging*: typical, cf. 4.467, 14.477.

269. *As sharp pangs* (**R-J**); *As when a woman* (**H**); *As the sharp sorrow* (**L**): a unique (D) simile for a unique occurrence (i.e. fighting till a wound forces retreat).

271. *Hera*: goddess of the family and childbirth. Artemis is goddess of childbirth too: gods have overlapping functions in the ancient world.

284-342: Hector enters the battle successfully, but Odysseus and Diomedes fight back.

292. *As (when) a/some hunter/huntsman*: two brief similes, of a hunter here and a squall at 297, introduce Hector into the fighting (see on 5.5).

301. *Asaeus ... Hipponous*: a 'catalogue' slaying (see on 5.677).

305. *as a storm force/west wind*: C-simile, with the main subject (apparently Hector) turning at the end into the people he killed (309), and the simile starting with the storm but focussing on its impact on the waves and the foam it sends flying.

312. *Odysseus*: the rallying call from Odysseus to Diomedes compares with that at 8.92-8, where Diomedes calls on Odysseus to no avail. They kill pairs, i.e. Trojans in retreat in their chariots (see on 5.144-65).

330. *prophet/seercraft/prophecy*: it is typical for a prophetic father to foresee death, cf. 5.148-51, 13.663-72.

336. *intensified* (**R-J**); *strained ... (taut)* (**H, L**): H, L translate accurately an image of stretching to represent the intensity of the fighting (cf. 12.436, 13.358-9, 14.390, 15.410-13, 16.662 and especially 17.401, preceded by its leather-stretching image).

338. *Agastrophus*: cf. 17.612-23, where Idomeneus, on foot, only just gets away when his charioteer is killed and Meriones comes to the rescue. It was the job of the driver to keep his chariot near the fighter in case he needed them for pursuit or retreat, and could be a very dangerous business (see on 15.447); cf. **GI** 13B(vi).

343-400: Diomedes stuns Hector, who retreats and recovers. But Paris shoots Diomedes in the foot. Diomedes leaves the field.

345. *was shaken/shuddered/shivered*: cf. 5.596.

353. *three-ply and hollow-eyed* (**L**): i.e. with three layers of protective material (bronze and/or leather), and eyeholes in the visor.

355. *sinking/dropped/dropping*: cf. Aeneas at 5.309-10, Sarpedon's fainting at 5.696 and Hector's recovery at 15.10, 240. It is strange that

Diomedes does not follow up with his sword at this point rather than chase his spear, but Homer must find some way of preventing Hector being killed.

362-7. *You dog … I can find* **(R-J)**; *Dog … others* **(H)**; *Once again … others* **(L)**: = 20.449-54.

368. *son of Paion* **(H, L)**: i.e. Agastrophus (338).

369. *Paris/Alexandros*: when Paris shoots, he always hits, cf. 580-2, 13.660-72. For this scene with its arrow-shot, boasting and withdrawal of weapon, cf. Diomedes and Pandarus, 5.95-105, 276-96. Diomedes is the second major Greek to be wounded and retreat (400), after Agamemnon. That he is (uniquely for the *Il.*) wounded in the foot has suggested (to some) a similarity to Achilles, killed by a shot from Paris in the heel. See 5/Intro.

385. *Typical archer* **(R-J)**; *You sorry* **(H)**; *You archer* **(L)**: archers are very effective fighters (e.g. Teucer at 8.273-6), but the heavy-armed spearman, fighting hand-to-hand with his enemy, would obviously feel contemptuous.

391. *But my weapons* **(R-J)**; *Far different is* **(H)**; *But if one* **(L)**: cf. Dione's consolation to Aphrodite at 5.410-15 about what might happen to Diomedes if he is not careful.

398. *arrow*: see on 5.95.

401-97: Odysseus, now stranded, fights back, but is wounded. Ajax and Menelaus rescue him. Ajax storms forward.

403. *reflected* **(R-J)**; *to his own great heart* **(H)**; *spirit* **(L)**: the first of a number of monologues, where a character talks to himself out loud as a result of some difficulty he is facing, and usually ponders what action to take (cf. internal pondering at 1.111-93, 5.670-76), though sometimes he merely reflects on the significance of what he has observed (e.g. 18.6-14). The monologue frequently features a question 'But why am I talking like this?' half way through it (408). The poet uses monologues to explore human motivation; they show that a character is perfectly capable of making a decision for himself without help from the gods. It is noticeable how they increase as the *Il.* drives towards its climax. They also occur at 17.91, 201, 443, 20.344, 425, 21.54, 553, 22.99, 197; see Willcock (1990).

408. *cowards*: Odysseus is no coward, but a hero who stands his ground – unusual when a warrior is heavily outnumbered and at a disadvantage, as he is here (cf. 471, where Menelaus calls him 'great/brave'). He calls for help at 462.

414. *As strong young* **(R-J)**; *As when hounds* **(H)**; *as when closing about* **(L)**: D-simile, emphasising the balance of advantage between boar and huntsmen/hounds, as the poet had indicated at 413 ('trouble/wound').

417. *the vaunt of his teeth uprises* **(L)**: i.e. there is a noise of gnashing teeth.

420. *Deïopites*: the first victim in a 'catalogue' slaying (see on 301 above).

427. *Socus*: the sequence here is much that like of Agamemnon against Iphidamas at 221ff., i.e. a Trojan killed (246/427), his brother comes to his defence (251/428), the brother scores a hit (253/437), the Greek counter-attacks and kills the brother (259-60/447-9), but his wound forces him to retreat (273ff./458ff.).

438. *Athene*: cf. 4.128-33, where she saves Menelaus in similar fashion.

455. *funeral honours/burial/bury*: Odysseus contrasts his fate with Socus', claiming the birds will tear Socus' body. This never happens in the *Il.*, but the threat of mutilation of the dead body is ever present (see on 1.5) and increases sharply from Book 16 onwards, reaching its climax when Achilles refuses to return Hector's body and drags it in the dust (22.395-404). But from Book 23 the savagery relaxes as the groundwork is laid for the return of Hector's body to Priam. See e.g. 11.391-5, 15.349-51, 16.499ff., 559-61, 836, 17.39-40, 125-7, 153, 557-8, 18.175-7, 271-2, 283, 334-5, 21.123-7, 203-4, 22.42, 66-71, 86-9, 254-67, 335-6, 346-54. Segal (1971) discusses this feature in detail.

462. *for help/shouted*: typical, e.g. 13.477, 17.120. Odysseus' death would indeed be a great loss, as Menelaus testifies (description by reaction, 471).

465. *Ajax*: he never leads an attack, but is the man to call on when stern defence is needed.

474-82. *like tawny/blood-red jackals* **(R-J, H)**; *like bloody scavengers* **(L)**: an extended, complex C-simile. A hunter (Socus) has wounded a stag (Odysseus), which escapes but is caught by jackals (the Trojans); but then a lion emerges and drives them off (Ajax and Menelaus). Observe how the mention of the lion foreshadows the successful attack of Ajax (485-6). Similes often have an anticipatory function.

488. *led him*: Odysseus is the third major Greek hero to be wounded and leave the battlefield.

492. *As (when) a river*: D-simile, describing Ajax in attack mode, sweeping all before him.

497-598: Paris wounds the Greek doctor Machaon; Nestor takes him back to the ships. Ajax slowly retreats before Hector and is helped by Eurypylus, but Paris shoots Eurypylus in the thigh. The Greek defence rallies.

497. *Hector*: last heard of at 360, in retreat, and now apparently doing combat with Nestor and Idomeneus' men 'on the left' (i.e. 'left' from the *Greek* point of view, which seems to be the position from which Homer sees things). This is not good news for the Greeks; Nestor is an old man, and Idomeneus is no spring chicken (13.361).

506. *Machaon*: the Greek doctor who saw to Menelaus (4.192-219).

His wounding – the fourth serious casualty – will attract Achilles' attention at 598.

508.   *whose wind was fury* (**L**): read 'breathing courage'.

515.   *herbs/medicines*: 'medicine(s)' has a modern ring to it. It is herbs that Machaon would actually be using. See on 4.191.

521.   *Cebriones*: Hector's half-brother, he became Hector's driver at 8.318-19.

523.   For the rebuke pattern, see on 5.471.

534-7.   *axle ... wheel(-rim)s*: repeated at 20.499-502 (of Achilles). This passage contains a rare reference to fighting *from* a chariot, cf. **GI** 13B(vi).

542.   *Ajax*: Hector has already fought a lucky draw with Ajax at 7.244ff. and been briefly knocked out by him at 11.355-6, so he is wise to steer clear of him. [For technical reasons **L**'s translation at this point drops one line behind other editions. Since I quote the text from **L**'s line numbers, **R-J** and **H**'s lines will be one ahead of the number quoted from here on to the end of Book 11.]

545.   *in retreat/drew back*: since Ajax does not retreat lightly, this is a major turning point in the battle. Hence the two extended similes describing the moment – Ajax as baffled lion (545-55) and stubborn donkey (556-64). Since only Hector could possibly bring about such a retreat but is avoiding Ajax, Zeus must intervene (543).

547.   *As dogs* (**R-J**); *As country farmers* (**H**); *as when the men* (**L**): D-simile, emphasising the efforts the lion (Ajax) makes to get among the cattle and his desire to do so, but his ultimate failure and retreat because the farmers and dogs (Trojans) drive him back and force him to retreat, much against his will (554).

556.   *As (when) a donkey*: the lion simile above suggested Ajax's frustration; this unique simile promotes the sense of his control. The donkey does retreat, but in his own time, whatever the efforts of those beating him (mere children) to speed him up. So Ajax remains in charge, combining retreat (567) with attack (565-7, cf. Antilochus at 13.550-9); the Trojans (568 'fend off/kept ... from advance/blocked') seem quite unable to impose themselves. This is Ajax's great strength – close, defensive combat, where even Achilles could not match him (13.321-5).

571-4.   *spears ... fill/flesh/body*: cf. 15.314-17.

573.   *thirsting/eager/straining*: personification of an inanimate object (a spear).

574.   *Eurypylus*: another (minor) hero, to be wounded at 582 (the fifth in all in this book), while (typically) carrying away armour, cf. Agamemnon at 246-52, Diomedes at 373-8.

580.   *Paris/Alexandros*: Paris makes his second hit in this book (see on 369).

586.   *Friends*: it is typical for a warrior to call to others for help, cf. 465, 8.93, 17.120, 708.

597.   *Machaon*: see on 506.

598-803: Achilles sees Nestor conveying Machaon from the field and sends Patroclus to find out what is going on. Nestor tells Patroclus a long story about his (Nestor's) youthful exploits – a revenge raid against the Eleans and defeat of the Elean counter-attack – and remembers Menoetius' advice to Patroclus. Nestor urges Patroclus to get permission to return to the fighting himself, in Achilles' armour.

603. *beginning of his end/doom/evil*: Homer signals a critical turning point in the *Il.* by interjecting a rare, authorial comment on the action (**GI** 10). As a result of his forthcoming encounter with Nestor, Patroclus in Book 16 will persuade Achilles to allow him to return to battle where he will be killed. Cf. 8.470-6.

609. *supplication*: but has the embassy not done this already in Book 9? Analytical scholars have used this passage to argue for multiple authorship, i.e. the insertion by an author of an embassy to Achilles in Book 9 that the author of Book 11 did not know about. That is possible, but the illogicality may also be a result of Homer's reworking and 'nodding'. On the other hand, the embassy in Book 9 did not come *in the first place* to supplicate Achilles, but to do a deal over compensation; it was only after that offer had failed that Phoenix tried to reconstruct the embassy as a supplicatory one (see on 9.502-14). Another line of argument would be to focalise these words through Achilles' eyes as an unthinking cry of triumph, that the Greeks might at last deliver whatever it is that he wants.

desperate straits (**R-J**); *need ... urgent* (**H**); *need past endurance* (**L**): is Achilles gloating over the success of his plan to ensure the slaughter of the Greeks?

619. *Eurymedon*: the useless driver of Nestor's chariot at 8.104, 114.

624. *Tenedos*: another memory of Achilles' past raids and seizure of women (see **GI** 1C), and the army deciding to whom the women should be given (see on 1.121-307). See **R-J** map 2.

628. *enamel/cobalt* (**H, L**): see on 11.24.

631. *cup*: this cup bears some resemblance to one (with doves and supports) found in a grave at Mycenae, cf. other objects of Mycenaean origin like Ajax's shield (see on 7.219, 6.117) and the boar's tusk helmet (see on 10.263).

638. *Pramnian*: no one knows where, or what, 'Pramnos' was. The vegetarian meal – bread and honey, an onion, and wine containing cheese and barley – would not excite modern taste-buds, but the combination of powerful sweet and sharp flavours like honey and onion seems to have appealed to ancient palates. Presumably the whole disgusting *mélange* was meant to have restorative powers.

645. *to sit down*: Nestor is trying to lure Patroclus with the full *xenia* routine. Patroclus is having none of it; in a few brief, exquisitely suggestive strokes, he tells us all we need to about the sort of person Achilles is, the hold Achilles has over Patroclus, Patroclus' feelings about Achilles and his (fully justified) unease at getting ensnared by Nestor (a wonderful example of description by reaction). But Nestor will not let go ... he sees an opportunity to get to Achilles through his dearest friend Patroclus.

665. *Is he waiting/going to wait*: cf. 9.650-3 – exactly what Achilles means to do!

669-802. *If only/Would that*: see on 7.132. This is the longest of Nestor's speeches. See 11/Intro.

1. Nestor's paradigm (670-763)

670. *Eleans* (**R-J**); *Epeians* (**H, L**): these are the same people, coming from the region around Elis. **R-J** calls them 'Eleans' throughout. The convoluted story is not easy to follow, but the outline is as follows: the people of Elis were at war with Nestor's town of Pylos (**R-J** map 4). The reason was that the Pylians had been weakened by Heracles' attack on them years ago (689-94) and the Eleans (led by Augeas) had taken advantage of this to raid them (693-4). Nestor therefore led a reprisal raid and killed the Elean Itymoneus (670-5), driving off much cattle into the bargain (676-80). Nestor's father Neleus was delighted at Nestor's victory (681-3) and invited the Pylians to share the spoils, seeing that so many were owed property plundered by the Eleans (684-8). Neleus in particular was owed a lot because on an earlier occasion he had sent a four-horse chariot to compete in games at Elis and Augeas had kept it, sending back only the driver (695-706, 702-4 picking up 684-8). On the third day of this distribution, however, the Eleans laid siege to Thryoessa. Athene warned us, and Neleus sent an army to take them on, though he did not want me (Nestor, his only remaining son) to fight and gave me no chariot – but that did not stop me! (706-20). A two day march took us, via the rivers Minyeius and Alpheus, to Thryoessa, and the next morning we attacked (721-35). I at once killed their leader Mulius, and the Eleans fled; I commandeered his chariot, captured and killed the occupants of fifty more and we chased them all the way to Buprasion, where Athene called a halt (736-60). See on 747 below.

690. *Heracles*: see on 5.392.

698. *competitors* (**L**): i.e. one four-horse chariot, with driver. Such a chariot was used in games, not war. This may somehow hint at the Olympic Games, founded at Olympia (in Elis) in 776 BC.

700. *Augeas*: he whose stables Heracles cleaned as a labour, by diverting the rivers Alpheus and Peneus through them. Augeas was father of Phyleus, father of the Greek warrior Meges (see 2.625-30).

708. *Moliones*: twins, possibly Siamese twins, who on another occasion beat Nestor in a chariot race (see 23.641-2).

710. *Thryoessa*: = Thryon, 2.592.

727. *sacrifices/sacrificed*: these are boundary sacrifices, offered as the troops cross into other territory, and the meal they take (729) is the one that always accompanies it.

747. *fifty chariots*: this is the only episode in the *Il.* where the fighting is carried out from chariots, by (apparently) chariot-squadrons. For the use of chariots in the *Il.*, see **GI** 13B(vi).

755. *Buprasion … Olenian … Alesion*: see 2.615-17 for these places.

2. What Menoetius said (764-88)

762. *advantage* **(R-J)**; *only one to profit* **(H)**; *enjoy his own valour* **(L)**: a point Patroclus makes forcibly to Achilles (16.31-2).

765. *From Phthia*: as a young boy Patroclus had accidentally killed someone, fled and been accepted into Achilles' home in Phthia (23.84-90). It is not clear why his father Menoetius should still be with him.

766. *Odysseus and I*: Nestor and Odysseus are on a recruiting mission for the Trojan war. See on 19.326-7 for a more discreditable account of Achilles' recruitment to the Trojan war, which Homer is 'correcting' here.

770. *(we) found*: a full *xenia* sequence (see on 9.188-244).

781. *giving/gave you (much) advice* **(R-J, H)**; *spoke to you* **(L)**: fathers always give their sons advice before they go to war, cf. 5.196-200, 6.207-10 (6.208 is the same advice as Peleus gives Achilles here at 783).

786. *older/elder*: one always thinks of Achilles as older than Patroclus, but no.

3. Nestor's proposal (789-802)

788. *to his own advantage* **(R-J)**; *for the best* **(H)**; *for his own good* **(L)**: irony. Menoetius was not to know what the consequences of this advice was to be – the death of Patroclus, and then of Achilles. Nestor makes the suggestion that Achilles or Patroclus should return to the fighting because (i) he does not know of Achilles' resolution to return (perhaps) but only when the ships are fired (see on 9.678); and (ii) Odysseus did report that Achilles might return home 'tomorrow' (9.682-3), but 'tomorrow' has now come and Achilles is still there, i.e. there is still hope. See Scodel (1989).

793-802. *But if he/there is … huts/shelters*: = 16.36-45 (with minor changes), where Patroclus makes the fatal suggestion to Achilles. Patroclus' response at 803 ('the words went straight to his heart/his feelings/heart was stirred/moved') indicates that Nestor's words have struck home.

804-48: Patroclus helps the wounded Eurypylus.

808. *Eurypylus*: wounded at 581-3.

815. *Wretched/You poor men/wretches*: note the sympathy in Patroclus' words and actions here (he is known as 'gentle Patroclus', see on 9.190); he is even prepared to forget the need to return to Achilles at once (838-9), which he had earlier insisted on (647-53). The plight of the Greeks and Nestor's example have hit home.

182

824. *All our former champions* **(R-J)**; *All (of) those who (were) before* **(H, L)**: i.e. Agamemnon, Odysseus and Diomedes in particular. They will not return to the fighting again in the *Il.*, though they will give advice and later compete in Patroclus' funeral games in Book 23.

831. *Cheiron*: see on 4.219, 9.168. He is probably 'most honest/most civilised/righteous' because he is the exception to the rule that the Centaurs were generally the opposite (see on 1.263-5).

832. *Podaleirius*: see on 2.732.

Book 12

Introduction

At the end of Book 11, Homer created the Patroclus-Eurypylus episode to give himself space in which to expand on the Trojan advance towards the Greek camp. The question he now faces is: how, precisely, will he organise it? Homer has already signalled that this day will see the return to the fighting and death of Patroclus (8.470-6); presumably, too, Patroclus will act on Nestor's suggestion that he should return in Achilles' armour. So between 'now' and the time when Patroclus returns to Achilles, arms, re-enters battle and dies, Homer has decisions to make.

The medium-term decision is: what will have to be happening to the Greeks to persuade Achilles that Patroclus should take to the field? The answer will turn out to be that the Trojans are on the point of setting fire to the Greek ships (15.743-6, with Ajax desperately holding the line). This is clever plotting, since that situation will approximate to the circumstances under which Achilles had indicated that he *might* be prepared to change his mind and return to battle *himself* (9.650-5); so even if Achilles is not persuaded by Patroclus to come back personally, it is reasonable that he should permit Patroclus to, as an interim measure. Between now and Book 16, therefore, Homer has to plot the Trojan advance, broadly in four stages: (i) over the ditch (ii) over or through the wall (iii) into the camp, and (iv) up to the ships.

The poet has already prepared one vital piece of stage machinery to help him pace the narrative: the Greek ditch and wall. These represent the first obstacles for the Trojans to overcome, and they are potentially severe ones. One could imagine lengthy battles developing round them. Slightly surprisingly, Homer plays the ditch + wall card here and now, both at once; Book 12 will end with Hector smashing down the gates and the Trojans pouring through into the Greek camp. One might subsequently expect, therefore, a rapid Trojan advance up to the ships in Book 13 and the prompt return of Patroclus to the fighting. In the event, we shall find that Homer has other plans.

As was observed in 11/Intro, Homer ensured that, even though some major Greek heroes were wounded, Zeus was still deeply involved in the action. Zeus continues to be engaged in Book 12. The poet himself comments that the Greeks are under the whip of Zeus (37); at 174 Trojan Asius complains that Zeus is not helping them at all, but the poet adds that Zeus is intent on giving *Hector* the glory; at 252-7, Zeus sends a hurricane that blows the dust straight into the faces of the Greeks, and at 290-4 the poet comments that the Trojans would never have broken through if Zeus had not launched his son Sarpedon (their Lycian ally) at the wall (and Zeus goes on to save Sarpedon from death at 402-3). When Hector comes into the fighting, Zeus is behind him all the way (437-8), making it easy for him to pick up a huge boulder (449-50) with which he will smash down the Greek gate. Zeus seems determined to see his and Thetis' plan for the destruction of the Greeks through to the end, personally. Note how Homer again reminds us of Zeus' instructions to all the other gods to keep clear of the fighting: they are in the depths of despair (179-80).

Homer signals the importance of the wall at this juncture in the battle by starting Book 12 with a description of how Poseidon was to destroy it in the future, after the Trojan war was over (Apollo will wreck part of the wall and ditch at 15.355-66). This is the most far-reaching example of the poet taking us beyond the end of the *Il.*, to the time not only when Ilium had been sacked but the Greeks had sailed for home as well; and also connecting the heroic past to the present of Homer's audience when, if Ilium was still visible in some form or other, the wall certainly was not. The tactic has a further aim: the evidence of the audience's eyes – look, no Greek defensive wall anywhere at Ilium – confirms Homer's account.

The first problem for the Trojan troops is the ditch and how their chariots are going to negotiate it (50-9). Polydamas' sensible advice is to abandon the chariots and cross on foot, which Hector accepts (75-80). Polydamas is to become a key player on the Trojan side, his advice being alternately accepted and rejected by Hector and thus throwing into relief the over-confident Hector's inability to discern what is in their best interests; see Willcock (1990). It is noticeable that Polydamas is not as convinced as Hector is of Zeus' good-will: 'If Zeus is really on our side ...' he says, being aware of the possibility that he may not be (67-74).

After a brief catalogue of the Trojan contingents (88-107), typical at key moments like this before a major attack, it is immediately made clear what happens to those who ignore Polydamas' advice. Asius decides not to attack on foot with the others but to launch his chariot at the Greek wall. The trouble he meets at the hands of the Lapiths (124-72 – note the prediction of his death at 113-15) marks the fate of those who will not listen.

The Lapiths continue their brief *aristeia*, so successfully that Hector and his troops hesitate to cross the ditch (199-200). But a bird of omen is seen, and Polydamas interprets it one way – if we fight round the ships we are doomed (215-29) – while Hector dismisses it out of hand, rejecting omens in favour of the promises of Zeus (231-50), a rich irony, since it was Zeus who had sent the omen (209). This is a heated exchange, hinting at tensions between the two in the past (cf. Achilles and Agamemnon, 1.90). But those who reject bird omens in the *Il.* are always wrong.

Zeus immediately spurs on the Trojans, and in a few lines the ditch (we must assume) is crossed and the wall reached (251-64). The Greeks, led by the two Ajaxes, put up a stern defence (265-89), but again Zeus intervenes to send into action his son Sarpedon, backed up by Glaucus (292-3, 309-28). The Greeks frantically summon the Ajaxes to defend that section of the wall (331-77), Glaucus is hit and retreats (387-91), but Sarpedon tears away a whole length of breastwork, exposing the top of the wall (397-9). Fierce battle is engaged, but then Zeus urges Hector into the fight, who smashes down the Greek gates, and the hordes pour through. The end seems to be at hand.

Three features stand out in Book 12. First, Homer maintains a careful balance in the fighting. The Trojans may attack hard, now assaulting the wall, now the gates, but the Greeks defend stoutly at all points, and Homer's 'camera' tracks dramatically from side to side. Note too the switching between action and talk, so typical of Homeric battles. Second, Homer uses the wall very imaginatively: men hurl rocks down from, and up at, it (154-61, marvellous simile at 278-89), tear away at it (257-60, 397-9), run along behind it for cover to defend a position elsewhere (373-4) or range up and down exhorting their troops from it (265-76). The dead fall from it (385-6, 394-6), either hit by spears (395-6) or flying rocks (379-86). Third, there is an absence of boasting between enemies that has characterised early books, because the fighting is of a different type now: not warriors in single combat out on the plain, fighting on or from chariots, but frantic defence round a wall, with the troops on both sides almost eye-ball to eye-ball (430-44, especially the two similes), smashing away at each other and the gates, and creating a din so terrible that people can hardly make themselves heard (337-41).

In the middle of this chaos stands a famous scene: Sarpedon's rallying call to Glaucus to remember why he holds the privileged place in society that he does (310-28) – because the Lycians reward him for it. It is an example of Homer's fair-mindedness that he puts this classic statement of a hero's duty in the mouth not of a Greek but of a Trojan ally from Lycia. But that raises the question – why is Sarpedon fighting in Troy, when Lycia is not threatened? Because that is what heroes do; see **GI** 4A.

Main sources for the commentary
Hainsworth (1993); Willcock (1978).

1-35: The future destruction of the Greek wall by the gods is described.

4. *ditch*: an amazing reversal in Greek fortunes, given that at 11.167-70 Agamemnon had pursued the Trojans right back to Ilium's Scaean gates.

6. *offerings/hecatombs/sacrifices*: whose absence Poseidon had complained about at 7.450.

17. *Poseidon and Apollo*: because they had built the wall round Ilium, and did not want the Greeks' wall to outshine it (7. 451-3, 21.441ff.).

23. *half-divine/half-god*: i.e. heroes like Achilles, with one immortal parent. But see on 1.1 (*Achilles*) and cf. on 10.50.

35-174: The Trojans cannot cross the ditch by chariot, and Polydamas suggests an attack on foot. Hector agrees; Asius' attempt by chariot fails.

35-8. *hue and cry...* **(R-J)**; *clamour* ... **(H)**; *battle and clamour* ... **(L)** ... *ships*: since the Trojans have not even crossed the ditch yet, this presumably indicates that the Trojans are hurling missiles at the wall from the other side of the ditch.

41. *As (when) a (wild) boar* **(R-J, H)**; *As when among* **(L)**: as usual, a (D) simile accompanies the entrance on to the scene of a great hero. It is slightly confusing. It looks as if Hector is a lion/boar taking on a 'wall' (43) of men (the Greeks), who attack with spears, while he continues charging and driving them back, though his own courage finally kills him (and when Hector does in fact die, Andromache also will say it was his own courage that killed him, 22.457-9, cf. her fears at 6.407); but the focus changes with the return to the narrative (49), when it appears the simile was about Hector going up and down urging his men to cross the ditch.

55. *surface of the floor ... palisades* **(L)**: read 'on top there was a row of pointed stakes' (i.e. on the Greek side of the ditch).

59. *the dismounted ... effort* **(L)**: i.e. the foot-soldiers wanted to attempt the crossing. All this prepares the way for Polydamas' advice.

60. *Polydamas*: A fine speaker, Hector's companion and warning voice, and sharing the same birthday (18.251-2, cf. on 3.146). He will offer four pieces of advice: two will be accepted (12.61-79, 13.726-47), two rejected (12.211-29, and most disastrously 18.254-83, cf. 22.100). Despite their closeness, tensions between Polydamas and Hector tend to run high, Polydamas sensibly assessing the pros and cons of every situation and advocating caution, Hector pursuing a path of honour and glory in (misplaced) confidence at the prospect of success, generated by Zeus' message at 11.200-9, and cf. 8.497-541.

64. *inside it* **(L)**: read 'along the edge' (the Greek says, lit., 'sharp stakes stand in it': presumably one is not supposed to take the 'in' too precisely).

87. *five contingents/divisions/battalions*: see on 2.876. They will attack the wall and gates of the Greek camp, on foot (175). The catalogue indicates the importance of the moment – the Trojans readying themselves to smash down the Greek defences (cf. the Myrmidons under Patroclus at 16.168-97). But while the contingents led by Hector, Asius and Sarpedon all feature, some have thought it odd that the two contingents led by Aeneas and Paris are given nothing to do. It may indeed be that there was once a plan for the five contingents to attack five separate gates (cf. the Seven against Thebes, see on 2.563-5); and it may be that cutting between five separate scenes of action presented too much of a challenge for the poet (see on 3.121-244), let alone of organising the Greek defence at each gate at the same time (cf. how much Homer relies on the Ajaxes here, 265ff., 333ff.). But the three contingents have their say, with Sarpedon being so successful that, when Ajax and Teucer leave the gate area (340) to defend the sector that Sarpedon is attacking, Hector can break through the gates. It is not compulsory on the poet to describe the activities of all five contingents at once.

117. *Idomeneus*: he will kill Asius at 13.383-93.

118. *where the Greeks/Achaians*: see on 11.47-52 for this presumed 'causeway'.

128. *Lapiths*: the gates remain open so that the Greeks in flight can find refuge behind the walls, and are defended by the two Lapiths (see on 1.263-5, 2.740).

132. *like ... oak(tree)s*: B-simile, emphasising the Lapiths' immovability.

146. *like(ness of) ... boars*: C-simile, again showing a change of focus when the narrative is re-joined at 151 – the simile does not liken the charging Lapiths to charging boars, but compares the clashing of the boars' tusks with the clash of the enemy's blows on the Lapiths' chests (nor are the Lapiths killed, as the simile might seem to suggest; for focus-changing, cf. on 41 above).

157. *like snowflakes*: B-simile, with no surprise twists.

165. *liar* (**R-J, H**); *lover of deception* (**L**): Zeus (173) does not rise to the charge (as if Zeus had made Asius any promises anyway). It is typical of men to complain of Zeus' treatment, cf. 9.21.

167. *like ... wasps*: D-simile, emphasising (to judge from 170-2) the determination of wasps-bees/Lapiths to fight to the death in defence of their own.

175-250: Zeus sends an omen – the eagle and the snake. Polydamas says it means the Trojans should retreat; Hector rejects his advice.

177. *fire*: round a stone wall? It is the ships that the Trojans talk about firing (e.g. 198), not the wall. But there were wooden foundations (12.29) and wooden outworks on the towers (36).

181-94. *Lapiths ... earth/succession*: the Lapiths enjoy a brief *aristeia* and are not seen on the battlefield again. For the brain-spattering (185-6), cf. 11.97-8; for spear + sword combination (189-90), cf. 11.108-9.

200. *bird (of) omen/sign*: bird omens are the most common type in the *Il.*, e.g. 8.247, 10.274, 13.821, 24.315, but snakes are also deployed, e.g. 2.308. Here the snake stands for the Greeks. Bird omens, most of which are sent by Zeus (209), never fail; those who reject them signal their own downfall, as Hector does.

212-13. *no good reason/for you, in your skill, to argue wrong, neither* (**L**): read 'it is, of course, entirely unfitting, for your humble servant (**R-J**)/a commoner (**H**) to disagree with you'.

214. *and ever to be upholding* (**L**): read 'he must always exalt'. Polydamas is being sarcastic. Past tension between him and Hector is emerging here (see on 60 above and cf. on 1.90).

236. *promise(s)/assented*: at 11.200-9. Hector does have Zeus' promise for the rest of that day, as he points out (241-2). While it could indeed be foolish to reject omens so absolutely, Greeks did not regard it as *necessarily* impious not to believe them, since it was acknowledged that the will of the god was difficult for a man to interpret accurately. Cf. 24.220-4.

247. *fight it out* **(R-J)**; *and fights* **(H)**; *nor a fighter's* **(L)**: this accusation is not supported by Polydamas' subsequent efforts in the field (see on 3.146). Hector in his confidence seems determined to do Polydamas down, come what may.

251-330: The Trojans storm the Greek wall, and the two Ajaxes stoutly defend. Sarpedon and Glaucus discuss the hero's duties and attack with their Lycian troops.

257-64. *tearing/They tore ... beneath/under the wall/it*: the only passage in the *Il.* which attempts to describe siege warfare in detail, though not against a fortified *town* (see **GI** 13B(ix), 9.529). The Trojans concentrate on breaking down the wall/gates (gates, 340-1), not scaling them, the Greeks on bombarding them from above. It was standard practice for the besieged to collect heaps of boulders to drop on their attackers (Thucydides 4.115).

263. *ox-hides/hides of oxen* **(H, L)**: read 'ox-hide shields', as if the Greeks were forming a battle-front on the ground.

265. *Ajaxes*: i.e. son of Telamon and son of Oïleus (see on 2.527), since Teucer is mentioned separately (336-7).

273. *for the sound of their blustering* **(L)**: read 'since you have your commanders' orders'.

278-89. *As snowflakes* **(R-J)**; *Like the flakes of snow* **(H)**; *as storms of snow* **(L)**: marvellous extended D-simile, describing the volleys of stones exchanged between the two sides (who do not wish to risk losing their spears). The sense of stillness generated by the simile – even the sea seems stilled – contrasts powerfully with the turmoil and noise (289) of battle.

281. *in the solid drift* **(L)**: delete.

286. *rain* **(L)**: read 'snow'.

290. *Hector*: looking forward to 12.457-62.

299-306. *like a mountain/hill-kept lion*: as usual with the entrance of a warrior onto the scene, a C-simile. This one expands on the shorter A-simile (like a lion falling on cattle, 293), fleshing out the need of the lion, its proud determination and do-or-die nature. It matches Sarpedon's forthcoming speech to Glaucus, which will reveal the same qualities.

307. *(Sarpedon's) courage/heart/spirit*: at the start of this episode it was Zeus (292) who launched Sarpedon against the Greeks. Now we are told it was Sarpedon's own courage – a good example of 'double motivation' (see on 9.702).

310-28. Sarpedon's speech is the classic statement of the heroic ethos in the *Il.*, i.e. the connection between the honour that a community bestows (most obviously in material terms) and one's obligation to prove worthy of it by laying one's life on the line in battle; the result is *kleos*, a glorious reputation that survives death. It is noticeable, however, that Sarpedon here is not fighting for Lycia; a hero is a hero, wherever he is. Note how everything else is forgotten when heroes talk to each other, even at the height of a loud and furious battle, cf. Diomedes and Glaucus, 6.119-236. See on 5.166 for the ensuing 'consultation' sequence.

311. *pride of place*: see 4.257-64 (and notes) for the honour attached to eating and drinking, and 7.319-22 for a special gift of meat.

313. *estate/land*: see e.g. the land given to Bellerophon at 6.193-5.

323. *ageless*: heroes seek *kleos*. If they were ageless and immortal, they would be gods, and have *kleos* automatically. So, naturally, they would not feel the need to get it by fighting. But they are mortal (326, 'demons/fates/spirits of death'), and in that sad condition, *kleos* has to be earned (cf. Hector at 22.304-5). But one does not have to be killed in battle to earn it. Odysseus and Diomedes, for example, return home, their *kleos* intact (cf. on 10.50). No hero in the *Il.* willingly invites death, except Achilles (18.98).

331-435: Ajax son of Telamon and the archer Teucer come to Menestheus' aid. Sarpedon tears down part of the Greek wall; Ajax and Teucer repel him.

331. *Menestheus*: see on 2.552 for his unimportant role.

335. *Ajaxes*: see on 265 above; for Teucer the archer (336), see 8.266-334. The removal of the Ajaxes from the gate sector (340) will allow Hector to attack it successfully (451-71).

366. *Lycomedes*: see 9.84, 19.240 for his small part, and on 11.824 for the thinness of the Greek defence in the absence of their wounded leaders.

372. *Pandion*: otherwise unknown.

379. *Epicles*: killed by a boulder dropped from the battlements (384-6); see on 257-64 above.

388. *Glaucus*: a leading Trojan ally, Sarpedon's second-in-command (2.876). At 16.492 the dying Sarpedon calls on Glaucus for help, but the wound Glaucus has received here hampers him, 16.517, till Apollo heals it.

389. *arm ... warcraft* (**L**): i.e. hit him on his exposed arm and ended his interest in the fight.

401. *shoulder-strap/baldric/belt*: cf. Menelaus saved by his belt (4.133, 186).

402. *Zeus saved/kept/brushed*: cf. 5.662, where we are again told that Zeus saved Sarpedon. He is being saved for death at Patroclus' hands (16.502), which will stir Zeus to tears (16.458-61).

421. *As two men*: D-simile, measuring the distance the two armies were kept apart – by the width of the battlements. But it also indicates the ferocity of the fighting and its importance to both sides: as any house-owner knows, when it comes to one's own territory (and that neighbour's extension into *my* garden), every inch is fiercely fought over, tape-measure in hand.

426.   *targes/guardskins* **(H, L)**: see on 5.453.

433.   *wool-worker/spinning woman/widow*: C-simile, the even balance of the scales of a poor working woman representing the even balance of the fighting (like Zeus' mighty scales, till they tip; see on 8.69). When the simile is picked up in the narrative ('tight/strained taut/pulled fast' 436), however, the poet seems to be thinking of a line pulled tight by opposing sides (see on 11.336).

436-71: Zeus intervenes, Hector smashes down a gate in the Greek wall and the Greeks turn and run.

437.   *Zeus*: Zeus' support glorifies Hector at this climactic moment, as does the way Zeus makes the rock light for him (450). So superhuman has Hector briefly become that only a god could have stopped him (466).

445.   *rock/stone*: presumably one hurled down from the battlements or perhaps (given its shape) used to wedge open the gate.

451.   *As (when) a shepherd*: unique C-simile, perhaps triggered by the wool-working woman at 433. A 'wether' **(L)** is a ram.

459.   *hinges* **(H, L)**: Homeric gates do not have hinges but are attached to posts which are fitted into pivots hollowed out in the threshold below and lintel above. Hector smashes the gates out of these pivots.

462-71.   *In leapt* **(R-J)**; *leapt inside* **(H)**; *burst in* **(L)**: one of the most dramatic moments in the *Il.*, as the Greek defences are breached for the first time and Hector and the Trojans pour inside. Note the vivid colour imagery: Hector's face dark as nightfall (463, cf. Apollo at 1.47), his armour gleaming balefully (465), eyes flashing with fire (466, cf. 1.104, 19.16-17).

Book 13

Introduction

Homer has now completed two of the stages by which the Trojans were to reach the Greek ships and fire them: they have crossed the Greek ditch and breached the wall. They are now in the enemy camp (cf. 39-43) and completely on top, with the Greeks retreating in terror to their own ships (cf. 12.469-71). It looks all over, but as indicated in 12/Intro, Homer has a card ready to play that will hold up the Trojan advance, and now he plays it. He makes Zeus decide the job is done and turn his attention elsewhere (1-9).

Since the poet has taken pains to remind us that the other gods have not enjoyed being kept out of the action (e.g. 11.75-9, 12.179-80, 13.15-16, 521-5), it is not surprising that, with Zeus' back (literally) turned, the pro-Greek god Poseidon should step in to take advantage of the situation. Disguising himself as the Greek prophet Calchas (45), he first inspires the two Ajaxes with the desire for battle (46-82) – these are major defensive players in the absence of the wounded Agamemnon and others – and, second, he berates a number of exhausted and demoralised minor heroes (83-90) for their unwillingness to fight back (naturally, their number does not include the major heroes Idomeneus and Menelaus, nor Nestor who is looking after Machaon, 11.595-7). As a result, they form up under the two Ajaxes in a massed defensive formation and prepare to meet the enemy (125-35).

The minor heroes are thus going to be given the chance to show what they can do, and Meriones and Teucer at once spring into action. Meriones misses with his spear, however, so goes off to fetch another, but Teucer scores and with Ajax's help strips the body (156-205). It is worth remarking here that a feature of these books will be the running battle that surfaces from time to time between the two major heroes on either side, Ajax and Hector. They had already fought a duel in Book 7, out of which Ajax had emerged the winner on points (7.279-312), and Ajax continues to get the better of the encounters that will now take place. But since Hector has yet to kill Patroclus (as Zeus had prophesied at 8.473-6) and will himself be killed by Achilles, Homer has to devise means by which this contest never reaches a decision. In this episode, the force of Ajax's spear-thrust merely drives Hector backwards (188-93), but Homer will continue to bring them into confrontation.

Homer now leaves Hector and the Ajaxes and changes focus to another part of the battlefield, thereby bringing the major Greek hero Idomeneus into the fray. He, we learn, has been helping a wounded companion out of the battle (210-15), and Poseidon, in the guise of Thoas, urges him to get back into the fighting (219-38). This Idomeneus eventually does in company with his attendant Meriones, after a long discussion with him about the nature of courage (249-329). All this is by way of preparation for a typical feature of Homeric battle, the *aristeia* (single-handed feat of arms) of a great hero, Idomeneus. After a picture of general fighting, Greek against Trojan and god against god (330-60), Idomeneus emerges for a number of exciting individual encounters against the enemy. It is noticeable how the nature of the fighting has now reverted back to the traditional: from the close-range scrapping round the wall in Book 12 to single, colourful duels between heroes, with boasting and counter-boasting, and so on, in the (relatively) open field of the Greek camp. Indeed, there is even a chariot encounter. Asius had earlier failed to break into the Greek camp with his chariot (12.109-72), but he has now apparently managed it (384-6). Little good it does him, as Idomeneus kills him while the minor hero Antilochus despatches his charioteer (387-401).

The fighting now becomes varied and very intense, with Homer deploying a full cast of warriors on either side. Idomeneus has a series of encounters with Deiphobus, who decides to bring in Aeneas and other Trojans to help him, and eventually this is enough to force Idomeneus to retreat, his *aristeia* done (514-16). But Idomeneus' attendant Meriones continues the good work, wounding Deiphobus (528-39), and Antilochus too comes to the fore again with a number of kills. They are now joined by the other absent hero Menelaus, and even though Paris intervenes with an arrow shot (660-72), the Greeks are getting on top, thanks to Poseidon's constant encouragement (674-8).

Time, then, for Homer to move back to Hector who is still fighting where he had first broken into the Greek camp (679-84), against the Ajaxes and their men, and with little success (685-22). We need a Trojan rally to even things out, and who better to set one up than Hector's adviser Polydamas? He suggests regrouping, and Hector takes the advice (723-53). Hector is appalled to find so many Trojan leaders dead or wounded (758-64), unfairly abuses Paris for it (765-88), and then reforms the Trojans for a serious combined assault on the Ajaxes (789-805). Ajax and Hector exchange insults in preparation for a second fight (which will be picked up at 14.402), and battle is joined again.

Main sources for the commentary and related reading
Edwards (1987) 238-45; Fenik (1968) 115-57; Janko (1992); Willcock (1984).

1-9: Zeus, confident that no god will interfere in the battle, looks elsewhere.

4-6. *Thracians … Abii/Abioi*: Zeus from Mount Ida (11.183) is looking due north and beyond (see **R-J** map 3). Thrace is in Greece, north of the Hellespont; the Mysians are not the Trojan allies of 2.858 but inhabit Bulgaria (Roman Moesia); the Hippemolgi (correct **L**'s spelling) are probably a Scythian tribe living across the Danube; the Abii are not otherwise known (but cf. on 1.423). Observe that, even though Zeus is king of the gods, if his mind is elsewhere he will not notice what other gods or humans are doing.

8. *He did not expect/think* **(R-J, H)**; *He had no idea* **(L)**: Zeus is fully confident that the gods will now obey his will, expressed at 8.5-9. He has no idea of the depth of their feeling for the Greeks or against him (15-16, Poseidon pities the Greeks and hates Zeus).

10-205: Poseidon takes advantage. He fills the two Ajaxes with re-newed vigour and rallies the rest of the Greeks. Ajax drives off Hector.

10. *Earthshaker*: i.e. the pro-Greek god Poseidon. He had refused to help the Greeks at 8.209-11, but now that Zeus is not watching, he sees his chance. His intervention will last till he is ordered by Zeus to leave the battlefield and withdraw into the sea (15.219).

12. *Thracian Samos* **(H, L)**: i.e. Samothrace **(R-J)**, an island to the north-west of Troy. See **R-J** map 3.

21. *Aigae/Aigai*: since Poseidon is visiting his magical palace under the sea (21-2) to fetch his golden chariot (23-7, cf. 5.720-32) on which he will then gallop towards the Greek camp (31: he parks between Tenedos and Imbros, 33; **R-J** map 3), there is little point is speculating where Aigae is; but there is a headland called Aiga on the south-west corner of Lesbos, which would fit well enough. The description of his journey makes for a magnificent picture of the power and majesty of the god, nature joyfully responding to him. The 'sea-beasts' (27) are probably dolphins **(R-J)**.

35. *fodder*: cf. 5.368-9, 775-7, 8.49-50, 433-5.

39. *Trojans*: we pick up the story from the end of Book 12 when the Trojans burst into the Greek camp.

45. *Calchas*: the Greek prophet (70) whom Agamemnon accused of constant ill-will (1.106-8). Poseidon adopts this form presumably because 'Calchas' is about to criticise Agamemnon again (111-14).

46. *Ajaxes/Aiantes*: i.e. Ajax son of Telamon and Ajax son of Oïleus (66-7). See on 2.406.

53. *like a raging fire* **(R-J)**; *madman ... like a flame of fire* **(H)**; *berserk flamelike* **(L)**: for Hector as raging, berserk ('rabid' is the basic image), cf. 8.299; for rage + fire, cf. 15.605-9.

54. *father was almighty Zeus/son of Zeus*: Hector has never made this claim, though he expresses the wish at 13.825-6 and cf. 13.153-4. Poseidon wants to encourage the Ajaxes by pointing up Hector's self-delusion.

62. *hawk*: B-simile. Poseidon does not turn into a hawk and fly off, as 71-2 prove; he simply departs with the speed of a hawk.

71. *heels ... knees* **(R-J)**; *feet ... legs from behind* **(H, L)**: a strange way to recognise a god, though cf. 3.396-7 for Helen's recognition of Aphrodite by her physical characteristics. Clearly Poseidon must have wanted to be recognised (it is typical for a god to reveal himself at the end of an encounter, cf. 13.71-2, 24.460). The fact that the two men are now itching for battle (72-5, 77-80) is further proof of the divine intervention at 59-61, where he strikes them with his staff, though they had been keen enough already (46).

84. *cooling the heat of their inward heart* (**L**): i.e. trying to recover their spirits.

88. *tears*: of fear, and therefore shameful; see on 1.349.

95-124. Poseidon's speech is a good example of ring-composition: A 95-6 – appeal to sense of shame; B 97-8 slackness will cause defeat; C 99-107 – the once cowardly Trojans are upon us; D 108-10 – because we are slack; D 111-17 – but Agamemnon's mistakes are no excuse for slackness; C 117-19 – you are cowards; B 120 – slackness will cause disaster; A 121-4 – appeal to sense of shame. Note the special emphasis on the demoralised troops' slackness/hanging back, with the implication that, to win through, all they have to do is get back into the fight. Appeals to men's pride and sense of shame are commonplace.

126. *Strong ranks* (**R-J**); *battalions* (**H, L**): the Greek are making a massed defensive formation, cf. 17.354-9; Albracht (2003) [I.36ff.]; see **GI** 13B(v)(b). The Trojans reply with a massed attacking formation (136 'in a mass/pack', cf. 16.212-17).

127. *the War-god* (**R-J, L**); *Ares* (**H**): in narrative as in similes, Homer sometimes imagines an observer looking on, in this case, a god. Cf. e.g. 13.343-4.

134. *spears … serried line* (**H**); *spears … jagged battle line* (**L**): the Greek seems to mean that their spears 'overlapped' (**R-J**), one on top of the other, as if in layers.

137. *like a boulder* (**R-J, H**); *like a great rolling stone* (**L**): a superb C-simile, the point being that Hector's energetic attack seems unstoppable but will be stopped (145-6). The simile also advances the action, starting with Hector sweeping forward, and ending with him threatening to reach the sea. Note the personification of the rock ('misbegotten/stubborn/un-willing' 'much against its will/for all its onrush/for all its energy').

143. *lightly* (**L**): i.e. 'easily'.

156. *Deiphobus*: a son of Priam and leader of the third Trojan contin-gent, 12.94. The massed charge having failed, a standing fight now ensues; see **GI** 13B(v).

159. *Meriones*: see 2.645-52. He is Idomeneus' attendant and second-in-command, and his departure here (167) will lead to a long conversation with him (246-97). He will take on Deiphobus again at 528.

162. *broke off* (**R-J, H**); *was broken* (**L**): cf. 17.607.

163. *at arm's length* (**R-J**); *away from him* (**H, L**): cf. 20.261, 278.

170. *Imbrius*: his description follows the a-b-c pattern; see **GI** 2(v). The details are typical: for 172 'before the Greeks came', cf. 9.403; for 173 'young husband', cf. 13.365, 428.

178. *like an ash-tree*: moving B-simile, cf. Simoïsius' death at 4.482ff.; see Friedrich (2003) 56ff. for a comparison of the two.

184.   *avoid(ed)*: cf. 17.305, 526. For missing A and killing B, as Hector does here, see on 4.491.

198.   *lions*: C-simile, cf. 18.579ff., 3.23ff., for lion + prey variations.

203.   *head*: it is rare for the head to be cut off, but cf. 11.261, 14.497, and see on 11.455 for the increasing violence of these later books.

206-525: Poseidon encourages Idomeneus to take the lead. Idomeneus meets Meriones: they exchange views on the meaning of bravery and make for the battle. Idomeneus enjoys success, and Deiphobus fights back.

206.   *angry* (**R-J**); *enraged* (**H**); *angered* (**L**): for a god's anger/grief at the death of a relative, cf. Ares at 15.113-18, Zeus at 16.458-61. Amphimachus was son of Cteatus (186, see **R-J** index of omitted father's names, 446-7).

210.   *Idomeneus*: see on 2.645. The reason for Idomeneus' retreat from battle, to help a wounded comrade, is honourable; but it appears that he is not wearing his armour (241), when he has only recently been fighting in the front line (11.501)!

216.   *Thoas*: see on 2.638.

219.   *threats*: cf. Apollo to Aeneas at 20.83-5, Aeneas to Pandarus at 5.171-3. Thoas is of a stature that allows the disguised Poseidon to offer a mild, impersonal criticism – more of an observation, really – without offending Idomeneus. Indeed, Idomeneus welcomes 'Thoas'' words and urges him to continue the good work (228-30). Idomeneus' gloomy analysis, that this is how Zeus must want it to be (226), is echoed elsewhere, e.g. Agamemnon at 9.23ff.

236.   *the pair of us* (**R-J**); *as a pair* (**H**); *being two* (**L**): in fact 'Thoas' does not link up with Idomeneus again; but the god has done the job he came to do (209).

241.   *armour*: Idomeneus arms, signalling the start of an *aristeia*, for which see on 5.1-8. See on 210 above for the implausibility of his reason for returning to his hut – feeble motivation for the conversation with Meriones which is about to ensue.

242.   *like the lightning* (**R-J, H**); *as a thunderbolt* (**L**): C-simile. Compare the 'fire' of Diomedes' armour at the start of his *aristeia* at 5.4, and cf. 13.330 'fire/flame'.

247.   *Meriones*: picking up Meriones' departure at 167.

249-294.   Idomeneus meets his attendant and second-in-command Meriones in a situation embarrassing to both – not on the battlefield, where things are going very badly for the Greeks, but lurking by their quarters. Both have to explain their presence there in order to make sure the other understands that it is not out of cowardice. Hence their protests about how brave they are and the weapons and armour they have to prove it, stripped from Trojans they have killed in battle. Whether their embarrassment is meant to be humorous, as some argue, is difficult to tell.

257. *left on your hut/shelter*: Meriones had originally intended to fetch a spear from his own hut (168), but now that he has met Idomeneus, whose his hut is nearer, he changes plan. Obviously he could have picked up a spear on the battlefield, but Homer has to motivate the meeting with Idomeneus somehow.

261. *polished* **(H)**; *shining* **(L)**: the mud-bricks at the entrance to Mycenaean buildings could be protected by white plaster façades. Hence **R-J** 'white-plastered'. Cf. 8.435.

263. *at a distance* **(R-J, H)**; *far away* **(L)**: Idomeneus, in other words, swoops in after a kill to try to collect his enemy's gear, a dangerous move; see **GI** 13B(v)(a). This seems to be a mild jibe at Meriones' *failure* to collect enemy spoils, since Meriones has said he has come to *Idomeneus'* hut to get a spear (256-7), as if he has none of his own.

268. *but not where* **(R-J)**; *not close by* **(H)**; *not near* **(L)**: Meriones answers Idomeneus' criticism – your hut is nearer than mine – and challenges him to be deny his bravery (273 'you've seen it'/'you (must) know (of) it').

277. *hidden position* **(L)**: i.e. ambush. See on 1.226-7.

278. *coward* **(H, L)**: the Greek *deilos* means 'wretched' in Homer **(R-J)**, i.e. in this context, a timid second-rater.

291. *intimacy* **(R-J)**; *dalliance* **(H)**; *meeting* **(L)**: the Greek *oaristus* is used elsewhere in the *Il.* of the whisperings of lovers (e.g. 6.616, 22.127-8) – an unexpected and powerful image to use of warriors grappling with each other in the front line (see also 17.228).

298-9. *murderous Ares … Rout* **(R-J)**; *Ares … Panic* **(H)**; *Ares … Terror* **(L)**: D-simile, likening Idomeneus to Ares and Meriones to his son Rout, going out to help one side or other in a battle. It is rare to find *extended* similes comparing men to gods (cf. 7.208-10).

301-2. *Ephyri … Phlegyans*: two towns in Thessaly, an area like Thebes rich in legends that became the subject of ancient epic (see on 9.529).

307. *Deukalides* **(L)**: = Idomeneus, son of Deucalion (13.451).

308-9. *right … left*: these always indicate the Greek point of view.

313-15. *Ajaxes … Teucer … Hector*: e.g. the fighting at 13.170-94.

324. *breaker of men* **(H)**; *who breaks men* **(L)**: i.e. who breaks through the battle-line **(R-J)** and so turns it to flight.

325. *run* **(R-J, H)**; *speed of feet* **(L)**: 'swift-footed' Achilles was unmatchable in the pursuit of fleeing opponents.

330. *These, as they saw* **(L)**: i.e. the Trojans.

332. *gathered about him* **(L)**: read 'attacked him'.

334-60. Homer here paints a superb general picture of the battle-scene before Idomeneus get to work: powerful images – storms and dazzling armour – are followed by the divine overview, Zeus' plan for a temporary Trojan success in order to honour Achilles, vs. Poseidon's pity for the Greeks (13.15) and desire to help them while Zeus is paying no attention (13.7-90).

334. *as … currents* **(R-J)**; *gusts* **(H)**; *winds* **(L)**: D-simile, cf. 3.10-14, 5.499-505. The confusion of the dust-clouds evokes the chaos of battle, as well as suggesting the dust that rises from the ground as troops engage, cf. 11.163.

341. *dazzle(d)* **(R-J, L)**; *flash* **(H)**: cf. 2.455-8.

343. *man*: see on 13.127.

347. *victory for the (…)Trojans*: see 8.470-6, 11.78-9.

350. *Thetis*: for the plan of Zeus, see 1.505-30.

355. *Zeus was the older*: see 15.165-6 and cf. *Od.* 13.125-48.

359. *rope(s)* **(R-J, H)**; *cable* **(L)**: the poet is saying that Zeus and Poseidon ensured the two sides fought an indecisive battle (as if Zeus knew what was going on, which he does not) but it is not clear how the rope image worked. Are the two gods engaged in a sort of tug-of-war over the battlefield? Cf. on 11.336 for the stretching image.

363. *Othryoneus*: introduced with the familiar a-b-c pattern; see **GI** 2(iv). See on 170 for the 'young husband' theme; the 'latecomer to war' theme is also typical, cf. 13.793-4.

371. *swaggered about* **(R-J)**; *pranced forward* **(H)**; *high stride* **(L)**: cf. on Paris at 3.17. This young man is an overconfident show-off (he does not even appear to have a shield, and cf. his boastful offer to Priam to drive off the Greeks). He pays the price.

373. *triumph(ed)* **(R-J, H)**; *vaunting* **(L)**: typical, cf. 11.450-5, 13.413-16, and 445-54.

376. *daughter*: one wonders how Idomeneus knows Othryoneus' history so intimately.

384. *Asius*: one of the Trojan leaders and keen on horses (12.96-7), he had ignored Polydamas' advice not to try to cross the Greek ditch by chariot (12.110-11) and his death was foreseen at 12.113-15. The poet left him cursing his luck at 12.173-4.

389-93. *crashed … dust* **(R-J)**; *fell … dust* **(H)**; *He fell … dust* **(L)**: = 16.482-86 (which see). And Asius loses his horses too (13.400).

394. *charioteer('s)*: for an interesting discussion of the charioteer episode and its variations (16.401ff., 5.576ff., 13.434ff. etc.), see Friedrich (2003) 7ff., though one would not wish to draw his conclusions about authorship.

402. *Deiphobus*: he resumes the fight after his brief encounter with Meriones at 156, presumably to avenge his fellow-leader Asius. A series of 'chain-reaction' deaths now ensues, cf. 4.457-504.

404. *Idomeneus … avoided*: cf. 22.274-5.

411. *Hypsenor*: throwing at A and hitting B is typical, cf. 184 above.

423. *groaning heavily*: this indicates that someone is still alive, but Hypsenor to whom it refers is definitely dead. Since it is typical for wounded, groaning warriors to be carried out of battle, e.g. 8.332-4, Homer has probably nodded here.

428. *Alcathous*: a Trojan leader (12.93), another newly wed (see 363 above).

435. *trance* **(R-J)**; *mazed* **(H)**; *bewitched* **(L)**: a terrifying moment, brought on by Poseidon as if by magic. Cf. the dream-like 22.199-201.

441. *He cried out ... in him* **(L)**: read 'the armour rang out drily as the spear cut through'.

443. *shook ... the ... butt* **(R-J)**; *quiver* **(H)**; *shake* **(L)**: see Saunders in Friedrich (2003) 140-1 for evidence that this could happen.

447. *three ... one*: i.e. Othryoneus, Asius and Alcathous as against Hypsenor.

450. *got by Krete Minos* **(L)**: read 'got Minos, lord of Crete'.

459. *Aeneas*: here begins a 'consultation' sequence (see on 5.166). Homer does not explain why Priam should fail to respect Aeneas, though at 20.300-8 Poseidon explains that Aeneas' line will survive, but not Priam's (for the different branches of the family, see 20.236-40). Homer may have enlarged on this theme, and perhaps the tension it caused between the families, in other versions of the *Il.* The family theme, at any rate, is dominant in Deiphobus' appeal to Aeneas.

466. *looked after you* **(R-J)**; *raised you* **(H)**; *nursed you* **(L)**: cf. Phoenix's care for Achilles, 9.485-95.

470. *fear* **(L)**: read 'desire for flight'.

471. *boar*: C-simile, concentrating on the boar/Idomeneus' determination to hold his ground, whatever the odds.

480. *calling/called*: cf. 11.461-84, where Odysseus calls for help and is likened to a stag at bay.

492. *sheep*: D-simile, starting with the men following Aeneas like sheep their shepherd, but moving on to the shepherd's pleased reaction, and ending with that – Aeneas was pleased to see them.

502-6. *first*: it is common for A to throw at B and kill C (like Deiphobus at 516-20), and then for B to kill D. Here the death of C is omitted. Cf. 17.304-13.

515. *quick*: Idomeneus is an older man (see 2.645), lacking the speed for the dangerous business of retrieving his own spear and his opponent's armour after a kill, cf. 4.532 and contrast Deiphobus at 527, Meriones at 532. See **GI** 13B(v)(a) and on 263 above for Idomeneus' boast. Idomeneus' *aristeia* ends here.

521. *heard/know*: Ares will find out his son has died at 15.111-18.

538. *carried him*: cf. Diomedes at 11.399-40.

540-672: General fighting ensues.

542. *it was turned* **(L)**: read 'he was turned'.

546. *vein*: there is no such vein, cf. 20.482-3 and see Saunders in Friedrich (2003) 147-8. Thoon is in flight, in contrast to Aphareus (542).

554. *Poseidon*: to remind us of his keen interest in the battle (352, 434). Also, Nestor's son Antilochus was a grandson of Poseidon (father of Neleus, father of Nestor).

560. *Asius*: killed at 392-3.

569. *painfully*: see on 5.59.

571. *as a (…) bull/ox*: striking B-simile. Cf. 17.521-4, 20.403-6.
gasped (**L**): read 'struggled' (and 573).

577. *sword*: Helenus (Trojan leader with Deiphobus, 12.94), combines this superior (cf. 23.807-8) Thracian weapon with a bow at 584, an odd combination. See on 3.17.

broke the helmet to pieces (**L**): read 'broke the helmet-strap'.

588. *As black beans* (**R-J**); *As when/along* (**H, L**): a homely, agricultural D-simile. The purpose is to separate the edible part of the vegetable from the husk. Cf. on winnowing grain at 5.499; but beans/chickpeas are bouncier, and better represent an arrow flying off armour.

603. *you*: see on 4.127. This battle between Menelaus and Peisander involves two exchanges of blows, a fairly rare occurrence, cf. 16.334-41. It follows a typical pattern, see on 11.233.

612. *axe*: used again in battle only at 15.711.

617. *eyes*: being held in by tendons, the eyes cannot drop out (cf. 16.741). See Saunders in Friedrich (2003) 145-7.

620-39. In the first half of his speech (620-30) Menelaus confidently describes the Trojans' disgraceful behaviour and forecasts their final defeat since they broke the laws of Zeus, god of guests and hosts (625, see **GI** 7E and cf. 3.353-4); but in the second he expresses his bewilderment that this same Zeus should allow the Trojans to fight on and win. Menelaus puts it down to the Trojans' propensity to go to extremes in everything (621, 635, 639). He does not know of Zeus' plans for Achilles. Cf. Book 3/Intro.

652. *bladder*: cf. 5.66-7.

654. *like a (dead) worm*: a humiliating A-simile. Living worms writhe and twist; dead ones lie stretched out.

658. *his father*: Pylaemenes (643), who was killed at 5.576-9!

663. *Euchenor*: a novel and moving life-story, uniquely exploiting the 'father as prophet' theme (cf. on 5.10) so that Euchenor can *choose* death in war rather than after a long illness at home. Since he is also killed by Paris, some see a similarity in story-pattern to Achilles – who had a choice about when to die and a prophetic mother in Thetis, and was killed by Paris (Fenik [1968] 48-9).

669. *heavy forfeit* (**R-J**); *heavy fine* (**H**); *troublesome price* (**L**): i.e. the deal he would have to make with the Greeks in order to avoid service in the army, cf. 23.296-9 (n.b. Homeric Greeks did not use money).

673-837: Hector finds many Trojans dead or wounded but leads the Trojans back to the attack. Ajax taunts Hector who, despite an omen, replies in kind. The Trojans charge, and general fighting breaks out.

675. *left*: where Idomeneus had entered the fighting (326-7) and where the recent action has been based. We last saw Hector driven off by Ajax at 193-4 in the centre of the fighting (312-16).

681. *Ajax*: son of Oïleus (701), whose ships were in the centre of the Greek line with Odysseus' (10.109-10, 11.5-6).

684. *Trojans ... ferocious* (H); *onslaught of the Trojans* (L): it is perhaps more likely that these words refer to the ferocity of the Greek defence rather than of the Trojan attack (literally, 'where most of all they themselves and their horses were powerful in battle'), since the Trojans had left their chariots behind the Greek ditch (12.85).

685-700. A brief catalogue of Greek troops, designed to remind us of the forces the Greeks had in this part of the field, to alert us to the stiff resistance the Greeks are putting up here and to provide some cannon-fodder (15.328-42).

701-2. *Ajax ... Ajax*: the two still together here as earlier at 46-80.

703. *as ... oxen*: a fine D-simile, the two Ajaxes standing alongside each other being likened to two oxen pulling the plough: they are inseparable (joined by the yoke), work as one (pulling equally hard), with great effort (sweat) and do the job (they reach the end of the furrow). See 17.720-1.

710. *shield*: see on 7.219.

712. *Locrians*: these are no cowards: they merely use different weapons, bows and slings (717), and with such success that the Trojans begin to lose their will to fight (722). This is the only time that the poet depicts the support that a differently armed force can give to the front line; see Albracht (2003) [I.33].

724. *Polydamas*: see on 12.60. For the critical opening of the speech (726-9), cf. the start of his earlier speech 12.211-14. Polydamas does not mince his words.

734. *but the man's ... others* (L): lit. 'he knows it best of all', i.e. the man who gives good advice knows better than anyone else how good it is.

744. *I fear/am afraid*: Polydamas praises Hector's achievements of 'yesterday' (745, i.e. in advancing so far as to be able to camp out on the plain, 8.489-565), but suggests that the Trojans must regroup at once (740) and even hints that withdrawal would now be the safest course (a message he will continue to deliver). To strengthen his case, he raises the spectre of the return of Achilles (746-7).

751. *while I go* (R-J, H); *I am going* (L): Hector agrees that the troops need regrouping, and tells Polydamas to rally one sector, while he goes off to rally the other. Hector does not respond to Polydamas' suggestion of retreat.

759. *Deiphobus ... Asius*: a roll-call of the major Trojan casualties in this book, the result of the Greek revival under Poseidon's intervention.

769. *Paris, you parody* (R-J); *Paris you pest* (H); *Evil Paris* (L): = 3.39. Hector is making assumptions about Paris' performance; he is not to know that Paris has been engaging hard (779-80) and doing well in this sector (e.g. 660-72). Paris himself is keen to show his ability (784-6). Paris features with one further kill on which no further comment is passed

(15.341) and then disappears from the *Il*. He goes out, then, with some martial credit to his name.

776. *it would be better ... than now* (**L**): i.e. I may have avoided fighting at other times, but not now.

789. *Cebriones ... Polydamas*: i.e. we return to the centre of the battlefield, where Trojan troops have been regrouped. Many in this brief catalogue will be killed in Book 14.

795. *like an angry squall* (**R-J**); *cruel winds' blast* (**H**); *racking winds* (**L**): C-simile, the march of the waves likened to the ranks of advancing troops, and their noise to the din of battle cf. 4.422-6, 11.305-9.

803. *rounded shield* (**R-J**); *circle of his shield* (**H, L**): see on 6.117.

810-32. Ajax son of Telamon and Hector challenge and insult each other. These two best fighters on either side (in Achilles' absence) will clash frequently in the following books (they have already at 189-94), as Hector drives forward to fire the Greek ships and Ajax desperately tries to defend them. This clash, however, stops almost at once, with exchange of insults but not of weapons, and resumes at 14.402ff. Some have thought the intervening section (13.833-14.401) has been inserted into an existing Ajax-Hector duel sequence. That may be; and it may be Homer who inserted it.

822. *eagle*: a bird of omen, but Hector always ignores them, cf. 12.237-40 and see on 12.200.

825. *son of/to Zeus*: Hector has toyed with this idea before (cf. 8.538-41) but it is hardly a sensible desire for a mortal to entertain. See on 13.54.

831. *glut the dogs*: ironically, this will (almost) be Hector's fate.

Book 14

Introduction

An important feature of Book 13, as of Book 14, is that, despite all the help Zeus has given so far, Hector cannot be allowed to appeal to Zeus for help, however disastrous the Trojans' plight. That would alert Zeus to Poseidon's intervention and the set-back Poseidon has caused to his schemes. However, Homer's device for keeping Zeus ignorant of what is happening on earth – he has been made to look away from the battlefield (13.1-9) – can hardly carry conviction in the long term. Zeus cannot be *that* careless, surely? Homer therefore invents a second scheme to keep Zeus away from the action: Hera will seduce him, and send him to sleep. This wonderful scene occupies the middle of the book, balanced by matching scenes on either side in a typical ring-composition format:

A 1-134: the Greeks look like losing
B 135-52: Poseidon rallies them
C 153-353: the seduction of Zeus
B 354-401: Poseidon leads the Greeks into battle
A 402-522: the Greeks look like winning.

Nestor's observation of the way things are going for the Greeks (very badly, 13-15) is reinforced by his meeting with the three wounded Greek leaders Odysseus, Diomedes and Agamemnon (27-9). Homer thereby gently reminds his audience of their absence from battle (cf. 11/Intro) and makes them stress the fact that they cannot and must not return to the fight (63, 128-30). Another absentee is also brought to mind in this book – Achilles. He has been there in the background all along – e.g. 12.10, 13.113, 324 and 348 – but now Homer brings him and his resentment against Agamemnon more strongly to the fore again at 14.50-1, 139-42, 366-9.

Agamemnon shows his usual incompetence in a crisis, but backs down with a good grace when Odysseus points out the hopelessness of his plan to prepare a departure from Troy (74-108). The youthful Diomedes, as ever, has a suggestion to make (110-32). When, after the seduction of Zeus, Homer returns the focus to the battlefield (354), he picks up the fight between Ajax and Hector that he had left at 13.810-32. Ajax's defeat of Hector is a signal for a major Greek offensive, and the book ends with the triumph of Ajax and the minor Greek heroes (442ff.) and the complete rout of the Trojans. It is time for Zeus to wake up to what is going on and reassert his will over disobedient gods.

Hera's seduction of Zeus is one of the high spots of the *Il*. The great theme of the battle of the sexes – woman's guile and sexual attraction, and man's inability to resist her – begins here in Western literature, prepared for by Homer's earlier hints of the tensions between the two (e.g. 1.536-

600). This sort of scene inevitably attracted the disapproval of later high-minded Greeks, who thought such behaviour corrupted men and demeaned divinities (e.g. Plato *Republic* 389e-391e), but Homer had no problems about the idea of gods enjoying themselves. What, after all, was the point of being a divinity if one could not make the most of it (e.g. 1.595-611)?

Such scenes are often described as 'light relief', as if the poet feels his subject-matter is becoming too heavy, and the audience will drop off unless he brings on the clowns. But the gods are not clowns; they are not brought on simply to provide a diversion from the story; they are an integral part of the world of the *Il*. The point is this: Homer has constructed his gods as a family, with Zeus attempting to control them as best he may, his ultimate sanction being force (see on 1.401). This is what families can be like, in our time as in Homer's. As human families argue, squabble and play tricks on each other, so too does the divine family. It may be intensely irritating when this happens on earth, but it is highly amusing to see the gods suffering, at least in this respect, from exactly the same problems as humans do and being able to do very little about it, all-powerful and immortal masters of the universe although they may be. Some problems, in other words, are universal, and families are one of them – some sort of consolation for struggling humanity. For other occasions when the divine family behaves all too like a human one, laughing and joking among themselves at the expense of other members of the family, see on 1.595 and 600.

Hera's seduction of Zeus is a particularly clever ruse because she can claim complete innocence of any wrong-doing: how can it possibly be *her* fault if Zeus suddenly feels passionate about her? In other words, Zeus will have only himself to blame if the result is that he continues to fail to spot Poseidon carrying on the good work (in Hera's eyes) of helping the Greeks. Hera knows her man and his weaknesses, and happily exploits them in her own interests.

Main sources for the commentary and related reading
Edwards (1987) 246-53; Janko (1992); Willcock (1984).

1-152: Nestor finds Odysseus, Diomedes and Agamemnon all wounded. Odysseus attacks Agamemnon for cowardice. Poseidon heartens Agamemnon with a speech.

1. *Nestor*: we left him and Machaon drinking Hecamede's (6) special potion and talking at 11.623-42, after Machaon had been wounded and driven back to the camp at 11.506-20. They had stripped at 11.620, so Nestor needs to re-arm here (9-12).

10. *Thrasymedes*: see on 10.255-7, though one wonders how a shield given to Diomedes came to be in Nestor's hut.

15. *Trojans*: it is not clear from the end of Book 13 that the Greeks are in flight at this moment (see e.g. 13.723-4, 835-7), but presumably, with the wall down, this is how it must have looked to Nestor (focalisation). Nestor had been in his hut with Machaon when the wall (built at 7.436-41) was breached (12.462).

16.   *As the great open sea* **(R-J)**; *As when* **(H, L)**: fine D-simile (cf. 9.4-8 for another image of the sea to illustrate a moment of mental agitation). **L** misses the 'sullen' **(H)** 'silence' **(R-J)** of the sea as it restlessly heaves about.

20.   *faltered* **(R-J)**; *pondered* **(H, L)**: see on 1.189.

28.   *wounded*: at 11.252, 377, 437. They limp in, propping themselves up on spears (37).

30.   *ships*: Homer takes us back to the time when the various contingents of Greeks and their ships first arrived in Ilium (see **GI** 1C). His description suggests that the ships were hauled up on the beach in rows in a curve around the length of the bay, like a Greek theatre (as the ancient commentator Aristarchus puts it). See **R-J** map 1, and cf. Agamemnon's plan to launch the ships at the bottom of the beach, lying closest to the sea, at 74-81.

43.   *turned your back on* **(R-J)**; *left the fighting* **(H, L)**: the leaders are even more demoralised at the sight of Nestor because they can draw only ominous conclusions from his absence from battle.

44.   *I am afraid*: Agamemnon under pressure, as often, sees only doom and gloom (cf. 9.17-28).

45.   *in the speech/assembly* **(R-J, H)**; *that he spoke* **(L)**: at 8.526-41. Cf. on 9.240.

50.   *furious with me* **(R-J)**; *anger (...) in their hearts* **(H, L)**: cf. 13.107-14 and see on 2.222. Agamemnon is uneasily aware that he does not command loyalty.

54.   *Zeus*: there is a fine irony in Nestor's observation that 'even Zeus' could not stop the Greek wall being breached: he was not to know that this was exactly what Zeus wanted to happen.

63.   *wounded*: Homer could have decided that these heroes had healed by now, but it suits his narrative plan to continue keeping them out of battle (see 11/Intro).

65-81.   More pessimism from Agamemnon, who makes the same suggestion to run for it as he had before (see on 44, above, and on 2.73, in the context of the 'testing' of the troops at 2.139-41). His state of mind can be gauged from the fact that he fears the Trojans may even attack at night (78-9) – a very rare occurrence in the ancient world.

82-102.   Odysseus' harsh rebuke can be compared with Diomedes' at 9.32-49, and his own to Agamemnon at 4.350-5 (where Agamemnon also backs down). Note that Odysseus does not accuse Agamemnon of cowardice (which he might have done: cf. Odysseus' heroic stand at 11.404-10) but only of demoralising talk (suggesting the army is willing to fight for him if only he will give them leadership) and poor tactical thinking. The result is that Agamemnon can agree that only his judgement was at fault and then appear in charge of the situation by asking for positive ideas instead (107-8).

109-32. The youthful (112) Diomedes, as often, has an idea to put forward when no one else does (cf. 7.40-2, 9.32-49, 697-709) and demonstrates his credentials with reference to his father (cf. on 4.376, and on 2.638 for the detail of Tydeus' settling in Argos, 119-20). He suggests leading by example, i.e. appearing on the battlefield and inspiring all the troops.

132. *indulging/favoured their anger* (**H, L**): the meaning rather seems to be 'those who had previously been loyal' (but are not currently fighting).

135. *an old man*: Poseidon's disguise is irrelevant since he indicates he is a god with his assurance (143-6) immediately followed by his inspiring (151-2) charge and shout at 147-50 (cf. 13.59-75). His verbal attack on Achilles (139-42) is well calculated to appeal to Agamemnon.

137. *(by the) right hand*: a friendly, calming gesture. Cf. 24.361.

153-360: Hera (on Olympus) decides to send Zeus (on Ida) to sleep by making love to him. She decks herself out, gets Aphrodite's love charm and persuades Sleep to join her. Hera and Zeus make love and Zeus falls asleep. Sleep tells Poseidon he can carry on helping the Greeks.

153-360. Hera's scheme ensures that Poseidon's pro-Greek intervention continues to be successful. Since the plot is the will of the poet, Homer did not *need* to invent this episode to prolong Zeus' absence from the action, but he clearly saw advantages to it. Perhaps Poseidon's great shout (150), raising fears that Zeus could sit up and take notice, acted as the motivation for it.

157. *sitting*: see 11.183, 13.1-9 and **R-J** map 1.

162. *deck/trick herself out* (**R-J, H**); *array herself* (**L**): this wonderfully sensuous, richly-elaborated dressing-up scene with its secret cleansing, anointing, hair-arrangement, ear-rings and so on has been (absurdly) likened to a warrior putting on his armour.

172. *oil of immortal sweetness … perfumed* (**H**); *sweet olive oil … beside her* (**L**): it seems more likely that this phrase means the 'immortal oil with which her dress was scented'. If this is so – **R-J** interprets like this – Homer goes on to describe how, when Hera moves it by walking, heaven and earth are filled with its fragrance, i.e. it is a very powerful perfume. Clothes are often described as 'shining' in Homer, i.e. treated with olive oil, which made them supple and shining, even after washing.

176-7. *arranged the … curls* (**L**): read 'plaited the … locks'.

188. *Aphrodite*: as goddess of sexual attraction, she alone can make absolutely certain that Hera's proposed seduction of Zeus will not fail. Note how Hera calls her 'dear child' (190), assuming seniority over her, and Aphrodite submissively calls Hera 'goddess, daughter of Cronus' (194). Aphrodite is willing to help her primarily because Hera is going to present her with a sexual problem (see 201 below).

192. *helping the Greeks* (R-J); *side with/defend the Danaans* (H, L): see on 3.380. Hera's plan will (amusingly) mean that Aphrodite is deceived into unwittingly helping the Greeks she hates.

201. *Ocean/Okeanos*: since sexual relationships are Aphrodite's domain, Hera has purposely designed this story of discord in the marriage between Ocean and Tethys with Aphrodite in mind.

203. *Rhea*: the story relates to the time when Zeus was battling against Cronus for superiority, which ultimately led to the burial underground of Cronus and his Titan supporters (see on 2.783). Hera was a daughter of Cronus and Rhea, and presumably Tethys 'took her in' during the battle. Cf. Thetis 'taking in' Hephaestus at 18.397-405.

215. *charm* (R-J); *band* (H); *zone* (L): since Aphrodite takes this item from her breast (214), it can hardly be a 'zone', which is a form of belt or girdle. Since the Greek *kestos* means 'strap, (breast-)band', one would rather like it to be something worn round the chest/breast, and perhaps it originally was; but Homer seems to imagine it as some sort of love-charm to be tucked away and carried (223), as if it were a pendant.

215-17. *magic ... turns even wise men into fools* (R-J); *magic ... seduces the heart even in those of good sense* (H); *beguilements ... steals the heart away even from the thoughtful* (L): gloriously sensual lines; the 'fools' will include even Zeus, wisest and most powerful of gods.

226. *Pieria ... Emathia*: Pieria is in Thessaly and Emathia in Macedonia.

231. *Sleep, brother of Death*: see on 11.241.

233. *if ever* (R-J, L); *before* (H): one god begs another god in a typical prayer-form (see GI 7A)!

246. *forefather* (R-J); *creator* (H); *whence is risen* (L): in some traditions (e.g. Hesiod and cf. *Il.* 5.898), Heaven (Ouranos/Uranus) and Earth (Gaia) were the parents of all, but Plato *Cratylus* 402b alludes to another tradition in which Ocean and Tethys fulfilled this function (cf. Plato's *Timaeus* 40e), and Aristotle tells of some poets who made Night the first being (cf. 261 – Zeus does not want to displease Night). Homer selects the tradition that suits him at the time. Near Eastern myth has stories of the same sort about Ocean, Earth and the Heavens; see West (1997) 382-4 on the whole seduction episode, especially 383.

250. *Heracles*: see on 5.638, and cf. 15.18-30. The reference to the gods being hurled/beaten about (257) is picked up at 15.23.

271. *Swear ... Styx*: see on 2.755 for Styx, and GI 7E for the theory of oaths. Hera swears by the Titans (279) because, as ancient enemies of Zeus (see on 2.783), they would be allowed to take revenge on her if she reneged on her promise – with disastrous consequences.

284. *Lecton*: a promontory at the foot of Mount Ida. Hera's route from Lemnos via Imbros to Ida is very roundabout, but she is only doing what any sea-going ancient Greek would have done – travel as close to land as possible at all times (R-J map 3).

307. *at the foot of Ida* (R-J, H); *in the foothills of Ida* (L): more lies from Hera, as is her wifely protestation that she has come to tell Zeus where she is going (309-11) – all calculated to proclaim her 'innocence' of any scheming and spur Zeus on (who clearly asked about the chariot only to check that none was easily available).

313-28. Zeus' come-on to Hera bears some comparison with Paris' to Helen (3.438-46). But the great joke about Zeus' speech is his long roll-call of previous lovers. These were a constant source of trouble between the two, but Zeus' lust has overcome any awareness he may have had about her sensitivity to the subject – he regards his recital as an index of his true feelings – while Hera, if she is to get her way, has to grin and bear the great list (in which she comes last) rather than go up in smoke about it. But she has the last laugh: Zeus thinks he is seducing her, to fulfil his desires, when in fact she is seducing him, to fulfil hers.

Ixion (317) tried to rape Hera, so Zeus got his own back by seducing Ixion's wife (Peirithous was a Lapith, 1.263); Zeus seduced Danae (319) by entering her chamber as a shower of gold (for Perseus, see 19.116-25); Demeter (326) bore him Persephone, and Leto (327) Apollo and Artemis.

332. *see everything* (**R-J**); *open to view* (**H**); *can be seen* (**L**): Hera continues to inflame Zeus with the prospect of delay. Cf. the embarrassment experienced by Ares and Aphrodite when they were exposed to public view by being trapped in bed by Hephaestus (*Od.* 8.266-366). Was Hera in fact planning to lock Zeus in her bedroom after they had made love there (cf. 166-8, 337-40)? Perhaps in some versions she did; if so, listeners missed out on the magnificent open-air love-making that now follows.

344. *Helios* (**H, L**): i.e. the sun.

346-53. A wonderfully erotic passage: all nature responds in fertile abundance when the king of the gods makes love. Alexander Pope (1743) surpasses himself here (Book 14, 393-406): 'Gazing he spoke, and kindling at the view / His eager arms around the Goddess threw. / Glad earth perceives, and from her bosom pours / Unbidden herbs and voluntary flow'rs; / Thick, new-born vi'lets a soft carpet spread, / And clust'ring *Lotus* swell'd the rising bed; / And sudden hyacinths the turf bestrow / And flaming *Crocus* made the mountain glow. / There, golden clouds conceal the heav'nly pair, / Steep'd in soft joys and circumfus'd with air; / Celestial dews, descending o'er the ground, / Perfume the mount, and breathe *Ambrosia* round. / At length, with love and sleep's soft pow'r oppress'd, / The panting Thund'rer nods and sinks to rest.'

361-439: Poseidon rallies the Greeks, and Ajax takes Hector out of the fighting with a rock.

363. *issued his orders* (**R-J**); *called loud to them* (**H**); *in a great voice* (**L**): is Poseidon speaking in his own person here, or still in disguise as an old man (136)? Given the energy with which he leads the advance – inspiring shout (147-52), verbal exhortation, and leading by example (374,

384-7) – presumably the former, though no Greek comments on the fact, and he was pretty active even as an old man (147-52).

371. *shields*: the men are surely swapping just weapons rather than exchanging all their body-armour?

381-2. *armour* **(H, L)**: if the above note is right, presumably this means 'arms'. On the other hand, cf. Diomedes and Glaucus exchanging body-armour at 6.234-6. This, after all, is epic, where people do unrealistic things.

392. *the sea*: Poseidon's element rushes up the beach.

394-9. The waves of the sea (Poseidon again), a wind-driven fire and the howling of a gale – three terrifying natural elements – cannot match the noise of the armies, now locked in an almost superhuman struggle.

401. *fearful shouts* **(H)**; *voice of terror* **(L)**: the men are not frightened or terrified; they are emitting terrifying war-cries as they charge.

402. *Ajax*: resuming the duel against Hector broken off abruptly in the last book (see on 13.810-32).

404. (*shoulder-*) *straps*: cf. 12.400-2.

410. *rock/stone/boulder*: for helping to support beached ships, see on 1.486. In battle, see on 5.503, and cf. Ajax vs. Hector at 7.264-72.

413. *spin/spun like a top*: a vivid and unexpected A-simile.

414. *As (when) a(n) (great) oak*: D-simile, Hector now being likened to a fallen oak (the most difficult tree to cut down), i.e. he has stopped reeling about and collapsed. The reference to Zeus' thunderbolt indicates the power of Ajax's throw. The shocked onlookers of the simile are presumably the Trojans, though they are not said to have reacted like that at the time. Indeed, the Trojans quickly gather to protect their leader and carry him out of the fighting (424-32).

425-6. *Aeneas ... Glaucus*: these make up virtually all the Trojan leaders left in the field; though Glaucus was wounded at 12.387-92 and had in fact retreated (he is still wounded at 16.508-12).

437. *vomit(ing)* **(H, L)**: read 'coughing'. Hector has internal injuries. For Hector's fainting, see on 5.310 and cf. Saunders in Friedrich (2003) 153-6.

440-522: With Hector gone, a series of killings ensues. The Trojans are routed and run.

A series of 'chain-reaction' killings now ensues (see on 4.457-504). After Ajax son of Oïleus kills Satnius (447), Trojan Polydamas kills Prothoenor and boasts over him; Ajax son of Telamon kills Archelochus and boasts back; Trojan Acamas kills Promachus and replies to that boast; and Greek Peneleos ends the sequence by killing Ilioneus and boasting over him too (for a similar exchange of boasts, cf. 13.373-454). This is too much for the Trojans, who turn and run (506-7), at which point Homer appeals to the Muses (508, see on 1.1) for information about the eight Trojans killed in the rout and Ajax's (son of Oïleus, see on 2.527) particular success. The scene is now set for Zeus to wake up at the start of Book 15 and redress the balance.

443. *Satnius*: described in typical a-b-c form; see **GI** 2(iv). For the rural setting of his birth, cf. 5.313, 6.21.

449. *Polydamas*: Hector's warning voice (see on 12.60).

462. *avoided/escaped*: for A throws at B, misses and kills C, see on 4.491.

467. *hit the ground*: Archelochus' reaction makes it look as if Homer is saying that his head was sliced off as a result of Ajax's throw – a most unlikely occurrence; see, on this and 494 below, Saunders in Friedrich (2003) 143-4.

473. *Antenor*: see on 3.146.

477. *drag (off) the body (away)*: always a dangerous moment, cf. 4.463.

479. *loud-mouths* (**R-J**); *bletherskates* (**H**); *arrow-fighters* (**L**): see on 4.242.

494. *eyeball*: another very grisly death, with beheading (496-7) and waving about of head (499-500) to follow. This precipitates the Trojan rout, an event that often follows a series of individual killings. See Albracht (2003) [I.27ff.].

499. *raised/lifting it* (**R-J, L**): i.e. the head.

508. *Muses*: see on 11.218 for appeals to them at important turning-points in the action.

515. *son of Atreus* (**H**): i.e. Menelaus, Agamemnon being among the wounded.

Book 15

Introduction

Zeus wakes up and reasserts himself in the same terms that he did at the start of Book 8, first threatening punishment for any god who crosses him (104-9, 135-7, 159-67); second, personally intervening in the battle, or prompting Apollo, to drive the Trojans back into the Greek camp, with especial help for Hector (236-62, 292-3, 318-22, 355-66, 377-80, 458-70, 488-93, 567, 592-602, 610-14, 636-7, 694-5, 717-25); and third, foreshadowing what is going to happen next (53-77, 601-2, 610-14) as if to confirm that the plan of Zeus to honour Achilles is now back in full swing (74-7), and nothing will be able to frustrate it. There is something amusing about the way Zeus sends Hera to carry out his orders, i.e. to warn off the other gods and tell Apollo and Iris to report back to Zeus. Hera is clearly furious about being humiliated like this, and takes it out on Ares with a malicious comment about the death of a son of his in battle (89-112), but there is nothing she can do about it, and the gods find nothing funny about Zeus' orders. They know they are back under the whip (cf. Athene at 121-41).

As in Book 8, Homer faces the problem of pacing the Trojan advance and ensuring that any victory is not too overwhelming, and he does this (as usual) by keeping the human and divine agencies in productive balance. So while it is clear to both sides that the Trojans have the upper hand – observe the Trojan response to Zeus' thunderclap designed to answer Nestor's prayer (377-80, cf. 467-70, 486-93) – Hector is still unable to get the better of Ajax, with whom he is brought briefly into contact at 415, and with whom he swaps rallying calls to the troops (484-513, 552-64, 715-41).

The Greek retreat is carefully sequenced:

218-345: Poseidon leaves the field, on Zeus' orders (218-19). Then Hector is revived by Apollo, and Greek hearts sink (236-80). A massed defensive formation is organised by Thoas to allow the main body of Greeks an orderly retreat (281-305), but this formation is routed when Apollo waves the aegis at them (320-7), and itself flees back behind the ditch and wall (343-5).

355-66: Apollo knocks down some of the wall, partially fills in the Greek ditch and allows the Trojan chariots successfully to penetrate the Greek camp *en masse* for the first time. This adds a new dimension to the assault on the Greeks in their own territory, allowing Homer to add variety to what, since 12.84-7, has been a clash between warriors on foot (with the exception of the foolish Asius, who had earlier tried, but failed miserably, to launch a chariot attack, 12.109-72, 13.384-8).

367-637: Nestor rallies the Greeks in front of the ships (367-77), where they fight back and form a second defensive line (565-6, 617-22). That too is broken by Hector's onslaught (629-37).

653-746: The Greeks regroup a third time round the sterns and huts of the ships drawn up at the highest point on the beach (653-7), with Nestor again urging them on (661-6). Ajax actually makes a stand from the decks of these ships, but even he cannot prevent Hector finally laying his hands on one and calling for the Trojans to bring fire (703-18); Ajax falls back a little (727-30), and still manages to keep the Trojans off – but for how much longer? The Greeks are unquestionably on the back foot, as they were in Book 8 when Zeus kept the Trojans hammering away at them, but they have not yet given up, especially not Ajax or Nestor. Note the cameo rôle given to Meges. He has scarcely featured up till now – another minor hero brought on stage for his hour of glory (302-543).

As the *Il.* approaches its climax, the sense of tragedy overhanging the proceedings increases. This feature will be dealt with in fuller detail in 16/Intro, but the note can be heard already in Book 15. We now know that Hector will kill Patroclus, and Achilles Hector, and Ilium will eventually fall (61-71), and the poet further announces that Zeus was glorifying Hector, but only for a short time before Athene and Achilles killed him (610-14). Thetis' demands were indeed unreasonable (598-9). Hector himself becomes increasingly frenzied as the action develops; note his threats at 347-51, the rabid dog image at 607-9, the overpowering confidence at 718-25 – all the more poignant when his death has just been signalled. Meanwhile, at 390-405, almost unnoticed, Patroclus too is on his way to a date with destiny: he leaves the wounded Eurypylus to return to Achilles, and death.

Hector in Book 6 was the epitome of a great warrior with a strong sense of duty to his family, but even more to the community which it was his duty to lead in battle (e.g. 6.492-3 – fighting is the job of men, and of him above all). But his duel with Ajax in Book 7 did not redound to his credit (the Trojans were delighted – and amazed – to see him return from it, 7.307-11), and the Trojan successes in Books 8-15 have been driven more by the plan of Zeus than any brilliance on Hector's part. The fact that Zeus supports him indicates that he is worthy of that support; but at the same time, it is as if he is simply an instrument of Zeus rather than a great warrior doing battle on his own terms (cf. Redfield [1994] 142). His confidence, too, in Zeus' support is excessive. It is not wholly misplaced – Zeus has given a clear enough indication of his support with Iris' message at 11.200-9 – but Iris promised him only one day's glory. Hector, however, seems to think this guarantees that he will drive the Greeks out of Troy once and for all – as the Trojans must, **GI** 13(ix) – and as a result he dogmatically rejects any advice contrary to that ambition (e.g. Polydamas' cautious warnings). Only when Zeus' plan is fulfilled – or abandoned – and Achilles has returned to the fighting will Hector become again the warrior we knew in Book 6.

Main sources for the commentary
Janko (1992); Willcock (1984).

1-261: The Trojans retreat in panic from the Greek camp. Zeus wakes up, furious, and turns on Hera, who claims innocence. Zeus foretells the deaths of Patroclus and Hector, calls off Poseidon (who reluctantly obeys) and orders Apollo to revive Hector and restore the Trojans' victorious assault.

3. *chariots*: which the Trojans had left behind the Greek ditch at 12.85.

4. *Zeus*: see 14.352-3.

9. *Hector*: see 14.436-9, and for 'vomiting' (11) read 'coughing' (see on 14.437).

12. *pity/pitied/felt pity*: as Zeus does frequently for those he admires, e.g. Sarpedon 16.431-61, Hector 17.200-8, 22.168-73, 24.66-70, 332, Achilles' horses 17.441-7, Ajax 17.648-50, Achilles 19.340-3; and sometimes for men in general, 20.21.

14. *Hopeless* (**L**): read 'incorrigible, impossible'.

15. *terrified* (**L**): read 'routed'.

19. *anvils*: Hera was punished by being hung up by her hands and with heavy anvils attached to her feet, to 'stretch' her and increase the agony (a common slave punishment). The king of the gods ultimately controls his family by force (1.401).

23. *hurl(ed)/throw*: see on 1.591; as becomes clear (25-30, cf. 14.249-62), Zeus is referring to the punishment he meted out to Hera for her treatment of Heracles.

37. *Styx*: see on 2.755.

39. *bridal couch* (**R-J**); *bed of … marriage* (**H, L**): it is a delicious irony that Hera should swear to her honesty by her marriage bed which she has just so ruthlessly exploited to deceive Zeus.

41. *Poseidon*: technically, Hera is correct – she had nothing to do with Poseidon's intervention on behalf of the Greeks (it was entirely his own doing, 13.10-16). Nor did she in fact instruct Sleep that, when Zeus was asleep, Sleep should tell Poseidon to continue with his support; it was Sleep's initiative (14.352-60).

47. *smiled*: why does Zeus smile? Because Hera (at last) agrees with him? Or because he knows she is being economical with the truth? His reply to her, an 'impossible' future condition (49-52 'Well, if you really were on my side, *of course* Poseidon would agree with the two of us'), and his follow up at 53 ('But if by any chance you are actually telling the truth …'), suggests perhaps the latter. But Homer does not tell us outright: we must draw our own conclusions. Cf. on 1.348, 1.595.

59-71. Zeus outlines the crucial events that will drive the *Il.* till Book 22, and even looks beyond the end of the *Il.* to the capture of Ilium, 70-1, though not to the death of Achilles. Such summaries of the future are typical, e.g. 8.470-6, cf. 13.345-60, and are characteristic of a *tragic* outlook. As in Greek tragedy, far from removing suspense, the audience's knowledge of what is to happen sharpens it, while increasing our sense of pathos because of the contrast between our knowledge and the characters' ignorance.

71. *Athene*: presumably a reference to the Wooden Horse.

75. *the promise I gave* (**R-J**); *as I promised* (**H**); *as I undertook* (**L**): see 1.500-30.

80. *Like the speed of thought* (**R-J**); *As (when) the thought* (**H, L**): unique D-simile, likening the speed of a flying god to the speed of thought: all one has to do is think of a place and you are there.

87. *Themis*: her name means 'Right', and she takes a leading role in summoning assemblies of the gods (cf. 20.5), where one assumes Right will prevail. She reaches Hera first with her cup (88-9).

95. *the gods' feast* (**R-J**); *their shared feasting* (**H**); *the feast's ... division* (**L**): Hera invites Themis to begin the feasting, but immediately spoils it all (cf. 1.573-6) by her obvious displeasure and revelation of Zeus' will. The feast is completely forgotten.

101. *no warmth* (**R-J**); *no softening* (**H**); *not at peace* (**L**): a fine description of Hera forcing a laugh to try to disguise her recent humiliation. See **GI** 10A.

112. *Ascalaphus*: see 13.516-23. Hera is trying to have it both ways – urging obedience to Zeus while provoking Ares to action with her news about his son.

119. *Panic/Fear and Rout/Terror*: cf. 4.440, 13.299. These are Ares' sons.

123. *Athene*: she has a reputation for dealing with Ares (e.g. 5.765-6, 21.391-417). Both are gods of war (Athene, see on 2.447, cf. 4.64-5), but she is also god of cunning intelligence, *Mêtis* (her mother: see on 5.880). Athene uses two arguments against Ares: Zeus' ruthless use of his power, and the impossibility of every son of a god being saved (presumably because there were so many of them, cf. 16.444-9).

143. *out of the palace* (**R-J**); *outside the house* (**H, L**): is Hera trying to save face in front of the other gods by passing on Zeus' instructions to Iris and Apollo *outside* the palace?

165-6. *stronger/superior ... senior* (**R-J, H**); *greater ... elder*: for Zeus' superiority over Poseidon, cf. 13.355.

170. *Like/as ... snow*: B-simile.

174-83. As usual, Iris' words virtually repeat Zeus' orders at 159-67. Cf. e.g. 2.28.

189. *three parts/ways*: see on 2.783.

197-9. *daughters*: cf. Ares' thoughts on the recalcitrant Athene, 5.875-80!

204. *Furies*: see on 9.454.

215. *Ilium*: unknown to Poseidon, Zeus has already agreed that Ilium shall eventually fall (15.70-1).

218. *withdrew/left*: Poseidon's abrupt withdrawal indicates his displeasure.

220. *Then/After this*: it is typical of Homer to report two events which *would* have happened simultaneously (i.e. Iris going to Poseidon and Apollo to Hector) *as if* they happened one after the other. See Zielinski's law, 3.121-244.

229. *aegis*: see on 1.202.

233. *Hellespont* (**R-J, H**); *crossing of Helle* (**L**): Helle escaped from her evil stepmother aboard a flying ram (the one with the Golden Fleece), which was taking her to Colchis in the eastern Black Sea. But she fell off into the sea named after her. Later Greeks understood by 'Hellespont' the straits we know as the Dardanelles to the north of Troy, leading to the Bosporus and the Black Sea (**R-J** map 2), but in earlier traditions it was also associated with the northern Aegean.

237. *hawk*: B-simile. Apollo descends with the speed of a hawk, not in the form of a hawk, cf. Hector's recognition of him as a god (247-8).

240. *no longer prostrate/lying/sprawled*: the poet left Hector unconscious at 14.436-9.

258. *cavalry* (**L**): neither Greeks nor Trojans have cavalry. Read 'chariots'.

262-389: Hector returns invigorated to battle. The Greeks panic and run. Apollo kicks down the Greek defences, and the Trojans swarm round the ships.

263-8. = Paris at 6.506-11 (see note there). Hector and Paris are brothers. Note that this simile ends with Hector urging on his men; at 6.514, it ends with Paris laughing.

271. *like rustics* (**R-J**); *As when country farmers/men who* (**H, L**): C-simile. The Greeks are first likened to rustics cornering a stag or goat (i.e. Greeks trapping Trojans – and the Greeks do currently have the upper hand); but then the simile foreshadows future action – the lion = Hector, who will indeed send them running. See on 11.474-82. A simile, as often, welcomes a hero back into the fighting; for a double simile (doubling the significance of the moment), see 16.351-67, and cf. 2.455-83, where a run of similes accompanies the Greeks as they go into battle for the first time in the *Il.*

281. *Thoas*: a minor leader (see on 2.638), but good enough to be one whose form Poseidon thought it worth taking (13.216).

295. *main body retreat* (**R-J**); *bulk of the troops return* (**H**); *multitude ... make its way*: Thoas' tactical advice here involves an important defensive move. While the rest of the Greeks retreat back to the ships, he and the other leaders will close ranks in massed defensive formation (303 'closed battle-line/formed a battle-front/closed their order', cf. 312) to face the Trojan massed assault (306). See on 13.126. This signals that the Greeks are now firmly on the back foot and prepares the way for Hector's assault on the ships and the entry of Patroclus into the fighting in Book 16. See Albracht (2003) [I.42].

312-19. The two massed formations meet, and a general picture of the fighting develops as they slog it out (cf. 4.446-56) until one sides breaks and runs (320-2, cf. 11.67-91). This is serious for the Greeks: their massed defensive formation (301-2) consisted of their best men.

323. *As (when) two wild* **(R-J, H)**; *as when in the dim* **(L)**: C/D-simile, describing a rout. The two wild animals stampeding the herds/flocks are (presumably) Apollo and Hector, though Apollo's action in waving the aegis is the primary cause (326-7); the shepherd who has left his flocks is Poseidon.

328-45. The bloody result of a rout: mass slaughter of the fleeing enemy, who do not know which way to turn in their panic (343-5). This is a major turning-point in the battle. From now on, the Greeks are in retreat. For 'catalogue-slayings', see on 5.677, though the Greeks killed here receive more detail than normal in such lists. This is our last sight of Paris (341) in action in the *Il.* (see on 13.769).

343. *victors were stripping* **(R-J)**; *Trojans/these stripped* **(H, L)**: see on 4.463 for this tempting practice, which naturally slowed up the attack; cf. Albracht (2003) [I.46-7]. No wonder Hector tried to stop it (345), cf. Nestor at 6.68-71.

351. *in/ front of/the space before Ilium/our city*: a grim fate for anyone, but especially humiliating for the Trojans, since their own families and friends will witness it.

355-66. A brilliant passage: first Apollo almost contemptuously kicks in the ditch, so that the Trojans can drive their chariots over it (cf. 12.82-3); then he wrecks the Greek wall at this point like a boy knocking over a sandcastle – an astonishing (and unique) image of effortless, wilful, childish destruction. So much for all the Greeks' 'arduous efforts/labour(ed)/hard work' (366-7). Now the Greeks are in real trouble.

356. *kicking them with his feet* **(L)**: 'them' means the edges of the ditch, not the Trojans.

358. *about as long as* **(L)**: read 'about as wide as'. How wide? Estimates vary from 50 to 250 feet, depending on the spear! But given this is a god at work and the Trojans come over in 'ranks/massed squadrons/ formation' (360), one must imagine a very wide way.

361. *and wrecked* **(L)**: read 'and *Apollo* wrecked'.

366. *terror* **(L)**: read 'panic' (i.e. fear + flight), as predicted by Zeus (15.62), all of whose plans outlined there are now coming to fruition.

372. *Father Zeus*: on prayer forms, see **GI** 7A. Zeus' thunderous reply (377-8) is a favourable sign (presumably preparing for Patroclus' return to battle), but the Trojans take it as favourable to them and attack even more keenly (379-80).

381-4. *As a great roller* **(R-J)**; *As a huge wave* **(H)**; *as when the big* **(L)**: fine C/D simile, likening the waves washing over ships to the Trojans sweeping over the wall. The battle is now beginning to advance towards the Greek ships (as Zeus ordered, 15.63).

386. *from their chariots* **(R-J, H)**: references to fighting *from* a chariot are rare, cf. **GI** 13B(vi). Correct **L**'s 'from their horses'.

390-405: Patroclus, hearing the noise, leaves the wounded Eurypylus and returns to Achilles.

390.   *Patroclus*: Homer left Patroclus interrupting his return to Achilles in order to tend the wounded Eurypylus at 11.803-47.

402.   *to make him fight* (**R-J**); *urge him into the fight* (**H**); *stir him into the fighting* (**L**): Nestor had suggested this to Patroclus at 11.789-92.

403-4.   *Who knows*: = 11.791-2.

405-564: Hector and Ajax rally their own sides: general fighting.

407.   *outnumbered/less/fewer*: the Greeks do seem to outnumber the Trojans (8.56), but 2.122-33 points out that the Trojans' allies make up the numbers to a large degree.

410.   *As a string/(chalk)line*: D-simile, likening the tautness of a string, used to guide a carpenter into cutting a straight line, to the closeness of the battle, neither side budging. Cf. on 11.336 for this common image, often representing the intensity of the fighting as much as its evenness. The string was coated with chalk or pigment and 'pinged' onto the wood to create the line for the carpenter to follow.

415.   *Hector … Ajax*: these two main men resume their duel (cf. on 14.402).

420.   *fire*: an important moment – the first time the Trojans have been close enough to attempt to fire the Greek ships, a long-held desire of Hector's (see on 8.182). The Greeks are aware of the threat – 9.242, 602, 653 – and Hector's desire intensifies as he approaches the Greek defences 12.198, 441, cf. 13.319.

426.   *narrow space/place/ pass*: presumably between the Greek ships and wall (8.476).

430.   *Lycophron*: see on 11.233 for this battle sequence; Lycophron receives a typical a-b-c description; see **GI** 2(iv). Cythera, his home island, was 'sacred' to Aphrodite, who landed there (*en route* for Cyprus) shortly after she was born from the waves (see on 2.205, 5.330).

440.   *arrows*: for Teucer's expertise with the bow, see 8.266-331, and for his attack here on Cleitus, cf. 8.309-29.

447.   *gave all his care to his horses* (**L**): read 'was in trouble with his horses'. See on 11.338. Cleitus, the driver of Polydamas' chariot, is dealing with horses who are nervous at being held closer to the thick of the action, 448, than they would normally be, to favour Hector, 448-9. Presumably Cleitus had turned his back on the enemy in trying to deal with them (451). See Albracht (2003) [I.21].

461.   *Zeus*: a good example of the distinction Homer generally maintains between his knowledge of what is going on and his character's. Homer as omniscient narrator knows it was Zeus who intervened; Teucer guesses it was some 'power/divinity' (467); Ajax ascribes it to a 'god'

(473); Hector, sure that Zeus is supporting him (11.200-9), confidently affirms it was indeed Zeus (489-90).

474. *spear ... shield*: Teucer fights well on foot (13.314).

486-513. *Trojans, Lycians*: Hector's exhortation is upbeat and patriotic: Zeus in on our side (493) and even those who die will have gloriously saved their fatherland (497). Ajax's reply (502-13) takes the 'now or never' line, arguing that they cannot win a war of attrition (512) and that the enemy is inferior (513). These two speeches introduce an extended period of fighting that will take the Trojans right up to the Greek ships.

502. *Shame*: for this 'exhortation' pattern, see on 4.464.

508. *dance*: a typical antithesis, cf. 3.392-4, 7.241, 16.617, 745, 24.261. Yet there is, too, an intimacy to battle (see on 13.291).

524. *Meges began to strip/was stripping*: a dangerous moment, cf. on 4.463. This is the first of a 'chain-reaction' sequence (Meges trying to kill Polydamas, who had killed his companion Otus, see on 4.A.457-504). Meges is a useful minor fighter, see on 2.627.

528. *son of Phyleus/Phyleides*; i.e. Meges.

532. *host/guest-friend*: it is typical for armour to be handed down like this (cf. 7.138-41, 10.266-70, etc.).

557. *either we (must) destroy/kill them*: Hector adopts Ajax's call at 502-3 – a mark of how tight the fighting has become, e.g. the equal number killed on each side at 515-23, but the death of Trojan Dolops tipping the balance.

561-4. *Fellow-warriors/ My/dear friends*: cf. Agamemnon at 5.529-32. Appeals to shame are typical, cf. 13.95-124.

565-746: Zeus spurs on Hector, and the Greeks retreat further back among their ships. Ajax defends the ships with a huge pike, but slowly has to yield.

567. *Zeus*: the climax of the Trojan effort is signalled by Zeus' determination here to drive them on to the ships, and Hector's willing acceptance of the help (but see on 610-14). This will continue for the rest of the book, e.g. 594-600, 610-14, 637, 694, 719, 724. The emotionalising increase in similes and special effects, e.g. Hector's terrifying look (607-9), the personal appeal (697), the report of the warriors' thoughts (699-703) etc., emphasise that a great climax is being reached.

569. *Antilochus*: swift (23.756, cf. 17.652-55) son of Nestor (see on 8.80), and close to Menelaus (see on 5.565); cf. the amusing *contre-temps* after the chariot-race, 23.566-611.

579. *like/as a hound/dog*: C-simile, the 'fawn' being Melanippus. Homer has changed the terms of the simile (one might argue Antilochus should be the hunter) to point up the speed and agility needed to strip armour, which is Antilochus' intention here.

583. *you*: see on 4.127. The poet sympathises with Melanippus' sad fate.

586. *like a wild beast*: C-simile, this time introducing a judgmental element on the beast which has 'done wrong/some bad thing': presumably because it should kill cattle and sheep, not men or dogs. One may ponder if this should reflect on Antilochus in some way. The 'crowd/group/gang of men' looks forward to the chasing Trojans (589-90).

592. *like ... lions*: A-simile.

598. *make completely ... prayer* (**L**): read 'make accomplished the unreasonable/disastrous (Greek: *exaisimos*) prayer'. In whose eyes is Thetis' prayer *exaisimos*? Does it indicate Zeus' feelings? The poet's?

602. *Greeks ... victorious* (**R-J**); *give the Danaans glory* (**H, L**): cf. Zeus at 15.69-70.

604. *without the god* (**L**): read 'as he was', 'already'.

605. *like Ares* (**R-J, H**); *as when destructive* (**L**): B-simile, the madness referring to *either* Ares *or* a raging forest fire (adjust **L**).

607. *foam* (**R-J, H**); *slaver* (**L**): foam, cf. 8.299 and the lion at 20.168; for flashing eyes, cf. Hector at 8.348-9, 12.466. At moments of high drama, Hector is a forbidding sight.

610-14. *Zeus ... Achilles/son of Peleus*: the poet foreshadows the plot again, indicating the role the gods are playing in Hector's impending death – a theme which (as in tragedy) becomes more pronounced the closer it comes. Hector will indeed die through a combination of Achilles and Athene (22.214-305, especially 299).

618. *wall*: the massed defensive formation, cf. 13.152, and on 13.126.

619. *like a ... cliff*: C-simile, signalling firm resistance.

623. *blazing with fire* (**H**); *lit about with flame* (**L**): i.e. Hector's dazzling armour, cf. Diomedes at 5.4, Achilles at 22.134-5.

625. *as (when) a (...) wave*: C-simile. The waves at 619 could not overwhelm the cliff, but they can a ship, as they nearly do here, cf. 15.381-6 (similes sometimes 'hunt' in topic-related groups). Note the change of direction the simile takes: it starts off with Hector as a wave breaking over a ship, but ends with the effect of this on the morale/courage of the crew, though at least they are (just) saved.

630. *Like/as a ... lion*: C-simile, emphasising the panic the one lion/Hector causes among the hundreds of cattle/Greeks, before it finally consumes a single ox/Greek (foreshadowing the death of Periphetes, 638), causing the cattle/Greeks to run for it (637). Note the way the simile advances the action; it begins with Hector's attack, but closes with the Greeks in flight.

634. *the first and the last* (**L**): read 'the first or the last'.

637. *in unspeakable/unearthly terror* (**H, L**): read 'miraculously' – Zeus and Hector are working together. The 'miracle' is not connected with the death of Periphetes (his death does not *cause* the flight) who is a better man than his father (641), a rare occurrence.

640. *Heracles*: see on 8.363 and cf. on 5.392, 638.

646. *shield*: presumably a tower-shield like Hector's (see on 6.117), which he had slung behind him.

653-6. *sterns/ships … huts/shelters*: see on 14.30, and cf. 14.74-81. The Trojans are now fighting it out among the first Greek ships to be beached, i.e. those highest up the beach, and the Greeks have 're-grouped/stood their ground' to form a new defensive line (656-7) to defend themselves round the ships and huts in which the men from those ships have been camped out.

666. *run* (**R-J**); *turned to flight* (**H**); *terror of panic* (**L**): Nestor's desperate appeal, put in the strongest terms (i.e. supplication, see **GI** 7D), is designed to ensure that at least *this* line is held, since if it is not, the Trojans will be able to fire these ships at will.

669. *mist*: Homer has not actually made us aware that there was a mist at this time; but divinely-induced mist over the battle is typical, cf. 17.269-70, 21.7, as is darkness cf. 5.506-8. Such 'mist' may reflect the reality of the dust-clouds thrown up by advancing armies, cf. 3.10-14, where the simile makes exactly this connection.

672. *those who had fallen back* (**H**); *whether they stood away* (**L**): lit. 'they [the Greeks] saw Hector, master of the battle-cry, and his men, both those who stood back … and those who were fighting', i.e. both the Greeks who were fighting (by the ships) and those standing back (by the huts), forming the new defensive line (656-7), could now see Hector and the Trojans clearly (correct **H**).

677. *pike*: mentioned at 387-9. Ajax is determined that the line will hold here.

678. *with clamps* (**H**); *by clinchers* (**L**): 'with pegs/bolts' is the more likely translation.

679. *As an expert trainer* (**R-J**); *As when a man skilled* (**H**); *And as a man who* (**L**): unique D-simile. The rider owns a stud-farm or training stable (for chariot races, 11.698) and is bringing four horses into a town for sale. He harnesses them together and moves from one to the other as they gallop along, presumably to save their energy. This obviously makes quite a spectacle (note the human angle, 682-3). It also makes for a splendid image of Ajax, leaping from half-deck to half-deck along the line of ships (i.e. the raised decks at the prow and stern).

684. *shifts his stance from one …* (**L**): this is not a trick-rider, standing up on the horses; read 'changes from one …'.

690. *eagle*: D-simile, commonly used of warriors on the attack, e.g. 16.582-3, 17.460.

693. *a blue/dark-prowed ship/vessel*: we find out whose at 705.

697. *you would think/say*: a rare 'personal' appeal from the poet to his audience, cf. 17.366-9. It draws the audience in and signals a particularly dramatic moment.

699-703. *this was/these were the attitude/thought(s)*: a very rare insight into the minds of the characters delivered by the omniscient third-person narrator. Homer usually allows these to emerge only in conversation. See **GI** 10.

705. *Protesilaus*: see on 2.693.

711. *axes*: cf. 13.612.

718. *give single voice to the clamour of battle* **(L)**: read 'raise the battle-cry' or, alternatively, 'charge!'

720-1. *against/in spite of the gods' will … cowardice*: neither claim, about the will of the gods or the Trojan elders' cowardice, is true, as far as our version of the *Il.* is concerned (unless Polydamas' caution is implied, e.g. 12.216, and see on 13.744). Hector is driving his men on by all possible means, but it does him no credit to set himself up as someone who had to fight against his own people to get his way.

729. *cross-bench/bridge/midship*: this is a bench/strut across the middle of the ship.

731. *beat off … vessels* **(L)**: i.e. beat off from the vessels any… .

733. *Friends*: see on 5.464. Note the two rhetorical questions at 735-6.

738. *and hold off this host that matches us* **(L)**: read 'and which could supply reinforcements'.

741. *Salvation's … battle* **(L)**: read 'So our only salvation is to fight. There is no tenderness in war'.

742. *spear* **(L)**: read 'pike'.

743. *crashed* **(L)**: read 'came up against'.

Book 16

Introduction

After the Greek retreat of Book 15, it is now the Trojans' turn to retreat before Patroclus' ferocious assault, which in terms of numbers killed is not matched even by Achilles in Books 20-2. Again, the poet sequences the battle carefully, in five stages, with the usual combination of human and divine agencies, single and mass attacks, boasting, advances, rallies and retreats, similes and so on:

Within the Greek camp: 122-3 Ajax withdraws as the Trojans fire the ship; 284-305 Patroclus attacks at that point and puts out the fire; the Trojans fall back, but still hold the line; 306-57 Greek successes force the Trojans to retreat further.

Outside the Greek camp: 364-72 Hector panics, and his chariot sweeps him to safety; many others follow and become ensnared in the ditch (370), i.e. the battle moves out of the Greek camp.

Around the dead Sarpedon: 394-553 Patroclus kills Sarpedon, but the Trojans rally; Patroclus' attack forces them back again (588), but Glaucus holds the line (593-4).

By the walls of Ilium: Zeus make a coward of Hector, who again takes to his chariot (657-8), not halting till he reaches the Scaean gate (712); Patroclus surges forward and reaches the very walls of Troy, where Apollo warns him off (698-711).

Outside Ilium: Apollo orders Hector to return to the battle (720-8), his charioteer is killed (742-43), the Greeks seize the body (781), and Patroclus launches his final assault, before Apollo disarms him, and he is killed.

Since the *Il.* is an epic, the hero's struggle for *kleos* lies at its heart. But *kleos* is won at a price, and that price is often paid in disaster – for the hero, his companions, or both. Achilles' demand for *kleos*, so urgent because he knows he is short-lived, brings disaster in its wake, so shaped by Homer as to lay the foundations for what was to become, in the hands of Greek dramatists two hundred years later, the form we know as tragedy; cf. Plato *Republic* 598d – 'tragedy and its path-finder, Homer'; see Macleod (1982) 1-8.

- In its literary sense tragedy tends to be characterised by a number of typical – though not necessarily exclusive – markers. These generally include prophecies and warnings (some involving the gods); irony (generated by an ignorance of the true state of affairs); over-confidence accompanied by self-delusion; and understanding too late to avoid disaster; all accompanied by a rich vein of sympathy for the tragic victim. The end result is a sense of self-inflicted, pointless, waste. These are hallmarks of much of the *Il.*, and are particularly concentrated in Book 16. For example:

- Patroclus' death has already been foretold by Zeus at 8.470ff., repeated at 15.64ff. At 11.604, the poet himself comments on the fatal moment when Patroclus answered Achilles' summons ('Hearing the call in his hut, Patroclus equal of Ares came out; and that was the beginning of his end.').
- Warning-notes sound at the very start of Book 16. When Patroclus suggests that, if Achilles will not himself return to battle, Achilles should send out him (Patroclus) in his (Achilles') armour, the poet intervenes to comment (46-7) 'So Patroclus spoke in supplication, the great fool. In doing so, he was simply invoking his own destiny and a dreadful death.' Achilles himself is aware of the danger Patroclus faces and begs him not to go too far (91ff.: note 'one of the eternal gods from Olympus may cross your path. The archer-god Apollo loves these Trojans dearly'); and when Achilles goes so far as to pray to Zeus for Patroclus' safe return, the poet tells us that half of the prayer will not be granted (250). Patroclus plunges into battle and meets with great success at first, but the poet alerts his listeners to the terrible truth: 'Had he kept to his orders from Achilles, he would have saved himself from the evil destiny which is dark death' (684).
- The book is rich in irony. Achilles expresses his hopes for himself and Patroclus when he prays they make take Ilium together (97); and he prays for Patroclus' safe return (246). Neither wish will be granted.
- Patroclus himself foolishly challenges the gods. The first time, he learns the lesson, retreating before Apollo (702ff.). But not the second time: 'But Patroclus, with murder in his heart, leapt on the enemy. Three times he charged with an intimidating yell, like impetuous Ares, and three times he killed nine men. But when he leapt in like something superhuman for the fourth time, then, Patroclus, the end was in sight. In the heat of the battle, Phoebus encountered you, Phoebus most terrible' (780ff.).
- Naturally, Patroclus was not able to see that this would be the outcome, deluded as he was (685); too late, he comes to understand what has happened to him: 'Zeus and Apollo handed you that victory. *They* conquered me. It was an easy task: they took the armour from my back' (844).
- Our sympathy for Patroclus is invited throughout the book. He feels deeply for his fellow-warriors' plight: 'Patroclus came up to Achilles shepherd of the people. Hot tears were running down his face like a dark spring trickling black streaks of water down a steep rock-face' (3ff.). He is all selfless nobility as he begs to be allowed to save them, unaware of what the eventual result will be: '... at least send me into battle with your Myrmidon troops – I might yet be the light of salvation for the Greeks. And give me your own armour to put on my back' (38ff.). Homer himself signals the warmth he feels for Patroclus by referring to

him in the second person singular in a predominantly third-person narrative. So, when Euphorbus moves in for the kill, Homer says: 'He was the first, then, to let fly at you, charioteer Patroclus. But he did not kill you' (812); as Patroclus dies, Homer prefaces his last words 'Fading fast you replied, charioteer Patroclus' (843). This, in other words, is tragedy in miniature, within the larger framework of epic. See further Rutherford (1982) in Cairns (2001) for the tragic thread running through the *Il.* from Book 9.

Book 16 brings Achilles back into the frame, the man who will take upon himself the responsibility for Patroclus' death (18.98-100). He is not the man he was in Book 9. Perhaps Patroclus' personal attack on him (29-35) or the Myrmidons' grumbles (200-9) have had their effect. Homer, as often, does not say; the precise cause and effect are left for us to infer. Whatever the reasons, Achilles still bitterly resents Agamemnon's treatment of him (52-8) and asserts that he continues to feel like an outcast from the community (59), but he acknowledges that his anger is not what it was (60-1) and gropes for a compromise of some sort (72-3, 'if Agamemnon had kindly feelings for me'). But since no further offer is forthcoming from the Greeks – and Achilles is not the sort of man to approach them himself (cf. 85-6) – all he can do at this crisis is to compromise his *own* position (see also on 16.61). He therefore continues to refuse to fight himself, but agrees to the Nestor/Patroclus plan, on two conditions: first, Patroclus must not to go too far (because of Apollo's love of the Trojans, 94-5); second, he must not take Ilium (because that would deprive Achilles of glory, 87-90). It is transparent that the compromise terrifies him, because he fears deeply for Patroclus' safety (cf. his prayer to Zeus at 233-48). No wonder he watches from his hut as Patroclus and the Myrmidons march out to battle (254-6).

In fact, the situation may be more complex than this. At 9.411-16, Achilles says he has an option to fight at Troy and win eternal glory but not come home. But at 17.406-9, 21.276-8, we will find out that the situation is more clearly defined than that: Achilles, it appears, knows very well that neither he nor Patroclus will see Ilium fall (a fact Apollo will also point out to Patroclus, 707-9). This, presumably, is another reason why Achilles forbids Patroclus even to try to take Ilium: he must be doomed to failure. Further, as he reveals at 19.328-33, Achilles knows that he will die in Troy but did not think Patroclus would. This makes the magnificent fantasy with which the speech ends – that Achilles and Patroclus should take Ilium alone (97-100) – all the more pathos-filled. Achilles surely *knows* it is a fantasy, at least as far as he is concerned; but is it also a cry of despair – to be free of the whole situation in which he finds himself, and able to carve out his own destiny, with Patroclus at his side?

At which point, a health warning. All these revelations are yet to come (Homer typically reveals such things piecemeal). Are we permitted to conclude that Achilles is making his recommendations to Patroclus on the basis of knowledge which we do not yet know that he possesses? Should we, in other words, read back into Achilles' speech in Book 16 a knowledge of his situation that will be revealed only much later? But if we should, why did Homer leave it to be revealed till much later?

At all events, the paradox of Achilles' whole position is that all he needs to do is return to the fighting *himself* to achieve everything he wants out of the present situation. But that would mean returning without gifts or apology (cf. 9.602-5): he still cannot forget, or forgive, Agamemnon. Alternatively, he could refuse to compromise; and then neither he nor Patroclus would return to the fighting at all. In the event, he takes the wrong decision, and pays for it, with Patroclus' death and, as it will emerge, his own.

Main sources for the commentary and related reading
Edwards (1987) 254-65; Fenik (1968) 190-218; Janko (1992); Segal (1971) ch. 3 deals with Books 16-20; Willcock (1984).

1-100: Patroclus tells Achilles that the Greeks are in serious trouble, and Achilles agrees Patroclus can return to battle in his (Achilles') armour.

1. *ship*: i.e. that of Protesilaus, which Ajax is defending (15.704-6, 727ff.).

2. *Patroclus*: last seen leaving Eurypylus at 15.405.

3-4. *like a (dark) spring*: = 9.14-15. See on 1.349 for heroic weeping.

7. *like a (poor) little girl*: wonderful C-simile, full of tender observation of a child's behaviour (cf. 6.466-73, 15.362-4, 16.259-65), arising from Achilles' pity for Patroclus (5). Does the child's plucking at mother's skirt suggest Patroclus is in some sense supplicating Achilles (see **GI** 7D)? See on 9.323. The simile relating to Patroclus' tears produced by Homer-the-narrator (3-4) is here exquisitely contrasted with the one Homer puts in the mouth of his character, Achilles, who sees his companion's tears in quite different terms, suggesting much about their relationship.

12-13. *Myrmidons ... Phthia*: the Myrmidons are Achilles' troops; Phthia is Achilles' home, where his father Peleus lives (15); Patroclus lives there too. See **R-J** map 4.

14. *Menoetius*: Patroclus' father: presumably any news about him would reach Patroclus from Phthia.

16. *Or perhaps/is it*: Achilles contrasts the grief they would feel at the death of a parent with what they would feel at the death of Greeks – nothing, since he claims it is all their own fault (18 'stupidity/folly/arrogance'). But was it not he himself who had asked Thetis for their destruction? Of course, but that make no difference. Achilles here is seeing things from his own perspective. He moves from pity for Patroclus' tears to a distinct lack of pity for Greeks. Does he anticipate what he might suspect Patroclus is about to say?

20. *you*: see on 4.127. Emotional 'apostrophe' for Patroclus occurs eight times in this book.

22. *don't be angry*: Achilles is not angry at the moment – Patroclus means 'don't be angry at what I am about to say', since he *does* feel pity for the Greeks, and he knows Achilles has a short fuse (11.651-3).

25-7. *Diomedes … Eurypylus*: see on 14.28, and 11.808. Patroclus begins by sketching the Greeks' plight.

30. *anger* **(H, L)**: this is the anger, or bitterness, arising from Agamemnon's insult in Book 1 (cf. 52-9).

31. *thank you for* **(R-J)**; *good will you do* **(H)**; *advantaged* **(L)**: see on 11.762.

33-9. *pitiless/cruel … to the Greeks/Danaans*: cf. Achilles' pity for Patroclus (5). Having explained the situation to Achilles, Patroclus now berates him, rhetorically seeing Achilles' parents as the unfeeling, inanimate sea and cliffs. Has Achilles' absence from battle been rankling with Patroclus all along? It has been rankling with the Myrmidons (200-9). Note that Patroclus does not accuse Achilles of cowardice.

40-5. *Give me … ships and huts/shelters*: the climax of the speech – Patroclus repeats Nestor's suggestion made at 11.793-802.

44. *with a mere cry … wearied* **(L)**: read 'drive men [i.e. the Trojans] weary from battle'.

46-7. *fool/innocence*: another terrifying intervention into the 'objective' narrative by Homer (see **GI** 10, and cf. 11.603 – another narratorial comment on the beginning of Patroclus' end).

50. *no/not / any prophecy*: see on 9.411.

52-9. *hurts me* **(R-J)**; *grievous thing* **(H)**; *bitter sorrow* **(L)** … *refugee/vagabond*: cf. Achilles to Odysseus (9.367-9) and to Ajax (9.646-8).

57. *girl … town/city*: the girl is Briseis, the town Lyrnessus (2.689-94, 1.346-8).

58. *Agamemnon*: see **GI** 10C.

61. *anger/angry … for ever*: cf. 9.649-55. It was Achilles' intention all along to return at some stage, as he reveals here (cf. Diomedes at 9.702-3). But he now goes on (62-3) to re-state what he *thinks* is well-known as his public position (i.e. that he will not return till the ships are fired), a position he does not feel he can back down from. In fact, however, the Greek army is not aware of this because Odysseus had not told them of it; see on 9.678, 11.788. As a result, Achilles sends Patroclus into battle.

72-3. *Agamemnon … kindly*: some have used this sentiment, and that expressed at 84-6, to wonder if the poet who composed this passage knew of the embassy to Achilles in Book 9. But Achilles, who resented being away from the fighting (1.490-2), had not given up on the possibility of a compromise, as he showed in Book 9 (see e.g. on 9.645, and on 61 above). See also on 11.609.

80-100. *Nevertheless, Patroclus* **(R-J)**; *But even so, Patroclus* **(H, L)**: Achilles, having explained why he has stayed away from the fighting himself (49-63) and why he now sees the need for Patroclus to save the situation (60-79), ends by adding a condition – Patroclus must limit his ambitions (87, 'come back', cf. 95-6 'leave/let the rest/others') and not take the fighting too far. The implication behind his prohibition at 92 not to 'lead ... on to Ilium/lead the way against Ilium' is that Patroclus could possibly lead the Greeks to outright victory. As a result, Achilles would never get the requital he demanded for Agamemnon's insult (the meaning of 90, 'you will diminish my honour/reduce my worth'), let alone any more battle-glory – he would indeed be redundant, as Agamemnon had so humiliatingly crowed (see on 1.186).

86. *gifts*: in his new frame of mind, Achilles now sees some point in these. Cf. on 1.408. Analysts argue that Achilles has already been offered gifts; indeed he has, but as the Meleager episode shows, it looks as if these are withdrawn if they are not accepted first time round (9.597-9).

94. *Apollo*: Achilles unwittingly predicts the fate of Patroclus.

100. *coronal* (**L**): i.e. with its walls/towers like a diadem or crown.

101-24: Ajax retreats, and the Greek ships are fired.

102-24. *Ajax ... stern*: we return to Ajax desperately defending the first line of ships (15.742-6), and finally being driven back from it, with the result that the first Greek ship is fired (124).

103. *Zeus*: see on 15.567 for this important theme, and cf. 16.120.

106. *shoulder*: cf. 13.709-11, where Ajax's followers allow him to rest occasionally – but he cannot rest now.

112. *Muses*: see on 11.218.

114. *spear* (**H, L**): but was not Ajax wielding a pike (15.677, 742-6)? It is quite true that *doru* normally means 'spear', especially when described as *meilinon* ('ash'), but its basic meaning is 'piece of wood', 'wooden shaft'. Correct also 117, 118 'spearhead'.

117. *headless/docked/lopped*; a wonderful image, Ajax still wielding the pike without realising it had lost it head, and the head clanging to the ground below.

124-418: Patroclus arms; the Myrmidons are readied. Achilles prays in vain to Zeus for Patroclus' safe return. They advance into battle and send the Trojans flying in panic.

126. *rider of horses* (**L**): read 'charioteer'.

130-144. *Patroclus ... death to warriors/fighters/fighting men*: for arming scenes, see on 3.328-38. Here Patroclus dons Achilles' armour. The important point is the emphasis Homer puts on the spear that Patroclus does *not* take, because (being Achilles') it is too heavy for him (140-4), cf. Armstrong (1958). Patroclus is not the equal of his young companion, but he will still create absolute havoc among the Trojans and slay the Lycian leader Sarpedon too (son of a god; only Hector is his better); he will slay twenty-seven Trojans in three attacks, unparalleled even by Achilles (784-

5); indeed, he will come within an inch of capturing Ilium itself, and it will take Apollo's intervention to stop him. It is not Patroclus' fighting ability that will be his undoing. Quite the reverse: it will be his desire to go too far and refusal to rein himself in that will kill him, as Achilles tragically foresaw (91-6, 242-8).

134. *Aiakides* (**L**): grandson of Aeacus, i.e. Achilles.

143. *Cheiron*: see on 4.219.

Pelian (**H, L**): Homer plays on words. The spear came from Mt Pelion (144), as a gift for Achilles' father Peleus (on his marriage to Thetis, with the rest of the armour, 18.83-5). It is 'Pelian' in both senses.

145. *horses*: a new item in arming scenes. The immortal horses were a gift from the gods to Peleus at his marriage (381). The highly respected (24.574-5) Automedon, one of Achilles' attendants (9.209), will drive the chariot for Patroclus (Patroclus normally was the driver for Achilles, cf. 126, 17.427), since he was absolutely reliable at keeping close to his fighter with the chariot at the ready (147; **L**'s 'stood most staunchly' means 'could be completely relied upon to answer his call immediately', see on 5.13 and cf. e.g. 17.501-2).

152-3. *trace(s) ... Eëtion*: on the trace-horse, see on 8.81; for Eëtion, see on 6.395.

156. *like/as ... wolves*: sensational D-simile, the point of which emerges at the end, i.e. in the Myrmidons surging round to fall in under Patroclus (165, **H, L**: 'lieutenant/henchman ... of Aiakides/Aiakos' stock'). The simile does not wander around the point, but moves towards it: the wolves have killed and fed, and then go *in a pack* to drink, fearless and satisfied. It is a brilliant anticipatory image to conjure up for men who have long been deprived of battle (cf. 2.778-9, 16.200-9) and are now about to have their urges fully satisfied, surging round their leader, eager for blood – with Achilles urging them on too (166-7).

168-97. A catalogue adds to the build-up to the attack – a sign of the importance of the moment, cf. on 12.87. The catalogue is organised in terms of the leaders of the five 'lines' of ships that Achilles had brought to Troy (and therefore should not really be called 'contingents' or 'battalions' (**H, L**; for Achilles' ships, see on 2.685). These ship commanders will also lead the ground troops. The first three ship commanders – Menestheus, Eudorus and Peisander – are not heard of again. The first two seem to have some connection by marriage with the families of Achilles and Patroclus (cf. Peleus 175, Actor's son 189). Phoenix is Achilles' old tutor (9.485); Alcimedon appears here as a Myrmidon leader at 197, as a charioteer at 17.467, and as an attendant of Achilles at 19.392, 24.474, 574 (under the shortened form of the name Alcimus).

174. *Spercheus*: Achilles' local river, here as the river-god (23.142; **R-J** map 4).

187. *Eileithyia*: goddess of childbirth.

195. *henchman* (**L**): i.e. Patroclus.

199. *bluntly/stern*: Achilles is reminding the Myrmidons of their past grumbles and warning them that they had better deliver. Is he gruffly concealing the concession he is making by allowing them to fight? Showing them they were wrong about him all the time? Urging them not to let him down? Or, mindful that he is sending Patroclus out in his place, terrified of what might go wrong? This is a fine example of Homer's ability to construct a superbly appropriate, crystal-clear speech, which leaves itself open to any number of interpretations.

212. *As a mason fits/as (when) a man builds*: the Myrmidons prepare for a devastating massed assault (276 'in close formation/in a mass/pack'); cf. 15.618; see on 13.126; and compare 215-17 with 13.128-35.

220-56. There is a grim irony that Achilles' prayer is to Zeus, who now above all is committed to helping the Trojans (see on 15.567) and overseeing Patroclus' death (15.65). Hence Zeus' ambivalent response (250-2). The prayer follows the usual prayer form; see **GI** 7A.

222. *Thetis*: ever the careful mother, packing fine, warm clothes for her short-lived (1.352, 416) son. They have served him for ten years – but not for much longer.

228. *sulphur*: sulphur, regarded as divine (perhaps because of its association with volcanoes and lightning, *Od.* 12.427), would be sprinkled into the cup before being rinsed away with water. Ritual cleanliness is an important feature of worship, cf. 1.313 and **GI** 7B.

233-5. *Dodona ... Helloi/Selloi*: there was an ancient oracle at Dodona (in north-western Greece, **R-J** map 4), consisting of a speaking oak-tree (oaks and sky-gods are commonly linked). The bare-footed Helloi (drawing mystical power from the earth?) interpreted what it said. Presumably there is some (family?) link between Achilles and Dodona to cause him to pray to Zeus as god of Dodona; he prays to Zeus as 'god of the Pelasgi' because Achilles' own homeland is also known as 'Pelasgian Argos' (2.681).

255-6. *wished to witness* (**R-J**); *eager/desire ... to watch* (**H, L**): why does Achilles want to watch? Pride? Envy? Trepidation?

259. *like wasps*: C-simile (cf. 12.167-70) and another insight into children's wilful behaviour. The emphasis is on the wasps'/Myrmidons' angry feelings and fierce response, as one, to any disturbance. Does Achilles = the boys, since he has been annoying the Myrmidons/wasps by refusing to allow them to go to battle (200-9), so that they/wasps are now all the more eager for it?

273-4. *Make wide-ruling Agamemnon ... Greeks* (**R-J**); *and so even the ... Achaians* (**H**); *so Atreus' son ... Achaians* (**L**): = 1.411-12. Patroclus is determined to carry out Achilles' wishes in ensuring that this attack will restore Achilles' honour, in the way Achilles outlined it at 84-6. The Myrmidons are clearly raring to go, as their immediate response (275) and the reaction of the Trojans shows, who start looking about for a way of escape (283).

281. *Peleion* (**L**): i.e. Achilles, whom the Trojans take Patroclus to be, dressed as he is in Achilles' armour. But the potential of this theme is not

Homer's Iliad

exploited; no one else makes this mistake. Sarpedon admits he does not know who Patroclus is, but he does not think he is Achilles (423-5).

286. *stricken* (**L**): read 'were fighting'.

286. *Protesilaus*: whose ship Ajax had been defending (15.705) and from which he had been driven (16.122).

287. *Pyraechmes*: 2.848.

293. *fire*: started at 122-3.

297. *Like/As when … Zeus*: C-simile, with a comparison between Zeus clearing the clouds from the skies, leaving a brilliant day, and the Greeks clearing the fire from the ships and enjoying a brief respite. Similes typically accompany fighting scenes (see **GI** 12). 299-300 = 8.557-8.

298. *stirs* (**L**): read 'removes'.

305. *forced (back)* (**R-J, H**); *gave way* (**L**): Homer is careful to pace the sequence of events. The Trojans are slowly falling back from the Greek ships, but are still within the Greek fortifications.

306-50. There now follows a sequence of Greek successes, leaving nine Trojans dead (and no Greeks). All the major Greek warriors of Books 13-15 bar Ajax feature, with Patroclus heading the list. Note that Areilycus is hit just as he is turning (308, cf. 5.40), Cleobulos trips up (331, cf. 15.645-7) and Acamas (see on 2.823) is killed as he is mounting his chariot (343), i.e. on the point of flight. See **GI** 13B(vi)(c) – the Trojans are well on the retreat. A number of the wounds are rather bloodthirsty, and some odd. See Saunders in Friedrich (2003) 144-5, 148-9.

313-16. *Meges*: cf. on 5.69. He hits Amphiclus where the muscle is very thick (not 'thickest'), i.e. the top of the thigh (not in the buttocks).

317-25. *Antilochus*: son of Nestor, saved by his brother Thrasymedes (321). It is typical for brothers to fight together, and for the one to try to avenge the other's death, e.g. 5.10, 20.

327. *Sarpedon*: leader of the Lycians (2.876) and soon to be killed himself.

329. *Chimaera*: see on 6.183.

334-44. *Peneleos*: see on 13.603, and cf. 13.617 for Lycon's equally grisly death here at 341.

345-50. *Idomeneus*: a horrific death-scene. For other teeth-wounds, see on 5.75.

352-6. *(Just) as … wolves*: C-simile, the wolves/Greeks picking off individual scattered animals/Trojans – though the Trojans have not quite broken and run yet. See on 15.271.

357. *terror* (**L**): read 'panic, flight' (as at 366, 373).

358-63. *Ajax … Hector*: they resume their lengthy duel, a central feature of Books 13-15 (beginning 13.189). But now, only Hector stands between the Trojans and a rout (363 'held/stood his position/ground').

364-6. *As Zeus unleashes* (**R-J**); *As when a cloud* (**H, L**): C-simile, another meteorological image (see 297 above). Here the clear weather of 297 is ended when Zeus brings on a hurricane; as the clouds race across

230

and darken the bright sky, so the Trojans run for it. The noise they make in so doing is commensurate with the noise of the storm.

369. *ditch*: now that Hector has fled (367-8), presumably via the causeway which Apollo had kicked in (15.357-60), the Trojans, scrambling in panic to get out of the Greek camp, become entangled in the ditch. Cf. Polydamas' warning words at 12.223-7, now fulfilled.

380. *cleared the ditch* (**R-J**); *straight over/across the ditch* (**H, L**): in epic, chariots can clear ditches with one bound. The battle now moves outside the Greek defences and onto the open plain, and Patroclus kills *from* his chariot, a rare occurrence cf. **GI** 13B(vi).

384-93. *As in autumn* (**R-J**); *As all the dark earth* (**H**); *As underneath* (**L**): D-simile, likening stormy downpours and their widespread effects to the noise the Trojans make as they run off, cf. Diomedes at 5.87-94. As often, the main point of connection – the noise – emerges only near the end of the simile (391).

388. *justice/righteousness*: one of the few instances in the *Il.* where Zeus is associated with human right-dealing and justice. It is hard to be certain whether the 'crooked dealing' is supposed to reflect on the Trojans.

397. *high (city-) wall* (**H, L**): this probably refers to the walls of Ilium, but it is tempting to take it as the Greek defensive wall, back towards which Patroclus is herding the Trojans to prevent them escaping into Ilium (396).

River: i.e. Scamander – see **R-J** map 1. The Trojans are boxed in between Scamander and the Greek camp.

399-418. Patroclus' killing spree continues (twelve victims).

402. *Thestor*: he is Pronous' driver. For losing one's wits, cf. 11.129, 13.394-7, 434-40 and cf. Friedrich (2003) 7-8.

406. *as a fisherman* (**R-J, L**): *as when a man* (**H**): B-simile, adding mockery to a gruesome death. Cf. 14.498-9, 16.742-50.

412. *Erylaus*: another very grisly death, cf. 578. Patroclus is ruthless in his execution.

415-17. *Erymas … Polymelus*: for similar 'catalogue' slayings, see on 5.677.

419-683: Patroclus kills Sarpedon, and Hector leads the Trojans back into the attack. General fighting. Zeus watches the battle keenly. He makes Hector flee; Apollo rescues Sarpedon's body.

419. *Sarpedon*: see on 2.876 and 5.685-6. His death was predicted at 15.67.

423. *find out*: the fact that Patroclus is wearing Achilles' armour does not identify him in Sarpedon's eyes.

428. *As two … vultures*: brief C-simile, featuring the same birds and showing that the warriors are evenly matched. The simile concentrates on the noisy attack of the two birds/warriors.

431-61. It is common for gods to watch the battle and reflect on its outcome, cf. 20.290-317, 22.167-81. These great heroes are worthy of the gods' attention, and pity (Zeus' tears of blood, 459, cf. 11.54. See on 15.12). For fate, see **GI** 8.

441-3. *Are you proposing* **(R-J)**; *do you intend* **(H)**; *do you wish* **(L)** *... approve (you)*: = 22.179-81 (and cf. 4.29).

447. *son of his/his own (...) son*: cf. on 15.123.

456. *burial*: as son of a god and great warrior, Sarpedon will receive special treatment. This device saves Homer the problem of an extended battle over his corpse at a time when he is saving up that theme for the dead Patroclus (cf. 17.156-9). For the theme of the burial and mutilation of corpses, see on 11.455, and Glaucus' fears at 16.545 and Greek hopes 16.559-60.

462. *advanced/advancing*: we return to the narrative at the exact point where we left it at 430.

463. *Thrasymelos* **(H, L)**: a name meaning 'bold-sheep' does not carry credibility. Read 'Thrasydemus'.

Patroklos threw first at ... Thrasymelos **(L)**: read 'P. threw first and hit Th.' – there is no indication that Patroclus *intended* to hit Sarpedon's driver. Note that this is the only battle where *both* warriors throw, miss and hit someone/something else.

467. *Pedasus*: the mortal trace horse (152-4).

471. *fouled* **(L)**: read 'entangled'. Cf. 8.85-8 and on 8.81 for dealing with a dead trace-horse.

472. *Automedon*: Patroclus' driver (16.144-7).

477. *Sarpedon missed/threw wide*: we now get a typical sequence – A throws at B and misses, B kills A. See on 5.17.

482-6. *as an oak ... dust*: C-simile, = 13.389-93.

487-9. *As a lion ... jaws* **(R-J)**; *like/as a (...) bull ... lion* **(H, L)**: D-simile, in which the point of contact is made in the last line, the *noise* of the bull as it dies likened to Sarpedon's 'bellowing/roaring' (486). In **L**, for 'claws' (489) read 'jaws', and for 'raging' (491) read 'struggling to speak'.

492. *Glaucus*: Sarpedon's second-in-command (2.876).

498. *blame ... disgrace* **(R-J)**; *shame ... disgrace* **(H)**; *shame ... reproach* **(L)**: Homeric heroes, aware that the eyes of the world are upon them on the battlefield, tend to judge their actions in terms of how they imagine others will react to them (**GI** 4). Glaucus challenges the Trojans in the same terms (544 'shame').

503. *stepping heel braced to chest* **(L)**: i.e. putting his foot on his chest.

507. *left/free of/ their master's chariot*: but Sarpedon's horses did not come free of the chariot during the battle. Homer has 'nodded' (see on 1.424).

510. *wound*: For Glaucus' wound, see 12.387-91 (though see the Homeric 'nod' at 14.425-6).

515. *wherever/anywhere*: Greek gods, like humans, are subject to time and space. See **GI** 5A.

530. *rejoiced/joyfully/was happy*: observe that Glaucus does not thank the god. His prayer was entirely self-interested; he did not humble himself, adore or revere (indeed, he was rather hard on Zeus, accusing him of not standing by his children, 521). In *Glaucus'* eyes, there is no numinosity or mysteriousness about Apollo. He is a god on the Trojan side. It is Apollo's duty and in his interest to help – and he does, 'at once' too (528). In other words, for Homeric heroes, gods are beings of superior power who will help or hinder you: they are either for or against you. See **GI** 6, and cf. the notes on the passages between 3.380-415.

537. *Hector*: for this 'rebuke' pattern, see on 5.471. See on 456 above for the 'death and burial' theme at 545-6.

543. *Patroclus*: Glaucus has recognised him, cf. on 423 above.

556. *Ajaxes*: they will play no part in the fighting over Sarpedon, whose body will anyway be spirited away by Apollo at 678. Homer's purpose here is to get the great Ajax out of the way while Patroclus is killed, otherwise he would be bound to leap to his defence. He will learn of Patroclus' death at 17.120.

558. *storm/break/scale ... the wall*: see 12.397-9.

563-643. Both sides clash over Sarpedon's body. Hector and Patro-clus score kills (569-87); the Trojan advance (569) becomes a retreat (588-92); Glaucus and Meriones score kills (593-607) and there is a Trojan rally, but the Greeks hold the line (601-3); Meriones and Aeneas exchange insults (608-25), before Patroclus urges Meriones to fight, not talk (626-31); and two similes bring us back to the body of Sarpedon.

567. *night/darkness*: typical during 'rebukes', cf. 5.506-8, 12.252-5, 17.269-70, etc.

571. *Epeigeus*: a-b-c description; note that, as a result of killing a relative, Epeigeus is a suppliant exile, welcomed in by Peleus. So too is Patroclus, 23.84-90; other examples of the theme occur at 2.661-7, 13.694-7, 15.430-9. Phoenix, 9.478-82, is welcomed in by Peleus too, though not for killing someone. For Epeigeus' death, cf. 412.

582. *like a hawk*: A-simile, cf. 17.755-9.

585. *you*: see on 4.127.

594. *Bathycles*: only here is a pursuing warrior killed immediately when his enemy turns on him.

595. *Hellas*: see note at 1/Intro.

604-5. *priest*: see on 5.10. He is priest of Zeus on Mount Ida (remove the comma after 'Idaian' in **L**).

610-13. *But Meriones/he ... its force/force from it*: = 17.526-9.

617. *dancer*: a common insult, cf. 4.392-4, 15.508, 24.260-1, and the diver/acrobat at 16.742; for Cretans as dancers, see on 18.592. War is seen as a dance of death at e.g. 7.241 and cf. 13.291 for the 'intimacy' of war. Exchanges of insults are typical, e.g. 14.453-505.

631. *talk/speeches*: cf. 20.211-12, 244-5, 366-8, 431-2.

633. *Like the crashing* (**R-J, H**); *As the tumult* (**L**): D-simile, the noise of lumberjacks likened to that of shields being struck.

641. *as (when) flies*: poignant C-simile, flies/soldiers swarming round the milk-pails/dead body. Spring, the season of new life, and milk, with all its maternal connotations, is used to illustrate death. Cf. 2.469-71.

644-55. *Zeus ... many lives* (**R-J**); *Zeus ... yet more men* (**H**); *Zeus ... life from many* (**L**): Zeus ponders (a typical scene, cf. on 1.189) about when Patroclus should die (not whether: that is already certain, 8.473-6). He decides Patroclus should die after being allowed to go too far, thus fulfilling all Achilles' fears (91-6).

656-83. *coward of Hector ... fertile realm* (**R-J**); *heart without courage ... broad Lycia* (**H**); *without strength ... broad Lycia* (**L**): Zeus routs the Trojans, and ensures that Patroclus gets Sarpedon's amour (663-5), but Sarpedon's body is spirited away by Apollo (678-9) and buried in Lycia, as Hera had suggested (16.453-7). This touching passage evokes a sublime response in Pope (1743) Book 16.823-36; it was also superbly depicted by Euphronios (late sixth century BC; Woodford [1993] 76).

658. *scales/balance*: see on 8.69.

684-867: Patroclus is warned off taking Ilium by Apollo. Patroclus kills Hector's charioteer Cebriones. Apollo strips Patroclus of his armour. Patroclus is stabbed by Euphorbus and finished off by Hector. Patroclus prophesies Hector's death at Achilles' hands.

685-91. *deluded ... into Patroclus* (**R-J**); *fatal error... Patroclus' heart* (**H**); *blind fury ... heart of Patroclus* (**L**): another intrusion by the poet into the narrative, cf. on 2.38, 11.603, raising the expectations and emotional temperature before the terrifying climax. For the double motivation (both Zeus, 691, and Patroclus are equally responsible for what happens), see on 9.702. For 'delusion', see on 1.412.

684. *with a shout* (**R-J, L**); *with a call to* (**H**): Patroclus is on foot; he called to Automedon to follow him with the chariot.

686. *Peleiades* (**L**): i.e. Achilles.

689. *terrifies* (**L**): read 'routs, drives off in panic'.

692-7. *(Then) Who ... run/flight/escaping*: more emotional apostrophe ('you') and narratorial intrusion precedes a 'catalogue' slaying. Note that the Trojans are now in flight before Patroclus, who is about to reach the very walls of Troy.

705. *fourth time*: Patroclus is almost superhuman now (705), on the brink of taking Ilium itself – and, going too far, is repelled by Apollo himself. Here, he obeys Apollo's command (cf. Diomedes at 5.436-44); when he sweeps forward like this for a second time (786), it will mean his death. Homer is preparing for the climax with great care.

712. *Scaean gates*: see on 3.145. This is a desperate scene for the Trojans – Hector is even thinking of withdrawing from the field completely (714).

715. *Apollo*: desperate situations require desperate remedies; as often, a god intervenes to rally routed troops, e.g. 6.106-9, 15.236-80, 17.319-23.

717. *Asius*: Homer makes Apollo take the guise of an experienced relative of Hector, whose words are bound to carry weight.

723. *So might you ... fighting* (**L**): read 'you would soon regret your withdrawal from battle', i.e. I would punish you for it.

727. *Cebriones*: Hector's charioteer since 8.318-19.

729. *mayhem/confusion*: Apollo ensures the Greek ranks are disorganised – as they would normally be after such a speedy and successful attack; see Albracht (2003) [I.45].

733. *from his chariot*: when Apollo ordered him away from Ilium, Patroclus presumably retreated back to the waiting Automedon (684, 710-11).

738. *Cebriones*: for this battle sequence, see on 4.491.

741. *eyes*: see on 13.617.

742. *like a diver*: A-simile, which Patroclus will develop in his mocking address. **L** says Cebriones 'vaults' from the chariot; but, hit on the forehead, he surely tumbles out backwards.

745. *acrobat(ic)*: Cebriones' dive to the ground puts Patroclus in mind of an acrobat; from this he develops the image of a man diving for molluscs (not 'oysters').

751-82. A fierce battle develops over Cebriones' body, its importance emphasised by three similes, two of lions, one of winds. Eventually the Greeks claim the body: Patroclus, in other words, is too strong for Hector.

752. *springing like/with the spring of/ a lion*: B-simile. Patroclus is likened to a lion which is killed by its own courage (cf. 12.46) – as Patroclus is about to be. See on 3.23.

756. *like (a pair of/two) lions*: B-simile. Hector and Patroclus are equally matched.

762. *got/had caught hold*: for warriors fighting like this over a body (Patroclus'), cf. 17.394-7.

765-9. *Like/As (the) east ... noisily/timber*: D-simile, the clash of branches in a storm likened to the weapons wielded and flying in battle, cf. 633-7.

775. *lay ... forgotten/horsemanship*: a superb change of viewpoint: from the ferocious tumult of warriors, heroically risking their all in battle (no retreat, 771), to the dead man, to whom now, for all his greatness and size and skill as a charioteer, it means nothing.

777. *high in the sky* (**R-J**); *centre of the sky* (**H**); *middle heaven* (**L**): see on 11.86. It is now getting into the afternoon of this momentous day (779).

780. *in defiance of destiny* (**R-J**); *beyond ... destiny* (**H, L**): see **GI** 8. This unprecedented occurrence and Patroclus' slaughter of an equally unprecedented 27 warriors (785) are almost the ultimate accolade for the warrior.

786. *fourth*: see on 705.

787-8. *Patroclus, ... you*: another moving apostrophe, as Homer prepares for the most terrifying scene in the *Il.* That it takes a god's intervention to bring about Patroclus' death *is* the ultimate accolade. Patroclus is too great a fighter to be killed by a mortal: it takes Apollo, Euphorbus, and Hector to do the job. The ruthlessness of Apollo's assault is quite chilling. Cross a hostile god, and this is the result.

791-804. *stood behind ... on his chest/off him/upon him*: Patroclus needs to be stripped of Achilles' armour because the armour, being divine, was impenetrable by mortal weapons (therefore, when Hector, wearing this armour, faces Achilles, Achilles finds a way *past* it – 22.324-7). So there is now a dis-arming scene. First Apollo knocks Patroclus into a daze, and then removes helmet, spear, shield and body-armour (no mention of greaves or sword). When the fight develops over Patroclus' corpse and armour, Homer rather fudges the fact that Apollo has knocked Patroclus' armour off piece by piece and treats Patroclus' body as if Hector stripped the armour from it whole in the normal way (e.g. 17.13, 125, 205).

800. *close to death/death was close*: does the poet 'compensate' for the shock of Patroclus' death by mentioning the impending death of Hector and Zeus' role in it? Achilles' helmet has now been dragged in the blood and dust; the head of Hector, who will be wearing that helmet when Achilles kills him, will suffer the same fate (22.401-4).

805. *Fatal blindness* (**R-J**); *Bewilderment* (**H**); *Disaster* (**L**): i.e. *Atê* grips him (see on 1.412). Even stripped, a quick-thinking Patroclus might have been able to get to safety. But he is blinded and dazed (cf. 13.394, 435) – he has even turned his back to the enemy (where Euphorbus hits him, 807) – and simply stands there, an easy target.

813. *ran back/away*: even a defenceless and wounded Patroclus terrified a man like Euphorbus (brother of Polydamas, see on 3.146).

816. *overcome/broken by the spear*: it is as if the spear-thrust rouses Patroclus from his daze to realise the danger he is in and try to retreat. He still stands a chance.

823. *As (when) a lion*: D-simile, pointing up the inequality of the contest: a boar stands no chance against a lion, nor does Patroclus in his present condition against Hector (cf. the equality of the simile at 756-8). But the boar is still 'panting/fights for breath'; Patroclus is not dead yet.

835. *finest spearman* (**R-J**); *renowned* (**H**); *conspicuous* (**L**): true, but a hollow boast in relation to Hector's minor part in Patroclus' death.

836. *the vultures*: cf. on 11.455. Hector is raising the stakes here. Achilles will make the same threat against Hector (22.335-6).

838. *I can imagine* (**R-J**); *he must have given/said* (**H, L**): Hector is wrong in his construction of Achilles' orders, which were the precise opposite (91-6). Hector continues to breathe tragic over-confidence. See on 22.330-66.

844-54. *Hector, boast ... son of Peleus* (**R-J**); *Yes, make ... Aiakos' stock* (**H**); *Now is your time ... Achilleus* (**L**): Patroclus has nothing to say of the 'unfairness' of Apollo's attack on him, though since Apollo came up behind him in a mist (790-1) one wonders how he knows of it. Patroclus acquiesces in it – Homer's heroes know the gods intervene, and accept it without concern or complaint (see **GI** 6, cf. on 16.530) – and turns the fact against Hector in order to belittle Hector's prowess, adding Zeus (845) and destiny/fate (849) to the list of his killers. Patroclus' closing warning is typical: the dying in the ancient world are often gifted with prophecy (as Hector will be, 22.358-60).

849. *Leto's son*: i.e. Apollo.

850. *third*: Patroclus' sums do not quite add up, since he lists five possible killers in all. Presumably he means those who actually manhandled him – Apollo, Euphorbus and Hector (cf. 18.454-6, 19.413-14, where Apollo is said to have killed Patroclus and given the glory to Hector: gods naturally come first in the pecking order when they intervene in human affairs).

855-8. *(As) he spoke ... left behind/must leave/behind her*: = 22.361-4 (lines that also finalise Hector's death).

860. *Who knows*: more over-confidence from Hector. Cf. Achilles' self-awareness in his reply at 22.365-6.

864. *Automedon*: the exultant Hector wants revenge on Patroclus' charioteer for the death of his charioteer Cebriones; but Hector's horses are no match for Achilles' (see on 16.145 and cf. 17.75-8). This pursuit is designed to keep Hector out of the action for a while.

Book 17

Introduction

Book 17 raises the question – more 'retardation' (see **GI** 9)? Certainly not. If the Trojans were to commandeer Patroclus' body, Achilles' one wish would be to retrieve Patroclus' body in order to give it proper burial. When, therefore, he killed Hector, he would have to offer Hector's body in exchange for Patroclus'. As a result, Homer would be unable to engineer the ending he desired for this version of the *Il.*, i.e. Priam coming by night to beg for Hector's return. Patroclus' body must therefore be won back by the Greeks. (So one wonders, idly, what an *Il.* might have looked like in which the Trojans *did* recover and keep Patroclus' body.)

But the Trojans are not going to give up such a prize so easily; cf. 160-5, where Sarpedon's second-in-command Glaucus argues that it could be used to swap for Sarpedon's body, which, in his ignorance of Zeus' intervention (16.666-83), he assumes the Greeks must have. A fierce scrap over the body is therefore fully justified, and the book is characterised by the intensity of the engagement, with a series of rebukes directed at fellow-warriors for not performing (e.g. 74-84, 148-78, 326-47, 556-66, 585-91), and calls for help in desperate situations (119-23, 183-7, 246-55, 335-41, 507). Homer's engagement can be judged by the fact that over 15% of the book is taken up with similes, a higher proportion than any other (Book 12 = 14.4%, Book 16 = 13.7%, Book 11 = 12.1%, Book 15 = 11.3%; see Edwards [1991] 39).

The location of the battle over the body is less clearly sign-posted than earlier episodes in which Greeks and Trojans are advancing and retreating over the plain. Patroclus' body is near the walls of Ilium, a long way from the Greeks' ships (403-5, explaining why Achilles had not yet heard he had been killed), and the action centres round the various efforts to seize it and drag it back to one side or the other:

1-124: Menelaus stands over the body to defend it against Euphorbus (1-69), but retreats when attacked by Hector and the Trojans (70-124).

125-39: Hector removes Patroclus' armour and begins to haul off the body but falls back when Ajax advances on him and stands over the body with Menelaus (125-39).

215-316: Both sides regroup and advance (215-73), and the Trojans again seize the body (277). Ajax scatters them and kills (279ff.).

318-65: The Greeks surround the body (355), while the Trojans are rallied by Aeneas (335ff.).

366-542: Homer offers a general picture of the fighting and the reaction of Patroclus' horses to events, with Hector's efforts to catch them.

543-761: Menelaus wins the body for the Greeks (582), and the rest of the book tells of the Greek retreat with the body and Antilochus' mission to alert Achilles to what has happened. The Greeks are 'at and around the ditch' by the end of the Book.

Menelaus is the star of this Book – some manuscripts call it 'Menelaus' *aristeia*'. He launches the defence of Patroclus' body at the start and plays the major role in its retrieval by the Greeks at the end. He is the first to protect Patroclus' body (1-8) and takes revenge on Euphorbus (45-9). He feels deeply that he owes it to Patroclus to defend him, since Patroclus fell 'fighting to avenge wrongs done to me' (92). It is a notable feature of this book how frequently Patroclus is referred to or remembered in warm terms, e.g. by his horses 426, by Automedon 459, cf. 477, 539, by Menelaus 557, 564, 670-3, 689-90. He is a man worth fighting over even, or especially, in death. In the face of Hector's attack, Menelaus summons Ajax and stands back to back with him over the body (119-33) and then rallies others Greeks (246-55). In the closing episodes, it is Menelaus who brings the body over to the Greek side (574-81), Menelaus who anxiously urges the Ajaxes and Meriones to watch over it (665-73), Menelaus who summons Antilochus (684-93), and Menelaus who, with Meriones, lifts the body and begins to carry it to safety (722-4).

Behind the action, however, looms the figure of Achilles. He is mentioned 24 times in this book. His absence is about to become a terrifying presence.

Main sources for the commentary and related reading
Edwards (1991), Fenik (1968) 159-89; Willcock (1987); Willcock (1984).

1-69: Menelaus moves in to protect Patroclus' body and kills Euphorbus.

4. *as a mother cow*: delightful B-simile, the mother determined to defend its first-born (there is no suggestion that the calf is dead). The 'parent-child' image is repeated with a lion and its cubs at 17.133-6 (with Ajax as the lion).

24-5. *Hyperenor ... insulted/taunted*: see 14.516-19, where no taunts are uttered. Menelaus says what suits a context in which he is trying to demonstrate what happens to the arrogant, and what therefore will happen to Euphorbus.

36. *widow(ed)*: a common theme, see on 13.170. On the desire of a brother for revenge, cf. 14.182-5.

40. *Phrontis*: wife of Panthous.

44. *bent back/turned in*: cf. 3.348.

52. *Like the shoot* **(R-J)**; *as when a man* **(H)**; *As some slip* **(L)**: D-simile. The youth, strength, growth and beauty of the tree all relate to Euphorbus (with his lovely hair and youthful prowess, 16.808-11), as does the tree's sudden uprooting. For **L**'s 'stand' (58) read 'trench'.

61. *As (when) a mountain lion* **(R-J, H)**; *As when in the* **(L)**: D-simile, the point of which emerges (66-9) in the fear of the herdsmen/Trojans at the prospect of facing the lion/Menelaus.

70-401: Hector leads a Trojan advance, but Ajax drives him off. Glaucus rounds on Hector, who promptly puts on Achilles' armour. Zeus pities his brief triumph. A full-scale fight develops over Patroclus' body, and a mist descends.

75. *Hector, at the moment/all this time* (**R-J, H**); *While you, Hector* (**L**): the first of a number of 'rebuke' patterns in Book 17; see on 5.471. Since Apollo decides to rebuke his favourite Hector for chasing horses (however fabulous), it is perhaps a sign that Hector is not keeping his mind on the job (has the killing of Patroclus gone to his head?). Hector chases them again at 483ff., and again Apollo has to call him back (582-90).

76. *Aiakides*: i.e. Achilles. For Hector's pursuit of the horses, see on 16.864.

difficult/hard: cf. 10.402-4.

88. *with a shrill scream* (**L**): Hector is yelling a war cry.

90-105. *Disturbed/in dismay/troubled*: the first of a series of 'debating' monologues in these later books. See on 11.403. Note Menelaus' typical concern with how others will react to him if he abandons Patroclus' body (**GI** 4). Menelaus' decision therefore to abandon the body may seem somewhat unheroic – cf. Odysseus, in equally desperate plight, at 11.407-10. But Menelaus is simply making a practical assessment of the situation. In the event he summons help from Ajax ('the pair/two of us/we two' 103), and together they return immediately and drive off Hector, with the loss of Achilles' armour (125). Calls for help are a common structural feature of Book 17, e.g. 245, 507.

109. *bearded lion*: C-simile, cf. 61-7, where the Trojans retreated from Menelaus, and see 657-64, where Menelaus is on the retreat again. Note that the lion withdraws 'against his will/reluctant', 112.

115. *Ajax*: we left him being urged by Patroclus to help capture Sarpedon's body (see on 16.556). The poet now invents a reason – that his men had been filled with 'panic' – why he had to stay there when Sarpedon's body had long been spirited away by Apollo (or was it Apollo's removal of the body that caused the panic?).

125. *armour*: see on 16.791-804. Given that it is so typical for warriors to strip armour from a corpse, it would be unwise to draw conclusions about multiple authorship because Homer did not say 'he gathered up the armour lying around the body'. Hector's boast at 187 that he stripped Patroclus when he killed him is a good example of Hector's focalisation of events, to impress his men.

126-7. *behead/ cut the/his head ... dogs of Troy*: see on 11.455 for the crescendo of violence against the dead developing here – on Hector's part, in this instance.

128. *shield*: see on 7.219.

133. *like/as a lion(ess)*: a delightful protective, defensive C-simile (cf. the cow and its calf, 4-5, and the lion that has *lost* its cubs at 18.318-22). The detail of the lioness's frown is especially fine. The animal is clearly female (correct **H, L**).

140. *Glaucus*: another 'rebuke' pattern (see on 5.471).

142. *looks/look at*: a jibe Hector often hurled at Paris, e.g. 3.39, 54-5, 13.769.

145-8. *with nobody to help/by yourself … day out/and on/enemies*: for the number of allies helping the Trojans, see 2.123-31; for Hector's lack of gratitude, cf. 5.472-92, 16.537-40.

160. *If that man's dead body* (**R-J, H**); *If, dead man* (**L**): Glaucus argues that, if the Trojans captured Patroclus' body, Achilles would demand it be exchanged for that of Sarpedon, and the Trojans would get Sarpedon back (the argument of 164-5 'such is the [importance of the] man', i.e. Achilles). Glaucus, of course, is assuming the Greeks have Sarpedon's body (for its removal by Apollo, see 16.678) – though they do have Sarpedon's armour (16.663-5). Body-swapping is an important theme of these later books and explains why Patroclus must be recovered by the Greeks; if he is not, Achilles will not be able to keep and mutilate Hector's body (because the Trojans would at once do the same to Patroclus').

176-8. *the will/mind of Zeus … battle/fight*: = 16.688-90. Is Hector losing his earlier supreme, if misplaced, confidence in Zeus, cf. on 15.567 and 610-14? Or is this just what one would say, to win the argument?

192. *(ex)changed (his) equipment/armour*: swapping armour, like body-swapping (160 above), is another important theme. Patroclus put on Achilles' armour (minus spear, 16.140-2) and was killed; now Hector puts on the same armour too (he originally intended to send it to Ilium, 130-1) – though it was not meant for him any more than it was for Patroclus (195-7, and cf. Zeus' comment at 205, 'improperly/wrongly/as you should not have done'). Note that Zeus will not grant Hector Achilles' horses as well (448-50).

197. *son*: Achilles is not to grow old in his father's armour, any more than Hector – an emotionalising comment by the poet, full of pathos (**GI** 10). Even immortal armour cannot save a man from death.

198-209. *(Now) When Zeus … confirmation/brows*: an intervention full of pathos – Zeus pities Hector and grants him glory for a *short* time, but Hector will never return home to Andromache. See on 15.12 for divine pity and cf. 9.410-16 for Achilles' choice of a short, glorious or long, inglorious life. Both will, in fact, share the same fate.

203. *There are others … him* (**L**): read 'before whom all others tremble'.

204. *brave/kind/strong and gentle/strong*: Patroclus is especially remembered for these qualities. See on 9.190.

218. *Chromios* (**H, L**): so says the Greek, but Homer means Chromis (2.858).

225-6. *gifts/presents and provisions/food*: the allies of the Trojans are not exactly mercenaries, but they need to be kept sweet (at considerable cost – 18.288-92). Hector's offer of a share of the spoils and glory for the man who captures Patroclus' body (229-32) is a further inducement (Hector can rightly claim the other half because he killed Patroclus in the first place). The allies' reaction to it (233-5) shows that it has worked.

228. *intimacy of battle* **(R-J)**; *dalliance of war* **(H)**; *sweet invitation* **(L)**: see on 13.291.

236. *Innocents/fools*: another narratorial comment on the action. See **GI** 10.

245. *Call*: see on 90-105.

250. *drink*: see on 4.345. The comparison with Hector's offer to the Trojans (above) is telling. The Greeks are all in this together; the Trojan allies are seen as a separate entity, requiring special treatment.

262-8. *mass/pack ... fence(d)*: massed Trojan attacking and massed Greek defensive formations are here on display; see **GI** 13B(v)(b).

263. *As (when)*: D-simile, emphasising the noise of the surf and river/Trojan attack, cf. 4.452-6.

270. *mist*: see on 15.669.

272. *loathed/hated*: for Zeus' pity, see on 15.12 and cf. on 16.431-61. The implication of this sentiment (uttered by the poet) seems to be that Patroclus was innocently caught up in Zeus/Thetis' plan for Achilles' triumphant return.

280. *next to ... Achilles* **(R-J)**; *after the excellent/blameless* **(H, L)**: a fine compliment to Ajax, see on 2.761.

282. *wild boar*: B-simile, boar/Ajax turning at bay as the hunters/Trojans charge.

290. *ankle*: as Achilles will drag off Hector's body, 22.396-7.

297. *brain(s)*: cf. 11.97-8, 12.185-6. Hippothous was bending over the body, and thus hit on the head.

302. *care*: cf. on 4.478.

306. *Schedius*: for A aims at B and hits C, cf. on 13.502-6.

316. *fell/gave back*: Ajax's success makes the Trojans retreat, and retreat looks like turning to rout (320-3, 332) until Apollo intervenes.

321. *will/destined/destiny*: see **GI** 8.

325. *Aeneas' old/aged father*: Anchises.

327. *Aeneas,/ if the gods/how could you*: another 'rebuke' pattern. See on 5.471.

328. *even against ... do it* **(L)**: i.e. 'if the gods were against you? I *have* seen men who could do it ...'.

342-60. *(So) Aeneas/he spoke ... such were (...) orders*: a series of individual slayings is followed by a rallying-call from Ajax to adopt a massed defence (355 'fence(d)', 359 'stick close/stand close/hard'). The discipline pays off, as Homer comments (364 'lost far fewer/fewer were killed/went down').

360-401. *earth was soaked/ground ran ... the battle for Patroclus/ Patroclos (on) that day*: a general description of the fighting – first over

Patroclus where there is a mist (see 270), then elsewhere, where the sun is shining (371); a fine simile returns us to the struggle for Patroclus and the ferocity of the fighting that Zeus brought on. The poet is adept at switching from the particular to the general, and imaginatively engaging his audience with a variety of different 'takes' on the fighting.

366. *you would/would you*: see on 15.697.

378. *Thrasymedes and Antilochus*: sons of Nestor (last seen 16.317-25), also fighting well away from the struggle over Patroclus. Homer invents a reason for their absence from the main battle (Nestor's orders, 381-3), cf. on Ajax, 115. Antilochus is mentioned here because he will soon be called upon to tell Achilles the news (651-93).

389. *As (when) a man*: the 'man' is presumably a tanner or leather-worker of some sort, but the process being described is obscure. The point is that the hide/body of Patroclus is being stretched/tugged by many standing round it, in a restricted space (394) i.e. with the result that there is no movement in any direction.

401-542: Achilles has heard nothing of Patroclus' death, but his horses weep for Patroclus. Zeus pities them and foretells Hector will not capture them. More fighting.

401-11. *Godlike/brilliant Achilles ... dearest/most loved companion/had perished*: the poet prepares for the moment when Achilles will be told of Patroclus' death, and reveals Achilles' thoughts.

406. *return(ing)/would come back*: cf. Achilles' orders to Patroclus at 16.91-6.

408. *mother*: the goddess Thetis. This is the first time we have heard that Achilles knew neither he nor Patroclus would take Ilium, let alone that Thetis gave him messages from Zeus all the time (though cf. 16.36-7, 50-1, which could be taken to imply it). Homer tends to reveal such things piecemeal, in accordance with their impact on the situation at the time. See on 16/Intro for the complex situation all this creates.

415-22. Greeks and Trojans, speaking simultaneously (one assumes, see on 3.121-244), urge on their own sides, cf. e.g. 3.297-301, 319-23, 7.178-80, 201-5. They are powerfully motivated because they understand the importance of the body to *Achilles*.

426-58. *Far from the conflict/But the horses ... Trojans/Achaeans and Greeks/Trojans*: a breathtaking aside, as Homer illustrates the impact of the death of Patroclus on Achilles' immortal horses (16.148-54), and how their grief affects even Zeus. So how will it affect *Achilles*, we wonder?

427. *their charioteer*: as Patroclus had been, before Achilles sent him into the fighting with Automedon as charioteer (see on 16.145). Patroclus' care for them is described at 23.279-84, where they are still grieving for him. See on 8.199-90.

429. *Automedon*: if pain, endearments and threats will not work with the horses, what will?

434. *gravestone/monument*: superb B-simile, associating the utter stillness of the grieving horses (in the face of Automedon's efforts, too) with that of Patroclus' own grave monument.

445. *unhappy men/mankind*: men are unhappy because, as explained in 446, they are in some way unique compared with all other creatures – presumably because they know they are mortal.

450. *armour*: see 125, 192-212.

455. *the sun goes down*: = 11.194, 209 – Zeus' plans for a day of victory for Hector are still on course.

460. *like a vulture*: A-simile.

467. *Alcimedon*: see on 16.168-97. Clearly one man cannot both control a chariot and fight, either in it or dismounted from it, at the same time. When Alcimedon takes over as driver (481), Automedon immediately dismounts to fight on foot (483), urging Alcimedon to keep the horses close at hand (501-2) in case they need to escape from Hector (502-6); see **GI** 13B(vi).

483. *Glorious Hector*: a 'consultation' pattern now follows: see on 5.166.

487. *incompetent/poor/weak*: Hector has observed that Automedon has taken over Patroclus' chariot, calling up Alcimedon to help, and reckons this 'second' team will be a soft touch. Hector has had his eyes on Achilles' highly desirable immortal horses (486) ever since Patroclus was killed (16.864-7), for which he was rebuked by Apollo at 75-81. For Dolon's desire for these horses, see 10.321-3; Diomedes lusts (successfully) after Aeneas' horses at 5.260-73, 319-27. See on 5.25.

494. *Chromios* (**H, L**): i.e. Chromis (and at 534); see 218 and on 2.858.

507. *called*: see on 90-105. In the event, the two Ajaxes only have to turn up to frighten off Hector and Aeneas (531-5) and then return to the fight. Note that Menelaus does not come: he is being held back for more important business.

520. *As (when) a strong (young/grown) man*: D-simile. Note how it advances the action. When the simile begins, Aretus has been struck in the belt. The simile describes how a struck ox springs forward and collapses, and the simile ends by pointing out that Aretus too sprang forward and fell back. See **GI** 12D.

527. *ducked/stooped/bent*: = 16.611-13.

538. *consoles/is relieved/put (...) sorrow*: a moderate 'boast', in contrast with e.g. 13.414-16, 446-7, 14.454-7.

542. *like/as a/some lion*: a brief and suggestive A-simile.

543-655: Athene encourages Menelaus, who drags Patroclus' body back to the Greek side. Zeus shakes his aegis, and the Greeks retreat. Zeus lifts the mist.

546. *changed his mind* (**R-J**); *purpose was/had shifted/changed* (**H,**

L): Zeus supports the Trojans throughout this encounter (453-4, 566, 593-6), but an important moment is coming up – Menelaus retrieving Patroclus' body – and this will justify his and Athene's intervention (Zeus does not want Patroclus to become carrion for the Trojan dogs, 272-3). Observe that Menelaus' effort is made easier in the absence of Hector, who had been lured away by the prospect of capturing Achilles'/Patroclus' horses (483-91). Hector returns to the 'front line' only when summoned by Apollo (592), after Menelaus has already seized the body.

547. *rainbow*: D-simile. It seems to be the shimmer/luridness of the cloud in which Athene wraps herself (551) that reminds the poet of the shimmer of the rainbow (547); but the rainbow is a signal of trouble to come (548-50) which Zeus soon sends (594-6), heralding a Greek rout.

555. *Phoenix*: see on 9.168. Since, in the temporary absence of the Ajaxes, Menelaus is leading the defence of Patroclus, it is right that he should be urged on, and who better than old 'Phoenix', Achilles' tutor (9.438-43), to do it? Note how Phoenix/Athene appeals to Menelaus' sense of shame, cf. 13.95-124, **GI** 4.

567. *Athene was happy/pleased/delighted*: ancient gods require acknowledgement – that is all. Menelaus will get his reward.

570. *fly/mosquito*: a clever image, signifying persistence (cf. 4.130-1) and the desire for blood. Athene is up to something.

574. *Patroclus*: Menelaus' position, standing over Patroclus, is significant. See following notes.

581. *the/his body* (**H, L**): whose body? **R-J** says 'Patroclus' body', though 'Patroclus' is not in the Greek. But clearly what has happened is serious, because Apollo, in disguise, immediately intervenes to try to correct it. See next note.

588-90. The Greek says, literally: 'As it is, he, alone lifting up [a/the] body out from under the Trojans, has got away, and he has killed your loyal companion Podes' etc. In other words, the Greek does distinguish between two bodies at this point. True, Homeric idiom could permit them to be the same body, as **H** takes it 'And now he has single-handedly carried a body out from the Trojan lines and got away – it was your trusted companion he killed … Podes' etc. **L** sticks more closely to the Greek: 'and now he has gone taking off single-handed / a body from the Trojans. He has killed your trusted companion / … Podes' etc.

The point is that (i) the Greeks now go on the retreat, effectively routed (596), and (ii) at 717-24 they lift up Patroclus' body and start to carry it. They could not possibly do that on the retreat unless they had control of the body *before* the retreat began. In other words, Menelaus at 581 drags back the body of Patroclus, beside which he was standing (574), to the Greek side; the Greeks are routed, taking the body with them; and at 724 they lift it up to speed their retreat.

Further, this capture of Patroclus' body is sanctioned by Zeus, even though he is still hostile to the Greeks. At 270-3 he pitied Patroclus, did not want him to become carrion, and urged on the Greeks. At 544-6 he has 'changed his mind' about the Greeks again, and sends down Athene to encourage them. So Athene breathes courage into Menelaus – to do what? Just kill Podes? Surely not. This retrieval of Patroclus' body gives Menelaus an important moment of glory. As Apollo says to Hector (588), Menelaus is not the greatest of fighters. But he has achieved greatness here, worthy of an *aristeia* (see 17/Intro). See Willcock (2002), who makes the central point that 'the body' (*nekros, nekus*) occurs twenty-five times in Book 17 and unambiguously refers to Patroclus twenty-three times – the only two possible ambiguities occurring in this passage (581, 589).

594. *aegis*: see on 2.202.

596. *terrified* **(L)**: read 'routed, panicked'.

597-601. *Peneleos … Leitus*: see on 2.494. Where death is the usual result of losing a fight, here both are only wounded.

605-25. *Idomeneus … frightened man* **(R-J)**/*entered his heart* **(H)**/*upon his spirit* **(L)**: a moving little sequence. Idomeneus hits Hector but does not penetrate (605-8). Coeranus, Meriones' charioteer, drives up to help Idomeneus (see on 5.13; Idomeneus was on foot that day, 612-13) but is killed when Hector aims at Idomeneus and misses (610-11). There is pathos in Coeranus' selfless rescue attempt which leads to his own death (615) – a particularly nasty one (see on 5.75, 292). The fact that fighters of the quality of Meriones and Idomeneus (companions in arms, 2.645) realise that there is no hope shows just how serious the situation is, but note that only Idomeneus gallops away – Meriones stays in the fighting. Cf. on 11.338 for a comparable episode.

608. *Deukalian* **(L)**: i.e. son of Deucalion.

611. *Lyctus*: in Crete.

640. *run with a/take/carry the message*: the last of the 'call for help' sequences, which will be answered by Achilles' great triple cry at 18.228-9.

644. *mist/fog*: see on 17.270. Ajax's call at least to die in the light is admirably heroic. For Zeus' pity, see on 15.12.

653. *Antilochus*: son of Nestor (fighting elsewhere, 377-83) known for his speed of foot. See on 15.569.

656-761: Antilochus runs to give Achilles the bad news. Menelaus and Meriones lift Patroclus' body, and the retreat continues.

657. *like a/as … some lion*: C-simile; cf. 11.547-556, where Ajax retreats in much the same way. The comparison lies in the lion's/Menelaus' unwillingness to go, after a long battle against farmer and dogs/Trojans, trying to get food/Patroclus.

671. *gentle*: see on 9.190.

674. *like an eagle*: C-simile, concentrating on the eagle's sight rather than speed of attack (e.g. 22.308-10).

679. *your (…) eyes/ you, Menelaus*: see on 4.127, and cf. 702.

695. *unable to speak/speechless*: Antilochus' inability to speak is more eloquent than any words.

698. *at a/on the run ... armour/war gear*: no other warrior strips like this, but speed is essential. One would have thought his chariot would have been quicker, but perhaps a chariot's mobility in battle was suspect; cf. Albracht (2003) [I.21].

699. *Laodocus*: the first we have heard of him as Antilochus' driver. He is rightly keeping close to his master. For **L**'s 'had turned' read 'was manoeuvring'.

705. *Thrasymedes*: Antilochus' brother, fighting with him (705). They are sons of Nestor, ruler of Pylos (hence 'Pylian').

711. *without (his)/bare of/ armour*: Achilles cannot fight because he had given his armour to Patroclus to wear. The poet prepares the ground for the making of new armour for Achilles (18.368-616).

719. *the pair of us/two of us/we two*: i.e. the two Ajaxes (who share the same name, 720). See on 13.703 for their joint efforts; for a neo-analytical insight, see on **GI** 2(vii).

722. *hoisted/lifted/lifting*: see on 588-90 for the significance of this moment.

725. *like hounds/dogs*: C-simile: the dogs/Trojans pursue a wounded boar/retreating Greeks, but retreat themselves when the boar/Ajaxes (732-3) turn on them (cf. 8.338-40). This is the first simile in a brilliant sequence of five, featuring 737 fire, 742 mules, 747 wooded ridge, 755 flock of birds. They indicate the importance and high drama of the moment.

737. *as (a) fire*: C-simile, the subject turning from fire's uncontrollability (737) and therefore destructiveness to its noise (the wind roaring the fire on, 739 = the din of battle, 740). The violence of the fire destroys cities and houses, as the Trojans threaten to destroy the Greek camp.

742. *as mules*: D-simile, the comparison being determined mules/Greeks, exhausted, sweating and struggling, to haul a heavy load/Patroclus down a mountain/to the ships.

747. *wooded/timbered (rock-) ridge*: precise C-simile, the ridge/Ajaxes spanning the country/line of retreat and holding back the floods/Trojans and dispersing them across the plain/battlefield, and not allowing them to flood through/break the line, even when they come in spate/full attack.

755. *as a flock/cloud*: D-simile, birds/Greeks, screaming/yelling and confused, see a falcon/Aeneas and Hector, threatening to kill their nestlings/them and their companions, and fly off/flee. The action will resume at 18.148 at the same point, with the Greeks still desperately trying to secure Patroclus' body, 18.150.

Book 18

Introduction

At the end of Book 17, the Greeks are in flight back to the camp with the body of Patroclus. There are two questions that Homer now faces. First, will Achilles get back his armour with Patroclus' body, or not? If he does, there will be no need to have new armour made. If he does not, new armour will be required. Homer opts for the latter. The poet must then choose whether to go into detail about this armour. He does not have to (he could simply report its manufacture and delivery). But if he chooses to, we shall have to see how he exploits the opportunity it offers.

The second question is: at what point will Achilles learn of Patroclus' death – after the body has been safely recovered, or before? If after, Achilles will (presumably) mourn him, have new armour made and return to battle. Nothing wrong with that, but if he hears that Patroclus has been killed *before* the body has been recovered, the poet can then involve Achilles in the actual recovery. Problem: Achilles has no armour. So if the poet *does* want Achilles to play a part in Patroclus' rescue – and surely he does, if possible – he must think of some way of doing it which does not involve Achilles joining battle against the Trojans. Hence the poet's invention of the dramatic episode in which Achilles, standing by the ditch, emits a great shout, just at the moment when it looks as if Hector is about to win back the body for the Trojans (165-238), followed at once by Hera hastening the day to its end – the one day when Zeus had promised Hector victory (see on 11.194).

Achilles therefore receives news of Patroclus' death before his body has been recovered (1-147); the battle for its recovery reaches a climax, and Achilles intervenes to save it (148-242). That scenario has the added advantage of giving the Trojans notice of Achilles' return. How will they react to it? We find out at 242-314; and then cut back to Achilles, mourning his lost friend, announcing what his intentions are now and preparing the body for burial (315-59). The divine reaction to events is recorded (360-7), and then comes the making of Achilles' new armour (368-616).

Book 18 is the great turning-point in the *Il.* The poet makes it the book of decision – (see Schadewaldt [1959b]) – Achilles' decision as to how he will respond to the death of Patroclus. This decision will shape the rest of the epic, and the crucial figure in it is to be Thetis. As in Book 1, we are back in the private world, unknown to anyone else, of Achilles and his mother. This again is a result of the poet's choice. Homer *could* have made Achilles hear the news and react (in whatever way) on the spot, without reference to anyone else. But Homer chooses to involve Thetis in the decision, to heart-stopping effect. She hears Achilles' terrifying scream when he is told the news of Patroclus' death and, as ever, rushes to be at his side (cf. 1.348-63). Not knowing what has happened (73; see below, 52-64), she is baffled at his despair: has not Zeus granted all his wishes in driving back the Greeks (74-7)? When she finds out the truth – that Patroclus is dead and Achilles' only desire is to avenge him by killing Hector – she is in a position to drop the bombshell: that if Achilles takes revenge on Hector, his death follows at once (96-7). What therefore will Achilles choose? Without a second's hesitation, he chooses death. It is an extraordinary decision in a world where life and the winning of *kleos* mean so much. Indeed, it is unique. No other *Iliad*ic hero embraces death in the way that Achilles does here. That is why Homer involved Thetis. She alone knows what the consequences of any decision will be. This revelation turns Achilles' decision to kill Hector from heroic revenge into heroic tragedy – all ultimately springing from Achilles' anger in Book 1, his decision to ask Thetis/Zeus to massacre the Greeks, and his self-willed refusal to rejoin the fighting after the embassy in Book 9.

The decision also ends Achilles' anger against Agamemnon and the Greeks. Already by the start of Book 16 – of which the start of Book 18 is something of a mirror (Patroclus = Antilochus, both bringing bad news to an expectant Achilles) – his anger was wavering (16.60-1); here in Book 18 he renounces it completely (107-13). He replaces it, first, with a different sort of anger, the desire for revenge against Hector (114-16, cf. the simile at 322) and, second, with the determination to set about winning the *kleos* which originally motivated his request to Thetis that the Greeks start losing (cf. 1.505-10) but now is the only compensation he has for his impending early death (120-1). In Book 9, no material compensation could equal the gift of life for Achilles (400-9). That is still the case: he dies to take revenge on Patroclus' killer and to win the *kleos* his pursuit of Hector will bring. The winning of *kleos* is the central subject-matter of epic; the *Il.* darkens and deepens that subject-matter by weaving tragedy into the heart of its epic texture.

The book is also a turning point for Hector. As we have seen, he has been driven on by Zeus in the fulfilment of Zeus' plan for Achilles' return, but was promised success for only one day. Since he did not know that his own death was to follow shortly (17.200-8), it is hardly surprising that, buoyed up with the success of the day, he should reject Polydamas' cautious advice to retreat into Ilium at once (273-9, cf. 303-9). As Hector implies, after years of debilitating siege, this is still the Trojans' best chance of ridding themselves of the Greeks for ever, 287-95, cf. on siege-warfare, **GI** 13B(ix). It is in fact a decision fatal for himself, as he will eventually admit (22.99-107); but at the moment he still has high hopes, in ignorance of the fact that Zeus' plan is now at an end and Zeus will support him no longer. Achilles, in other words, makes the fatal decision knowing what the consequences will be (cf. e.g. 330-3, 19.420-2, 22.365-6, etc.); Hector, not knowing (cf. e.g. 16.859-61, 18.305-9, etc.).

That leaves the plan of Zeus. But *where* does it leave it? At the end of Hector's day of success, which has indeed brought Achilles back into battle as Zeus had foretold the day before (8.470-6), Zeus himself seems oddly cagey about his 'plan' now that it has run its course. He seems to want to blame *Hera* for what has happened, as if it were all her doing, and he now wishes to wash his hands of responsibility (see on 358). One can, however, rather see why. The purpose of the plan was to bring Achilles back into the fighting, covered with glory, leaving Agamemnon humiliated. But the consequence for Achilles of the string of victories that Zeus granted to the Trojans has been not only the mass slaughter of Greeks (as Achilles indeed demanded) but also the death of Patroclus and (as a result of Thetis' revelation) Achilles' early death too. Was this what the plan was for?

Not that Achilles sees the plan of Zeus in that light. He points no finger of blame at Zeus. He simply admits that he himself was wrong in the first place (107-13) and that Patroclus' death was his personal fault, for which he must now pay the full price (98-104). One might call that some sort of (rough) justice for Achilles' 'accursed anger' (1.2) and desire to see fellow-Greeks pay with their lives simply so that he might be honoured; even more so when Achilles remains in denial of his direct responsibility for the mass Greek slaughter at e.g. 19.273-4, where he blames Zeus for their deaths, and 21.134, where he says it was all the Trojans' fault (it is worth remembering that Achilles never tells anyone it was actually all his responsibility). But the 'rough justice' analysis would be hard to justify from the evidence of the text: it is not a 'lesson' that Homer or his characters draw. So who was 'at fault'? Achilles for requesting that Greeks be slaughtered? Thetis for conveying it to Zeus? Zeus for agreeing to it? As ever, Homer draws no conclusions. This is what happened. That suffices.

At 369, the scene switches from the conversation of Zeus and Hera on Mount Ida to Hephaestus' forge on Olympus, where Thetis has gone to ask him to make new armour for her son. How is Homer to describe the moment? He could merely report Thetis' request and Hephaestus' compliance. In fact he chooses to go into detail, beginning with a wonderfully civilised scene of divine *xenia* as Hephaestus welcomes Thetis to his home, full of delightful character touches (especially of Hephaestus as blacksmith), and quite different in tone from the recent harrowing events on earth. This can hardly be by mistake. But why does Homer concentrate on the shield, and say nothing about the rest of the armour except that it was made (609-12)? Because only the shield gave the poet the physical space on which to depict the scenes of human activity which he had decided to illustrate there. He could hardly place these on the greaves or helmet.

But one has to ask – why these scenes? Especially as the images Homer describes are never referred to again in the poem (but see Alden [2000] who thinks that they are supposed to reflect on incidents in the poem itself, e.g. the court case to the issues lying behind the embassy to Achilles in Book 9, etc.).

First, this is a shield produced by the great blacksmith god for Achilles. The poet constantly reminds us that this is not the real world we are observing, but a world of gold and silver and tin; on the other hand, 'static' scenes are envisaged as stories, alive with sound, colour and movement (e.g. 492-5, 523-30, 567-72). The shield is a miracle, created by a divine hand (e.g. 548-9, 561-3). Yet what it creates is images of a living human world. The human and the divine meet here as nowhere else in the *Il.*

Second, Homer's chosen subject-matter for these scenes is social and every-day, drawn from many walks of life, and universal (the people on it are not said to be Greek or Trojan): marriages, festivals, law-courts, sieges, ploughing, herding etc., in which the pleasure of the participants is a significant feature (e.g. 496, 556-7, 604). That Hephaestus should illustrate scenes predominantly of peace and pleasure on a shield made for the Greeks' greatest war-monger to shake in the face of his enemies, when he himself is doomed shortly to die in battle, is not only a delicious irony in itself; it represents a typical Homeric reflex. The *Il.* may be a poem in which force is the major determinant of human action, but it is shot through with images of peace (e.g. Hector and Andromache in Book 6), of worlds far from the battlefield (especially in the similes, see **GI** 12), and memories of what Ilium was like before ever the Trojan war began (see e.g. 22.156). The scenes on the shield exemplify this reflex on the largest scale in the *Il.* The comparison with Aeneas' shield (Virgil, *Aeneid* 8.626-731) is instructive. Since Virgil was serving a political as well as a historical agenda in the composition of the *Aeneid*, Aeneas hoists on his shoulder depictions of the future history of the Roman people.

Main sources for the commentary and related reading
Edwards (1987) 267-86; Edwards (1991); Schadewaldt (1959b); Taplin (1980); Willcock (1984).

1-147: Antilochus brings news of Patroclus' death. Achilles collapses in grief, and his mother Thetis, hearing his cries, arrives with her Sea-nymphs to lament. Achilles says he will have his revenge by killing Hector and ignores Thetis' warning that his death will follow soon after Hector's.

2. *Antilochus*: picked up from 17.685-701.
3. *found*: see on 2.167 for scenes of arriving and finding.
in front of ... his ships: Achilles, of course, is watching the fighting (16.254-6), but he is too far away to see what has happened (17.401-4).
5. *disturbed/in dismay*: see on 11.403 for such monologues.
11. *leave the light*: another of Thetis' prophecies of which we had not yet specifically heard, cf. on 16/Intro.
13. *Unhappy!* **(L)**: read 'Hot head!' or 'Obstinate man!'
I ordered/told him: see 16.87-96.
17. *tears*: see 17.696. Antilochus can barely blurt out his message, cf. 17.695.
22. *black cloud*: Achilles can *say* nothing. All he can do is react. He

does so by mourning and, in collapsing, disfiguring himself and mingling with the dust (26-7, as fallen warriors do), he announces that good order is at an end (see **GI** 7B) and even, perhaps, enacts his own death. The shock of imagining the worst is as nothing to knowing it.

31.   *beat their breasts*: the slaves seem to be mourning for the prostrate Achilles, as if *he* were dead; see **GI** 2(vii). Cf. the lament of Hector's household for him while he was still alive, 6.497-502; and see on 24.720 for 'official' lament-singers, whose role the slaves seem to be adopting here, in the absence of anyone else to do it.

34.   *let/gave out a (…) cry* **(R-J, H)**; *he cried out* **(L)**: Thetis responds at once to her son's cries of anguish. See on 1.352. Her fears are related to the early death she knows he must suffer (59-60) – how early, she is now about to find out.

39-48.   *Glauce … Emathia*: a gloriously harmonious litany of names. Nereids were daughters of Nereus (old man of the sea, and Thetis' father), famous for their beauty and fickleness (like the sea) and endowed with the gift of prophecy. Their sympathetic presence (65-7, 138-5) might have been intended as something of a consolation to the distraught Achilles. They certainly make magical listening for the audience.

52-64.   *Listen/Hear … from the fighting*: Thetis mourns in advance for her dear son, all the more sharply because she knows that he is doomed to die young (59-60, cf. 1.352) but, immortal though she is, can do nothing to help him (62) except (like any mortal mother) listen (63-4). Compare Hecabe's laments and her pride in Hector (22.432-6, 24.749-59). As usual, Thetis is not omniscient about Achilles' present troubles (see on 1.365).

71.   *took her son's head*: a traditional gesture when mourning the dead (see on 22 above, and cf. 23.136, 24.712, 724).

74.   *has been fulfilled/brought about* **(R-J, H)**; *brought to accomplishment* **(L)**: Thetis points out that all Achilles wishes have been met. So what can possibly be the trouble? Herein lies Achilles' tragedy – all his desires turn to ashes, with the most dreadful consequences for *others* as well as himself. His greatness lies in his unblinking confrontation with and acknowledgement of what he alone has brought about.

82.   *I have lost him* **(H, L)**: the Greek *apôlesa* also means 'I have destroyed' him, which **R-J** prefers. This is a genuine ambiguity – it means both at once, and neither meaning can take preference. Cf. on 9.318.

85.   *brought/drove you to the (…) bed*: Thetis married Peleus, a mortal, under protest (18.432-4). See on 1.352.

88.   *(But) as it is*: see on 9.356.

89.   *lose your son* **(R-J)**; *death of a son/your son's death* **(H, L)**: Achilles argues here that he will die because he does not want to live. He then adds the condition – unless he kills Hector. We may argue that he will almost certainly succeed in this (and therefore that his desire for life may be rekindled), but Achilles at the moment is in the depths of the blackest despair.

96.   *you are doomed* **(R-J)**; *your own doom* **(H)**; *it is decreed* **(L)**:

Thetis' bombshell, the secret she has been keeping from Achilles – if he kills Hector, he dies next. In other words, far from rekindling the desire to live, Hector's death will guarantee his own. Thetis' worst fears are now being realised. Note that she does not suggest to her son what he should do. She knows (cf. 126 'you will never/not persuade me'). Or does Achilles cut her off by interrupting her here (cf. **R-J**'s punctuation, and see on 1.292 for another example)?

98-102. *let me die/I must die … defence/saving light/safety for Patroclus*: Achilles confronts his responsibility for his decisions and accepts it and the consequences – his own death. A fragment of Aeschylus' *Myrmidons* talks of an eagle, struck by an arrow, saying, as it saw the arrow-feathers, that it had been caught not by others but by its own feathers. If that refers to Achilles lamenting the death of Patroclus, it is an exquisite summary of Achilles' situation in the *Il.*

104. *idle/useless burden/weight*: the full pointlessness of what he has done strikes home to Achilles – this hero, so swift-footed, an idle burden on the earth.

106. *others are better in debate* (**R-J**); *better skilled at speaking* (**H**); *better in council* (**L**): cf. 11.785-8. Achilles thinks through issues with quite extraordinary intellectual intensity (e.g. before the embassy in Book 9 and with Patroclus in Book 16), but acknowledges that his strength does not lie in dealing with others in the give-and-take of everyday debate. Cf. on 1.247.

107-10. *rivalry/quarrels/strife … smoke/honey*: Achilles does not attempt to justify his past feelings. All he can do is wish them away. The two images of 'anger', sweet as honey and growing like smoke, are quite extraordinary, but typical of Achilles' colourful language. See Griffin (1986b).

113. *curb the feelings* (**R-J**); *forcing down the passion* (**H**); *beat down … the anger* (**L**): as others had already told him to, in vain e.g. Peleus 9.255-6, Phoenix 9.496, cf. 19.216-20. It is a lesson Achilles will not learn, however, since his anger will now be transferred from Agamemnon to Hector (cf. 322, 337, 22.395ff.).

114. *dear life*: presumably Patroclus, but it could (in a broader sense) mean either Achilles' own life in the sense that Hector has destroyed his reason for living, 89-90, or even in the (less likely) sense that, when he kills Hector, his own death will follow immediately, i.e. Hector will have (in a way) 'killed' him.

117. *Heracles*: an interesting choice of example. Heracles was a sort of 'superman', the only mortal to be deified at death, and (like Achilles) a hero of volcanic passions. For his activities and the anger of Hera, see on 5.392, 638.

121. *glory*: what all warriors desired – a great reputation that will survive death. The quarrel with Agamemnon, Achilles' feelings of humiliation and all thoughts of gifts and compensation are now forgotten; the epic priority, the search for glory, asserts itself over everything else.

123. *Dardanian*: Dardanus, son of Zeus, founded the Trojan race, 20.215-16.

125. *from battle too long* (**R-J**); *too long out of the fighting* (**H, L**): it is now the sixteenth day since Achilles walked out, but only the third day of fighting.

130. *armour*: see 17.189-97, cf. 17.711.

148-242: Achilles makes an appearance on the battlefield and with Athene's help routs the Trojans with a shout. Patroclus' body is brought back to the Greek camp [night before 27th day].

151. *drag*: we must assume the Greeks have reverted to dragging the body of Patroclus (cf. 17.722-3); or that 'drag' means 'drag away from the carrying party'; or that Homer has 'nodded'. The references to the two Ajaxes (157, 163), however, do recreate the situation at 17.719-21.

161. *As (…) shepherds/herdsmen*: C-simile, the lion and Hector both being equally 'hungry' to drag the kill/Patroclus from the shepherds/Greeks.

167. *to arm* (**H, L**): but Achilles had no armour. Here it means 'to prepare for battle', as **R-J**.

without telling (**R-J**); *unknown* (**H**); *secretly* (**L**): as the plan of Zeus is still technically in operation, Hera continues to act in secret from her husband.

172. *beside/in front of the ships*: the fight has moved on past the ditch (17.761).

177. *palisade/stakes*: Hector has considered cutting off Patroclus' head (17.126-7), but Iris adds the gloss about sticking it up on display to motivate Achilles all the more. See on 11.455.

178. *(a)shame(d)/disgrace*: a typical appeal, cf. 13.95-124.

182. *which of the gods/what god*: Thetis had told Achilles not to join the fighting (134-5).

203. *rose up*: simple, but electric, words. Achilles returns – and a goddess immediately 'arms' him, with an aegis (see on 1.202) and halo in place of body-protection/shield and helmet. Achilles is worthy of divine help.

207. *Just as/As when the/ smoke* (**R-J, H**); *As when a flare* (**L**): superb D-simile, the scene being pictured from a distance ('far away', 208), starting with the smoke (correct **L**'s 'flare') going up during the *day* from a burning town (the desperate Greek camp/ships) besieged by enemies (Trojans) and ending with beacon-fires (Achilles) lighting up the *night* (see 241), signalling that help is at hand. Achilles is regularly associated with fire in these later books, e.g. 19.16-17, 365-6, 373-83, 398, 20.371-2, 490-4, 21.12-16, 522-5, 22.25-32, 134-5.

209. *who* (**L**): read 'and the city's inhabitants'.

215. *ditch*: the Greeks' defensive ditch, built outside the wall (7.438-41) – what there is left of it, after it had been filled in by Apollo (15.355-66)

– even though the fighting seems now to be going on round the ships (172 above).

219. *Like the piercing sound* **(R-J)**; *As when the voice* **(H)**; *As loud as* **(L)**: C-simile, continuing the image of the besieged city from 207 above. It is hard to know what the purpose of blowing the trumpet is: to rally the troops?

224. *pull their chariots round* **(R-J, H)**; *turned their chariots about* **(L)**: the chariots and their drivers are presumably following the advancing Trojan line. When the horses hear Achilles' shout, they turn round, their terrified drivers cannot control them (cf. 13.394-6) and are themselves terrified by the flames from Achilles' head (226); and in the ensuing chaos, as the fighters scramble to get aboard to flee (229), twelve are killed in the chaos (230) either 'falling down or being crushed by the wheels or impaling themselves as they try to mount the chariots pulled by horses which have gone wild'; see Albracht (2003) [I.23].

231-8. *Meanwhile/And then (…) the Greeks … on his return/to be welcomed*: Homeric restraint makes the passage almost unreadable. Patroclus is finally saved and brought home, in silence except for the tears (234-5). Homer changes the focus from one image to another, adding no comment himself; but surely 'he had sent…' focalises the action through Achilles' own, appalled thoughts at the consequences of what he had done.

239-42. *Now the/Ox-eyed/lady Hera … leveller/war/battle*: night, as usual, brings the day's fighting to a close (e.g. 7.282). Hera's intervention makes it a dramatic conclusion to an even more dramatic day, which had begun at 11.194 (see note there). Note the sun is 'unwilling'. After Hector's Zeus-given day of triumph (11.191-4, 17.206-8), Hera wants her revenge, and soon. These two last scenes – the return of the dead Patroclus and the setting sun – make an unforgettably brilliant ending to the day. As usual, Homer 'merely' reports.

243-314: Terrified by Achilles' return, the Trojans hold an assembly. Polydamas recommends withdrawal to Ilium; Hector, wrongly convinced Zeus is on his side, rejects this advice and wins Trojan approval to continue the attack next morning.

245. *meeting/assembly*: the last Trojan meeting was at 8.489-542, when Hector's confidence was greeted with shouts of approval and the Trojans camped out on the plain (Polydamas refers to the occasion at 259-60). It is a very different situation now.

249-283. *Polydamas*: see on 12.60. His speech falls into two halves: 254-66 – retreat back into Ilium because, with Achilles on the loose, our town and women are at risk (note ring-composition on the 'retreat' theme, 255/266); 267-83 – since Achilles will wreak havoc if he finds us out here, we should hold Ilium and let him exhaust himself riding up and down outside the walls, to no effect.

264. *sunder between them* **(L)**: read 'share between them', i.e. fight it out on equal terms.

274. *strength* **(L)**: i.e. troops.

285-309. Hector answers Polydamas point by point, in two halves: 285-96 – our town has lost everything because of the war, but now Zeus gives us a chance of winning the war once and for all (and, by implication, recouping our losses); 297-309 – we must take our position on the plain, not worry about our possessions in the city, and in the morning arm for battle; I may well kill Achilles if he comes out to fight. Observe that Hector is still buoyed up by the promises of Zeus which have yielded such success during the past day of battle, culminating in the death of Patroclus. But Zeus promised him success only for that day, as Iris informed him (11.206-9). Hector is quite unaware that Zeus' will is now the very reverse of what it had been (17.206-8) and still has all the confidence of e.g. 15.718-25.

290. *emptied of treasure/vanished*: because of the need to pay the allies over the course of the ten-year war (17.225-6).

295. *fool*: Hector's scorn for Polydamas will be matched by the poet's for the Trojan approval of Hector's speech (310, 'fools' – a rare judgmental intervention by the third-person narrator; see **GI** 10).

307. *not ... run away/from him*: but Hector will (22.136ff.).

314-68: Achilles laments Patroclus, foreseeing his own death but anticipating revenge on Hector. The body is washed, anointed and clothed, and lamentation continues throughout the night. Hera gloats to Zeus over her success in bringing Achilles back into the fighting.

318. *like a (...) lion*: C-simile, the lion/Achilles groaning at the loss of cubs/Patroclus to a huntsman/Hector; lion/Achilles was too late to save them/him, grieves, but pursues the huntsman/Hector in anger (here the simile looks to the future). The feelings of lion/Achilles in this simile are as important as its actions. For the parent-child relationship between Achilles and Patroclus, see on 16.7 and cf. on 9.323.

325. *in his house* **(H)**; *in his halls* **(L)**: this is what the Greek says, but presumably Achilles is referring to the assurances he gave Menoetius at *Peleus'* palace before they set out for Troy, cf. 9.252-9, 11.764-89.

326-42. *I said/told him ... towns of men/cities of mortal(s) (men)*: observe how Achilles' thoughts move back and forth – to the deep past ten years ago, when he remembers a promise made to Patroclus' father (326-8); to the present, as Achilles consciously now links himself in death with Patroclus (329-32); to the immediate future and his new promise to kill Hector and only then bury Patroclus (334-40); and to their past together at Troy (340-2). Note that Achilles does not attempt to justify his actions or excuse himself in any way (by pointing out, for example, the various prophecies of the gods which have intervened, e.g. 17.406-8). Regret for the past mingles with determination about the future.

335. *head*: Achilles' threat parallels Hector's (see on 17.126).

the great man (**H**); *your great-hearted* (**L**): **H** and **L** refer the epithet 'great (-hearted)' to Hector. That is perfectly possible; **R-J** prefers to refer it to Patroclus.

336. *cut the throats/behead*: correct **L**'s 'behead'. This most un-Homeric slaughter – a blood payment for the death of Patroclus – will be prepared for at 21.26-32 and carried out at 23.175-6. Acts of brutality of this sort are normally reserved for the battlefield, but the whole funeral of Patroclus (23.166-77), with its offerings of horses, dogs, etc., is unparalleled anywhere in Homer. It is clearly supposed to be a very special event, designed to demonstrate the intensity of Achilles' grief.

351. *ointment/unguents*: this and other passages suggest that the Greeks knew something about embalming. Cf. 19.123-9, 23.187.

358. *roused* (**R-J, L**): *stirred* (**H**): since it has been Zeus' plan all along to get Achilles back into the fighting, it is strange that he says Hera achieved it herself, in a tone that suggests it is her 'fault'. Is Zeus referring to her supposedly secret message to Achilles at 167-201, which cannot then have been secret from him? It almost seems as if Zeus is admitting that his own plan has failed. And, arguably, it has: Achilles has not returned, loaded with honours and gifts, from a humiliated Agamemnon.

367. *trouble for them/angered me/I hate them*: Hera's anger against the Trojans has remained implacable throughout, and Zeus is well aware of it (4.31-6). See also on 4.21, 40. Observe that Hera is quite happy to justify her actions by drawing an analogy between divine and human behaviour (362-3): anything humans can do, gods can and should do even more thoroughly. This scene signals the end of Zeus' help for the Trojans.

369-467: Thetis arrives at Hephaestus' home and asks for armour.

369. *made her way to/came*: an adapted scene of arrival + *xenia* (see on 9.182-224 and cf. the arrival and reception of Nestor at 11.768-80). Note how Thetis arrives 369 and finds 372 (description of Hephaestus); then Charis his wife goes up to her, greets her and offers hospitality (i.e. food) 382-7, leads her in 388, seats her 389, Hephaestus calls for hospitality for her 408 (perhaps given to Thetis while he gets ready?), and then questions are asked and answered 424. After the recent dreadful events, the Thetis-Hephaestus scene offers a delightfully different perspective on the gods, one where civilised discourse is the norm. In the *Od.*, Hephaestus' wife is Aphrodite, but that would not do in the *Il.*, where Hephaestus is pro-Greek and Aphrodite pro-Trojan.

373. *tripods*: see on 8.290 – fitted with wheels, and self-propelled too! Cf. Hephaestus' automated female attendants (417-21), intelligent robots made of gold. This is the master-craftsman Hephaestus at his most miracle-working, but there is nothing easy about it: it involves sweat 372, fitting and forging 379 (for **L**'s 'beating the chains' read 'forging the rivets'), though Hephaestus has automated the bellows to do his bidding (469-73).

395. *threw me out/great fall*: see on 1.591, where Zeus threw

Hephaestus out of heaven, but not (presumably) causing the lameness for which Hera threw him out of heaven on this occasion, since in Book 1 Hephaestus had been trying to help Hera.

402. *Ocean*: see on 1.423, and cf. 18.606-7.

410-21. A delightful, carefully observed description of Hephaestus hurriedly clearing away and then smartening up to greet Thetis: he gets up from the anvil, panting (being a smith is hard work), he puts away his bellows and tools, sponges his face (not 'forehead', **L**), hands and chest, puts on a tunic and limps off with his staff, supported by his golden robots.

410. *took the huge blower off from the block of the anvil* (**L**): read 'raised his monstrous, panting bulk from the anvil'.

428. *Thetis replied/answered*: notice that Thetis never calls Achilles by his name throughout this speech: it is always 'he/him/his' and 'my son'. From 444-56 she outlines the plot of the *Il.* to date. Note the key moments: 444-5, Agamemnon takes Achilles' girl chosen for him by the Greeks; 446-50, Greek defeats lead to the embassy with its gifts, which Achilles rejects; 451-6, Achilles sends out Patroclus in his armour, but he is killed by Apollo, with glory for Hector.

434. *against my will*: see on 18.85.

437-43. *warriors/heroes ... to his side/go to him/to help him*: = 18.56-62.

453. *Scaean gate*: not *all* the fighting went on there, but 16.712 associates the gate with Patroclus' death (and Achilles will die there too, 22.358-60).

454. *Apollo*: see on 16.850.

468-617: Hephaestus returns to his forge to make armour for Achilles. The shield is described in detail.

The description of the construction and decoration of Achilles' shield is often taken to be a sort of extended 'arming' scene, and comparisons are drawn between the decorations on Achilles' shield and those terrifying images on Agamemnon's shield (11.32-40). But it is the differences that are important. Agamemnon carries a shield created by a human, but Achilles one created by a god. Hephaestus' shield represents the ultimate glorification of Achilles as a man worthy of carrying on his shoulders the finest work that the supreme craftsman god can create. As a result, the shield is given a place all to itself, and described quite separately from Achilles' actual arming scene, which takes place much later (19.367-99)

In describing the shield as he does, Homer probably had in mind contemporary decorated shields and dishes of the sort which have survived till today. **Fig. 1** is from a Phoenician silver dish found in Cyprus. Observe the siege at eleven o'clock and the workers in the countryside at ten o'clock, and cf. 18.509-50. A possible *schema* for Achilles' shield might look something like **Fig. 2**.

Fig. 1. Phoenician dish from Cyprus, *c.* 700 BC.

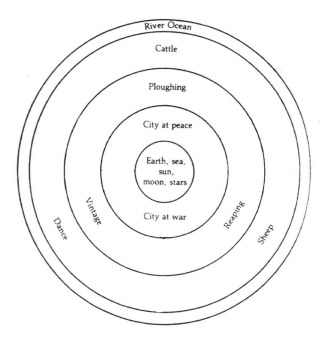

Fig. 2. Possible reconstruction of Achilles' shield, based on
Willcock (1976), 210.

470. *on the crucibles* (**H, L**): preferably, 'through the nozzles'.

477. *hammer … tongs/pincers*: tools used for working iron rather than the soft metals Hephaestus will be using here.

483-9. *earth … wary eye/Ocean*: scene 1 – the world and its constellations. Since Orion is a hunter, it is no surprise that the Bear keeps an eye on him. The Bear never sets – hence it does not plunge into Ocean, i.e. sink below the horizon (see on 1.423).

490-6. *two towns/cities … admire(d)/admiring*: scene 2: town I, in which a marriage is being celebrated. For **L**'s 'court', 496, read 'house'.

497-508. *(But) the men/people … soundest/straightest judgement/opinion*: scene 3: town I, in which proceedings relating to murder are being heard (see on 9.633). There seem to be two possible interpretations: (i) the murderer is claiming to *have* handed over the blood-price, but the other family is denying it; or (ii) the murderer is claiming the right to settle the dispute by handing over the blood-price, but the other family is refusing to allow him to. Whatever the issue at hand, both parties have put forward a talent of gold in lieu of judgement, and expert arbitrators have been called in. Both sides and their supporters rush from one expert to the other to hear their various judgements (on the use of the staff/sceptre, see on 1.234). It is not clear how a final decision is reached: perhaps the whole crowd decides.

509-40. *other town/city … real warriors do/those who were killed/those who had fallen*: scene 4: town II, which is under siege. The besiegers are debating whether to continue with the siege or accept the town's offer of surrender and half their goods (cf. 22.120). But the townspeople decide to act first and ambush the suppliers of the besieging army, which rushes to their defence. A pitched battle ensues.

509. *two armed forces/armies/forces of armed men*: presumably this means one army, split into two for the purposes of the siege.

531. *debate/assembly-place/councils*: perhaps discussing the tactical issues raised at 510-12.

535. *Strife/Hate … Panic/Confusion*: common participants in battle, e.g. 4.440-1.

541-9. *field … piece of work/craftsmanship/forging*: scene 5: ploughing. Hephaestus now depicts scenes from the farmer's year. Ploughing and sowing took place in November, but the poet may be referring to the spring (and summer) ploughing of fallow land.

550-60. *estate/precinct … supper/meal/barley*: scene 6: reaping (cf. 11.67-9), watched over by the local land-owner (556), with a meal being prepared for the workers. This is a summer occupation.

555. *boys/children*: these are probably removing the bound sheaves to be stored, rather than (**H, L**) handing the cut swathes to the sheaf-binders for binding.

559. *trimmed* (**L**): read 'were busy with'.

560. *barley*: the women may be sprinkling barley over the meat (**R-J**), or preparing a separate meal of porridge for the workers **(H, L)**, leaving the ox to the lord.

561-72. *vineyard ... dancing feet/music*: scene 7: the vintage. Grapes were harvested in the autumn.

564. *inlay/dark metal/enamel*: see on 11.24.

570. *Linus*: a mythical minstrel and composer who invented the dirge, and was, in one version of his death, killed by Apollo for boasting that he was as good a musician.

573-86. *herd ... avoid them/keeping/kept clear*: scene 8: herding cattle. It would complete the calendar if this were winter, i.e. when the cattle were kept in the byre and taken out to water. The attack by the lions evokes the world of the similes, cf. 17.61-7.

587-9. *grazing ground/pasture ground/meadow*: scene 9: sheep-flocks. Another winter scene?

590-605. *dancing-floor ... among the people/at the centre/among them*: scene 10: dancing. The beautiful (593-4) participants are in their finery (594-8), dancing now in circles (599-601), now in rows (601-2).

592. *Daedalus*: mythical inventor, held in Crete by Minos king of Cnossus. Ariadne was Minos' daughter. She helped the Athenian Theseus to kill the Minotaur, the monster to which tributes of Athenian boys and girls were sacrificed every year. After the Minotaur was dead, Theseus and Ariadne performed a dance celebrating the event (cf. 16.617 for the Cretan Meriones as dancer).

596. *oil*: see on 14.172.

604-5. *A godlike singer of tales sang with them to the lyre* **(R-J)**: Athenaeus (second century AD) tells us that the ancient commentator Aristarchus omitted these lines (for another omission by Aristarchus, reported this time by Plutarch, see on 9.458-61). If they are Homeric, they should be inserted between 'dance:' and 'and' in **(H)**, and 'watching,' and 'while' in **(L)**.

606-7. *rim/Ocean ... Ocean/shield/structure*: scene 11: Ocean, running round the edge of the shield as it does round the flat disc of the world. See on 1.423.

608-16. *shield ... Olympus/Hephaestus*: only the shield receives descriptive elaboration. The rest of the armour is swiftly dealt with.

615. *swooped/plunged/came*: the first element of an arrival scene, see on 2.167.

Book 19

Introduction

Now that Achilles has his armour (12-17), with his usual single-minded impetuosity all he wants to do is arm and fight (23). Only the possibility of the decay of Patroclus' body gives him any pause (23-7), and Thetis solves that problem at once (29-33). However, as Thetis sees (34), the return of Achilles from private to public life is, like his original walk-out, a matter of the highest importance for himself as well as the whole Greek army. However independently heroes behave on the battlefield (**GI** 13B(iv)), Achilles is either with the army or he is not, and if he is now with them, he must publicly demonstrate it (see e.g. on 20.357). The assembly, therefore, which witnessed that walk-out (1.304-7), must be summoned to witness the end of the dispute that caused it, and see Achilles brought back into the public fold.

One might expect a man like Achilles to use the occasion at least to demand recompense for Agamemnon's insult, or even an apology from Agamemnon, if not actually to humiliate Agamemnon to his face. Nothing, however, could be further from Achilles' thoughts. He makes no reference to gifts or apologies. Having renounced his anger (67-8), all he wants to do is hurl himself into battle and avenge Patroclus' death (68-70), a demand he repeats time and again (148-50, 199-214, 275). As he says at 18.106 (see note), he is not very good at this sort of debate; one feels he is having to restrain himself severely throughout (cf. on 24.560-70).

The Greeks are delighted to hear that Achilles is back (74-5), but Agamemnon must now have his say, and a lengthy, tortuous, self-justifying say it is (78-144): one can almost feel the steam rising from Achilles as the leader bangs painfully on for what seems like hours. Agamemnon ends by agreeing that he was deluded (137) and will therefore make recompense (138), and offers the same gifts as he proposed to the embassy in Book 9. Achilles responds at once by taking the same attitude to the gifts as he did then – he virtually dismisses them as irrelevant (147-8). Achilles, it seems, wants it to be made clear, in public, that he feels about Agamemnon as he did in Book 9 (see e.g. 9.378), i.e. he has no interest in being 'bought off' by him (cf. 9.157-61, and 18/Intro on gifts). He will remain his own man and will bow no knee to any Agamemnon. One can feel the tension rising between the two: Book 1 all over again? No. Odysseus quickly steps in and takes control.

Odysseus realises that the issue between Agamemnon and Achilles has to be sorted out, now. The assembly, he sees, must witness an act of *public* reconciliation involving gifts and that requires *both* sides to play the game. On this occasion, Achilles simply cannot be allowed to do his own thing (cf. 9.700-3). Tactful, quick-thinking Odysseus therefore insists, by patient, unthreatening argument, that Achilles joins in, despite Achilles' continued insistence that all he is interested in is immediate action (199-208) and that he personally will take neither food nor drink till revenge against the Trojans is complete (208-14). Eventually Odysseus sees to it that, first, Agamemnon's gifts are duly handed over and, second, Agamemnon swears an oath that he did not touch Briseis (171-7, 243-75). Whatever their personal feelings, Agamemnon and Achilles are now publicly 'all square'. The dispute has been officially resolved. Only now can the assembly be dismissed (276-7). Agamemnon's oath at 258-65 represent the last words that are put directly into his mouth in the *Il*. From now on, he drifts out of the story, as Achilles come to the fore.

Some have felt that the long discussions about food become a little wearisome: 'More than 180 lines have now passed since luncheon stole the limelight, and nothing has been achieved', says Page (1959) 314. It is true that food does not make for a scintillating epic subject (any more than inspecting sentries, see on 10.56), but it is the usual, sensible practice for the army to eat before battle (2.381, 8.53), and it indicates at this early stage how divorced from normal human needs and behaviour Achilles has become. Self-absorbed, single-minded, overcome with grief, all he can think of is revenge for Patroclus: nothing and no one else matters (213-14, 305-8, 312-13). The fact that Zeus has to send Athene to feed him (342-54) indicates how extreme his behaviour has become.

Homer has to fill in time while the army eats, and he does so with the handing over of Agamemnon's gifts (277-81) and two further laments: one by the newly returned Briseis (282-300) for Patroclus and another by Achilles (315-37), in whom the issue of food prompts memories of the way Patroclus used to serve him (315-21). It is significant that Achilles and Briseis exchange no words. It was her seizure by Agamemnon that caused the quarrel in Book 1. She has now been returned, but that no longer means anything because Patroclus is dead. Achilles' concerns are elsewhere (cf. Achilles' wish that he had never captured her in the first place, 58-60).

After the Greeks get ready for battle and march out (351-2, 363), Homer turns the spotlight back to Achilles. He arms in his new armour (367-91) – a powerful and terrifying scene – and his horses are yoked (392-98). A quite extraordinary moment now follows: Achilles berates his horses for not rescuing Patroclus (400-3), and the horse Xanthus replies (404-17). Homer normally goes out of his way to avoid grotesque, monstrous or bizarre interventions of this sort in ordinary human life (see on 6.119-236). This incident is a major exception, but it works. Xanthus is an immortal horse (16.154), one that stood grieving for Patroclus before Zeus took pity (17.426-59). Achilles has now accused this magnificent creature of failure, and no immortal takes kindly to that. Further, Achilles shows no surprise: in Homer one takes divine interventions, even equine ones, in one's stride. So, therefore, do we. Xanthus rebuts Achilles' charge (411-14) and goes on to remind Achilles that he is mortal and doomed to die *whatever* they do (415-17), because destiny decrees it, and soon (409-10). Achilles' reply

– that he knows all this and it will make no difference – gives a further insight into his current state of mind. Compromise is a word with which he is not, at the moment, acquainted. He has a debt to discharge on behalf of Patroclus, and that is all he can think about.

Main sources for the commentary
Edwards (1991); Willcock (1984).

1-144: [27th day: fourth day of combat] Thetis delivers Achilles' new armour. Achilles summons an assembly, expresses his regret for the past, his willingness to renounce his anger and his desire to return to battle. Agamemnon blames Delusion for his actions, describes how even Zeus was deluded by Hera and agrees to hand over the compensation.

1. *Dawn*: Eos, married to Tithonus (see on 11.1).

3. *[Thetis] reached/came*: the Greek says 'she came', meaning Thetis in the *previous* book (18.614). There is a debate about whether the book-divisions as we have them were made by Homer (surely not; see Richardson [1993] 20-1 and Taplin [1992] Appendix, for discussions of each book division). At all events, it is most unlikely that this one was, given that it interrupts a regular scene of arrival (see on 2.167). Since books often begin with dawn (e.g. Books 8 and 11), it may be that, when this book division was made, 1-2 were inserted.

4. *Achilles/son*: the poet left Achilles remorsefully mourning over Patroclus with the Myrmidons (5; see 18.354-5).

16. *anger*: against Hector now, not Agamemnon, as **R-J** interprets it (Hector is not referred to in the Greek). Note how Achilles is associated with fire here; see on 18.207.

23. *So/therefore now*: see on 9.356.

25. *flies*: Patroclus will not be buried till Hector is dead.

39. *ambrosia and red nectar*: cf. Sarpedon (16.680) and Hector (23.186-7). See on 5.340 for this immortal nourishment of the gods.

42. *assembly/assembled*: see on 2.87 for mustering the troops before battle. Note how everyone comes along, even helmsmen and stewards: the return of Achilles is a moment of high importance.

47. *limping*: we last saw these heroes, leaning on spears, at 14.28-9, 37-9. See on 14.28.

52. *Coön*: see on 11.248-53.

56. *Agamemnon/Son of Atreus*: it is brilliant move by Achilles to begin with a rhetorical question relating to the quarrel between him and Agamemnon. It immediately reduces the tension because it does not place the blame anywhere.

59. *Artemis*: this is not as cruel a sentiment as it seems: see on 6.205. Nevertheless, with Patroclus dead, Briseis is no longer relevant to Achilles' immediate interests.

60. *Lyrnessus*: see on 1.184.

65-6. *But however ... choice* (**R-J**); *But all this ... hearts* (**H**); *Still ... us* (**L**): = 18.112-13.

67. *renounce/end(ing) my anger*: Achilles' fight with Agamemnon is now at an end. But he has not *resolved* the issue at stake; he has been overtaken by events of his own construction. Further, in reaching this position, he has already lost Patroclus, and will shortly lose his life too, though not in the course of the *Il*. In other words, his angry departure from the battle, however principled, has turned into a disaster for him, not to mention for the Greeks killed in battle as a result. In the light of this, it is noteworthy that Achilles here expresses a wish that the quarrel had never happened (compare his attitude towards Briseis now with e.g. 9.334-45) and acknowledges his regret at Greek losses and Trojan success (62-4), but points no finger of blame at Agamemnon, nor at himself. For Achilles *now*, that is all past. Blame is not an issue. This is an unexpectedly tactful speech.

71. *by/beside our ships*: cf. Polydamas at 18.267-72.

72. *rest where they are* (**L**): i.e. back in Ilium, if they get there after facing a rampant Achilles.

77. *from/in his seat/place*: much disputed – does this line mean 'Agamemnon stood up to speak from his place, not moving to the middle' (**H**)? Or does it mean 'Agamemnon spoke from where he was sitting and did not stand up in the middle of them' (**R-J, L**)? Whatever Homer meant, it is clear Agamemnon is edgy, as if he feels upstaged already. See next note.

79-80. *when a man stands ... to give him a hearing* (**R-J**); *when a man is standing ... not right to interrupt him* (**H**); *it is well to listen ... break in on him* (**L**): Agamemnon is saying that he wants to be heard in silence, but there are two possible interpretations of how it means this, depending on one's understanding of 77. **H** understands that Agamemnon is standing to speak, but his wound prevents him from moving into the middle (where one would expect him to speak). **R-J** and **L** prefer to have him sitting because these lines can then be seen as a jibe at Achilles, i.e. Agamemnon is saying 'It's OK for someone like Achilles who can stand – unlike myself, who have been injured fighting – but even if I can't stand, you must still listen without interrupting'. After 'stand to speak', **R-J** adds 'as Achilles has just done' (not in the Greek) to make the point clear. For **L**'s 'speaker', 79, read 'one who is standing'. Of course Agamemnon can in fact stand: he walked to the assembly (51), and will stand to sacrifice at 250.

85-138. *The Greeks have often ... immense compensation* (**R-J**); *The Achaians before this ... limitless reparation* (**R-J**); *This is the word ... gifts in abundance* (**L**): Agamemnon starts by claiming that Achilles' speech laid the blame on him, when it did nothing of the sort; and then needlessly defends himself, in a massive excursus, by arguing that it was not he but first, Zeus, Destiny and the Fury (87), and then *Atê*, Delusion (88-94), that were responsible for his actions. It is as if Agamemnon had been expecting a rancorous attack on him from Achilles and prepared his defence accordingly, but finding nothing of the sort, is caught on the hop, unable to change tack. His inflated, self-justifying response ('What could I *do*?' he whines, 90) is quite out of proportion to what the occasion demands – and at the end of it all, he agrees to compensate Achilles anyway, but still leaves the impression that he really did not believe he had been at fault at all. It is also noticeable that he can hardly bring himself to address Achilles directly, even in the second person singular, let alone by his usual titles. He does not find it easy to apologise to a man he still loathes.

87.   *Fury/Erinys*: see on 9.454. It 'walks in darkness/mist' because it lives in the underworld. For 'Destiny/Fate', see **GI** 8.

89.   *Achilles' prize/prize from Achilleus*: see **GI** 10C.

91.   *Delusion*: see on 1.412, and cf. Agamemnon's use of Delusion as an excuse at 2.111 = 9.18, 116-19.

93.   *ground/earth … heads*: i.e. *Atê* visits a man undetectably.

95-133.   *even Zeus … set him by/tasks for Eurystheus*: a long mythological paradigm (see on 1.247), arguing that if Zeus could be caught out by *Atê*, no wonder he, Agamemnon, was. The story relates to the birth of Heracles, son of Zeus by Alcmene (98-9). Zeus boasted a child born of his blood that day would dominate all his neighbours (103-5). Hera, who hated Alcmene for her affair with Zeus, made Zeus swear to it (108-13), then held back Heracles' birth and brought on Eurystheus' (114-19). Zeus, realising he had been tricked, hurled Delusion out of heaven (126-31, cf. on 1.591). So, Agamemnon suggests, he too was victim of his own words, that led to him taking Briseis (de Jong [1987] 173). Eurystheus was to be the king who forced Heracles to carry out the twelve labours (131-3, cf. 8.361-5).

103.   *Eileithyia*: see on 16.187.

139.   *lead/rouse*: Agamemnon is making the point that he is wounded and cannot fight.

141.   *Odysseus*: the gifts were listed at 9.122-56 = 9.264-98.

145-278: Achilles wants to return to battle at once, but Odysseus says the men must be fed. Agamemnon's gifts are fetched, an oath sworn, and the assembly dismissed.

146-8.   *Agamemnon … keep them (with)*: Achilles continues to show no interest in his past quarrel with Agamemnon (see 67 above). All that counts now is revenge, which is why he wants to get into battle at once (148-50). Achilles is as single-minded as ever.

154-277.   *Odysseus … scattered*: an episode featuring the need for the men to eat before going into battle and the handing over of Agamemnon's compensation to Achilles, accompanied by an oath that he had not slept with Briseis. Note how Odysseus insists on Achilles showing a gracious and forgiving spirit (178-80 'gracious … short' **(R-J)**, 'reconciled … due to you' **(H)**, 'gracious…due you' **(L)**) and goes on to demand that Agamemnon feasts Achilles in his hut as well. However little Achilles may want this at the moment, Odysseus is determined to do everything by the book.

161. *food and wine*: food is an essential element in preparations for battle, cf. on 2.381.

177. *as is the way/natural ... women* (**H, L**): this verse is not very appropriate here and may be an interpolation added from 9.132-4, where the offer of an oath to this effect was first made. **R-J** omit it.

180. *Feast/meal*: this will take place at 23.35-57.

181-3. *Agamemnon, you/you, son of Atreus ... begun/angry*: there is no doubt in Odysseus' mind who started the trouble between Agamemnon and Achilles, but his rebuke to Agamemnon is mild.

185. *delighted/welcome/pleased*: there is a distinct note of relief as well as gratitude in Agamemnon's voice here. Odysseus seems to have pulled off the public reconciliation which Agamemnon knew was needed but could not bring himself to articulate with any conviction.

197. *boar*: to seal the proposed oath (175).

209. *no food or drink* (**R-J, H**); *neither drink nor food* (**L**): Achilles' refusal to eat is a sign of his sense of shame at Patroclus' death. He is punishing himself for what he has done – see 315-21.

212. *feet lying/turned towards the door* (**R-J, H**); *turned against the forecourt* (**L**): it was the normal custom for the feet of the body to face the door (modify **L**). Rohde (1925) p. 47 note 26 claims that this is to prevent the spirit of the *uncremated* dead from returning back into the house. Cf. on 6.418.

214. *slaughter*: typically ruthless, single-minded Achilles, cf. 1.177. For **L**'s 'in the hard work' read 'dying' or 'in pain'.

221-4. *Men have soon ... small* (**R-J**); *Men grow tired ... scales* (**H**); *When there is ... fighting* (**L**): Odysseus is arguing that men need food because battle is hard work, they tire of it quickly and the reward for it is meagre. War here is likened to harvesting thin crops, cf. 11.67-71.

223. *poised* (**L**): read 'tipped', i.e. given victory to one or other side, when the killing really starts.

225-9. *You wish ... suffice* (**R-J**); *Starving ... of a day* (**H**); *There is no ... the day* (**L**): one cannot mourn on an empty stomach either, observes Odysseus – and too many die for that anyway (i.e. not only Patroclus). So we must bury the day's dead (he hints at Patroclus), while those still alive must eat now and then start fighting again. Odysseus pleads the case of normal behaviour for normal mortals, as against an Achilles who goes to extremes whatever he is doing – even mourning.

244. *Briseis*: the 'cause' of the final break between Achilles and Agamemnon is now returned. See on 1.184, 348.

252. *knife*: for oath and sacrifice, see on **GI** 7E, 3.275.

270. *delusions/blindness*: now that Agamemnon has admitted the quarrel was all his fault, Achilles can publicly agree with him without causing offence (see on 67 above for Achilles' tact in this matter) and even mitigate the charge by blaming *Atê*, as Agamemnon had, and Zeus (273-4)

– though in fact, as Achilles knows very well (but no one else does), it was his idea, which Thetis transmitted to Zeus, that the Greeks should be killed so that he could have revenge on Agamemnon (cf. also 21.134-5). Achilles is interpreting the issue for public consumption.

276. *assembly*: the assembly over, the army is to eat before battle is joined. Homer must therefore fill in time while this is happening (see on 3.122-244), and does so with the delivery of Achilles' gifts, Briseis' lament, another lament from Achilles and his feeding by Athene. At 350-1, the Greeks start to arm.

279-351: Briseis laments for Patroclus. At Zeus' suggestion, Athene secretly feeds Achilles with ambrosia and nectar.

287-300. Briseis' speech begins with a greeting to the dead Patroclus (287), recalls the situation when she left Achilles' hut (288-9), generalises about her sufferings (290-4) and paints the hopes she once had, now dashed by Patroclus' death (295-300). The reflections that move from past to present and back, and the pervading sense of loss, loneliness, and frustrated hopes, are typical. This speech is Briseis' sole utterance in the *Il.*, and no less moving for it; for her, Patroclus' death overrides any feelings related to her return to Achilles.

295. *Achilles*: see on 1.184, and Briseis' part in the chain of death linked to Achilles. Cf. Andromache's experience at 6.414-24.

296. *Mynes*: presumably Briseis' husband, see on 2.685.

298. *wife*: hardly possible, since she was a slave. Patroclus was showing the kindly, encouraging side of his nature; after all, Briseis *did* look like Aphrodite (282, see on 1.113).

300. *gentle/kind*: see on 9.109.

311. *Phoenix*: major heroes stay with Achilles (not Diomedes, cf. 9.700-3), and Phoenix too, his sympathetic old tutor who played such a part in Book 9 (432-622).

315-37. *How often you ... am dead* (**R-J**); *Oh, there was a time ... am dead* (**H**); *There was a time ... been killed* (**L**): Achilles' lament follows the same pattern as Briseis' – after an introductory salutation, he recalls the past and compares it with the present (315-21), generalises about other sufferings relating to his father and son (321-7) and describes dashed hopes in relation to them (328-37).

316. *meal/dinner*: cf. 9.205-17.

320. *food/meat and drink*: see on 209.

322. *father*: because Achilles now knows he will die at Troy, his thoughts constantly turn to his old father Peleus, abandoned and alone at home in Phthia, e.g. 18.101, 330-1, 19.334-7. This reflection will play a vital role in his meeting with Priam in the last book.

326-7. *Scyros ... Neoptolemus*: the story was that Achilles (disguised as a girl) was hidden on Scyros by his parents, who did not want him to go to the Trojan war. During that time he fathered Neoptolemus by Deïdameia, daughter of Lycomedes, king of Scyros. Homer nods to that tradition here, but gives an alternative, and far more creditable, account of Achilles' send-off to the war at 11.769-88. During the Trojan war Achilles captured Scyros in a raid (9.667-8).

329. *I alone would perish/die*: this seems to suggest that Achilles had long known that he would die *at Troy*. But this 'knowledge' has never been made explicit, and even here it is expressed in term of expectation rather than prophetic certainty (cf. 17.403-11).

347-8. *nectar … ambrosia*: food of the gods, used also to preserve human flesh (19.37-9). See on 5.340.

351-424: The Greeks come out for battle – bronze armour flashes, the earth resounds – and Achilles arms himself, taking his father's spear. The horse Xanthus prophesies Achilles' death.

357. *snowflakes*: D-simile, the snowflakes/men's armour pouring down/emerging from a clear sky/brightly (363 the brightness of the armour lights up the sky). Similes typically accompany the advance to battle of troops, cf. 2.455-73, especially 455-8, where the glitter of the armour is likened to a forest fire.

364-98. *Achilles armed … shining sun* (**R-J**); *Achilleus began to arm … beaming sun* (**H**); *Achilleus helmed him … crosses above us* (**L**): the final arming scene, see on 3.328-38. It is notable for emphasising the feelings of Achilles, his emotions (rage) being, as usual (see on 1.44), played out as physical reactions (grinding teeth, blazing eyes), 365-7. Note the other expansions (indicating the importance of the moment) in the simile describing the shield and helmet, the fitting of the armour (cf. Hector at 17.210-12), the uniqueness of the Pelian spear (which Patroclus could not wield, 16.139-44, see notes on the lines between 16.130 and 145) and the extra detail of the chariot (cf. 16.144-54).

375. *Like the gleam* (**R-J**); *As when sailors* (**H**); *And as when from* (**L**): D-simile, the gleam of the fire/helmet seen from the sea/in the sky. The expansion referring to the sailors driven unwillingly over the seas who see the light (i.e. hope of safe landfall) calls to mind the Greek army, who see in the return of Achilles the light of salvation. Such light gleaming from armour often precedes an *aristeia* (cf. 398, Achilles' armour shining like the sun); see on 5.1-8 and on 5.5.

382. *like a star*: cf. 22.313-20.

386. *like (…) wings*: Achilles is swift-footed enough as it is; the new armour seems to give him added speed.

392. *Alcimus* (**H, L**): i.e. Alcimedon (see on 16.168-97). Automedon (392) had been Patroclus' driver (16.148), and took over the chariot when he was killed (16.864-7).

400. *Xanthus and Balius … Podarge*: see 16.149-51. **L**'s 'Bay' and 'Dapple' are not two extra horses: the terms translate 'Xanthus' and

'Balius'. An impassioned Achilles addresses them with a sharp rebuke about their failure to save Patroclus.

404-17. *(Then) from under/beneath … and a man/mortal*: an amazingly daring moment – one of the horses that had so movingly grieved for Patroclus (17.426-40) answers Achilles. Note the ring-composition: A 408-10 death is near, B 411-12 our slowness did not kill Patroclus, C 413-14 Apollo killed him, B 414-16 we are swift, A 416-17 you are destined to die.

413. *Apollo/child of Leto*: Achilles had not been told that Apollo played a major role in Patroclus' death, though he had feared it (16.91-5).

418. *Furies*: see on 9.454.

420-3. *Xanthus, why … battle/war/fighting*: cf. compare Hector's hopeful reply to Patroclus' prophecy at 16.859-61, and Achilles' analysis at 21.110-13 and 22.365-6. Achilles prepares for terrible revenge on the Trojans while facing his own impending death, unflinching.

Book 20

Introduction

With Achilles about to return to battle and the plan of Zeus played out, the poet has to decide where the gods are going to fit in to the scheme of things from now on. Since Zeus no longer has an overall controlling interest in the action, it makes sense for him to renounce his restrictions on divine interference in the war. Homer therefore begins Book 20 with an assembly of gods, paralleling that of men at the start of Book 19, in which Zeus gives the gods a free hand (24-5); and then depicts the consequences of this decision – the world physically shaken to its roots by the collision of divinities in conflict (54-74). The gods are back, and the world knows it. See further Bremer (1987).

Homer now faces an especially difficult example of a permanent problem, cf. **GI** 13B(viii). The *aristeia* of the great Achilles is at hand. Who will be his first victim in the *Il.*? Homer decides that, after all that build-up to Achilles' return, he cannot be a non-entity, but must be someone worth fighting. But since there is only a limited number of great Trojan heroes to go round, will Achilles be permitted to kill him? And if the tradition forbids that, how can Homer ensure that this first encounter will not fall somewhat flat? Homer bites the bullet and goes for Aeneas. Since he is the man who will take over the Trojan succession after the death of Priam and fall of Ilium, the audience at least will be under no illusion that he is about to meet his death. Homer is therefore going to have to work on the detail of the encounter if he is to make it a contest worthy of Achilles.

He does this in a number of ways. First, he makes it an encounter between the gods as much as between the two heroes. Apollo inspires Aeneas so effectively (79-111) that Hera, in terror for Achilles, appeals to Poseidon and Athene to intervene; they refuse, but agree to keep an eye on things (112-52). This, then, is an encounter that attracts the closest attention from the warring deities. Second, the preliminaries to the fight are heavily expanded, with similes, extensive boasting on both sides, genealogies, and so on (161-258). Third, the fight itself (259-90) is fairly complex, with an exchange of spears and detailed descriptions of them (259-83), and preparation for another exchange with sword and rock (284-90). Finally, the fight ends with Aeneas being rescued by (of all people) the pro-Greek Poseidon, who fears that Zeus' plan for Aeneas' succession to the kingdom of Troy is about to be foiled (300-8). Hera strongly disagrees with his decision (310-17), but Poseidon goes ahead, removing Aeneas from the action and giving him a lecture too (320-40), while Achilles dismisses Aeneas, curses his luck and looks for his next opponent (341-52).

The net effect of all this is to show what sort of a fighter Achilles is, even though he has not scored a kill – one to whom the gods have to pay the closest attention. He drove off a hero who had been inspired by Apollo; and it took another god, Poseidon, to rescue that hero when Achilles had him cornered. In other words, the poet has announced Achilles' return with a suitably heroic, even if kill-free, encounter against a major opponent.

That first fight out of the way, Achilles can now go on a full-scale rampage (381-503), but the poet decides to bring Hector briefly into the picture. We know Hector's death is to form the climax of Achilles' return to battle, and the poet clearly sees advantages in whetting the appetite for the final encounter with some false starts, a common technique (see last paragraph of 8/Intro). First time, Homer makes Hector boast of taking on Achilles, but Apollo warns him off, and he duly retreats (364-80). But Achilles' deadly assault on the Trojan rank-and-file includes Hector's brother Polydorus (407-18), and Hector can no longer stand by and watch. Heroically, or foolishly, he steps forward to challenge Achilles, and Apollo has to whisk him away to safety in a mist (as Poseidon had done Aeneas), leaving Achilles frustrated again (419-54). It is noticeable that in this clash Homer makes Hector more aware of his vulnerability, admitting he is the weaker but still prepared to risk all (434-7). Hector grows in stature as a result. It is the last time we shall see him before he faces Achilles in Book 22.

Meanwhile, Achilles slaughters unstoppably on, cutting down everyone in his path with clinical brutality, and the book ends in a welter of blood as a gore-drenched Achilles drives ruthlessly over the heaps of dead in search of – glory (502-3). It is noticeable how rigorously, and in keeping with his practice elsewhere, Homer focuses the audience's attention on the subject in hand, i.e. Achilles. No other Greek hero gets any look-in on the battle-field in Books 20-22; no Trojan makes any serious attempt to hold up his onslaught. How could they, when the greatest epic hero of them all is about his business, at last?

Main sources for the commentary
Edwards (1991); Willcock (1984).

1-74: Zeus summons an assembly of gods and, worried that Achilles might immediately storm Ilium, tells them that they can now intervene. The gods march out to battle, and nature is so shaken by the onslaught that Hades almost cracks open.

2. *you*: see on 4.127.
5. *Themis ... assembly*: the return of Achilles and Zeus' abandonment of his plan are of such significance that virtually all the gods respond by turning up, right down to even the most minor rivers and nymphs, apart from Ocean (7-9). Cf. on 18.203 and 19.42.
8. *nymphs*: see on 6.22.
18. *For the onset ... broken to flame* (**L**): i.e. battle is about to flare up.
23. *delight/pleasure my heart* (**H, L**): **R-J** translates 'enjoy the divine spectacle' to emphasise that it is the sight of the *gods* doing battle which

Zeus hopes to enjoy (cf. 21.389-90, 508) not the slaughter of humans, for whom he has just expressed his concern (21 'they do concern/I do care/I think of'). See on 15.12. At any rate, Zeus' prohibition on the gods from helping one side or the other, which has been in force since 8.5-27 though occasionally subverted by pro-Greek gods (e.g. Books 13-14), has now been abandoned

27. *Peleion* **(L)**: son of Peleus, Achilles.

30. *destiny/fate*: see **GI** 8.

33-40. *Hera ... Aphrodite/Xanthos*: a 'catalogue of gods' precedes their engagement in battle, cf. 2.494ff.!

40. *Artemis ... Leto*: Leto was mother of Artemis but also of Apollo, and that, presumably, is why she is on the Trojan side.

53. *Callicolone* **(R-J, H)**: wherever Homer envisaged that to be (R-J map 2 has a guess). In **L** read 'running towards Callicolone, beside the river Simoïs'.

57. *Poseidon*: we know Poseidon predominantly as god of the sea, as Homer does (15.190), but all his regular epithets in Homer refer to him as earth-shaker or earth-encircler. Here he unleashes the terrifying power of the earthquake (cf. 63). See 21.387-8 for another example of nature's physical response to the clash of gods – not surprising, since all aspects of the physical world (trees, rivers, springs etc.) have their own deities.

59. *feet of Ida* **(L)**: i.e. the foothills of Mount Ida.

61. *Aidoneus* **(H, L)**: i.e. Hades, lord of the dead.

65. *loathing/horror/shudder*: gods, being immortal, tend to keep themselves at a distance from anything to do with death.

69. *Enyalios* **(L)**: = Ares.

75-155: Apollo persuades Aeneas to face Achilles. The gods decide not to take sides.

79. *Aeneas*: except for this episode and at times in Book 5, Aeneas features only sporadically in the *Il.*, though he is second in command to Hector (2.819-20).

81. *Lycaon*: to be killed by Achilles at 21.34-135. It is typical of a god to disguise himself as a human and harangue someone, e.g. Poseidon disguised as Thoas urging on Idomeneus at 13.206-20 (note the 'threats' motif again).

84. *wine*: it is typical to boast on vinous, social occasions e.g. 8.228-34; for warriors and wine, cf. 4.257-263, 12.310-21.

92. *Lyrnessus ... Pedasus*: cf. 6.34-5 and on 2.685 (**R-J** map 2; note that **R-J** adds 'where the Leleges live' after 'Pedasus' to explain the reference to them at 96). Achilles refers later on to this incident between him and Aeneas at 20.188-94, where (not surprisingly) he gives a far fuller account than Aeneas does here.

107. *Old Man/sea's ancient*: = Nereus (see on 1.358).

112-55. *Hera ... Zeus*: it is typical for gods to intervene in important battles to debate the destiny of their favourites, e.g. Zeus and Sarpedon, 16.431-61. Hera's fear for Achilles is fully justified, since Apollo (who has already done for Patroclus in Book 16) is filling Aeneas with determination (110, cf. Hera at 129-31). Poseidon will intervene again at 291.

127. *Destiny/Fate*: see **GI** 8.

133. *angry/anger/aggressive*: Hera has been arguing that the gods should intervene on Achilles' side, or at least do something. Poseidon feels it is best to let humans get on with it, though if pro-Trojan gods intervene, he agrees they should too (138-41).

145. *Heracles*: see on 5.638. His fort/stronghold is 'located' on **R-J** map 1.

152. *you, (lord) Apollo*: it is odd for the poet to use apostrophe of an almighty god.

155. *Zeus*: cf. his instructions at 23-5.

156-352: Achilles and Aeneas meet. Aeneas is rescued by Poseidon, to Achilles' disgust.

164. *like a lion*: C-simile, fittingly the longest in the *Il.* since it accompanies Achilles' return to the fighting (see on 5.5). The lion/Achilles, being set upon by a horde of villagers/Trojans, ignores them contemptuously/stays out of the fighting until, hit by a spear/provoked by the death of Patroclus, it growls/laments; then, in a fury, it/he charges, to kill or be killed. The changing emotions of the lion are the main point of the simile, though the immediate connection is the pride and determination of lion/Achilles.

183. *he has sons*: for the tension between Aeneas and Priam, cf. on 13.459. Achilles is in confident, mocking mood here for his first encounter since returning to fight, cf. his mockery of Lycaon, 21.54-8.

184. *land*: see e.g. 12.314-15 for the rewards of service.

197. *get/go back*: typical, cf. 17.13, 30.

200. *words*: Aeneas returns to this 'words vs. deeds' theme at the end of his speech (248-57), cf. 16.629-31, 20.367-8, 431-3, 22.280-2.

206-41. *Peleus ... as/call mine/born from*: a complete genealogy of the Trojan royal line, from Dardanus to Hector (see **R-J** p. lxix). It is typical of warriors to boast about their parentage, e.g. Glaucus at 6.150-211, Diomedes about his father Tydeus at e.g. 13.112-25, etc. (see on 4.376). Possibly this genealogy was composed to honour some local Troad dynasty which claimed descent from Aeneas' family, whether of Homer's time or earlier (if earlier, it had become firmly fixed in the tradition by Homer's time). On the other hand, Aeneas (who is a son of immortal Aphrodite, as Apollo points out at 105-7) survives the Trojan war (302-8) while Hector and Achilles (though a son of immortal Thetis) do not; the purpose of the episode may be to draw attention to that feature of the Trojan war myth (Homer typically makes references to events that take place after the *Il.* ends; cf. **GI** 1D).

219. *Erichthonius*: his horses and their divine offspring by the North wind presumably helped to give rise to the 'horse-taming' epithet of the Trojans. Achilles' horses were offspring of the West wind by Podarge (16.149-51). It is the gods of these winds who impregnate the mares, cf. on 5.544 for the activity of river gods.

232. *Ganymedes*: see on 4.2. His abduction to heaven explains why he has no children.

242. *gift from Zeus/Zeus (who) increases/builds up*: see on 3.66.

247. *locks* (**L**): i.e. oars.

248-52. *Man's tongue ... asked for/spoken to* (**R-J, H**); *The tongue ... to you* (**L**): these three lines explain why Aeneas and Achilles could exchange a shipload of words (246-7) if they wanted to.

252. *wives/women*: cf. our 'fish-wives' for women quarrelling angrily in public.

256. *will put me off/not deter/not by talking*: gently ironical, given that it is Aeneas who has been babbling on for the last nearly sixty lines.

260. *pike* (**L**): read 'spear'.

264. *Fool*: Achilles is afraid and thinks Aeneas' spear might get through because he has temporarily forgotten that he is holding a divine, and therefore impenetrable, shield. The poet then goes on to explain its impenetrability with references to the layers of bronze, gold and tin of which it was constructed. Such a shield may seem odd, since Homeric shields are usually made with layers of ox-hide and a top layer of bronze, e.g. 7.219-23; and further, tin and gold are both soft metals. But Hephaestus is a metal-worker, not a tanner, and this is a divine shield, using precious materials in which the god always worked (cf. 18.474-82); of course such metals will stop mere human shots, even a soft metal like gold (the gold layer stops a further shot at 21.165). Whether the ordinary gold armour sported by some ordinary mortals (2.872, 6.236, 10.439) was as effective is doubtful.

286. *rock/boulder/stone*: see on 5.303 and cf. 5.302-4.

291-308. *Poseidon*: it is most odd that he, a pro-Greek god, should intervene to save a Trojan, but he excuses himself by claiming that he is doing so to avoid the anger of Zeus, whose dynastic plans demand that Aeneas shall live (300-8). Hera, naturally, will have no truck with this (310-17, cf. 4.20-67) but does not try to stop Poseidon.

297. *innocent/guiltless*: because Aeneas is not descended from the god-defying Laomedon (see on 5.638), whom Poseidon hated.

299. *gratifying offerings* (**R-J**); *gifts that are pleasing/please* (**H, L**): cf. 4.44-9, 24.66-70 for the gods' appreciation of offerings.

316. *(on the day) when*: Homer looks beyond the end of the *Il.* to the time when Ilium is destroyed.

323. *spear*: typically returned, cf. 22.276-7, and Diomedes' whip 23.382-90.

325. *swept Aeneas off* (**R-J**); *Aeneas he/lifted Aeneas* (**H, L**): Aphrodite saved Aeneas similarly at 5.311-18. For the 'mist' motif (321), cf. on

3.380. It is remarkable how unfazed the heroes are by such miracles, accepting them as a feature of everyday life. Cf. on 3.448. This is the last time Aeneas appears in the *Il.*; cf. Achilles' ironically prophetic words at 349-50 ('To hell/let him go'). Achilles has a grim humour about him.

329. *Caucones*: note that different contingents go into battle at different times; there is no sense of a 'united front' at the start of an engagement. See Albracht (2003) [I.25] and cf. **GI** 13B(iv).

336. *destiny/fate(d)*: see **GI** 8.

353-454: Apollo advises Hector to withdraw. Achilles' rampage begins, and Apollo has to rescue Hector.

357. *take them all on/fight with them all/all of them*: Achilles realises he cannot do it all on his own, and rebukes the Greeks who (presumably) have been standing back admiringly while he gets on with it.

359. *take the edge of* (L): read 'could throw themselves into the jaws of'.

364. *Hector*: the poet continues to tease us with the prospect of the Achilles-Hector duel, but this time Apollo warns Hector off (376-8).

372. *like fire/flame*: for Achilles and fire, see on 18.207.

382. *Iphition*: the a-b-c pattern shapes this slaying; see **GI** 2(iv). There is the usual pathos associated with the detail of the dead man's background (the poet does not explain how Achilles knew it, 390-2), and the gruesome follow-up as the chariot wheels slice him to pieces (394-5).

384. *Naiad/nymph*: see on 6.22, and cf. on unfortunate sons of nymphs 4.473-9, 14.442-5, 7.21-6.

389. *Here you fall/you lie there*: taunting the dead is typical, e.g. 13.374, 16.745 etc.

395. *Demoleon*: for his grisly death, cf. 11.96-8, 12.184-6.

401. *Hippodamas*: he had left his chariot and was running on foot – presumably because he could not turn the chariot round quickly enough. Was he Demoleon's driver?

403. *bellowed/bellowing*: B-simile; for the bull, cf. 17.516-24.

404. *Helice*: see on 8.203.

407-18. *Polydorus ... guts/entrails/bowels*: the first of three sons of Priam that Achilles kills (Lycaon and Hector being the others). For beloved sons refused permission to fight, cf. 11.717-21. For warriors fleeing on foot, cf. 11.338-42. See Saunders in Friedrich (2003) 149-51 for this and other deaths here.

410-11. *favourite/loved ... innocence/young folly/thoughtlessness*: two emotionalising comments from the poet, to heighten the pathos of the young man's death. However swift, Polydorus was no match for swift-footed Achilles.

419. *brother*: it is typical of brothers to support each other; see on 5.20.

422. *Achilles*: another non-encounter with Hector, cf. on 364 above.

431. *words*: see notes on 200-56 above. Now that he is face to face with Achilles, Hector's admission of weakness (434) and determination to fight are courageous. Cf. his inflated hopes at 16.860-1.

439.   *blew against it*: cf. 4.127-31 and 5.853-4 for similar interventions by Athene; Athene will restore Achilles' spear in his final duel with Hector at 22.276-7.

443-54.   *Apollo ... I can find/others*: see on 325 above, where Poseidon rescues Aeneas in the same way. For Achilles' feelings of exasperation, cf. Diomedes' identical words at 11.362-7: but Achilles' words are prophetic of what he will do when he kills Hector in Book 22, when Athene *will* help him (20.366, 22.214ff.), and Apollo will abandon Hector (22.213). We next meet Hector outside the walls of Ilium, preparing to meet his fate (22.5).

455-503: Achilles' rampage continues, his chariot red with blood.

A chilling sequence of slaughter now ensues, nine Trojans ruthlessly dispatched, with much variation of horrific detail.

460.   *sons*: see on 5.10.

462.   *spear ... sword*: cf. 5.144-7 and 20.480-82 for this combination.

464.   *knees*: the first of a number of (failed) supplications of Achilles; see **GI** 7D. No words are exchanged, but note the poet's (rare) comment on Achilles' mind-set – not sweet-tempered or tender, but in a fury (466-7).

473.   *pike* (**L**): read 'spear'. For Mulius' death cf. 4.501-3.

476.   *warming/warmed/smoking*: cf. 16.333-4.

481.   *looked death in the face/over his eyes ... death*: a unique moment, as is the (impossible) spurt of marrow (482-3).

484.   *Peiras* (**H**); *Peires* (**L**): for this father of Rhigmus, read 'Peiros' or 'Peiroos' (see 2.844; he is killed at 4.527-31).

487.   *Areïthous*: it is typical for a driver to die as he turns his chariot, e.g. 5.580-2.

490-503.   A typical summarising scene, decorated with two similes, ends this grisly sequence of slaughter on the plain (cf. Agamemnon at 11.147-80, likewise after a series of grisly individual slayings, again decorated with two similes). The next book runs seamlessly on into Achilles' slaughter of those trapped in the river Scamander/Xanthus as he drives the Trojans back towards Ilium.

490.   *As (...) fire*: D-simile, the extent and urgency of Achilles' slaughter likened to a wide-ranging fire, driven on by the wind.

495.   *As (when) a farmer/man*: D-simile, the farmer's/Achilles' oxen/horses, yoked/attached to his chariot, crushing/trampling the barley/men (so that the barley/bodies are squeezed of their contents, cf. the blood spattering the chariot rails at 500-2). See on 5.499 for other techniques of separating chaff/husks from grain.

499-502.   *trampled ... wheel-(rims)*: cf. Hector's assault at 11.534-7.

Book 21

Introduction

How far will Homer make Achilles go in his thirst for revenge? Almost too far, the poet decides. The end of the last Book saw Achilles, spattered in gore, driving over heaps of the dead. He now crowds the fleeing Trojans into the river Scamander (1-3) and continues the slaughter there (17-26). His programme, as he says, is to kill Trojans all the way to Ilium, till they have paid the full price for the death of Patroclus and other Greeks during his absence (128-35, cf. 224-6); and the programme is fleshed out by Athene and Poseidon, who add that he is to kill Hector and then return to the ships (295-7). But in a daring move, the poet (who had quietly prepared for this moment at 20.73-4) decides that the pro-Trojan god of the river Scamander shall stand in his way.

Scamander has hardly featured up till now. When Patroclus drove the Trojans back to Ilium, for example, it did nothing to block his path. But it is characteristic of Homer to call up at one moment, and ignore at another, physical features of the Trojan plain, as he needs them, to describe the course of the battle (see on e.g. 11.47-52). Now the river god is to loom large. Homer decides that the god will become involved because Achilles insults him, claiming there is nothing the river can do to stop him in his pursuit of blood (129-32, cf. 192-3). A god insulted by a human does not stand idly by. Scamander first encourages Asteropaeus, offspring of the river Axius, to kill Achilles (145-7). When Asteropaeus fails, Scamander personally commands Achilles to desist (211-21). Achilles refuses (223-6 – note the reference to his programme of action, which now includes Hector), and Scamander floods in an attempt to drown him. Athene and Poseidon encourage Achilles (284-300), but Scamander calls on the river Simoïs to help him (307-23), and only the intervention of Hera prevents Scamander from burying the hero deep in silt (316-23): she persuades Hephaestus to turn his divine flame-thrower on the rivers and dry them up (328-82). It is a dramatic incident, but Achilles has been saved only because of divine intervention. His willingness to insult a god surely raises questions about the control he has over his actions: as Scamander says, he is now 'a savage ... who thinks himself a match for the gods' and even Hera is made by the poet to admit she has gone too far in injuring a fellow god to help a mere mortal (379-80).

The epic hero deals in death. That is what he is for. But the way he deals in it is an index of the man himself, and in these books Homer portrays a hero testing the limits. The first victim of Book 21 is one of Priam's sons, Lycaon. Like Tros (20.463-72), he attempts to supplicate Achilles and fails (the theme of supplication is building to a climax). Lycaon claims he has a bond with Achilles, which Achilles should respect – the bond generated by the meal they shared when Achilles first captured and then ransomed him abroad (75-8). In an icily self-aware reply, Achilles sardonically agrees with Lycaon, calling him *philos*, 'friend' (106), a word in Greek that indicates someone with whom you have a bond and with whom (in normal circumstances) you would make common cause. But Achilles, with terrible irony, goes on to explain that this bond consists in the early death that both he and Lycaon will share with Patroclus. Nor does Achilles spare himself: as he unflinchingly points out, his own birth, greatness and splendour cannot save him (108-13) any more than Lycaon's birth (not a son of Priam by Hecabe, 95-6) can save him.

This is a truly magnificent speech. What follows is less so. Quite gratuitously, Achilles hurls Lycaon into the river and invites the fish to consume him (122-7), an act in defiance of all normal human conventions relating to the treatment of corpses (see on 1.5, and cf. on 11.455 for the 'mutilation' theme, now also drawing to a climax). The poet is preparing us for Achilles' treatment of Hector.

Achilles' next victim, Asteropaeus, actually grazes Achilles and draws blood (167). This is typical: a hero in mid-*aristeia* usually suffers some kind of set-back (cf. on 5.1-8), though this is a minor one compared with Achilles' battle with Scamander. The fight with Asteropaeus is particularly marked by mutual boasting about divine ancestry (153-60, 184-99). This helps to lay the groundwork for the Scamander incident. Achilles sneers that the river is no match for a descendant of Zeus like himself, 192-3, but that claim will soon be put to the test, and Achilles will be found wanting. Any mortal is unwise to imagine that divinity in the blood, even from Zeus, gives him *carte-blanche* to behave as he will. It did not save Sarpedon (16.431-61; cf. on 1.1). Achilles is walking a perilous tight-rope. But at least he merely leaves Asteropaeus to be eaten where he fell (200-4) instead of hurling him into the stream, as he did to Lycaon.

The subsequent battle between Achilles and Scamander turns eventually into a battle between Hephaestus and Scamander, which the river loses (342-82). As we have seen, this and other battles between the gods were prepared for by Homer in Book 20, and the scene now shifts to Olympus where these other battles are played out before a hysterical Zeus (388-90). It is pure knockabout, with the pro-Greek gods beating the pro-Trojan gods across the board. It is easy to miss Homer's point here. As Apollo says, god is fighting god, *on Olympus*, over men. What good can that do anyone, god or mortal (463-7)? Quite apart from the fact that fighting can do no serious damage to gods anyway (unlike to mortals). Hephaestus made the same point at 1.574-6. In other words, when gods fight among themselves on Olympus, it is a meaningless and faintly ridiculous exercise. No wonder Zeus falls about. What one must not do is to confuse that with the seriousness with which the gods support their favourites *on earth*. When they compete against each other on behalf of men, on earth, it is a quite different question. Humans, Homer seems to be telling us, can really count for something in the gods' eyes.

While this farce is being played out on Olympus, the Greeks have driven the Trojans yet further back, and from the walls of Ilium Priam can see Achilles approaching (527). Homer now has a decision to make: in what circumstances is Achilles going to face Hector? If Homer opts for the turmoil of mass battle, it is difficult to see it being a straight one-on-one fight: the issue is too important for others, especially the Trojans, not to intervene. He must therefore engineer a situation in which Achilles and Hector meet face to face, alone. If that is to be the case, Homer must clear the battlefield. He therefore has Priam open the gates of Ilium to allow the fleeing Trojans access (537-8, 606-11), while Agenor (454-94), and then Apollo disguised as Agenor (595-605), divert Achilles away from the town and prevent him getting access too. The stage is now set for the grand finale – or at least, the grand finale of the present plot (see **GI** 9).

Main sources for the commentary and related reading
Richardson (1993); Segal (1971) ch. 4; Willcock (1984).

1-204: Achilles slaughters Trojans hiding in the river Scamander, including Lycaon and Asteropaeus.

2. *Xanthos* **(H, L)**: the alternative name for Scamander (20.74). This is the first time that the river separating Ilium from the Greek camp **(R-J** map 1) has been brought fully into play.
5. *previous day/before*: perhaps 15.325ff.
7. *fog/mist*: see on 15.669.
12. *As a cloud* **(R-J)**; *As when locusts* **(H)**; *As before* **(L)**: D-simile, locusts/Trojans evading an unexpected fire/newly returned Achilles by huddling in the river. For the link between Achilles and fire, see on 18.207.
22. *As (the other) fish* **(R-J, H)**; *As before a* **(L)**: D-simile, fish/ Trojans attempting to escape from dolphin/Achilles who will eat/kill anyone it/he catches by crowding into nooks and crannies of the river. In the previous simile, Achilles was chasing men *into* the river; here he chases them *in* the river.
27. *twelve*: see 18.336.
35. *Lycaon*: see on 11.104, 20.81. As a son of Priam by Laothoë (85-8), he was a half-brother of Paris (3.332-3) and Hector, and full brother of Polydorus, killed by Achilles at 20.407-18.
37. *night raid/expedition/foray*: see **GI** 1C for such raids.
41. *Jason's son/son of Jason*: the son is Euneus, a trader; see on 7.467-8. Euneus gave Patroclus a mixing bowl (23.740-9) worth 100 oxen (21.79) to buy Lycaon.
43. *Eëtion*: a friend of Priam's from the island of Imbros **(R-J** map 2), no relation of the father of Andromache (for whom see on 6.395). Eëtion evidently paid 300 oxen for Lycaon (80), so Euneus (see above) made a useful 200% mark-up on the deal. Arisbe is on the Hellespont **(R-J** map 2). We are not told why Eëtion should have sent Lycaon to Arisbe.

50. *unarmed/naked*: Lycaon's plight is all the more pathetic for his inability to defend himself.

54-63. *astonishing/astonishment/strange ... him too/strongest of men/strong man*: a grimly sardonic, mocking speech from Achilles, especially the reference to Lycaon's final journey to Hades, to see if he will come back from there too; cf. on 20.325.

67. *spear*: Achilles had left this in a tamarisk bush (17-18).

71. *supplicate/beg for mercy/supplication*: see **GI** 7D.

76. *yield of Demeter* (**L**): i.e. bread. Lycaon says he and Achilles have broken bread together and therefore should be friends.

85. *short-lived/short life*: a richly ironic appeal, in view of Achilles' own decision to meet an early death (see on 18.96 and cf. 1.416).

86-7. *Leleges ... Pedasus*: see on 20.92.

89. *two sons/two of us/we are two*: i.e. Lycaon and Polydorus (see on 35 above).

101. *spare/ing (of) the Trojans*: see e.g. Isus and Antiphus at 11.101-12.

103. *not a single man/no(t) one*: e.g. Tros (20.463-72), who also tried in vain to supplicate Achilles.

115-16. *stretching out/spreading wide both hands* (**R-J, L**); *arms outstretched* (**H**): in an appeal for mercy, but Lycaon has thereby broken physical contact with Achilles (see on supplication, **GI** 7D).

122. *fish*: another hideously humiliating death; see on 1.5 and cf. on 11.455.

131-2. *bulls ... horses*: for bull-sacrifice, cf. 11.726-7; and see 21.237, where the river roars like a bull. Greeks did not normally sacrifice horses to rivers. Presumably this is meant to be a Trojan speciality.

134. *death/ravage/slaughter of the Greeks*: but it was Achilles who had asked Zeus for them to be slaughtered in the first place, cf. 18/Intro.

136. *river* (**H, L**): i.e. the god of the river Scamander/Xanthus. The god will take action at 212ff.

140. *Asteropaeus*: see on 2.848.

142. *Axius*: called the Vardar in Macedonia; it flows into the sea at Salonica (Thessaloniki).

145. *two spears*: typical, cf. Paris at 3.18. They are mentioned here because Asteropaeus, being ambidextrous, will throw both at once, a unique trick, 163.

162. *Mount Pelion/Pelian*: see on 16.143, 19.364-98.

165. *gold*: see on 20.264.

167. *grazed*: it says much for Asteropaeus that he manages to wound Achilles, who had raised his elbow to throw his spear (note, though, that he does not penetrate the divine armour: the elbow, like the ankle, would be exposed). The wound is not mentioned again.

178. *break*: a heroic but vain effort by Asteropaeus to render Achilles' great spear useless. Achilles recovers his spear at 200.

184-99. *river(-god) ... heaven/sky/crashing*: such contemptuous insults from Achilles about the weakness of rivers, and even of Ocean itself, are guaranteed to infuriate the listening river-god Scamander even more.

194-5. *Achelous … Ocean*: Achelous was the longest and most important river in Greece, and sometimes stood for 'rivers' in general; see **R-J** map 4. For Ocean, see on 1.423.

203. *eels*: see on Lycaon's death, 122 above.

205-382: The River-god of Scamander tells Achilles to desist and pursues him with a massive flood. Hera, terrified for Achilles, tells Hephaestus to turn his fire on the plain and burn up the river. Scamander gives up.

209. *Thersilochus …*: a typical list of slayings (see on 5.677).

223. *your will* (**R-J**); *what you ask* (**H**); *All this* (**L**): Achilles seems to agree that he will leave Scamander alone, as Scamander had requested, but then does nothing of the sort by jumping in (233-4), presumably to kill even more Trojans, as he had vowed (224-5).

230. *orders/wishes/counsels of Zeus/son of Cronus*: Zeus has not given any specific orders to Apollo, but he has invited the gods to fight for their favourites (20.23-5), and Scamander is justified in saying that Apollo, who supports the Trojans, has been failing in his duty to help them, even if he says it in somewhat exaggerated terms.

234. *in spate/seething swell/boiling surge*: there follows a most imaginative, vivid and exciting sequence, as the river sends wave after wave smashing down on Achilles in an effort to drown him, and he desperately tries to get away. But since gods are stronger than men (264), in the end even mighty Achilles has to appeal to the gods for help.

257. *Like a gardener/As (when) a man*: enchanting D-simile, the wave catching up Achilles being likened to water from a spring which a gardener is carefully guiding round his plot, but suddenly it takes on a life of its own and runs away from him. The idyllic picture of the busy, constructive gardener, mattock in hand, hard at work, is in strong contrast to the violence of Scamander's attack; its detail is almost impossible to connect with the narrative. Homer builds up the picture of the simile independently of its surroundings (though the details of the pebbles, 260, may anticipate Achilles' feet slipping from under him 271), and reveals the point of comparison only at the end.

275. *Uranian* (**L**): i.e. sky-gods; see on 1.570.

278. *Apollo*: further revelations about Achilles' knowledge of his end. See 16/Intro, and cf. Patroclus at 23.81.

279. *Hector*: death at the hands of a great warrior was at least heroic; death in a river certainly was not. Cf. 22.304-5, and Odysseus' plea not to be drowned at sea at *Od.* 5.306-12.

282. *(like) a (little) boy*: B-simile, emphasising the humility and meanness of the end that the mighty hero Achilles sees for himself.

285. *human form/like mortals*: a pointless form to take, given that Poseidon immediately announces who they are (289-90).

296. *Hector's /life/of Hector*: Achilles has been assuming that he will kill Hector since 18.95-8.

307. *Simoïs*: see **R-J** map 2, but cf. map 1, where Simoïs is shown feeding into Scamander, as Homer must envisage it doing here if the rivers are to unite their efforts against Achilles.

323. *burial/grave/funeral mound*: a superb conceit on the part of Scamander, imagining the rivers will bury Achilles so deep he will never be found.

325. *foam ... bodies/corpses*: a sensational image, the climax of the rivers' efforts to kill Achilles – buried, ironically, under the dead he has himself killed.

328. *Hera*: she comes to the rescue once again (cf. 1.195, 2.156) bringing into play the line-up of gods at 20.33-40, where Hephaestus is listed on the Greek side and Xanthus/Scamander on the Trojan. Hephaestus is to dry up the river.

336. *heads of the Trojans* (**L**): read 'bodies'.

346. *As (...) the (...) north wind*: brief D-simile, the wind/fire drying out the previously wet garden/river. Note the human perspective in the delight of the gardener (347), cf. on 4.275.

353. *eels ... fish*: cf. 203.

360. *Why should I* (**R-J**); *what need for me* (**H**); *What have I* (**L**): gods, like humans, know when they are beaten; Scamander goes even further at 373-6, promising not to interfere even when Ilium, the city which the river god serves, is destroyed, if only Hephaestus will relent. This battle between gods represents the preliminaries of the wider conflict between them which is about to break out (385ff.). Note that Hephaestus pays no attention to Scamander's plea: he is under orders only from Hera (340-1).

367. *As a cauldron*: D-simile, the cauldron/river boiling up fat/bodies (?) as a result of the logs/Hephaestus.

376. *fire(s)*: another indication of events occurring beyond the end of the *Il.* – the destruction of Ilium, cf. on 3.302, 4.40, 6.440, etc.

380. *to help/for the sake of/mortals*: see **GI** 5C, and cf. Apollo at 21.462-7. Hera's point is not that one does not help mortals – what has she just been doing? – but that one should only go so far in maltreating a fellow god on earth.

383-513: The gods now take sides and fight each other. Ares takes on Athene and is flattened, as is Aphrodite. Apollo refuses to fight Poseidon over mere mortals. Hera boxes Artemis' ears. Hermes refuses to fight Leto. Artemis goes sobbing to Zeus.

389. *laughed/amused*: Zeus sanctioned this battle at 20.22ff., and clearly envisaged it as being fun (see on 20.23). For significant Near Eastern parallels with this 'divine comedy', see West (1997) 177-90.

396. *Diomedes*: see 5.825-63.

400. *aegis*: see on 2.202.

409. *triumph(ing)*: Athene, a war-goddess, usually has the better of Ares (see 5.765-6).

412. *mother's (= Hera) curses/furies*: see on 9.454.

413. *deserting/abandoned the Greeks*: see on 5.832.

418. *Hera*: Homer hardly refers to the story behind the *Il.*, i.e. the judgement of Paris, when Paris offered the golden apple to Aphrodite, not Hera or Athene (see **GI** 1C and on 3.380). But its influence is still felt from time to time, especially when Hera and Athene gang up on Aphrodite as they do here (see also on 5.419). See Reinhardt (1960) and Jones and Wright (1997) 18-20.

420. *Atrytone*: see on 2.157.

443. *Laomedon*: see on 5.638; cf. 7.452-3, a slight contradiction to the story here which says that Poseidon built the wall while Apollo herded the cattle (448-9).

464. *leaves*: cf. 6.146-50.

468. *improper/respect/too modest*: Homer informs us of the real reason for Apollo's refusal to fight: nothing to do with the evanescence of mortals, but his respect for an older relative. Apollo will, in fact, continue eagerly to support the Trojans – as he does immediately the gods have stopped fighting (515-17) – until Hector's time is up (22.213).

475. *boast(ing)*: there is no record of such a boast in the *Il.*, but it is a typical charge to make against someone who is not living up to their reputation (cf. 3.430-1, 5.472-4, 13.219-20, 20.83-5).

484. *kill women/destroy*: see on 6.205. Hera says that Artemis may kill women and hunt beasts (cf. on 5.51), but she will meet her match in Hera.

491. *smiling*: this is all a great joke for Hera. It is a delightful picture of a naughty little girl having her ears boxed by mum.

493. *as a pigeon*: B-simile, the pigeon/Artemis, attacked by the hawk/Hera, flying/running for protection to the rocks/her father Zeus (as it will emerge, 505-7).

497. *the Guide* (**L**): i.e. Hermes, amusingly rejecting battle with Leto (Artemis' mother, who fusses about picking up Artemis' 'toys' after her, 502-3) and offering her the chance to claim that she, being the stronger, defeated him (501).

508. *laugh(ed)*: Zeus is having great fun watching his family fighting away among themselves, to absolutely no purpose whatsoever (which is why it is fun, cf. 20.23, 21.389-90). For this scene, cf. on 5.371, where Dione comforts Aphrodite, and Zeus' amusement at 5.426-30.

514-611: The gods return to Olympus, but Apollo enters Ilium to protect it. Priam orders the gates to be opened. Apollo in disguise leads Achilles away from the town while the relieved Trojan army floods back in.

520. *Achilles*: we left him being rescued from the river by the gods at 356-82. He has now resumed his killing spree, and the Trojans are stampeding in rout before him (533).

522. *as (when) smoke*: D-simile, looking forward to the future destruction of Ilium at the hands of men and gods. Note how the connection of the simile with the narrative emerges only at its end; the central point of the simile is not the smoke, but the suffering and hardship. Cf. 18.207-14, 22.408-11.

526. *Priam ... tower/bastion*: the wall round Ilium (built by a god, as the poet reminds us here) is punctuated with towers integral to its defence, cf. 3.153-4, 6.386. Such places also act as vantage points from which people can look out over the plain. This tower has a gate built into it, to which Priam now descends.

531. *Hold the gates*: as the Trojans run for it from Achilles, everything that Polydamas said – and Hector rejected – is coming true (18.254-313).

545. *Agenor*: one of the leaders of the Trojan army (see 12.93). Since Homer makes Apollo eventually take over the chase in the guise of Agenor (597-600), why does he introduce Agenor at all? Could not Apollo have done it all himself from the start? But if the poet had done that, there would have been no monologue, debating whether to stand or run (553-70), and therefore no point of comparison with Hector (22.99-130). Achilles may be carrying all before him, but Agenor shows that a mortal can take him on. Indeed, he even hits Achilles (591-4). There is hope for Hector yet.

549. *oak tree*: next to the Scaean gate; see on 6.237, and cf. 7.22. There are a number of landmarks like this; see on 11.167-70 and cf. on 558 below.

552-70. *reflected*: see on 11.403 for this typical monologue format. Note how Agenor weighs options in rather a loose, meandering format (giving a realistic sense of thinking the issue over), rejects them, and finally settles on his decision; observe too that he considers flight a perfectly good option, but rejects it because he knows it will not save him (555, 565, cf. Menelaus at 17.89-105, and see on 5.252 for the opposite reaction). He might as well chance his arm – and comes up with reasons why he could win (568-70).

558. *Ilian plain/plain of Ilion*: perhaps the plain associated with the tomb of Ilus (**R-J** map 1).

568. *vulnerable* (**R-J**); *can be wounded* (**H**); *might be torn* (**L**): heroes in the *Il.* are thoroughly human and therefore do not possess magic powers, or flesh that cannot be penetrated, etc. Cf. on 1.1. But Achilles' divine *armour* cannot be penetrated (593-4, cf. 20.264-72, 21.164-5).

573. *As a leopard(ess)*: D-simile, the leopard/Agenor emerging from her lair/out to fight, hearing/seeing the hounds/Achilles, not running before the huntsman/Achilles but taking him on or dying in the attempt. Does this simile indicate the result of the combat for Agenor? No – he is rescued and replaced by Apollo (597-601).

586. *plenty of us/many of us*: see **GI** 13B(ix) for the way in which Homeric 'sieges' were conducted.

592. *shin-guard/greave*: see on 1.17.

597. *mist*: a common tactic on the part of the god, see on 3.380. Apollo can now lure Achilles temporarily away from the battle while the Trojans get safely back into Ilium.

Book 22

Introduction

In lines 1-6 Homer announces that the battlefield has been cleared of Trojans and only Hector is left outside the gates. All the poet now has to do is to disengage Achilles from Apollo (6-24), and the duel with Hector can begin.

But not yet. At 21.526 the poet positioned Priam on the walls of Ilium and described how he could see Achilles advancing, threatening disaster (531-6, a fear that will be fulfilled, as the poet implies, at 22.410-11). Priam, therefore, cannot miss seeing his son preparing to take a lone stand against Achilles. This enables Homer, first, to describe Priam's reactions to what he sees – it is a terrifying sight (25-32) – and to report his appeal to his son to retreat inside the walls of Ilium, as everyone else had done (38-76); and, second, to add the appeal of his mother Hecabe – suddenly appearing from nowhere – with her vision of her son being left to feed the dogs (82-9). Their pleas fail. All they can do is watch. Homer does not tell us what their reactions are as they witness the death of their son – the poet forgets about everything else to focus entirely on Achilles and Hector – but when Achilles has dragged Hector away he does return to them to report their feelings after the event. So speeches from Priam (415-28) and Hecabe (431-6), matching the earlier ones, follow up the death of Hector, to be capped by the reaction of Andromache. She was working at the loom at the time and knew nothing of what was going on until she heard the cries and rushed out to see her husband being dragged off behind Achilles' chariot (437-515). It is an intensely moving scene: Andromache's ignorance – she is at work (440 cf. 6.490-1), a bath is being run for Hector (444) – turns into premonition (451-9, cf. 6.406-10) and then revelation (463-5). The day of her marriage, now ended, is recalled (470-2), and all the fears she expressed in Book 6 are here realised, for herself and her son. But her fears about her husband's burial will not, in fact, be realised (508-14). In Book 24 Hector *will* be coming home.

Why in Book 22 does Homer pay all this attention to Hector's family? Because he is already laying the groundwork for the new turn that the story is about to take. It was the death of Patroclus in Book 16 that changed the story from being about the consequences of Achilles' anger (when, if at all, will Achilles return to the fighting?) to being about Achilles' desire for revenge (when, and with what consequences, will Achilles kill Hector?). With the death of Hector, therefore, Book 22 brings the revenge theme to a close. At the same time, it lays the groundwork for the story of the *consequences* of revenge – will Achilles return Hector's body? – in which Priam and his family have a crucial part to play through their burning desire to see their son properly buried. Book 22 is therefore rich in unsettled issues, preparing for the new twist to the story that will finally be resolved in Book 24: will Priam supplicate Achilles? (no 22.412-13, yes 24.485); will Achilles accept gifts? (no 22.348-52, yes 24.593-5); will Hector be buried? (no, 22.352-3, yes 24.788-804). Homer makes further preparations for this turn of events in Achilles' immediate reaction to his triumph: though he has killed Hector and briefly thinks about taking Ilium (378-84), he puts all this behind him (385) and turns his thoughts back to Patroclus, whom he will never forget (387-90). Achilles still has unfinished business, and it will turn out to involve Hector as much as Patroclus. See **GI** 9.

To return to the battle. The poet chooses to have Hector ignore the pleas of his mother and father begging him not to fight. Hector's mind is elsewhere, and in turmoil. Homer illustrates this by inserting a powerful simile to describe his determination (the snake awaiting the traveller, 93-5) – this is what he looks like, to the external eye – but at the same time giving him a monologue that indicates his internal struggle as he weighs up the options (99-130). This is not the brash, over-confident Hector of Books 8-18 but the brave, self-aware Hector of Book 6, facing the harsh reality of a situation for which he blames no one but himself, even though (as *we* know) he has been ruthlessly exploited by Zeus into helping to further a (disastrous) divine scheme. But even as Hector reflects, Achilles is racing towards him at speed, looking like the War-god Ares himself (131-5). Hector turns and runs (136-8). Why? Homer does not say. But what would you do? Is it that Hector lacks courage? Or is it that he never expected it to be quite like this? Or what?

Achilles' attack is likened to that of a hawk on a dove (139-42), and is one of a complex series of interrelated images with which Homer makes this climactic contest real to his audience. When Achilles arms at 19.369ff, his armour flashes like a fire (376) and a star (382). At 22.26-32, Priam sees Achilles as an evil star; at 135 Achilles approaches with his armour shining like a blazing fire or sun; at 317-20 he moves in to kill Hector with a spear shining like a star (the spear, of course, belonging to his original armour, which Patroclus left behind because only Achilles could wield it, 16.139-44). Images of the race and the hunt abound: at 22.22-4 Achilles is likened to a prize-winning race-horse pulling a chariot, at 162-6 Hector and Achilles are engaged like race-horses for a prize; at 139-42 Achilles swoops like a hawk on a dove; at 189-92 he chases Hector as a dog does a fawn (cf. the Trojans at 1); at 308-10, Hector swoops like an eagle on a lamb or hare. Now add the images of Hector as a snake (93-5) and the two men running as in a dream (199-201) for the full hand.

The whole episode is, in fact, a demonstration of the oral epic poet's art at its finest. The longest fight-description in the *Il.* – not surprising, since it is the *Il.*'s most important battle – it begins at 131 and ends with the removal of Hector's/Achilles' armour at 369. The fight itself is wholly typical – A misses B, B hit but fails to pierce A, A kills B; see on 11.233 and **GI** 2(iii). But it takes up barely sixty lines 272-327, and fewer than half of those are to do with the actual exchange of weapons. The episode as a whole is dominated by imagery (those seven similes) and descriptions (the washing-places of Ilium, the chase round the walls) but most of all by speeches (two from Zeus, four from Athene, six from Hector, four from Achilles). Action-packed as the *Il.* is, nothing in it is as dramatic or intense as the interaction between the characters, human and divine, through what they say to each other.

One of the most satisfying features of the book is the strong sense it gives us of having been here before: it both summarises and closes the revenge theme (see **GI** 9). We see the Achilles of Book 9, intent only on avenging the dead Patroclus, rejecting compromise, rejecting gifts, rejecting negotiation, almost as if he owes it to the memory of Patroclus not to negotiate (22.261-72, 348-54). When Achilles says he would eat Hector raw if he could (22.346-8), he seems to have cast off the last vestiges of humanity. We see the Zeus of Book 16, wondering there if he must lose his son Sarpedon (yes, says Hera, 16.440-4), now wondering if Hector too must die (yes, says Athene, 22.178-81). We see the Apollo of Book 16, coolly stripping Patroclus of his armour (16.791-804), now slipping away (22.213) to be replaced by Athene, coolly tricking Hector into standing his ground (22.229-47). But gods are there to support their human favourites, and humans welcome that support. Most intricate of all, Achilles' and Hector's exchange of speeches in Book 22 bears a striking resemblance to Patroclus' and Hector's exchange in Book 16 (see on 330-66 below). The major difference is that in Book 16, Hector thought he knew what the situation was and might be, but was deluded on all counts; in Book 22, while Hector's eyes are finally opened to the truth, Achilles is under no illusion as to his own impending death (at which point we recall Book 18, where Achilles made his fatal decision to take revenge on Hector).

The last word must go to Hector. His speech at 297-305 is the epitome of the heroic ethos. He knows he has been cheated by Athene (299) and abandoned by both Zeus and Apollo, who, as he says, once supported him so willingly (301-3). But that counts for nothing *now*, since he sees his death is at hand (297, 300-1). Nothing for it, then, but to win that *kleos* which is the hero's sole consolation in death (304-5) – and drawing his sword, he charges. Now re-read 6.440-502; cf. Schein (1984) 175-9, Taplin (1992) 120-7.

Main sources for the commentary and related reading
Edwards (1987) 287-300; Richardson (1993); Segal (1971) ch. 5; Willcock (1984).

1-24: The Trojans recover within the walls, but Hector remains outside. Apollo mocks the furious Achilles, who races back towards Ilium.

1-3. *Trojans ... battlements/thirst*: the physical effects of flight also suggest the Trojans' emotional state.

4. *sloping*: are the shields being used as protection against missiles thrown from the walls above?

5. *Hector*: last seen being rescued from the fighting by Apollo at 20.444-5. He may be 'shackled by fate', but that does not mean he has no desire to fight – far from it (as 36 indicates, his determination is implacable).

8-13. *why ... death/fate(d)*: there is a heavily mocking, almost sarcastic, tone to Apollo's speech. Note the ironic reference to the Achilles' swift feet – not swift enough to catch Apollo.

18. *glory*: one does not need to kill other great heroes to win glory; sheer numbers of victims are enough.

20. *I would ... power/strength*: an extraordinary threat for a human to make to a god, even though that human is Achilles. See West (1997) 393.

22. *(race-)horse*: B-simile. Add 'prize-winning' to **L**'s translation: Achilles is a winner because he is so fast.

25-130: Priam and Hecabe appeal to their son Hector not to take on Achilles. Hector decides he must fight.

25. *Priam*: the poet's preparations for Achilles' climactic battle against Hector include showing us reactions from as many sides as possible – here, Hector's parents Priam and Hecabe, and at 92-130, Hector himself.

26. *like a star*: C-simile (cf. on 5.5, 11.62: this is Sirius, the brightest of stars, while Hesperus is brightest of planets – see on 317 below). It is the bronze on Achilles' chest that is shining, as the end of the simile tells us (32) – that is what the simile is 'about' – but note its internal development: the star is a sign of no good for mortals (30), i.e. the simile is focalised through the thoughts of Priam: this is how *he* sees Achilles (25), and he is a deadly threat. See on 18.207 for the fire/light imagery associated with Achilles. The 'fever' it brings to mortals (31) may well refer to the deadly malaria, as Robert Sallares argues (*Malaria and Rome*, Oxford 2002, p. 21).

34. *supplication/entreaty*: yet another example of a supplication that will receive no response (see **GI** 7D).

41. *he is ... ruthless* (**R-J**); *you stubborn man* (**H**); *a hard man* (**L**): **R-J** and **L** prefer to apply *skhetlios* 'ruthless, stubborn' to Achilles, since he is the subject of this extended passage; but it is possible to apply it, with **H**, to Hector.

42. *dogs and vultures*: see on 11.455 for development of this 'mutilation' theme; cf. Priam's horrible vision of his own death at 69-76 below and Hecabe's fears at the end of her speech, 89.

45. *sold*: e.g. Lycaon, 21.34-41.

46. *Lycaon ... Polydorus*: killed at 21.118-19 and 20.416-18; cf. 21.82-91.

48-51. *Laothoë ... Altes*: cf. 21.82-9.

50. *bronze and gold*: there is no chance of ransom with Achilles in his present mood (21.99-105).

56. *inside the wall(s)*: cf. 84, and see **GI** 13B(ix) for siege tactics. Compare Andromache's defensive advice at 6.431.

59. *pity on me*: after appealing to Hector in terms of Hector's personal safety, backed up with evidence in the number of sons already killed by Achilles, Priam leaves the most emotional appeal to the end: to pity Priam. The bond between sons and fathers is frequently depicted as the closest of all in the Homeric world (cf. on 6.440), and Priam turns up the emotional pressure in the rest of this speech with his increasingly ghastly vision of what will happen to his family (sons, daughters, children, in-laws) and, finally, him, if Hector is killed. The image of his own lapdogs, wild with the smell of blood (70), tearing at the old man's genitals (74-5), is quite dreadful. Homer's audience would presumably know of the rape of Cassandra (62, 'daughters raped/dragged off'), Astyanax thrown from the walls (64, see on 6.403) and Priam slaughtered by Achilles' son Neoptolemus at the altar of Zeus.

73. *beautiful*: one wonders how 'beautiful' Priam will find the dead Hector, as the Greeks mutilate him (see on 371).

81. *breast*: with this powerful physical gesture Hecabe appeals to the most basic ties binding a son to his mother, the giver of his life, soother of his troubles.

86. *ruthless/obstinate/hard*: see on 41 above. Again, **R-J** prefers to apply the word to Achilles; this time **H** and **L** opt for Hector.

87. *weep for/mourn you*: laying out the body and conducting the official mourning at the burial was a woman's work in the ancient world: they see man into, and out of, life. This therefore is an appropriate reflection from Hector's mother.

92. *Hector*: we now turn to his feelings about the situation he faces.

93. *as a (mountain) snake*: D-simile, the snake/Hector awaiting a man/Achilles by his hole/walls of Ilium, full of anger/determination. Cf. 3.33-6. Hector's determination will fail him when Achilles does actually attack (137).

98. *troubled/in dismay*: the final monologue; see on 11.403, and compare the format and content with Agenor's at 21.553-70. There is the same sense of groping for a decision, in sentences that fade away without grammatical resolution.

100. *Polydamas*: see his recommendation to retreat at 18.254-84, on which Hector poured scorn.

102. *night*: 18.203.

104. *reckless(ness)/folly*: without self-pity Hector assesses where he went wrong (103-4), realises the consequences for his public position – the very common 'shame' theme – (99-107), confronts the choices he can now make (108-21), and makes one (122-30). There is no cloying sentiment here, nor does Hector try to pass himself off as a 'victim'. He is quite open about the foolishness of his decision to reject Polydamas' advice, and feels the obligation to make up for it now by facing the ultimate challenge, one he has constantly invited (e.g. 16.859-61, 18.305-9). At least that may bring him glory, and therefore respect, even if he is killed by Achilles in the attempt (110).

105. *feel (...) shame*: cf. 6.441-3.

114. *Helen ... property/possessions*: cf. the oath agreed at 3.284-5, and Polydamas at 18.509-12.

120. *divide/distribute*: cf. on 18.509-40.

126. *'from an oak/tree or (a) rock'*: this seems to refer to a saying well-known to Greeks, but mysterious to us, presumably to do with some idyllic setting in which young lovers whisper their private intimacies to each other (see next note).

127. *intimacies/murmuring/whispering*: are we supposed to remember the time when Hector was at the Scaean gate, as he is now (6), but exchanging intimacies with Andromache (6.516), and even then realising that the war was unwinnable (6.447-9, 464-5)? The juxtaposition of images of young lovers whispering together and of Hector's dawning realisation that he is about to fight Achilles to the death is a brilliant stroke (cf. on 13.291).

131-213: Achilles charges, and Hector runs. They complete three circuits of the walls. The scales of destiny weigh against Hector, and Apollo leaves him.

132. *Enyalios* **(H)**: another name for the War-god Ares.

133. *Pelion/Pelian*: see on 16.130-44 and 16.143.

134. *glowed/shone/shining*: see on 26 above.

137. *Hector ... ran in panic/terror/fled*: no surprise; the description of the charging Achilles (132-5), surely focalised through Hector's eyes, reveals no sign of a human being, but only a nodding helmet, a brandished spear and the blinding light of the armour.

139. *hawk*: D-simile, the hawk/Achilles, with its speed/his swift feet, determined to kill, swoops after/flies at a timid dove/terrified Hector, which runs for it/who turns in flight. The shriek of the hawk (Achilles' battle cry) and its strikes at the dove foreshadow what is about to happen. Note the precision in Homer's observation of the dove, darting *under and away* after an attack from above.

145-6. *lookout/watching point ... waggon track/way*: two new 'signposts', cf. on the fig tree 11.167-70. The look-out post must be near the fig tree, i.e. near the wall, and presumably the waggon-track skirts the wall as well.

147. *springs*: there were indeed hot springs in the Mount Ida region, and there may have been some near Ilium (there are still some springs near it, but not hot; some have recently been found *under* the town). Whatever Homer knew about these springs' location or existence – clearly they are based on *some* ancient reality – he places them near Ilium in order to make the moving contrast between the days of peace, when the women could safely do the washing there, and the present war (147-56).

162. *As (when) powerful/champion/ horses*: D-simile, cf. the horse-racing simile at 22-4 (and note the turn round the post at the end of the course, 162, like the turning round the walls of Ilium). The prize for which the two men are racing is life or death. The poet has prepared us for this image of life-or-death competition by his observation about the purpose of the 'race' (a foot-race in this instance) at 159-61. Note the reference to the funeral games at 164, looking forward to the funeral games of Patroclus in Book 23, or hinting at Hector's impending funeral?

165. *whirling* **(L)**: add 'three times'.

166-87. *gods*: at important moments it is typical for the poet to intro-duce the divine perspective; see on 16.431-61. The debate here signals divine approval for Hector's death, cf. 17.198-209.

170. *oxen*: cf. 4.44-9, 24.33-70, where Zeus is adamant that Hec-tor's/the Trojans' sacrifices should count for something.

175-81. *save/rescue ... approve (you)*: cf. 16.435-43, where Zeus has much the same debate, with the same response.

182-5. *Zeus ... at once/longer*: cf. 8.38-40.

189. *As (when) a hound/dog*: D-simile, the dog/Achilles tracking a fawn/Hector which tries to take cover/seek the protection of the walls (foreshadowing 194-6) but is always nosed out/cut off back towards the plain (197-8).

194. *Dardanian*: i.e. the Scaean gate? See on 3.145.

199. *Like a chase/in a dream*: D-simile, likening Achilles' and Hec-tor's inability to catch or shake off the other to a dream in which both parties are frozen and cannot move a limb.

208. *fourth*: cf. 'three times' at 165. The climax approaches. For the dramatic 'three times ... but on the fourth' see e.g. 5.436-8, 16.702-5, 784-6, 20.445-7. For the springs, see on 147 above.

209. *scales*: another glance up to the gods. See on 8.69.

213. *Phoebus Apollo*: a coldly terrifying half-line – after all the help Apollo has given Hector, he cannot be associated with failure and now simply deserts him (though he will help to preserve his body, 23.188-91). Nothing more needs to be said. Hector is on his own.

214-366: Athene tricks Hector into fighting. Achilles rejects Hector's suggestion that the loser's body should be returned, charges and kills him. Hector prophesies Achilles' death.

214. *Athene*: as soon as Apollo leaves, Athene is there on the spot to continue her support for her favourite, Achilles. Gods support winners only; and the heroes are magnified, not diminished, by divine help. Note how Achilles welcomes Athene's help (224 'was delighted/happy/glad'). Achilles objected to humans interfering with his personal prospect of glory (205-7); but he has no objection to divine intervention ('you and I/we two' will kill him, as Athene says, 216; cf. Homer's comment on Athene's role at 22.446). The moment is depicted by the 'Berlin painter' (490-480 BC); see Woodford (1993) 82.

220. *grovelling/wallow*: even humans do not grovel before gods, let alone a god before a god (see **GI** 6). Athene is maliciously revelling in her triumph. These gods love winning, and rejoice in others losing, as much as humans do.

227. *Deiphobus*: last seen in retreat after being wounded by Meriones (13.527-39).

233. *closest/I loved most/dearest*: there is something quite chilling about Athene's ruthlessness in exploiting family ties to persuade Hector to fight; her outrageous lies at 239-42, bringing Hector's parents into the equation as well, take the breath away. Equally, it is pitiful to see Hector so utterly deceived.

255. *agreement(s)*: Hector looks for the same burial terms as he did in his duel with Ajax at 7.76-86, where they were accepted.

262. *lions … men*: Achilles shows how far beyond the reach of human society he is when he argues that he and Hector are the equivalent of animals when it comes to the human convention of burial.

270-1. *Athene is waiting/will beat/kill*: cf. on 214 above.

274. *avoided/crouched down*: for this battle pattern see on 11.233.

276-7. *brought/gave it back*: more help from Athene, quite as grotesque as at 20.438-40.

281. *glib/talk/speech*: cf. Aeneas (on 20.200), and Hector (on 20.431-3) – a typical 'words vs. deeds' antithesis.

295. *long spear*: warriors often carry two spears, but in this case they have only one each. Achilles' has been returned, but there is no one to give Hector another.

297-305. *It's over/Oh, for sure/No use … hear of/know of it*: Hector analyses the situation coolly and rationally: it was Athene who deceived him and Zeus and Apollo must have deserted him. This is the moment of realisation, so typical of tragedy. It is characteristic of Homeric heroes never to call 'foul' when a divinity is involved. What does one expect of divinities? Cf. on 16.844-54. Hector's response is to determine to do whatever he can, in his own right, to ensure that he gains the *kleos* that all Homeric heroes longed for (see on 1.1). So he draws his sword (306) and charges, in a futile effort to take on Achilles who wields his great Pelian spear (319). Cf. 8/Intro.

297. *It's over/Oh, for sure/No use*: the Greek *ô popoi* is an exclamation, variously interpretable.

308. *like a high-flying/flown eagle*: C-simile, the eagle/Hector swooping down on a cowering lamb or hare/Achilles. The simile is clearly focused through Hector's eyes: he is 'psyching' himself up for a final effort, picturing himself as the winner and Achilles as the loser.

314-16. *helmet*: cf. 19.381-3. This is the impenetrable, divine armour made by Hephaestus.

317. *Like/As the (...) star*: D-simile, the point of Achilles' Pelian spear, as he charges, shining like Hesperus (the planet Venus), the graceful evening 'star' (cf. on 26 above), that moves through the heavens; the beauty of this planet and Achilles' murderous intent (320) are poignantly juxtaposed. The spear is Achilles' original spear, too heavy for Patroclus to wield (16.141-2). Patroclus was lent Achilles' armour; Hector captured it; neither of them could live up to it. See Armstrong (1958).

330-66. *triumphed/vaunted ... wish it to be/to bring it on me/accomplish it*: the parallels with the death of Patroclus are sharply pointed. Both Hector in Book 16 and Achilles here boast (829/330); both speculate on what their enemy's hopes had been, the fool (830-33/331-3); both claim the vultures will have the body (836/335-6). Hector in Book 22 – but not Patroclus in Book 16 – begs for burial (337-43) and Achilles refuses. In their final speeches, both dying men prophesy their enemy's death (851-5/358-60); both die in the same way (855-7 = 361-63); and both victors talk of their future, Hector full of confidence (16.859-61), Achilles in the sure knowledge that he will die (365-6).

338. *I entreat/beseech*: the climax of the failed supplications in the *Il.* – and it is not even an appeal from Hector to be allowed to live (as it normally is in these circumstances) but only to be properly cremated. Achilles' words at 260-72 suggest he will not be granted his wish.

347. *eat you(r) raw/flesh*: Achilles' wish that he would, if he could, eat Hector raw, as if he (Achilles) were a vulture or dog, is further evidence of Achilles' descent into the almost bestial (cf. on 262 above, and compare Hera at 4.34-6, and Hecabe at 24.212-14).

349-51. *not (even) if ... not (even) if*: Achilles had used this extreme language before in rejecting the embassy, and been wrong (9.379-87), as he will be now.

358. *angry gods* **(R-J)**; *anger* **(H)**; *curse* **(L)**: why should the gods be angry? Because Achilles threatens to maltreat Hector's body? On the whole scene, cf. Taplin (1992) 240-7.

359. *Paris and Phoebus Apollo*: Achilles knows most of this already (21.278), but the mention of Paris' involvement comes as a bombshell – the feckless seducer who started the war will kill the mighty Achilles!

367-404: Achilles strips the dead Hector, the Greeks stab his body. Achilles tells the Greeks to return to camp, and drags Hector's body back by the ankles behind his chariot.

369. *armour*: i.e. Achilles' own armour that he gave to Patroclus (16.130-54) and which Hector took and put on (17.192-7). Homer shows no interest in the implications of Achilles' possession of *two* sets of armour, i.e. the story that, when Achilles died, the Greeks decided to offer Achilles' armour as a prize to their greatest hero, and awarded it to Odysseus (with the result that Ajax committed suicide out of shame).

371. *stab*: it is not only Achilles who horribly mutilates the body of the dead man (as Achilles is about to, 395). For Priam's view of the beauty of the young warrior in death, cf. 22.71-3; it is not a sentiment he repeats now that Hector is dead.

374. *fire/flame/firebrand*: at 16.122-3.

381. *under arms/armed attack/go in arms*: it looks as if Achilles is about to launch an immediate assault on Ilium and thus bring about his own death, which is fresh in his thoughts anyway (cf. 365-6, and the prophecy at 18.95-8). But he changes his mind when he realises he has yet to bury Patroclus (386).

395. *foully/shameful*: = 23.24. Is this Homer's *moral* judgement on Achilles' behaviour? Probably not, since Achilles himself says that this is what he will do (335-6) – and he is hardly going to condemn himself in this way – and Zeus himself is said to allow it to happen (404). In other words, Homer is simply describing the shame it represented for Hector's body. Nevertheless, Achilles' behaviour will be condemned by the gods at 24.33-54.

396. *holes*: dragging off a body by winding a strap round the ankles was not unusual (17.290), but surgically drilling holes through the 'Achilles' tendon' was.

401. *dust … hair*: Homer is focusing like a camera closely on the head, seeing the dust rise from it and the hair spread out behind as Achilles gallops off, cf. Patroclus at 16.795-800.

405-515: Priam and Hecabe lament Hector. When Andromache hears of his death she faints, recovers and offers a third lament, emphasising her fatherless child Astyanax's fate.

405-11. *mother … father … people … smouldering/fire*: the worst fears of Priam and Hecabe, expressed at 38-91, are fulfilled; and the people's lamentation adds to the sense of tragedy for the whole city (cf. Priam's awareness of this at 54-5). Homer at once draws out the implications: it is *as if* Ilium had fallen, its ruins smouldering. Soon it will have (though not in the *Il.*).

406. *veil*: discarded in times of distress, as if the conventions of normal life no longer have point or purpose (cf. on 23.46).

414. *dung/muck*: this is a world of chariots pulled by horses and carts pulled by oxen; waggon-ways (146) too lead from the gates out to the fields. Priam befouls himself, on the ground, as Achilles does at the news of Patroclus' death (see on 18.22).

418-21. *supplicate/supplication/suppliant … Peleus*: Homer prepares us for Priam's night visit to Achilles in Book 24 and his appeal to Achilles in Peleus' name (24.486-506).

430. *Hecabe*: Priam's thoughts turned to how he might retrieve Hector's precious body. Hecabe remembers what a man her son was, a dream come true, looked up to like a god, and gives no indication that she sees any hope.

437. *Hector's wife*: i.e. Andromache, whom we left at 6.490-502, being instructed by Hector to return to the loom and to see to the maids' work; and returning home and lamenting Hector as if he were dead. Here in Book 22 she is at the loom (440-1), ordering her maids to prepare for Hector's return (442-4), 'the (poor) innocent/child' (445). Her ignorance of what has happened to her husband is all the more moving for her own fears of its occurrence (6.406-31) and her awareness of Hector's vulnerability (6.460-1, 487-93) – the notes below show how many of the themes of Andromache's speech in Book 6 are reprised here. It is as if we, and she, have been waiting for this moment; but when it comes, it is far more terrible than could ever have been expected.

448. *dropped the shuttle/shuttle dropped*: a significant physical gesture, paralleling the emotional state; cf. her beating heart (452) and frozen limbs (452-3).

457. *over-confidence/pride (of courage)*: see on 12.41.

460. *like a mad/raving/woman in frenzy*: cf. 6.388-9.

462. *tower/bastion*: when she had last been there – the tower by the Scaean gate (6.391-5) – she had been looking for Hector, and failing to find him (6.386-7).

466-76. *Black night/darkness ... sobbing/mourning*: more physical reactions responding to Andromache's emotional state. Note the loss of her head-dress. **R-J** suggests it fell off as she fainted, **H, L** that she threw it off, as Hecabe did at 406. Homer tells us it was given to her on her wedding day (470-2); she was still wearing it; and its removal now signifies the end of her marriage.

477-80. *same star/fate/single destiny ... Eëtion*: cf. 6.395-8, 409-16. Andromache contrasts her and Hector's previous state – he in Ilium, she in Thebe, soon to be married (478-80) – and their present state – Hector in Hades, herself in grief, a widow (482-4).

484. *widow*: cf. 6.406-8, 432.

487. *If he survives* (**R-J**); *Even if he lives* (**H**); *Though he escape* (**L**): cf. Hector's hopes for his son at 6.476-81. Andromache's fears for her son expressed in this speech are justified, given that other sons of Priam will now take priority in the inheritance stakes. Ultimately Aeneas was destined to rule the kingdom (see on 13.459, 20.79).

496. *feast/banquet*: on the importance of such occasions, see on 4.262.

500. *who used to/before now/in days before*: cf. Phoenix's loving description of his care for the young Achilles, 9.485-91.

509-14. *worms ... honour/Troy/Trojan women*: Andromache repeats others' fears over Hector's treatment in death. Note the touching reference to the burning of what would have been Hector's burial clothes: since Andromache will never (she thinks) recover the body, she can at least 'cremate' the clothes in his honour, a moving gesture indicative of her faithfulness and despair.

Book 23

Introduction

Whatever Achilles intends to do with Hector, the poet has already signalled that mourning for Patroclus is not at an end, and his burial comes next (22.386-90). Throughout Book 23, the memory of the living Patroclus burns bright, both in the moving dream sequence with its story of how Patroclus and Achilles met in the first place (65-107), and in the games (e.g. 279-84, cf. 619, 646). That memory sharpens more keenly Achilles' sense of loss, and the lamentation is as intense as ever it was in earlier books (10-23, 60-3, 108-10, 135-7, 153-5), culminating in the moving simile of the father mourning for his son (221-5); so too is the extreme behaviour (rejection of civilities, 38-46, excessive mourning 154, the abnormal slaughter at the pyre 166-77). If the simple act of revenge on Hector was meant to resolve Achilles' grief at Patroclus' death, it has not succeeded.

Meanwhile the poet keeps the issue of Hector firmly before our eyes during the funeral ceremonies for Patroclus by reminding us of what Achilles threatens (by contrast) to do to Hector (20-6, 180-3); and by then describing how the pro-Trojan gods intervene to prevent it (184-91). In other words, the gods themselves will make sure that Achilles does not succeed in any plans he has to deface the body. By this means Homer assures us that the story of Hector is not yet over, and neither, therefore, is the story of Achilles, except in one respect: throughout the ceremony, the poet reminds us that Achilles' death comes next, and that Achilles knows it (46-7, 80-1, 126, 150-1, 248). In burying Patroclus, Achilles is also preparing to bury himself. From Books 2-16, Achilles has felt himself to be an outcast (9.648, 16.59); from Books 18 to the end, he knows he is a dead man. The question is: will any of this change his mind about his treatment of Hector?

The games in honour of Patroclus (257-897), however, are a different matter. Taking six hundred lines to describe, they make for a monumental commemoration of Patroclus, worthy of Achilles' feelings for his beloved companion, and they reveal a very different sort of Achilles. Anger, denial, self-obsession melt away from him, and he turns into a generous and tactful master of ceremonies, firmly sorting out the nasty quarrel between Idomeneus and Ajax son of Oïleus (491-8), rescinding his judgements where necessary (535-65, but not 824-5), kind to Nestor (618-23), responsive to the crowd (540-1, 735-7, cf. 721), charmingly open to flattery from Antilochus (795-6), even finding a compliment for Agamemnon (890-4), who has been noticeably co-operative throughout (49-54, cf. 110-11; 155-62; 236-49). Running his own show to honour Patroclus and under orders from no one else, Achilles is transformed.

The games serve another purpose too: they allow the poet to show us the Greek heroes in action for the last time. They have not featured in battle since Book 17, the wounded ones (Odysseus, Diomedes, Agamemnon) since Book 11. Now, on the playing-field, against their own side, they compete as ferociously as ever they did in battle, with just as much awareness of issues of honour and its material rewards (566-613), and the gods support their favourites with just as much intensity, as the competitors well know (382-406, 768-84, 863-73). The rank-and-file remain on the sidelines enjoying the show, by turns hushed (676), bored (721), amazed (728, 881), partisan (766-7), amused (785), terrified (822-3), thrilled (847, 869).

Patroclus is buried. In contrast to the events leading up to and during the burial, the games have revealed an Achilles apparently at ease with himself and with others, even Agamemnon. In the dreadful modern clichés, has the 'grieving process' done its work? Has the 'process' brought Achilles to 'closure'? Is he now 'reintegrated back into the community'? Or even 'moving on'? Or is he still in a 'downward spiral'? Fortunately, Homer does not deal in clichés.

Main sources for the commentary and related reading
Richardson (1993); Segal (1971) ch. 6; Willcock (1984).

1-108: The Greeks withdraw to their ships. Patroclus is mourned, and his ghost visits Achilles in his sleep [night before 28th day].

9. *honour/right/privilege*: the ritual of saying farewell to Patroclus, ending in cremation and the deposition of his bones, begins here with the triple circuit of the body (13) and a funeral meal (29).

15. *sands*: Patroclus' body has been moved out from the hut (where it was left at 19.339) on to the beach, ready for cremation.

21-2. *Hector's body … dogs … throats*: see 18.333-7, 21.27-32 and 22.354. For **L**'s 'behead' (22) read 'cut the throats of'.

26. *took off each man* (**L**): i.e. each man took off.

29. *funeral feast*: this usually followed the cremation of the dead (cf. Hector at 24.803). Presumably Homer placed it earlier so that it would not interfere with the funeral games (257ff.).

34. *The blood ran off and was caught in cups* (**L**): this is possible; **R-J** and **H** prefer to make the blood an offering to the dead, translating 'Blood in cupfuls was poured'.

38. *Agamemnon's hut/shelter*: the meal with Agamemnon fulfils the proposal made by Odysseus at 19.179-80 as part of the settlement between Agamemnon and Achilles.

46. *shorn/cut my hair*: a traditional mourning gesture (see 135-43), a characteristic of which is to reverse usual social customs (Homeric heroes normally let their hair grow long).

49. *Agamemnon*: the first of a series of commands that Achilles issues to Agamemnon (who obeys without a murmur) as he takes charge of Patroclus' funeral, cf. 156, 236.

59. *on the shore/along the beach*: Achilles wants to be near Patroclus.

69-92. *You sleep/are asleep ... our bones/mother gave to you/our ashes*: Patroclus' speech begins with a sharp reminder to Achilles that he needs burial because without it he could never enter Hades properly and would simply roam endlessly along the banks of the Styx (the 'river' of 73). He then links his and Achilles' fates and requests they be buried together (75-83); and finally recalls what brought them together in the first place (84-92; for Opous, 85, see **R-J** map 4). There is a strong sense here of Patroclus reviewing the circle of their joint life, and closing it in their joint death. The simple 'Give me your hand' (75) signals the end of their earthly relationship. Achilles wants more (98 below).

79. *from birth/was born*: see **GI** 8.

81. *to perish/be killed*: see 16/Intro.

89. *Peleus*: for other stories of suppliant exiles, including those arriving at Peleus' house, see on 16.571.

98. *hold each other/embrace*: the living Achilles needs more than a farewell handshake from the dead Patroclus; but all physical contact is denied (99-100).

104. *real heart of life* (**L**): i.e. real (physical) existence or being. Achilles can communicate with the spirit, but it remains otherwise intangible. Note that Homer in the *Il.* has no concept of judgement in the after-life, no vision of punishment or paradise, nothing to fear or look forward to. These ideas will emerge later in classical thought.

109-257: [28th day] Firewood is collected, and Patroclus' body taken in funeral procession. Achilles dedicates a lock of his own hair, and the pyre is lit. Aphrodite and Apollo preserve Hector's body. Winds are summoned to prevent the pyre going out, and [29th day] Patroclus' bones are gathered and placed temporarily in a golden vessel, awaiting Achilles' death.

132. *sideman* (**L**): i.e. the fighting warrior.

135. *hair*: see on 46 above.

136. *head*: see on 18.71.

142. *Spercheus*: the river of Achilles' home territory, **R-J** map 4. The god of the river is being addressed.

150. *I shall never see* (**R-J**); *I shall/do not return* (**H, L**): the thought of his own death presses ever more closely on Achilles as he oversees Patroclus' funeral, cf. 244, 248.

167-77. *sheep ... devour everything/feed on them*: the animals are a sacrifice to the gods; the fat is intended to encourage the burning of the body; the oil and honey are offerings to the dead (as is the wine, 218-21); the horses and dogs will accompany Patroclus on his journey to the dead;

and for the twelve Trojans and the especially horrific nature of the whole event (cf. 176 'murderous/grim purpose/evil … thoughts'), see on 18.336.

187-8. *oil … cloud/mist*: Aphrodite and Apollo join forces to preserve the mortal body of the Trojan hero – the gods, in other words, do have a continuing interest in the fate of Hector, cf. 24.18-21 and most importantly 418-28, where that interest is associated with Hector's ritual piety, cf. on 22.170. Aphrodite's oil preserves the body when Achilles drags it up and down, Apollo's cloud keeps the sun off. Cf. on 18.351.

195. *Boreas … Zephyr*: cf. on 5.544. This amusing little scene is very different in tone from its sombre surroundings. See on 5.544.

198. *Iris*: she is a messenger of the *gods*; her response to an appeal from Achilles highlights the status he enjoys.

203. *sit beside him*: an agreeable little touch – courtesy, or something more?

205-7. *Ocean … banquet/feast/sacrifice*: so Iris was called when she was attending a banquet for the gods in the Ethiopians' land (see on 1.423) – or is this an excuse she invented on the spot so that she can get away?

207. *sacraments* **(L)**: Homer's is not a Christian world. Read 'sacrificial banquet'.

215-21. *Troy/Troad … poor/unhappy Patroclus*: an astonishingly graphic scene – the howling winds, the raging pyre and the lone figure of Achilles, all night long, drenching the ground with libations and calling on Patroclus. The subsequent simile allows us a further glimpse into Achilles' feelings – mourning as a father does a son.

221. *As a father*: D-simile, another simile linking Achilles and Patroclus as father and son. Grieving fathers are to play an even more important in the *Il.* when Priam in Book 24 appeals to Achilles in the name of Achilles' father Peleus.

243-4. *vase/jar … fat*: the bones are to be stored as Patroclus ordered (91-2), specially protected with a double layer of fat. They will be kept in the vase, presumably in Achilles' hut, till Achilles dies and both he and Patroclus are buried together.

245. *(grave-)mound*: the mound, set in a base of stones (255), is to act as a marker of the burial-place. It will cover the huge funeral pyre, and will act as a cenotaph ('empty tomb') to start with: when Achilles and Patroclus are finally buried there together, it will be turned into a huge monument (246-8). It was common in Homer's time to mark burial places with vast mounds.

251. *ash*: an acute observation, the delicate ash piles collapsing as they are disturbed.

257-652: Achilles seats the army in readiness for Patroclus' funeral games. The chariot race is first up: Nestor exhorts his son Antilochus 262-361, the race includes Eumelus' crash and Antilochus' sharp manoeuvre against Menelaus 362-447, Diomedes' victory and the dispute between Antilochus and Menelaus 499-652.

259. *games*: these are set up in honour of the dead Patroclus (646). Competition, in peace and war, was an important part of Greek life. The gods had won their way to power by defeating opponents; gods loved to watch humans compete on the battlefield and to support their favourites; so too did humans. Once dead, one no longer competed, because there was nothing to compete over (cf. Achilles in the underworld at *Od.* 11.487-93). So special games in the dead man's honour were, perhaps, felt to be a consolation for him as well as a celebration of everything he held dear. Homer faces the same problem in the games as he does on the battlefield – see **GI** 13B(viii) – i.e. ensuring that the great heroes win, and if they are fighting each other, that they draw. He therefore needs to conjure up a number of losing stooges. Sophilos (570 BC) depicts the crowd watching the race; see Woodford (1993) 83.

264. *ears* (**L**): i.e. handles.

273. *in the place of games* (**L**): i.e. here, where the games are to be contested. The Greeks had not built a special arena.

276. *my horses*: these were immortal (16.148-51, 866-7; cf. 2.769-70).

281. *grooming/pour/anointed*: cf. Andromache at 8.185-90.

283. *grieve(-ing)*: see 17.426-40.

288. *Eumelus*: see on 2.714.

290. *Diomedes*: inactive since being wounded by Paris at 11.376-8.

292. *Aeneas ... Apollo*: see 5.222-73, 319-27, 344-6, 445-7.

297. *Echepolus*: he gave Agamemnon the horse to avoid joining the army in Troy; cf. 13.669-70.

304. *Nestor/his father*: Nestor, often called *hippota* 'charioteer', is an experienced horseman, cf. his advice about chariot fighting (4.297-309), his account of fighting from chariots (11.716-60), etc.

306. *Poseidon*: god of horses and great-grandfather of Antilochus. Cf. on 13.554.

315. *wood-cutter*: cf. 3.61 for the skill required.

323. *post*: round which the chariot turned to start back for home on the second and final 'lap' of the race. Nestor goes on to enlarge on the importance of the manoeuvre round the turning-post, describing the post (327-33) and then the best way to round it (334-43).

341. *wreck/smash/break*: cf. the chariot-race in Sophocles' *Electra* 700-56, especially 743-6, when Orestes is said to have failed to control the left-hand rein properly and smashed the chariot into the post.

346-8. *Arion ... Adrestus ... Laomedon*: Arion was an equine offspring of Poseidon; his owner Adrastus – Adrestus in Homeric dialect – was king of Argos and one of the Seven against Thebes, see on 2.563-5; for Laomedon, see on 5.638.

352. *deposited the lots* (**L**): add 'in a helmet' (to be drawn out).

360. *Phoenix*: he had brought up Achilles (9.485-95).

368-9. *earth ... high/air/clear*: a vivid picture – the chariots are very light and therefore hard to control at speed over rough ground.

373. *final stretch/last (part)*: surprisingly, nothing happens at the turning-post!

375. *the field of horses strung out* (**L**): read 'and they forced the pace'.

376. *son of Pheres* (**L**): read 'grandson of Pheres' (omitted by **R-J**).

383. *Apollo*: Eumelus' horses had been bred by Apollo (2.766), who did not like to see them being beaten.

390. *gave (...) back*: cf. Athene returning Achilles' spear to him (22.276-7). She then proceeds to smash up Eumelus' chariot, adding further insult to Apollo (cf. her treatment of Ares and Aphrodite, 21.403-33). Diomedes is, of course, one of Athene's favourites (see e.g. 5.115-32).

408. *Aethe*: see 295.

415. *find some way* (**R-J**); *think out a way* (**H**); *contrive it* (**L**): Antilochus uses his judgement here – not to round the post without crashing (the subject of Nestor's earlier advice), but to work out how to overtake Menelaus on the home strait.

419. *narrow(ed)*: presumably the direct track for home led at this point along a narrow 'road', made ever narrower by part of the road being swept away by winter rains and thus deepened. Menelaus is in front, holding his position along this narrow stretch and taking it rather slowly; Antilochus therefore decides to abandon the 'road' and take a diversion or short cut before getting back on the track, risking crashing his chariot and Menelaus' too (hence Menelaus' concern about them both being wrecked, 428).

434. *eased the pace*: (**R-J**); *eased/slackened his driving* (**H, L**): i.e. Menelaus gives way to prevent a crash: Antilochus has 'carved him up'. Menelaus promptly lets him have it verbally (439-41) and vows to catch him up (443-5). It is all very much like Friday evening on the Basingstoke by-pass.

448-98. *The Greeks/Argives ... first and/come/run second*: Homer whets our anticipation of the result by turning our attention to the crowd and depicting a pointless argument between the spectators about who is winning. His observation is, again, wonderfully true to life: spectators always know better than even the players, let alone other spectators (especially when they have no evidence to go on), and Homer depicts the escalation of the argument to perfection.

450. *Idomeneus*: he would have had a particular interest in the fortunes of his attendant Meriones in the race (see on 2.645).

462. *(turn-)post*: Idomeneus' analysis is wrong – Athene had smashed up Eumelus' chariot – but his instinct about the danger of the turning-post (as Nestor showed) is right. Note how cautious he is about who is now in the lead (469-73).

473. *Ajax son of Oïleus*: see 2.406, 527. During the sack of Ilium he enraged Athene by dragging Cassandra from Athene's shrine and raping her. On the voyage back from Troy she sank his boat, but he swam to safety to a rock, where he boasted of cheating the will of the gods. Poseidon at once smashed the rock and drowned him (*Od.* 4.502-11). Ajax's arrogant, ignorant, boastful character is perfectly suited to the part of the moronic spectator who always knows best. His accusation that Idomeneus is a loud-mouth (474, 478-9) is especially rich coming from him (and typical).

485. *bet/wager*: further typical crowd behaviour – 'wanna bet on it, squire? Name yer price'.

490. *quarrel*: Idomeneus and Ajax have reached the 'you wanna step outside?' stage of the argument.

491. *Achilles*: it is no surprise that Achilles steps in to sort out the argument ('You ought to feel ashamed of yourselves. Now just shut up and sit down', 494-5). These are games in honour of his beloved Patroclus. He is not having them ruined by this sort of behaviour ('not right/improper/unbecoming').

511. *Sthenelus*: Diomedes' attendant, eager to seize the prize on his master's behalf. See on 2.563-5.

514. *Neleian* (**L**): Antilochus was grandson of Neleus.

527. *dispute/argument*: Homer prepares us for Menelaus' accusation of cheating against Antilochus.

532. *son of Admetus* (**H, L**): i.e. Eumelus.

536. *best driver/man*: Achilles is prepared to award prizes by status, not performance: if Eumelus is 'the best', he *deserves* a good prize, wherever he has actually come in the race – an argument Achilles used to attack Agamemnon in Book 1 on the grounds that, even though leader, he was *not* the best (see 1.121-307). The ensuing argument is all about what one is due – should it be decided on the strength of who one *is*, or of what one has *achieved* (status vs. performance)?

551. *larger/greater (prize) than mine*: Antilochus argues that Achilles can give Eumelus any prize he likes, of any 'monetary' value he likes: it is the *status* of winning second prize, on the strength of his *performance*, that he is claiming as his due. Cf. on 6.234, where the status of owning Diomedes' armour, even though it is bronze as against gold, is what seems to count for Glaucus. No wonder Achilles smiles (556), for the only time in the *Il.* – he recognizes the argument (536 above).

560. *Asteropaeus*: see 21.182-3.

563. *Automedon*: see on 16.145.

566. *Menelaus*: his argument is one from performance – Antilochus won only because he cheated by cutting in (571-2). Note that Menelaus specifically denies that he is using his *own* superior status to claim second prize (578, the Eumelus argument), i.e. what he is *due* relates to nothing but to his own performance, balked by Antilochus' fouling.

584-5. *who encircles the earth/encircler* (**H, L**): i.e. Poseidon, god of horses as well as Antilochus' great-grandfather. For oaths, see **GI** 7E. Menelaus rejects human arbitration – one way of settling disputes – possibly because of the objection he himself foresees being used against him (574-8), and goes for the theoretically more serious challenge to the other party, an oath before the gods.

590. *judgement*: Antilochus does not *directly* admit that he cheated, but he agrees that a young man can go too far (i.e. he did not show the judgement he should have, cf. Nestor's advice at 313-18) and that his judgement is unsound (cf. 3.106-8), and indicates that he does not intend to fall out of favour with the gods. Nevertheless, he still says that the mare is the prize 'I won' (592).

595. *fall out of/from your favour*: Antilochus and Menelaus are, in reality, good friends, e.g. they joined together to repel Aeneas at 5.561ff., Antilochus was inspired by Menelaus to attack at 15.568ff., etc. It is clear from Menelaus' reply (601-11) that he feels kindly towards the young man.

598. *like/as with the dew*: B-simile, seeing a comparison between the dew warming on ears of corn and Menelaus' heart warming to Antilochus' reply.

600. *your/you*: see on 4.127 for this 'apostrophe'.

610. *(mine) though she is mine*: Menelaus rejects Antilochus' claim to the mare, but still generously hands it over. Menelaus, in other words, feels that he has received his due because of Antilochus' admission that he (Menelaus) should have come second; he does not see the necessity of proving it by having actual possession of the mare. This makes for an interesting commentary on Homeric heroes' desire to produce tangible evidence of their achievements (see **GI** 4A, 4.463) and their willingness to be flexible where friendship is concerned (cf. Menelaus pointing out that he would not have done it for anyone else, 606).

615. *the fifth prize*: this is now redundant because Achilles had already rewarded Eumelus (560-5). Achilles awards it to Nestor for services rendered, i.e. *past* achievements, since he can no longer perform in the present (as Eumelus was able to).

626-45. *Yes ... in a class by myself/hero among heroes/young heroes*: Nestor's last story of his own past achievements; see on 1.247. He ends by agreeing with Achilles' analysis that past achievements have their own value, which should continue to be respected (647-9).

630. *Amarynceus*: father of Diores (2.622, killed 4.517-26). Note the Elean/Epean and Buprasion connection with Nestor's tale at 11.669-760.

638. *two Moliones/sons of Actor*: see on 11.708.

653-99: The boxing: Epeius knocks out Euryalus.

653. *dangerous/painful*: boxing was known to be more dangerous than e.g. all-in wrestling, where virtually no holds were barred, because it takes only one blow to kill, whereas a wrestler has time to signal his submission. There were no rounds: men fought to a knock-out or submission.

655. *jenny* (**L**): a female mule.

660. *Apollo*: god of boxing in particular (at which he was an expert) and of athletes in general.

665. *Epeius*: presumably the carpenter who made the Wooden Horse (see on 3.202) and, as he admits, no star on the battlefield (670).

667-75. *Step forward ... finished with him* (**R-J**); *Step forward ...*

have broken him (**H**); *Let the man ... beaten him under* (**L**): a speech ringing with clichés still to be heard in the mouths of today's boxers – 'Who's coming second?' 667, 'I am the champion/the greatest' 669, 'I'll tear him apart' 673, 'He'll need the undertaker when I've finished with him' 674-5 – and quite enough to silence the crowd (676).

677.   *Euryalus*: see on 2.563-5 – he is Diomedes' cousin – and 6.26.

679.   *of him* (**L**): i.e. Mecisteus, who attended Oedipus' funeral games and beat all-comers (cf. Nestor, above).

683.   *boxing-belt* (**L**): read 'loin-cloth' (only later did Greek athletes compete naked).

692.   *As (when) a fish/in the water*: D-simile, the end of it clinching the comparison, i.e. the way Euryalus was lifted off the ground by the blow.

695.   *set him on his legs/feet/upright*: a sporting gesture from 'great-hearted' Epeius, followed by acute observation of a groggy boxer (696-8).

700-39: The wrestling: Ajax son of Telamon and Odysseus fight a draw.

701.   *wrestling*: it looks as if the purpose is to remain upright while throwing your opponent to the ground (718-20), but even when both parties agree to give each other a free lift, in turn, to see if they can do it (724), they are still foiled, and both tumble to the floor. There is no point in trying to decide who has 'won' when, transparently, neither has. It could, of course, be the case that the fight was decided on falls *caused*, even if the one who caused the fall fell himself. In that case, Odysseus won – but no winner was declared. No wonder the troops became bored (721) and Achilles quickly ended the contest (735-7). The purpose of competing was to find a winner, not fight lengthy draws, and Achilles sensed the mood of the crowd. Homer understood crowd psychology.

703.   *worth/valued*: the crowd tots up what is at stake, as crowds do when prizes are on offer.

712.   *like /as when (the) ... rafters*: B-simile, the hands of both wrestlers being raised up and locked like the gable-end rafters of a house at this opening stage of the fight.

714-16.   *backs ... ribs/sides ... shoulders*: the two wrestlers are trying varieties of holds and grips but cannot make the decisive move.

736.   *share the prizes* (**R-J, H**); *take the prizes in equal division* (**L**): but how do you share out equally a tripod, worth twelve oxen, and a woman, worth four?

740-97: The foot-race: Athene helps Odysseus beat Ajax son of Oïleus.

743.   *Sidon*: see on 6.291.

745.   *Thoas ... Euneus*: see on 7.467-8.

747.   *Lycaon*: see on 21.41.

756. *Antilochus*: he was sent to Achilles with the message about Patroclus' death, 17.653-18.21.

760. *like the rod* (**R-J**); *close as the weaver's rod* (**H**); *as near as to the breast* (**L**): C-simile, another homely image taken from everyday life.

765. *breath(ing)*: cf. Diomedes' horses breathing down Eumelus' neck, 380-1.

769. *Athene*: she will obviously help her favourite (see on 10.245) when he calls on her (see e.g. Menelaus at 17.567-8, and cf. Antilochus' accusation against Eumelus, 546-7). Athene does so in two ways (i) she increases Odysseus' speed and (ii) she ensures Ajax slides over in the dung. Gods never do things by halves when helping their favourites – as Ajax acknowledges (782-3). Cf. on 390, where she helps Diomedes similarly.

781. *spat/spitting (out) the dung*: an appropriate result for the foul-mouthed Ajax (see on 473 above) who has, amusingly, won an ox as a prize. 'I wuz robbed' comes to mind. The Greeks laugh at him (784) because they had wanted Odysseus to win (766-7) and he had, with maximum discomfort to Ajax – a double bonus.

787. *Antilochus*: cf. 586-611 – again Antilochus explains away his lack of success, this time with an amusing quip about Odysseus' age (789-91: cf. 3.215, where Menelaus is said to be younger than Odysseus), and quite without any resentment (cf. Ajax); and again he gets rewarded for it, this time by Achilles (795-6). The young Antilochus knows how to appeal to his elders and betters.

798-825: Armed combat: Ajax son of Telamon and Diomedes fight a draw.

800. *Sarpedon*: see 16.663-5 – another reminder of Patroclus in whose honour the games are being held.

808. *Asteropaeus*: see 21.182-3.

806. *and reach his innards through his armour and his blood* (**H**); *to get through ... reach to the vitals* (**L**): R-J omits this line, as the ancient commentator Aristarchus did. Is Achilles really inviting Ajax and Diomedes seriously to wound, even kill, each other? Indeed, the whole episode looks suspiciously like a later addition, inserted by someone who knew that single combat, resulting in death, was an important feature of some funeral games (perhaps the origin of gladiatorial games). At any rate, the Greeks call for it to be stopped when things look like getting out of hand (822-3). On the other hand, Achilles is a brutal man – and *he* certainly does not want it stopped, nor does he agree with the crowd's demand for a draw, but awards the prize to Diomedes (824-5).

826-97: Throwing the lump of metal; archery; and spear-throwing, in which Achilles gives the prize uncontested to Agamemnon.

826-49. A lump of iron (826) may not seem an attractive prize, but metal was precious and Achilles was offering a five-year supply of it (note the homely reference to the difficulty of travel into town, 834-5; see **GI** 3).

827. *Eëtion*: see on 6.395.

836-8. *Polypoetes ... Leonteus ... Epeius*: the first two are giant leaders of the Lapiths (see on 2.740), while Epeius had won the boxing (689-95).

840. *whirled/swung it round*: did the Greeks all laugh because the weight should have been 'put' rather than thrown like a discus?

846. *throwing-stick*: evidently some sort of stick with string and weights attached, thrown at cattle to catch them or separate them out from the herd.

850-83. Achilles provides two different prizes for the archery, one for the man who hits the dove, the other for the man who misses the dove but hits the string tethering it. Since the purpose of the contest can hardly be to hit the string – a far more difficult task anyway – why does Achilles *set up a prize* for doing this? He could easily have awarded such a shot 'marks for effort' when the contest was over. One can only guess that the poet wanted to whet the listeners' expectations that this would happen – and it duly does. It is also hard to see what purpose is served by the arrow that Meriones shoots falling back to his feet when it has hit the bird (876-7) or the wounded bird falling back onto the mast-head from which it had originally been tethered, before expiring and dropping to the ground (878-81).

859-60. *Teucer ... Meriones*: these are the only two Greeks to use a bow in the *Il*. Teucer uses it regularly (e.g. 8.266-334), while Meriones uses it once at 13.650-2.

863. *forgotten to promise* **(R-J)**; *had not vowed* **(H)**; *did not promise* **(L)**: failure to invoke the gods, with the inevitable result, is a common theme of these games. See on 769 above. Meriones, naturally, gets it right with a prayer to Apollo, and wins (872-3).

884-97. Achilles awards the prize for spear-throwing to Agamemnon without further ado, even admitting to Agamemnon's superiority over everyone else (890). There is a reconciliatory note to Achilles' actions here.

897. *Talthybius*: see on 1.321.

Book 24

Introduction

Lines 1-18 of Book 24 make it clear that 'no' is the answer. The public display as genial master of ceremonies for Patroclus' funeral games did not represent any change of heart in Achilles. The 'grieving process' has not led to 'closure'. Far from 'moving on', Achilles is back to where he was, incapable of reconciling himself to Patroclus' death. It is a brilliant coup by Homer, but it leaves the question – what next?

Throughout the *Il.*, Homer has depicted an Achilles who is not as other men – son of a goddess, passionate, obsessive, impatient, absolute in his demands on himself and others and now, as a result of his own decision, doomed to an early death. It is the mark of the extraordinary nature of the hero he has created that Homer can see no other way for Achilles out of his dilemma except through the intervention of the gods. To Olympus, therefore, the poet removes us for the resolution of the *Il.* This is what it takes to deal with an Achilles.

The motivation that Homer discovers for the gods' intervention is a rareish commodity in the *Il.* – pity (23). Apollo's argument is that Hector has done nothing to deserve such barbaric treatment from Achilles (33-8), who is simply destroying pity by acting like a wild animal (41-4), and gaining nothing by it either (52). If the gods can show pity, so can humans. Hera angrily objects, but Zeus reinforces Apollo's argument with his own testimony to Hector's piety (66-70). Gods and men, in other words, must reciprocate, and Zeus goes on to say that, since the body cannot be stolen (71-3, cf. 24), Achilles must be persuaded to relent, and Thetis, his mother, is the person to do it (74-6).

This, then, is Homer's solution to the problem, and an elegant one it makes too, since it means that the beginning of the *Il.* is reflected in its ending, giving a satisfying sense of resolution. Thus, the issue with which the *Il.* begins – an old man brings gifts to Agamemnon for the return of a girl and is rejected – is reflected at the end – an old man brings gifts to Achilles for the return of a body and is accepted; and the series of interactions which gets the main plot of the *Il.* under way in Book 1 (Achilles summons Thetis who appeals to Zeus to destroy Greeks) ends the *Il.* in reverse in Book 24 (Zeus summons Thetis who appeals to Achilles to return Hector). So the divine rationale is laid out for what we now guess is to be the climax of the *Il.* – the return and burial of Hector. But how is it to be brought about? And will Achilles play along? And if he does, why?

Zeus' instructions to Thetis contain a clarification of the means by which all this will be achieved. At 76 Zeus had said the return of Hector would involve a ransom from Priam. At 117-19, he drops a small bombshell – Priam will actually *go himself to Achilles with the ransom*. We know from Book 9 what Achilles is like with embassies, even with one consisting of his dearest friends (9.197-8). What on earth will happen when the aged father of his most bitterly hated enemy turns up in his hut, begging for his body? Is this another plan of Zeus' that is going to fall apart, like the first one (see 18/Intro)? Apparently not: Zeus, obviously aware of the problem, makes it clear to Priam (via Iris) that Achilles will treat the suppliant Priam with the proper consideration (155-8 = 184-6). It is worth emphasising that there was no *need* for Priam personally to deliver the gifts. Messengers could have done the job just as well. The poet *wants* Achilles to have to confront Hector's father – but why?

Meanwhile Thetis has delivered her message to Achilles. This is an important moment. Achilles does not take orders easily from anyone, even gods; one remembers the somewhat grudging tone in which he yielded to Athene at the start of the *Il.* (1.215-17), and she was supposed to be on his side. The point is that Zeus is not going to force Achilles to return the body. He has to make the decision to do so himself. So when Thetis reports Zeus' feelings to him (133-7), the atmosphere crackles with tension: will he or won't he? Achilles' terse, two-line agreement (139-40) says it all. Achilles has blinked. Zeus' plan can go ahead.

When Priam receives the message from Iris that he is to supplicate Achilles for the return of his son's body (159-87), he ignores objections from Hecabe (188-227), berates townsmen and sons alike (237-64) and leaves with an omen from Zeus (281-328), while Zeus sends Hermes to accompany him (334-8). The poet is emphasizing, first, the gods' pity and concern for the old man and his family, e.g. Iris' kindly approach to him 171-4, the omen 320-1, the protection afforded by Hermes during the journey 374, and the gods' care for Hector 422-8 (and note too the number of references to Priam as an 'old man'); second, Priam's courage, as he moves from grovelling in the dung (163-5) to making a journey of great difficulty and danger 'as though he were going to his death' (328), e.g. 171-2, 181, 207-8, 287-8, 364-7; and third, the value the family places on Hector, willing as they are to pay a ransom for a dead son when ransoms were normally paid for the living (cf. 224-7). Throughout it all, Priam feels that in this cause, at any rate, the gods are on his side (compare his feelings when Hector is killed: all he wants to do is die, 22.426-8). Homer, then, creates overwhelming sympathy for Priam and his mission. We feel his appeal to Achilles simply *must* be accepted. But that is the point: he is appealing to Achilles, and no real-time supplication by anyone in the *Il.* has yet been successful.

Homer knows his man, and he makes the dramatic night encounter between Achilles and Priam a desperately fraught affair. For one terrible moment it looks as if Achilles will reject the old man's supplication (see on 509); when Priam pleads to be given the body at once, Achilles has great difficulty restraining himself and warns the old man not to push him too far (see on 560-70); Achilles remains on edge while Patroclus' body is prepared (581-6); and he has to make his peace with Patroclus about what he is doing (592-5). But this tension must be set against the tears to which their fates reduce them both (507-12), the compassion Achilles feels for Priam (516), their mutual admiration (629-32), the care Achilles takes over Hector's body (587-91, cf. 619-20), the meal they share (601-19), Achilles' concern for the old man's safety (650-5) and his commitment to ensuring a truce while Hector is buried (669-70). We are in Achilles' private world again, but this time the issues are not those of personal honour, status and revenge, but of compromise and a degree of shared sympathy.

For Achilles' famous speech of consolation to Priam, see notes to 486-506 and 518-51. How much of a consolation it is for Priam remains open to doubt. Priam does not respond to it; instead, he immediately begs for Hector's body, a request which does not go down well. Since everything Achilles says to Priam is even more relevant to himself, is Achilles' sharp reply more about his own feelings than Priam's? Can one account for Achilles' anger because he is attempting to reconcile himself to handing over the body of Hector? Comparisons with Achilles' self-absorbed reply to Odysseus in Book 9 may be relevant here. Nevertheless, Achilles does see that his and Priam's fates are linked by their mutual sufferings, and this brings him to feel compassion for the old man. If Book 1 of the *Il.* centred on an Achilles bent on revenge for his own slighted honour at the hands of Agamemnon and willing to see Greeks slaughtered *en masse* to get it, Book 24 shows us an Achilles acknowledging that grief at the death of loved ones can make even enemies see the other's point view, for certain purposes. But there is no suggestion that this will prevent Achilles continuing to slaughter Trojans on the field of battle when the fight resumes.

The *Il.* ends with the Trojans and the burial of their greatest champion Hector. As often, Homer has a surprise for us. One could have expected laments from Andromache and Hecabe, the one peering into a Hector-less future in which she can see only disaster for herself and the Trojans (725-45), the other finding some comfort in the return of her son for burial (748-59). But who would have thought that Homer would give the final lament to Helen – who started the whole war – and put in her mouth such a loving tribute to the protective kindness she experienced from Hector and Priam (762-75)? One can understand why the Trojans, as she admits, hate her (768-70, 775). That Hector and Priam should have been so solicitous says much for their understanding of human failings. One (pointlessly) wonders how, under the same circumstances, an Achilles or an Agamemnon would have treated her.

Main sources for the commentary and related reading
Edwards (1987) 301-16; Macleod (1982); Richardson (1993); Segal (1971) ch. 7; Willcock (1984).

1-21: Achilles cannot sleep for thinking about Patroclus. He drags Hector's body round Patroclus' tomb, but Apollo protects it from disfigurement. [Eleven days of Hector's mistreatment, which began from the day of his death, cf. 24.107-8]

4. *began to weep/wept*: neither the death of Hector, nor the funeral, nor the games have brought peace of mind to Achilles after Patroclus' death – nor will his maltreatment of Hector (15-18).

5. *tossed*: Achilles' physical actions delineate his mental and emotional turmoil. His restlessness is superbly drawn in 5-18 ('in the dust').

16. *grave-mound/tomb*: note that Patroclus is not in the grave-mound at the moment – see on 23.243-4.

18. *Apollo*: see on 23.187-8 for his protective care, and cf. 24.406-23.

23. *pity/compassion/pitied*: cf. on 15.12. The gods' argument will turn on the feeling that they should reciprocate with humans: Hector gave them many offerings, as Apollo says, and they give him nothing in return (33-54).

22-142: [39th day] The other gods pity Hector, but Hera, Athene and Poseidon remain hostile. Apollo pleads Hector's case, and Zeus instructs Thetis to tell Achilles he must return the body. Achilles agrees.

27-30. *hated/hatred ... lust (for women)/to disaster*: the only clear reference in the *Il.* to the judgement of Paris, which was the ultimate cause of the Trojan war and the reason for Hera and Athene's hatred of the Trojans (see on 21.418 and cf. on 1.352). Poseidon comes into the equation because of his dealings with Laomedon (see on 5.638). Reinhardt (1960) argues that the reason why the story does not bulk large in the *Il.* is that a rather trivial episode from folklore does not accord with the spirit of Homer's transformation of the Trojan war into a mighty epic centred on the wrath of Achilles, far removed from the knockabout of beauty contests on mountain-tops. See also Davies (1981).

33. *Hector*: for his ritual piety, see on 22.170.

41. *like a lion*: for Achilles' almost bestial behaviour, cf. on 22.347.

45. *[shame, 44] which can both help and hurt a man* **(H)** (and **L** similarly): line 45 'which ... man' occurs in Hesiod *Works and Days* 318, where *aidôs*, 'shame' is the main subject, as it is here in the *Il.* (in line 44). Now 'shame' can, indeed, help or hurt a man. But here in the *Il.*, Achilles' 'shame' is not the issue, but his 'respect for others'. That, as it so happens, is a perfectly good translation of *aidôs*. Problem solved? No – since it makes *no* sense to say that 'respect for others' can both help or hurt a man. As a result, the ancient commentator Aristarchus omitted l. 45; so does **R-J**, who translates *aidôs* in line 44 as 'respect for others', omitting line 45 'which can ... a man'.

46-9. *(Many) a man ... enduring heart/heart of endurance*: cf. 19.228-9, where Odysseus says that soldiers can weep for their dead comrades for a day, but must then get back to the business of war, and 24.518, 549-50. See too 15.128-41, where Ares is rebuked by Athene for not being able to endure the death of a son of his.

52. *honour or credit/good*: Apollo argues that Achilles does not serve even his own interests by treating Hector as he does.

54. *dumb clay/earth*: i.e. Hector's dead body. Cf. 7.99, where Menelaus wishes the Greeks would all become 'water and clay/earth' because of their cowardice.

55-63. *Hera ... friends/traitor/forever*: Hera cattily replies that Hector was a mere mortal, while Achilles was the child of an immortal who happened to be a friend of hers. But this does not deal with Apollo's accusations that, because of his offerings, Hector deserves better than to be treated by someone acting like an animal, who has lost all feelings of pity and respect. For Hera, Thetis and Peleus, see on 1.352, and cf. Hera's warmth to Thetis at 102.

74. *Thetis*: Zeus agrees with Apollo about Hector's offerings, and sees that the only way to get a change of heart in Achilles is through his mother.

77-87. Note the arrival scene: Iris goes 77, arrives 80, finds 82, Thetis is described 83-6, Iris addresses her 87. See on 2.167. Further arrival scenes start at 122 and 160.

80. *like (...) lead*: B-simile, Iris plunging into the sea to fetch Thetis like a weighted fishing-line sunk to catch fish. The 'horn' was either a protection for the line, fastened above the hook, or an artificial bait.

82. *Thetis*: she is among her sea-nymph sisters, cf. 18.36-51, lamenting Achilles' death even though he is still alive (cf. Andromache among her servants lamenting Hector, 6.497-502, and Priam at 24.328). There is comfort in numbers.

100-2. *Athene ... from it/the cup*: a warm, sympathetic welcome for the grieving Thetis, cf. 15.84-8.

102. *accepting* (**L**): read 'gave back after she'.

110. *but I still put upon Achilles the honour that he has* (**L**): i.e. I intend to grant Achilles glory – an important promise from Zeus. It may refer simply to the great ransom Priam will bring for Hector's body; it may go further than that.

122. *came/made her way*: another arrival scene.

125. *sacrificed* (**L**): read 'slaughtered'.

129. *forgetful of/no thought of/remember neither food*: a pointed observation to make when food was being prepared at that very moment (but did not Achilles eat at 23.29-30, 48?). See next note.

130. *make love/join/lie with a woman*: evidently Achilles has not made love to Briseis (or any other captive woman) since Patroclus' death. The poet's purpose is to show how cut off from everyday life Achilles has become. Thetis' advice is to enjoy earthly pleasures while he may. After all, there will be none in Hades (see on 23.104).

134. *wishes you to know/he says*: Thetis repeats Zeus' words of 113-15, cf. on 2.28.

140. *If the Olympian*: note that Zeus will not impose divine sanction on Achilles. Achilles has to agree willingly to return the body himself. That said, the fact that the proposal comes from Zeus himself would, of course, be persuasive, all the more since his mother is the mouthpiece. Does Achilles' reply here indicate resignation? Indifference? Relief? Whatever we may read into it, Achilles realises he cannot go on like this, and the return of the body is crucial to a resolution of his situation.

141-2. *exchanged/spoke/conversed*: a heart-stopping two lines – Homer at his richly suggestive best. Are these the last words mother and son spoke together before Achilles' death (cf. 85-6)? What one would give to know what they talked about ... .

143-87: Zeus tells the mourning Priam to take gifts to Achilles and ransom Hector.

145. *Tell him*: Zeus plots the next sequence. Priam is to take a ransom to Achilles. An elderly herald will go with him, driving a waggon containing the ransom, on which the body of Hector can then be brought back. Hermes (Argeiphontes) will guide him. The instructions at 147-58 will be repeated by Iris at 176-87.

160. *lamentation/mourning*: cf. Thetis at 82 above.

163. *dung*: cf. on 22.414 and see **GI** 7B.

174. *pities you/is pitiful*: unlike Achilles, who has destroyed pity (44). See on 15.12. Note the gentle voice in which Iris addresses Priam, trying not to terrify him (170).

188-321: Priam, after rounding on his sons, sets off, with an omen from Zeus.

192. *cedar*: a precious wood (mentioned nowhere else in Homer) known for its durability, fragrance and resistance to woodworm and beetle – ideal, therefore, for a storeroom in a rich palace like Priam's.

208. *at/in our home/palace*: one of the functions of women in the *Il.* is to restrain their men from excessive danger, cf. Andromache at 6.431. Hecabe's pessimism, already evident from 22.431-6, is even more marked in this speech, and her language powerful and agitated. Cf. her equally pessimistic 'libation' speech at 287-98.

210. *thread (of life)/life line*: see **GI** 8.

213. *liver*: see on 22.347. Hecabe's wish is more specific and so more terrifying than the other examples. The sentiment may seem primitive, but a mother whose child has been so treated may well not disagree.

216. *without any/with no thought of/ flight*: a good example of focalisation. Hector did turn and run (22.137), but in Hecabe's eyes, he was a hero.

220. *any human/mortal man/one of the mortals*: see on 12.236.

239. *Get out*: a telling portrayal of an old man under intense emotional pressure, carrying not only the burden of losing his son but also about to set out, alone, on a dangerous mission to get his son's body back from his greatest enemy. He turns with equal fury on his lazy sons at 252-64.

245. *town/city plundered/destroyed*: Homer again looks beyond the end of the *Il.* to the sack of Ilium, during which Priam will be killed. Cf. on 6.460.

249-51. *Agathon ... Pammon, Antiphonus ... Hippothous ... Dius*: whoever these sons may be. They have not featured elsewhere in the poem and do not feature in other tales of the Trojan war. Priam turns on them because he had ordered them to get the waggon ready (189-90) and nothing had been done. For other criticisms of Hector's brothers, cf. 3.106, 75.472-6; for the accusation of being a 'dancer' (261), see on 16.617.

257. *Mestor ... Troilus*: neither of these features in the *Il.* either, though their stories are told in later accounts of the Trojan war by other writers.

279. *Priam's chariot/for Priam*: i.e. Priam is travelling separately from the herald who will drive the waggon.

287. *libation*: see on 1.471. It is a sign of Hecabe's fear that she suggests Priam seeks an omen from Zeus, involving Zeus' own bird, the eagle (292-3, cf. 315).

303. *water*: for purification before ritual, see **GI** 7B.

309. *for love and pity* (**L**): i.e. to be received with love and pity.

316. *black eagle* (**H, L**): better 'golden eagle', whose wingspan reaches seven feet and would fit the dimensions suggested by the comparison with the entrance to a chamber in a rich man's house (317-18). See on 12.200.

322-469: [Night before 40th day] Hermes in disguise accompanies Priam safely to Achilles' quarters.

324. *Idaeus*: he is the old herald driving the waggon (149-50). He has featured before at 3.248, 7.276-416.

328. *to his death*: cf. on 6.500.

334. *Hermes*: see 153-4.

344. *eyes*: see on 445-6.

349. *Ilus*: see on 11.167-70, cf. on 21.558.

350. *river*: i.e. Scamander.

356. *with our horses* (**L**): read 'in the chariot' (far quicker than in the waggon).

361. *(by) the hand*: see on 14.137.

371. *like a beloved father* (**L**): read 'like my own father'. The whole point is that, with great psychological astuteness, Hermes presents himself to Priam as the sort of son that Priam had lost in Hector. This clearly strikes a chord with Priam, as he compliments the 'young man' on his looks and intelligence and calls his parents 'blessed' (375-7). Has Priam forgotten that Zeus told him he was going to send Hermes to accompany him (182-4)? Has Homer nodded? No: first, Zeus has indeed sent Hermes; second, Priam does not recognise him since he is disguised as a young man. Homer's purpose here is two-fold: first, to emphasise the sheer courage of Priam in undertaking the journey; second, in the light of Priam's state of mind, to create a moving and pathos-filled narrative involving the human interaction between Hermes as a 'son' figure and Priam as 'father' figure.

384. *greatest warrior/best man*: Hermes cleverly repays the compliment by praising the dead Hector in glowing terms.

387. *who are you*: Priam cannot answer Hermes' questions – Priam is interested only in how he knows about Hector (388).

390. *You're testing me* (**R-J, H**); *You try me out* (**L**): Priam is indeed testing him, since he has to establish Hermes' credentials. Hermes now supplies them, with further compliments to Hector's abilities (392-4); the 'information' that he is an attendant of Achilles gives Priam further scope for questioning.

401. *(on)to the plain*: cf. the purpose of Odysseus' and Diomedes' night expedition (see on 10.208).

411-23. *sir/old man … dear/loved*: for the preservation of Hector's body, cf. 23.184-91, 24.18-21; for its stab-wounds (420-1), see 22.371. The moral that Hermes draws – that Hector must be loved by the gods – is even more re-assuring for Priam: if even a (potential) mortal enemy, an attendant of Achilles, recognises that, there must be hope that he will be sympathetically received.

427. *never neglected/forgot*: cf. on 22.170.

435. *I fear*: a clever touch, which stops Priam giving a present to a deity while assuring Priam of Hermes' closeness to Achilles. Cf. Patroclus on Achilles at 11.647-53.

444. *sentries*: the guards posted at 9.79-88 and inspected at 10.180-9.

446. *gates*: i.e. those built into the fortification walls (7.438).

452. *enclosure/yard/courtyard*: Achilles' 'hut' or 'lean-to' is an impressively extensive building, as it will need to be if Hector's body is to be kept out of Priam's sight. The size of the hut, seen through Priam's eyes, must have made it seem an almost insurmountable obstacle.

460. *god*: see on 13.71.

466-7. *father … mother … son/child*: in the event Priam will supplicate Achilles only in the name of his father. Achilles' son is Neoptolemus (see on 19.326-7).

469-571: Priam's supplication of Achilles succeeds. They both weep, and Achilles consoles him, comparing Priam's fate with that of his own father, Peleus.

471. *walked/went/made straight*: the start of an arrival/*xenia* scene (see on 9.182-224), adapted to circumstances, e.g. Priam 'finds' people (472-6), but naturally does not wait to be welcomed in (cf. 9.192-3); Priam enters (477); stands near (477); supplicates (the normal sequence here – the guest waits to be received – is altered to allow for a supplication); then, eventually, is seated (522 – 553 – 571 – 597); food is taken (621); conversation (635); bed (673).

474. *Automedon*: see on 16.145; *Alkimos* (**H, L**): i.e. Alcimedon (see on 16.168-97). These two now 'stand in' for Patroclus at Achilles' table, 19.315-18.

476. *eating*: cf. 124-30.

476. *Great/huge/tall Priam*: Priam is never described like this else-where. Old as he is, he makes for an imposing figure at this critical juncture – perhaps inspired by Hermes' help and the gods' approval of Hector? Homer does not say.

478. *knees ... hands*: the full supplication ritual. See **GI** 7D for this ritual and its unique significance here.

479-80. *Terrible/dangerous ... sons*: words surely focalised through Priam's thoughts – note the reference to 'his' sons, and cf. Priam's reference to 'the man who killed my sons' at 506. The impact of this focalisation is almost shockingly powerful at this, one of the most dramatic moments in the whole *Il.*; cf. 505-6, 520-1.

480-4. *As (when) ... glances/each other*: D-simile, accompanying (as often) a moment of high emotion. The subject – exile for homicide – is a common one (see on 16.571). The point of contact, emerging (as it often does) at the end of the simile, is the wonder that Achilles and his men/the rich man experience at seeing Priam/the outcast. But how can Priam be, in any sense, a murderer? Similes, as we have seen, do not necessarily reflect with any exactitude the situation they illustrate in the narrative. That may be the case here. On the other hand, it is possible to construct a comparison. It depends on making assumptions, first, about the closeness of fathers and sons and Hector's (unexceptional) view that he is seeking *kleos* for himself and his father (6.446); and second, taking seriously Achilles' view that all Trojans must pay for Patroclus' death (21.103-5 is an especially sharp expression of the view). In that light, it may be possible to argue that, *in a sense*, and *in Achilles' eyes* in particular, Priam himself is construed as a killer, as the father of the Hector who killed Patroclus; in that case, delusion, *Atê* (480-1) had overtaken Priam the 'killer' in the sense that he was father of both Paris, who started the war, and Hector; and Priam, likewise, is the equivalent of an outcast in the Greek camp. Likewise, the outcast of the simile came to be purified of the murder; and there will be something of a reconciliation between Achilles and Priam in this scene (cf. 9.632-8, where Ajax accuses Achilles of being like a man who would *not* be satisfied by such a reconciliation).

486-506. Priam's speech depends for its effect on his observation that he and Achilles' father Peleus are in the same situation: both have 'lost' their sons, though at least Peleus can *hope* his son will return alive. In the name of pity, then, for all fathers without sons, Priam makes his plea. Observe the structure:

A 486-7: *The plea*: remember your father, who is old like me.
B 488-502: *Sorrow*:
   I 488-92: Peleus
      (a) 488-9 His misfortune (there is no one to defend him)

(b) 490-2 His fortune (he knows you are alive and hopes you will return)

II 493-502: Priam

(a) 493-8 Misfortune (all my sons have been killed)

(b) 499-502 Misfortune (Hector, the city's protection, is dead)

A 503-6: *The plea*: honour the gods, pity me and remember your father, than whom I am even more pitiable.

488. *tormenting/pressed by/afflict him*: cf. Phoenix on the care which the old look for in their children, 9.492-5.

492. *from Troy/Troad*: ironic, since Priam is not to know that Achilles will never return home from Troy.

494. *not one*: not strictly true (see e.g. 248-51). For his fifty sons, see on 4.499.

496. *mother*: i.e. Hecabe. See on 8.304-5.

506. *raised/brought/put to my lips the hands*: the Greek here would seem rather to mean 'reached out my hand to the lips', i.e. reached my own hands out towards Achilles' lips, rather than taking his hands and kissing them with my lips. The former is a typical gesture of supplication (see **GI** 7D, cf. 1.501); but the Greek could bear the latter meaning (which is offered in all three translations) and it is strongly indicated by the fact that this is what Priam actually did (478-80).

509. *gently*: a heart-stopping moment, since by pushing Priam away, Achilles is breaking the supplication contact (cf. 6.62-3). Is he about to kill him? 'Gently' tells us he is not.

512. *Patroclus*: as Priam weeps for his son Hector, Achilles weeps both for his father and his 'son' Patroclus. Achilles, in other words, can understand Priam's and his own father's loss in a deeper way because of his loss of Patroclus. Cf. 19.321-7, where Achilles says the death of Patroclus is for him even worse than would be the death of Peleus or his (actual) son, and the father-son simile at 23.221-5.

516. *compassion/pity*: from the man who had destroyed pity (24.44).

518-51. Achilles' reply is structured in precisely the same way as Priam's and point by point re-assesses Priam's claims, arguing that both Priam *and* Peleus have suffered a mixture of good *and* evil. But whereas Priam's speech was shaped as an appeal, Achilles – who has taken pity on the old man (515-16) – shapes his as an attempt to console. Given, however, the coldness of the comfort he offers, 'counsel' might be a better term. After all, Achilles is still 'seeing to' Priam and his children (542), and the killing round Ilium continues (548). Nor does Achilles say the killing will end. His 'consolation' consists simply in pointing out that grief achieves nothing (523-4, 549-51, cf. 19.229, where Odysseus recommends grief for one day, and Hecabe at 756-7); and that life and lamentation are inseparable (525). Pretty cold comfort indeed, both for himself *vis-à-vis* Patroclus and for Priam. But this may be the point: Achilles is not a man to go soft on himself, and he is not about to go soft on Priam either. Achilles has come to see that grief (like anger, 18.112-13?) cannot go on for ever.

This, perhaps, is why there is nothing in the speech about Patroclus. Achilles is struggling to control his shame and grief over Patroclus' death, which are bound to be sharpened by the release of Hector's body, and is intentionally trying to rein in his feelings (see on 560-70 below). To introduce Patroclus into the speech at this moment would be to wreck it as a means of bridging the gap between himself and Priam.

A 518-33: *Consolation*: brave man, there is nothing to be gained by grieving, since the gods ordained grief for mortals.
B 534-48: *Sorrow*:
  I 534-42: Peleus
    (a) 534-7 Fortune (gods gave Peleus gifts and an immortal wife)
    (b) 583-42 Misfortune (but they gave him a single son who will not protect him in his old age)
  II 543-48: Priam
    (a) 543-6 Fortune (Troy previously rich in wealth and children)
    (b) 547-8 Misfortune (gods brought war and death to Troy)
A 549-51: *Consolation*: do not grieve. It will not bring your son back.

On the two speeches, see D. Lohmann, *Die Komposition der Reden in der Ilias* (Berlin 1970), 121-4. An earlier section of this excellent book, Lohmann (1970), is translated in Jones and Wright (1997).

528. *evils … blessings*: there is a strong thread of pessimism running through Greek literature – Zeus may give a man mixed good and evil (530), or all evil (531), but never all good.

544-5. *Lesbos … Phrygia … Hellespont*: i.e. Lesbos out to sea to the south, Phrygia inland to the east, and Hellespont to the north. See **R-J** maps 2, 3.

544. *Macar*: legendary king of Lesbos.

560-70. It is clearly a very great struggle for Achilles to hand over Hector's body. Achilles knows that he himself is under divine compulsion (561-7) and has no desire to break the god's commands (567-70). Nevertheless, he wishes (as ever) to remain in control as far as he can, and does not welcome Priam telling him what to do. Again, his unspoken feelings for Patroclus, which he does not wish to provoke, lie behind all this. Cf. the further precautions Achilles takes at 583-6.

561. *messenger/message*: 126-40.

570. *suppliant*: cf. 186-7.

571. *did as he was told/ordered/told him*: i.e. sat down (522, 553).

572-691: Priam's gifts are unloaded, and Hector's body placed on the waggon. Achilles and Priam eat together. By night Hermes leads Priam secretly away.

572.   *like a lion*: a brief reminder of Achilles' darker side (cf. 41-3)?

577.   *herald*: Idaeus had been left outside (470-1).

585.   *his own feelings/heart/deep heart*: see on 560-70 above.

589.   *Achilles (himself) lifted it*: Achilles is treating the body with great respect, overseeing its (strictly unnecessary) washing and himself lifting it on to the waggon.

592-5.   *Patroclus*: out of sight of Priam, Achilles can explain his actions to the spirit of Patroclus (though he is not certain if Patroclus will find out, 592). Note that Achilles does not say he was forced into action: as usual, he takes full responsibility for what he has done.

601-17.   *food/supper ... gods dealt/gave her*: another example of the poet's manipulation of a myth to make it fit the requirements of the present situation (cf. on 9.529, last paragraph). Niobe was famous for having twelve children, boasting that she was superior to Leto (who had had only two – Apollo and Artemis), and finding all twelve children killed; as a result of which she turned to stone for grief. Achilles adapts this myth by claiming that, even though her children had been killed and despite her grief, Niobe still remembered to eat (613); and by adding that her children lay unburied for nine days too because the people had been turned to stone (! 610-12). So Priam should eat, despite both his grief and the fact that Hector had not yet been buried. See Willcock (1964).

Note the ring-composition (**GI** 11) within which the story is set: A 599-601 your son is free; B 601 you must eat; C 602 Niobe ate; D 603-12 Niobe's story; C 613 Niobe ate; B 618-19 you must eat; A 619-20 take back your son.

615-16.   *Sipylus ... Achelous*: Sipylus is a mountain in Asia Minor (near Smyrna); for Achelous see on 21.194-5. See **R-J** maps 3, 4.

621-8.   *slaughtered ... satisfied/drinking*: a typical eating sequence, cf. 7.317-18, 9.216-22.

633.   *their fill of gazing/pleasure in looking*: a wonderfully suggestive moment – did Achilles see something of Peleus in Priam? And Priam something of Hector in Achilles? Homer comments only on their mutual admiration for their physique and utterance.

636-42.   *bed ... tasted nothing*: like Achilles at the death of Patroclus (128-31), Priam too had experienced disruption of life's normal patterns after the death of Hector (lack of sleep, fasting, self-defilement). Some sort of return to normality is now being experienced.

649.   *causing him some agitation* (**R-J**); *dissembling his thought* (**H**); *sarcastic* (**L**): it is not clear what the Greek *epikertomeôn* 'speak provocatively' means in this context. The poet's purpose in having Achilles ask Priam to sleep outside is that Priam can take Hermes' advice and slip away by night (679-91); the poet therefore has to motivate the request. Homer does so by making Achilles argue it would be dangerous for Priam to sleep inside (650-5), an argument Hermes repeats at 686-8. It is hard to see how this explanation can be sarcastic (**L**) or deceptive (**H**). Since Priam's reaction to being led outside is one of fear (671-2), **R-J** prefers to see in *epikertomeôn* a meaning based on its roots (*kêr* 'heart' + *tom-* 'cut'), meaning 'cut to the quick, agitate, raise fears in'. In fact, 'outside' in the forecourt (*prodromos*, 673) is precisely where a guest normally would sleep – if we were talking of a proper Homeric palace (e.g. *Od.* 3.397-403). But we are not.

652. *discuss tactics/make/plans*: as was done by the leaders in council before they held a general assembly and launched their troops into battle, e.g. 2.53-86.

657. *funeral/burial*: Achilles continues to show respect for his bitter enemy; the poet here lays the groundwork for the ending of the *Il.*, with Hector's funeral.

663. *afraid/frightened*: cf. 778-81, 799-800. The Trojans, being cooped up in the town a long way from the woods of Mount Ida (662-3, cf. 23.117), are afraid of being attacked while they prepare for the funeral.

675-6. *Briseis*: this is our last sight of Achilles – asleep with Briseis, presumably for the first time since Patroclus' death (129-31), over whose seizure by Agamemnon the whole story of Achilles' anger and its tragic consequences began. It is another wonderful example of Homeric reticence, of which we make whatever we will.

679. *Hermes*: he negotiated Priam into Achilles' quarters, at night; he must now negotiate him out by night as well, for the reasons he gives (686-8, cf. 653-5). He accompanies Priam and Idaeus as far as the crossing of Scamander/Xanthus (693-4).

686. *ransom*: cf. on 3.305 for the value that Priam as a hostage would represent to the Greeks.

691-776: [40th day] Cassandra sees Priam approaching. Andromache, Hecabe and Helen utter laments.

699. *Cassandra*: mentioned by name (and only for her beauty) at 13.365-7, but implicit elsewhere (see on 1.113, 23.473). In later literature she was the prophetess who always told the truth and was never believed, a punishment visited on her by Apollo, god of prophecy, for rejecting his advances. Homer in the *Il.* does not take advantage of this story about her: there is no indication here, for example, that Cassandra had climbed Pergamus (see on 4.508) because she had had a premonition. Is it implied?

702. *him too, lying* (**R-J**); *Hector lying/drawn* (**H, L**): the Greek says 'him'. The scene is being focalised through Cassandra' eyes, and she sees first her father, standing in the chariot, then the herald, then – him, lying on the bier, all the more dramatic for not being named.

706. *from battle*: a poignant irony – Hector *is* returning from battle.

710. *wife … mother*: see on 22.87, 509-14. In fact the women will, after all, be able to mourn and bury Hector properly.

712. *head*: see 724 and on 18.71.

720. *(dirge-)singers*: in classical times mourners could be hired to lament the dead; here these 'professionals' – if they were such – sing formal laments for the dead, on top of the laments from Hecabe, Andromache and Helen. The Greeks had no such 'professionals' with their army, so they drafted in slaves to do the job, cf. 18.28-31, 339-42, 19.301-2.

712-45. Andromache's lament. She concentrates on what her and Ilium's future will be now that Hector is dead. She is most specific in linking the death of Hector not just to the destruction of Ilium and her own enslavement but now also to the early death of Astyanax (729-39, much exploited in later art and literature, e.g. Euripides' *Trojan Women*); cf. her and Hector's premonitions at 6.406-10, 450-65 and (now ruined) hopes at 6.476-81, and compare her lament at 22.482-5, 487-506. This public lament ends on a note of intimacy – the 'memorable word' Hector might have uttered to her, alone, on his death-bed, but now denied her, cf. Achilles and Thetis at 24.141-2. See Schein (1984) 189-91. Note that in the Greek world it is the women's role to lament the dead (see on 22.87). There is therefore nothing especially significant about the mere fact of their appearance at the end of an epic which closes with a funeral.

748-59. Hecabe's lament. She sounds, for the first time in her mouth, a note of optimism and comfort, because of the condition of her son's body (757-9), in defiance of everything Achilles could do to it (753-6). She associates this with the gods and Apollo's care for him (749-50, 759; see on 22.170, 23.187-8).

752. *sent them/sell (them)*: see 21.100-2.

756-7. *(back) to life*: cf. Achilles to Priam, 550-1.

759. *Apollo*: see on 6.205.

762-75. Helen's lament is the last – a surprising choice of mourner, perhaps, but Homer was never predictable (for Helen, see on 3.173). She concentrates on what Hector meant to her as the woman who caused the war (763-6) – and therefore, ultimately, his death – and focuses on his protection of and kindness to her, even when others were abusing her (including Hecabe, but not Priam, 770). Since it was Hector who bore the brunt of the fighting, his kindness to her says much for his magnanimity. Helen's outsider's view of Priam's family adds an important alternative perspective.

764. *wish I had perished/died/should have died*: cf. Hector and Helen's exchange at 6.343-60.

770. *father*: cf. Priam's kind words to Helen at 3.162-5.

777-804: Wood is collected. [Nine days to build Hector's pyre] [49th day] Hector is cremated and [50th day] buried, and a grave-mound set up. A funeral feast is held in Priam's palace.

780. *assured/promised*: see 670.

784-803. *wood/timber ... feast*: the sequence is much the same as for the burial of Patroclus: thus 784 wood cf. 23.110-26; 787 pyre cf. 23.164; 791 wine cf. 23.250; 793 bones cf. 23.252; 795 casket cf. 23.253, which will be the equivalent of a coffin for Hector; 799 grave-mound/barrow: cf. 23.255-7; 803 feast cf. 23.29.

804. *funeral rites/burial*: the *Il*. opened with Achilles' anger (1.1). It ends with its results, the death and burial of Hector – and Achilles next...?

Appendix
The 'truce' in Book 3

It is generally taken for granted that the oath taken by the Greeks and Trojans in relation to the duel between Menelaus and Paris (276-301) constitutes an *official* truce, whose breaking by Pandarus in Book 4 constitutes a major crime against Zeus, see e.g. Edwards (1987) 189, Kirk (1985) 331.

I can see no evidence for this. Truces are perfectly possible to ratify officially (e.g. Agamemnon at 7.411-12: ' "A truce, then; and let loud-thundering Zeus, husband of Hera, witness it." With these words he sealed the oath by lifting up his sceptre to all the gods.') But this never happens in Book 3. There is clearly an *unofficial* truce, but when characters talk of 'the oath(s)', they refer only to the oath taken in relation to the outcome of the duel, not to any truce, official or otherwise. In other words, it is the duel-oath which, in Greek eyes, the Trojans have broken. The evidence is as follows:

(a) When Hector proposes a cessation of the fighting in Book 3, he expresses the intention that a duel will take place, in order that the issue be settled and 'we others can *then* [my italics] swear solemn oaths of friendship' (94), i.e. when the duel is over, we can agree a truce. Menelaus consents, and the troops on both sides 'were delighted at the prospect of a reprieve from the painful business of fighting' (111-12). Nothing is said about a truce to cover the period of the duel. Why should it be? It needs no official truce to persuade soldiers to stop fighting. They do not want to lose their lives anyway (cf. 2.401, where each man 'prayed that he might come through the grind of battle with his life'); and now a duel has been proposed *which should end the war once and for all*. They need no truce to opt for that.

(b) The oath itself deals only with the outcome of the duel (276-309). The terms of the oath are:

- if Paris kills Menelaus, he keeps Helen and the Greeks sail home (281-3);
- if Menelaus kills Paris, the Trojans return Helen and pay compensation (284-7);
- if Paris falls and the Trojans are still unwilling to pay compensation, Agamemnon will fight on till they do (288-91).

Nothing about a truce there either; but the troops, naturally, express the hope that the right man is killed, so that *then* a truce can be made and the fighting stop ('and let firm oaths of friendship be made' [322-3] – a pointless thing to say if a truce had *already* been made).

(c) The duel is fought, and Menelaus is about to win, when Aphrodite whisks Paris away (373-82). So what now? Is this a result? It may not be a knock-out, but Agamemnon proclaims a win on points for Menelaus:

'Trojans, Greeks and allies, listen to me. Menelaus has clearly won. Now give up Helen from Argos and all her property and pay compensation on a scale that future generations will remember' (456-60) – a win which Zeus ratifies on Olympus at 4.13: 'victory has certainly gone to warlike Menelaus, and we should now consider what to do next.'

In other words, in *Greek* eyes, and with some justification, the contest is over and the terms of oath can be delivered: the Trojans must hand over Helen and pay compensation. What happens? Pandarus takes a shot at Menelaus, and nearly kills him. No wonder the Greeks in Book 4 regard that as 'trampling on the oaths' (157, 236, 271) – the oaths controlling the terms of the duel between Paris and Menelaus. Hector, not surprisingly, blames Zeus for not bringing the oath to fulfilment (7.69).

At the start of Book 4, the scene switches to Olympus, where the whole issue is discussed in the divine conclave at which Zeus ratifies the Greek win. Zeus has nothing to say about a truce but wonders whether to start the fighting again ('Are we to stir up evil war again, with all the sound and fury of battle, or shall we make peace between the two sides?'); further, when Hera sends Athene to restart the fighting on the ground and she races down like a meteor (4.78-80), the troops at 4.82-4 have nothing to say about a truce either. They see the portent and glumly remark that it may mean fighting will recommence.

There may be an objection to the no-truce theory at 4.66 = 71, where Hera urges Athene to make sure that the Trojans break the oath *first*. Now, what does that mean? If there were a truce, Hera's orders would create no problem – one or the other side could obviously break a truce first. But there is no truce. So what can Hera mean? How could the *Greeks* break the oath first?

I make the point that the question is purely hypothetical. The issue is never raised. If anything, I would regard Hera's comment as having rhetorical rather than legal force. But assuming the issue is not hypothetical, I refer back to the original oath, which states that if Menelaus kills Paris, the Trojans return Helen and pay compensation (284-7); and if they refuse compensation, Agamemnon will fight on till he gets it. The critical point is that *Paris is not killed* as a result of the duel. Clearly, therefore, in *Trojan* eyes, any resumption of hostilities by Agamemnon could be condemned because there had been no outcome to the duel. Agamemnon therefore could not trigger clause three. If he did, they could claim that *he* had broken the oath. But, as I say, we float in the realm of the purely hypothetical at this point.

Conclusion: there is no official truce in Book 3. There was no need for one, any more than there will be to cover the duel between Hector and Ajax in Book 7. There are only oaths relating to the duel, and these are sufficient to explain why the Greeks and Trojans make the claims and act as they do when the duel ends as it does. The clinching evidence comes with Antenor's speech to the Trojans at 7.350-3: 'Enough is enough: let us give Helen back to Agamemnon and Menelaus, along with all the property that came with her. By fighting on as we are doing, we have cheated on the oaths.' In other words, Antenor agrees that Menelaus won the duel and that the Trojans are therefore bound to return Helen: by not so doing, they have cheated on their oaths. Which oaths? Obviously the oaths relating to the duel.

Bibliography

Albracht (2003): F. Albracht, *Battle and Battle Description in Homer*, translated and edited by P. Jones, M.M. Willcock and G. Wright, Duckworth; originally published as *Kampf und Kampfschilderung bei Homer*, Naumburg 1886-95.

Alden (2000): M. Alden, *Homer beside Himself: Para-narratives in the Iliad*, Oxford.

Andersen, etc. (1995): O. Andersen and M. Dickie (eds), *Homer's World: Fiction, Tradition, Reality*, Bergen.

Armstrong (1958): J.L. Armstrong, 'The arming motif in the *Iliad*', *American Journal of Philology* 79.

Beye (1964): C.R. Beye, 'Homeric battle narratives and catalogues', *Harvard Studies in Classical Philology* 69.

Boardman, etc. (1986): J. Boardman and C.E. Vaphopolou-Richardson (eds), *Chios*, Oxford.

Bremer, etc. (1987): J. Bremer, I. de Jong and J. Kalff (eds) *Homer: Beyond Oral Poetry*, Amsterdam.

Bremer (1987): J. Bremer, 'The so-called Götterapparat in *Iliad* XX-XXII' in Bremer, etc. (1987), 31-46.

Cairns (1993a): D.L. Cairns, *Aidôs: The Psychology and Ethics of Honour and Shame in Ancient Greek Literature*, Oxford.

Cairns (1993b): D.L. Cairns, 'Affronts and quarrels in the *Iliad*', *Papers of the Leeds International Latin Seminar* 7, 1993, in Cairns (2001).

Cairns (2001): D.L. Cairns (ed.), *Oxford Readings in Homer's Iliad*, Oxford.

Camps (1980): W.A. Camps, *An Introduction to Homer*, Oxford.

Clarke (1981): H.W. Clarke, *Homer's Readers*, London.

Claus (1975): D.B. Claus, '*Aidôs* in the language of Achilles', *Transactions of the American Philological Association* 105.

Dalley (1989): Stephanie Dalley, *Myths from Mesopotamia*, Oxford.

Davies (1981): M. Davies, 'The judgement of Paris and *Iliad xxiv*', *Journal of Hellenic Studies* 101.

de Jong (1985): I.J.F. de Jong, '*Iliad* 1.366-92: a mirror story', *Arethusa* 18, reprinted in Cairns (2001).

de Jong (1987): I.J.F. de Jong, *Narrators and Focalisers*, Amsterdam.

Dickinson (1986): O.T.P.K. Dickinson, 'Homer, poet of the dark age', *Greece and Rome*, April, reprinted in McAuslan, etc. (1998).

Donlan (1981-2): W. Donlan, 'Reciprocities in Homer', *Classical World* 75.

Donlan (1998): W. Donlan, 'Dark Age Greece: Odysseus and his *hetairoi*' in Gill, etc. (1998).

Edwards (1987): M.W. Edwards, *Homer: Poet of the Iliad*, Baltimore, MD.

Edwards (1991): M. Edwards, *The Iliad: A Commentary*: vol. V, *Books 17-20*, Cambridge.

Emlyn-Jones, etc. (1992): C. Emlyn-Jones, L. Hardwick and J. Purkis (eds), *Homer: Readings and Images*, London.

Emlyn-Jones (1992): C. Emlyn-Jones, 'The Homeric gods: poetry, belief and authority' in Emlyn-Jones, etc. (1992).

Fenik (1968): B. Fenik, *Typical Battle Scenes in the Iliad*, Hermes Einzelschriften 21, Wiesbaden 1968.

Fenik (1978): B. Fenik (ed.), *Tradition and Invention*, Leiden.

Foxhall, etc. (1984): L. Foxhall and J.K. Davies (eds), *The Trojan War: Its Historicity and Context*, Bristol.

Fränkel (1921): H. Fränkel, 'Essence and nature of homeric similes' in Jones and Wright (1997).

Frazer (1993): R.M. Frazer, *A Reading of the Iliad*, Lanham, MD.

Friedrich (2003): W.-H. Friedrich, *Wounding and Death in the Iliad: Homeric Techniques of Description*, translated and edited by P. Jones, K.B. Saunders and G. Wright, London, originally published as *Verwundung und Tod in der Ilias*, Göttingen 1956.

Gaisser (1969): J Gaisser, 'Adaptation of traditional material in the Glaucus-Diomedes episode', *Transactions of the American Philological Association* 100.

Gill (1990): C. Gill, 'The character-personality distinction' in C.B.R. Pelling, *Characterisation and Individuality in Greek Literature*, Oxford.

Gill (1996): C. Gill, *Personality in Greek Epic, Tragedy and Philosophy*, Oxford.

Gill, etc. (1998): C. Gill, N. Postlethwaite and R. Seaford, *Reciprocity in Ancient Greece*, Oxford.

Gould (1973): J.P. Gould, 'Hiketeia', *Journal of Hellenic Studies* 93.

Griffin (1977): Jasper Griffin, 'The Epic Cycle and the uniqueness of Homer', *Journal of Hellenic Studies* 97, reprinted in Cairns (2001).

Griffin (1980): J. Griffin, *Homer on Life and Death*, Oxford.

Griffin (1980/2001): J. Griffin, *Homer*, Oxford 1980/Bristol 2001.

Griffin (1986a): J. Griffin, 'Heroic and unheroic ideas in Homer' in Boardman, etc. (1986) and in Emlyn-Jones, etc. (1992).

Griffin (1986b): J. Griffin, 'Words and speakers in Homer', *Journal of Hellenic Studies* 106 (the index title: the heading to the article is 'Homeric words and speakers').

Griffin (1995): J. Griffin (ed.), *Homer Iliad IX*, Oxford.

Hainsworth (1991): J.B. Hainsworth, *The Idea of Epic*, Berkeley and Los Angeles.

Hainsworth (1993): J.B. Hainsworth, *The Iliad: A Commentary*: vol. III, *Books 9-12*, Cambridge.

Hooker (1979): J.T. Hooker, *Homer: Iliad III*, Bristol 1979.

Hooker (1987): J.T. Hooker, 'Homeric society: a shame-culture?' *Greece and Rome*, October, reprinted in McAuslan, etc. (1998).

Janko (1992): R. Janko, *The Iliad: A Commentary*: vol. IV, *Books 13-16*, Cambridge.

Jenkyns (1992): R. Jenkyns, *Classical Epic: Homer and Virgil*, Bristol 1992.

Jones (1995): P.V. Jones, 'Poetic invention: the fighting round Troy in the first nine years of the Trojan War' in O. Andersen, etc. (1995).

Jones (1996): P.V. Jones, 'The independent heroes of the *Iliad*', *Journal of Hellenic Studies* 116.

Jones and Wright (1997): P.V. Jones and G.M. Wright (eds), *Homer: German Scholarship in Translation*, Oxford.

Jones (2000): Peter Jones, *An Intelligent Person's Guide to Classics*, London.

Kirk (1962): G.S. Kirk, *The Songs of Homer*, Cambridge.

Kirk (1978): G.S. Kirk, 'The formal duels in Books 3 and 7 of the *Iliad*' in Fenik (1978).

Kirk (1985): G.S. Kirk, *The Iliad: A Commentary*: vol. I, *Books 1-4*, Cambridge.

Kirk (1990): G.S. Kirk, *The Iliad: A Commentary*: vol. II, *Books 5-8*, Cambridge.

Latacz (1996): J Latacz, *Homer: his art and his world*, Ann Arbor.

Lee (1964): D.J.N. Lee, *The Similes of the Iliad and Odyssey Compared*, Melbourne.

Lesky (1961): Albin Lesky, 'Divine and human causation in Homeric epic', translated by Leofranc Holford-Strevens, in Cairns (2001).

Lohmann (1970): D. Lohmann, 'The "inner composition" of the speeches in the *Iliad*' in Jones and Wright (1997).

Lord (1960): A.B. Lord, *The Singer of Tales*, Harvard.

Lowe (2000): N.J. Lowe, *The Classical Plot and the Invention of Western Narrative*, Cambridge.

Macleod (1982): C.W. Macleod, *Homer Iliad Book XXIV*, Cambridge.

McAuslan, etc. (1998): I. McAuslan and P. Walcot (eds), *Homer* (Greece and Rome Studies vol. 4), Oxford.

Morris (1986): Ian Morris, 'The use and abuse of Homer', *Classical Antiquity* 5, reprinted in Cairns (2001).

Morris, etc. (1997): I. Morris and B. Powell (eds), *A New Companion to Homer*, Leiden.

Morrison (1992): J.V. Morrison, *Homeric Misdirection*, Michigan.

Moulton (1977): C. Moulton, *Similes in the Homeric Poems*, Hypomnemata 49.

Owen (1946): E.T. Owen, *The Story of the Iliad*, Clarke, Irwin 1946, Ann Arbor 1966.

Page (1959): D.L. Page, *History and the Homeric Iliad*, London.

Parker (1983): R. Parker, *Miasma: Pollution and Purification in Early Greek Religion*, Oxford.

Parker (1998): R. Parker, 'Pleasing thighs: reciprocity in Greek religion' in Gill, etc. (1998).

Parry (1971): A.M. Parry (ed.), *The Making of Homeric Verse*, Oxford.

Pelling (1990): C.B.R. Pelling (ed.), *Characterization and Individuality in Greek Literature*, Oxford.

Pope (1743): Alexander Pope (translator), *The Iliad of Homer* (1743), edited by Steven Shankman, Penguin 1996.

Pulleyn (2000): S. Pulleyn, *Homer: Iliad Book 1*, Oxford.

Redfield (1994): J.M. Redfield, *Nature and Culture in the Iliad*, Durham, NC.

Redfield (1979): James Redfield, 'The proem of the *Iliad*: Homer's art', *Classical Philology* 74, reprinted in Cairns (2001).

Reece (1993): S. Reece, *The Stranger's Welcome*, Michigan 1993.

Reeve (1973): M.D. Reeve, 'The language of Achilles', *Classical Quarterly* n.s. 23.

Reinhardt (1960): K. Reinhardt, 'The Judgement of Paris' in Jones and Wright (1997).

Richardson (1993): N. Richardson, *The Iliad: A Commentary*: vol. VI, *Books 21-24*, Cambridge.

Rohde (1925): E. Rohde, *Psyche* (8th ed.), London.

Rutherford (1982): R.B. Rutherford, 'Tragic form and feeling in the *Iliad*', *Journal of Hellenic Studies* 102, reprinted in Cairns (2001).

Rutherford (1996): R.B. Rutherford, *Homer* (Greece and Rome: new surveys in the Classics 26) Oxford.

Schadewaldt (1959a): W. Schadewaldt, 'Hector and Andromache' in Jones and Wright (1997).

Schadewaldt (1959b): W. Schadewaldt, 'Achilles' decision' in Jones and Wright (1997).

Schein (1984): S.L. Schein, *The Mortal Hero*, London.

Schofield (1986): Malcolm Schofield, '*Euboulia* in the *Iliad*', *Classical Quarterly* 36, reprinted in Cairns (2001).

Scodel (1982): R. Scodel, 'The autobiography of Phoenix: *Iliad* 9.444-495', *American Journal of Philology* 103.

Scodel (1989): R. Scodel, 'The word of Achilles', *Classical Philology* 84.

Segal (1971): C. Segal, *The Theme of the Mutilation of the Corpses in the Iliad*, *Mnemosyne* suppl. 17, Leiden.

Silk (1987): M.S. Silk, *Homer: The Iliad*, Cambridge.

Sissa, etc. (2000): G. Sissa and M. Detienne, *The Daily Life of the Greek Gods*, Stanford.

Slatkin (1986): Laura M. Slatkin, 'The wrath of Thetis', *Transactions and Proceedings of the American Philological Association* 116, reprinted in Cairns (2001).

Slatkin (1991): Laura M. Slatkin, *The Power of Thetis: Allusion and Interpretation in the* Iliad, California.

Strasburger (1982): H. Strasburger, 'The sociology of the Homeric epics' in Jones and Wright (1997).

Taplin (1980): Oliver Taplin, 'The shield of Achilles within the *Iliad*', *Greece & Rome* April, reprinted in McAuslan, etc. (1998) and Cairns (2001).

Taplin (1990): Oliver Taplin, 'Agamemnon's role in the *Iliad*' in Pelling (1990).

Taplin (1992), O.P. Taplin, *Homeric Soundings*, Oxford.

Toohey (1992): P. Toohey, *Reading Epic: An Introduction to Ancient Narratives*, London 1992.

van Wees (1996): H. van Wees, 'Heroes, knights and nutters: warrior mentality in Homer' in A.B. Lloyd (ed.), *Battle in Antiquity*, London 1996.

Wace, etc. (1963): A. Wace and F. Stubbings, *A Companion to Homer*, Cambridge 1963.

West (1997): M.L. West, *The East Face of Helicon*, Oxford.

Willcock (1964): M.M. Willcock, 'Mythological paradeigma in the *Iliad*', *Classical Quarterly* 14, reprinted in Cairns (2001).

Willcock (1976): M.M. Willcock, *A Companion to the Iliad*, London.

Willcock (1977): M.M. Willcock, '*Ad hoc* invention in the *Iliad*', *Harvard Studies in Classical Philology* 81, 41-53.

Willcock (1978) M.M. Willcock, *The Iliad of Homer I-XII*, Macmillan 1978.

Willcock (1984): M.M. Willcock, *The Iliad of Homer XIII-XXIV*, Macmillan 1984.

Willcock (1987): M.M. Willcock, 'The final scenes of *Iliad* XVII' in Bremer, etc. (1987).

Willcock (1990): M.M. Willcock, 'The search for the poet Homer', *Greece and Rome*, April, reprinted in McAuslan, etc. (1998).

Willcock (1995): M.M. Willcock, 'The importance of *Iliad* 8' in Andersen, etc. (1995).

Willcock (1997): M.M. Willcock, 'Neoanalysis' in Morris, etc. (1997).

Willcock (2002): M.M. Willcock, 'Menelaus in the *Iliad*' in M. Reichel and A. Rengakos (eds), *Epea Pteroenta*, Stuttgart.

Wilson (1996): C.H. Wilson, *Homer: Iliad Books VIII and IX*, Warminster.

Woodford (1993): S. Woodford, *The Trojan War in Ancient Art*, London.

Index

The Index identifies the subjects discussed in this commentary. **R-J** and **H** both have thematic indexes where further subjects are listed, and further exemplary passages may be found. **H** and **L** also have full people and place indexes.

Index

APHRODITE, **2.**820; birth **2.**205; comforted by Dione **5.**371; Cyprus **5.**330; from Cythera **15.**430; Helen **3**/Intro; laughter **3.**424; powers **3.**66; saves Aeneas **5.**313; saves Paris **3.**380; sex **5.**349, **14.**188; tricked by Hera **14.**192; wicked ways **5.**374

APOLLO, aegis **1.**202; and Ares **5.**455; and Laomedon **5.**638, cf. **12.**17; attacks Patroclus **16.**787-8, 791-804; characteristics **1.**9; deserts Hector **22.**213; hates Greeks **6.**88; helps Hector **7.**244-73; killed Patroclus **16.**850, **18.**454; Lycian **4.**101; peaceful death for men **6.**205; plague god **1.**39, 48, 453; protects Hector **23.**187-8, **24.**18; rallies Trojans **16.**715, **17.**316, cf. **21.**468; wrecks Greek ditch and wall **15**/Intro, **15.**355-66

APOSTROPHE, **4.**127, **7.**104, **16.**20, 692-7, 787-8, **17.**679, **20.**2, 152, **23.**600

APPEARANCES, **2.**212, **3.**197

ARCESILAUS, **2.**495

ARCHELOCHUS, **2.**823

ARES, agrees with Athene **5.**30; hated by Zeus **5.**890; re-enters battle **5.**455; sons **15.**112, 119; uniquely kills a mortal **5.**844; vs. Athene **15.**123, 197-9, **21.**409; yells **5.**858

ARGIVES, **1**/Intro, 'A note'

ARGOS, **1**/Intro, 'A note'

ARISTEIA, **5.**1-8, **19.**375

ARMING, Achilles **19.**364-98; Patroclus **16.**130-44, 145; pattern **3.**328-38

ARMOUR, **4.**132, 463; Achilles' **18**/Intro; as gift handed down **15.**532; decoration **11.**16-46; gleams **5.**5, **11.**62, **13.**242, 341, **15.**623, **19.**357, inlay **11.**24, **18.**564, swapping **17.**192

ARMY, distributes prizes **1.**121-307, **11.**624, reviewed **4.**223-421

ARRIVAL/FINDING PATTERN (see also '*xenia*'), **1.**167, **3.**121, **4.**89, 200, **9.**182-224, **18.**3, 369, 615, **19.**2, **24.**77-87, 122

ARTEMIS, **5.**51, peaceful death for women **6.**205, snubbed **9.**537, **19.**59

ASCALAPHUS, **2.**512, **15.**112

ASCANIUS, **2.**862

ASIA, **2.**461

ASIUS, **2.**837, 876, **12**/Intro, **12.**165, **13.**384,

ASSEMBLY, pattern **1.**54, **2.**279, **9.**10, **19.**42

ASTEROPAEUS, **2.**848, 876, **21.**167

ASTYANAX, **6.**403, **22.**59

ATÉ, **1.**412, **6.**356, **9.**115, 537; Agamemnon **19.**91, 93; Furies **9.**454; *Litae* **9.**502-14; Patroclus **16.**685-91, 805; Zeus **19.**95-133

ATHENE, agrees with Ares **5.**30; birth **5.**880; deals with Ares **15.**123, **21.**409; encourages Menelaus to remove Patroclus' body **17.**546, 570; epithets **2.**157, **4.**8, 128, 515; hates Aphrodite **5.**419; hates Trojans **4**/Intro, **4.**21, **6.**88; helps Achilles **22.**214, 276-7; helps Diomedes **5.**116, **23.**390; helps Odysseus **10.**245, **11.**438, **23.**769; inspires troops **2.**447; protects Menelaus **4.**130; rebukes Diomedes **5.**800; rejects prayers **6.**311; ruthless lies **22.**233; sent by Hera to help Greeks **1.**194, **2.**167; supports Agamemnon **11.**45; warns Nestor **11.**670; Wooden Horse **15.**71

ATRUGETOS, **1.**316

ATTENDANTS, function **1.**321

AUGEAS, **11.**700

AUTOMEDON, **9.**209, **16.**145, 472, 864, **17.**429, **19.**392, **24.**474

AXYLUS, **6.**12

BABYLONIAN EPIC, **GI** 3, 8, 12, 13; **2.**783, **11.**241, **14.**246, **21.**389

BATTLE, see also 'Chariots', 'Defensive wall', 'Massed assault/defence', 'Standing fight': A misses B, B hits but does not pierce A, A kills B **11.**233, **22**/Intro; A misses B, B kills A **5.**17, **11.**233, **16.**477; A misses B, hits C **4.**491, **13.**184, 411, 502-6,

EXHORTATION PATTERN, **5.**464, 528, **15.**502

FATE: see 'Destiny'
FATHERS AND SONS, **4.**376, **5.**635, **7.**128, **22.**59, **23.**221; advise sons **5.**197, **11.**781; win glory for father **6.**440, **8.**285, **9.**438
FEASTS, **4.**262, 345, **8.**162, **9.**71, **10.**212, **12.**311, **20.**84, **22.**496, **23.**29
FIG TREE, **6.**433, **11.**167-70
FOCALISATION, **GI** 10, **1.**370-92, **3.**28, 128, **4.**/Intro, **5.**414, 832, **6.**343, **7.**212, 244-73, **9.**411, **10.**27, **11.**242, 609, **14.**15, **15.**598, 699-703, **17.**125, **18.**231-8, 295, **22.**26, 137, 308, **24.**216, 452, 479-80, 702
FORCE, **1.**401, **2.**222
FURIES: see 'Erinyes'

GAMES, **11.**698, **23.**259
GANYMEDES, **4.**2, **5.**266, **20.**232
GARGARUS, **8.**48
GATES OF ILIUM, **3.**145, **6.**237, **7.**20, **11.**167-70, **16.**712, **18.**453, **22.**127, 194, 462
GIFTS, for Achilles **1**/Intro, **9**/Intro, **9.**120, 598, **19**/Intro
GLAUCUS, active **14.**425-6; and Sarpedon **16.**492, 510; catalogue, **2.**876; Diomedes **6.**119; life story **6**/Intro, **12.**388; rebukes Hector **17.**142
GODS, **GI** 5-7; admit defeat **21.**360; ambrosia **5.**340, **19.**39, 347-8; angry at death of relative **13.**206; as abstractions **4.**440; as family **GI** 5; as natural forces **5.**544; avoid contact with the dead **20.**65; blamed by humans **3.**164; bow to force **8.**428, **11.**73-83; create phantom **5.**449; desire sacrifice **GI** 7, **4.**48-9, **20.**299; disguise **3.**122, 380, **5.**462, **13.**62, 71, **20.**81; distant **6**/Intro; divine perspective on earth **16.**431-61, **22.**166-87; enjoy life/feast **1.**610-14, **15.**95; fickle **1.**574, **3.**414-15; humour **5.**408, 419, **21**/Intro; ichor **5.**340;

incestuous **4.**60; inform mortals **7.**44; inspire men **13.**71; intervene **GI** 6; men fear gods? **5.**434; 'miracles' **3.**448, **20.**325; moral? **GI** 7C; not omniscient **1.**213, 365, **5.**892, **18.**52-64; nymphs **6.**22, **20.**384; only Ares kills a mortal **5.**844; only Diomedes attacks a god **5.**438; quarrel **GI** 5; rally troops to stop rout **16.**715, **17.**316; reach agreement **5.**30, **7.**20; 'real' **GI** 6; **3.**414-15; **14**/Intro; recover self-esteem **5.**905; ruthless **4.**40; same gods for Greeks and Trojans **6.**88; subject to restrictions of time and space **GI** 5, **8.**48, **13.**4-6, **16.**515; suffer at hands of men **5.**382; support favourites **GI** 6, **6.**147, **20.**112-55, **22**/Intro; thrown out of Olympus **1.**591, **15.**23; travel by chariot **5.**365-9; will irresistible **8.**143, **13.**219
GORGON, **5.**741, **8.**348
GREAVES, **1.**17
GREEKS, all in it together **17.**250; do not take captives **6.**45; Homer's name for **1**/Intro 'A note'; long hair **2.**11; outnumber Trojans **2.**130, **8.**56, **15.**407; silent advance **4.**429; top-ranked fighters **7.**161; used to threaten Trojans **13.**219

HADES, a god **1.**3, **2.**783, horses **5.**654, unyielding **9.**158
HEBE, **4.**2, **5.**905
HECABE, **6.**87, advises Hector **6.**255, **22.**81; bestial **24.**213; death of Hector **22**/Intro; laments Hector **24**/Intro, **24.**748-95; pessimism **22.**430, **24.**208
HECTOR, **2.**816, 876; accuses Trojan elders **15.**720-1; admits folly **22.**104; and *kleos* **GI** 4, **6.**440; and Polydamas **12.**60, 247, **13.**751; as son, brother, husband **6.**238; attacked for looks **17.**142; berserk **13.**53, **15.**607; boasts **17.**125; body preserved **23.**187-8, **24.**18, 411-23; breaches Greek gates **12.**462-71; buried **24.**784-803; character **6**/Intro, **7**/Intro, **15**/Intro,